TinyML
Machine Learning with TensorFlow Lite on Arduino and Ultra-Low-Power Microcontrollers

Pete Warden and Daniel Situnayake

Beijing · Boston · Farnham · Sebastopol · Tokyo

TinyML

by Pete Warden and Daniel Situnayake

Published by O'Reilly Media, Inc., 1005 Gravenstein Highway North, Sebastopol, CA 95472.

O'Reilly books may be purchased for educational, business, or sales promotional use. Online editions are also available for most titles (*http://oreilly.com*). For more information, contact our corporate/institutional sales department: 800-998-9938 or *corporate@oreilly.com*.

Acquisitions Editor: Mike Loukides	**Proofreader:** Rachel Head
Development Editor: Nicole Taché	**Indexer:** WordCo, Inc.
Production Editor: Beth Kelly	**Interior Designer:** David Futato
Copyeditor: Octal Publishing, Inc.	**Illustrator:** Rebecca Demarest

December 2019:   First Edition

Revision History for the First Edition

2019-12-13:   First Release
2020-08-07:   Second Release

See *http://oreilly.com/catalog/errata.csp?isbn=9781492052043* for release details.

978-1-492-05204-3

[LSI]

Table of Contents

Preface

Something about electronics has captured my imagination for as long as I can remember. We've learned to dig rocks from the earth, refine them in mysterious ways, and produce a dizzying array of tiny components that we combine—according to arcane laws—to imbue them with some essence of life.

To my eight-year-old mind, a battery, switch, and filament bulb were enchanting enough, let alone the processor inside my family's home computer. And as the years have passed, I've developed some understanding of the principles of electronics and software that make these inventions work. But what has always struck me is the way a system of simple elements can come together to create a subtle and complex thing, and deep learning really takes this to new heights.

One of this book's examples is a deep learning network that, in some sense, understands how to see. It's made up of thousands of virtual "neurons," each of which follows some simple rules and outputs a single number. Alone, each neuron isn't capable of much, but combined, and—through training—given a spark of human knowledge, they can make sense of our complex world.

There's some magic in this idea: simple algorithms running on tiny computers made from sand, metal, and plastic can embody a fragment of human understanding. This is the essence of TinyML, a term that Pete coined and will introduce in Chapter 1. In the pages of this book, you'll find the tools you'll need to build these things yourself.

Thank you for being our reader. This is a complicated subject, but we've tried hard to keep things simple and explain all the concepts that you'll need. We hope you enjoy what we've written, and we're excited to see what you create!

— *Daniel Situnayake*

Conventions Used in This Book

The following typographical conventions are used in this book:

Italic

Indicates new terms, URLs, email addresses, filenames, and file extensions.

`Constant width`

Used for program listings, as well as within paragraphs to refer to program elements such as variable or function names, databases, data types, environment variables, statements, and keywords.

`Constant width bold`

Shows commands or other text that should be typed literally by the user.

`Constant width italic`

Shows text that should be replaced with user-supplied values or by values determined by context.

This element signifies a tip or suggestion.

This element signifies a general note.

This element indicates a warning or caution.

Using Code Examples

Supplemental material (code examples, exercises, etc.) is available for download at *https://tinymlbook.com/supplemental*.

If you have a technical question or a problem using the code examples, please send email to *bookquestions@oreilly.com*.

This book is here to help you get your job done. In general, if example code is offered with this book, you may use it in your programs and documentation. You do not need to contact us for permission unless you're reproducing a significant portion of code. For example, writing a program that uses several chunks of code from this book does not require permission. Selling or distributing examples from O'Reilly books does require permission. Answering a question by citing this book and quoting example code does not require permission. Incorporating a significant amount of the example code from this book into your product's documentation does require permission.

We appreciate, but generally do not require, attribution. An attribution usually includes the title, author, publisher, and ISBN. For example: "*TinyML* by Pete Warden and Daniel Situnayake (O'Reilly). Copyright Pete Warden and Daniel Situnayake, 978-1-492-05204-3."

If you feel your use of code examples falls outside fair use or the permission given above, feel free to contact us at *permissions@oreilly.com*.

O'Reilly Online Learning

For more than 40 years, *O'Reilly Media* has provided technology and business training, knowledge, and insight to help companies succeed.

Our unique network of experts and innovators share their knowledge and expertise through books, articles, and our online learning platform. O'Reilly's online learning platform gives you on-demand access to live training courses, in-depth learning paths, interactive coding environments, and a vast collection of text and video from O'Reilly and 200+ other publishers. For more information, please visit *http://oreilly.com*.

How to Contact Us

Please address comments and questions concerning this book to the publisher:

O'Reilly Media, Inc.
1005 Gravenstein Highway North
Sebastopol, CA 95472
800-998-9938 (in the United States or Canada)
707-829-0515 (international or local)
707-829-0104 (fax)

We have a web page for this book, where we list errata, examples, and any additional information. You can access this page at *https://oreil.ly/tiny*.

Email *tinyml-book@googlegroups.com* to comment or ask technical questions about this book.

For news and more information about our books and courses, see our website at *http://www.oreilly.com.*

Find us on Facebook: *http://facebook.com/oreilly*

Follow us on Twitter: *http://twitter.com/oreillymedia*

Watch us on YouTube: *http://www.youtube.com/oreillymedia*

Acknowledgments

We'd like to give special thanks to Nicole Tache for her wonderful editing, Jennifer Wang for her inspirational magic wand example, and Neil Tan for the groundbreaking embedded ML work he did with the uTensor library. We couldn't have written this book without the professional support of Rajat Monga and Sarah Sirajuddin. We'd also like to thank our partners Joanne Ladolcetta and Lauren Ward for their patience.

This book is the result of work from hundreds of people from across the hardware, software, and research world, especially on the TensorFlow team. While we can only mention a few, and apologies to everyone we've missed, we'd like to acknowledge: Mehmet Ali Anil, Alasdair Allan, Raziel Alvarez, Paige Bailey, Massimo Banzi, Raj Batra, Mary Bennion, Jeff Bier, Lukas Biewald, Ian Bratt, Laurence Campbell, Andrew Cavanaugh, Lawrence Chan, Vikas Chandra, Marcus Chang, Tony Chiang, Aakanksha Chowdhery, Rod Crawford, Robert David, Tim Davis, Hongyang Deng, Wolff Dobson, Jared Duke, Jens Elofsson, Johan Euphrosine, Martino Facchin, Limor Fried, Nupur Garg, Nicholas Gillian, Evgeni Gousev, Alessandro Grande, Song Han, Justin Hong, Sara Hooker, Andrew Howard, Magnus Hyttsten, Advait Jain, Nat Jeffries, Michael Jones, Mat Kelcey, Kurt Keutzer, Fredrik Knutsson, Nick Kreeger, Nic Lane, Shuangfeng Li, Mike Liang, Yu-Cheng Ling, Renjie Liu, Mike Loukides, Owen Lyke, Cristian Maglie, Bill Mark, Matthew Mattina, Sandeep Mistry, Amit Mittra, Laurence Moroney, Boris Murmann, Ian Nappier, Meghna Natraj, Ben Nuttall, Dominic Pajak, Dave Patterson, Dario Pennisi, Jahnell Pereira, Raaj Prasad, Frederic Rechtenstein, Vikas Reddi, Rocky Rhodes, David Rim, Kazunori Sato, Nathan Seidle, Andrew Selle, Arpit Shah, Marcus Shawcroft, Zach Shelby, Suharsh Sivakumar, Ravishankar Sivalingam, Rex St. John, Dominic Symes, Olivier Temam, Phillip Torrone, Stephan Uphoff, Eben Upton, Lu Wang, Tiezhen Wang, Paul Whatmough, Tom White, Edd Wilder-James, and Wei Xiao.

## CHAPTER 1

Introduction

The goal of this book is to show how any developer with basic experience using a command-line terminal and code editor can get started building their own projects running machine learning (ML) on embedded devices.

When I first joined Google in 2014, I discovered a lot of internal projects that I had no idea existed, but the most exciting was the work that the OK Google team were doing. They were running neural networks that were just 14 kilobytes (KB) in size! They needed to be so small because they were running on the digital signal processors (DSPs) present in most Android phones, continuously listening for the "OK Google" wake words, and these DSPs had only tens of kilobytes of RAM and flash memory. The team had to use the DSPs for this job because the main CPU was powered off to conserve battery, and these specialized chips use only a few milliwatts (mW) of power.

Coming from the image side of deep learning, I'd never seen networks so small, and the idea that you could use such low-power chips to run neural models stuck with me. As I worked on getting TensorFlow and later TensorFlow Lite running on Android and iOS devices, I remained fascinated by the possibilities of working with even simple chips. I learned that there were other pioneering projects in the audio world (like Pixel's Music IQ) for predictive maintenance (like PsiKick) and even in the vision world (Qualcomm's Glance camera module).

It became clear to me that there was a whole new class of products emerging, with the key characteristics that they used ML to make sense of noisy sensor data, could run using a battery or energy harvesting for years, and cost only a dollar or two. One term I heard repeatedly was "peel-and-stick sensors," for devices that required no battery changes and could be applied anywhere in an environment and forgotten. Making these products real required ways to turn raw sensor data into actionable information locally, on the device itself, since the energy costs of transmitting streams anywhere have proved to be inherently too high to be practical.

This is where the idea of TinyML comes in. Long conversations with colleagues across industry and academia have led to the rough consensus that if you can run a neural network model at an energy cost of below 1 mW, it makes a lot of entirely new applications possible. This might seem like a somewhat arbitrary number, but if you translate it into concrete terms, it means a device running on a coin battery has a lifetime of a year. That results in a product that's small enough to fit into any environment and able to run for a useful amount of time without any human intervention.

 I'm going to be jumping straight into using some technical terms to talk about what this book will be covering, but don't worry if some of them are unfamiliar to you; we define their meaning the first time we use them.

At this point, you might be wondering about platforms like the Raspberry Pi, or NVIDIA's Jetson boards. These are fantastic devices, and I use them myself frequently, but even the smallest Pi is similar to a mobile phone's main CPU and so draws hundreds of milliwatts. Keeping one running even for a few days requires a battery similar to a smartphone's, making it difficult to build truly untethered experiences. NVIDIA's Jetson is based on a powerful GPU, and we've seen it use up to 12 watts of power when running at full speed, so it's even more difficult to use without a large external power supply. This is usually not a problem in automotive or robotics applications, since the mechanical parts demand a large power source themselves, but it does make it tough to use these platforms for the kinds of products I'm most interested in, which need to operate without a wired power supply. Happily, when using them the lack of resource constraints means that frameworks like TensorFlow, TensorFlow Lite, and NVIDIA's TensorRT are available, since they're usually based on Linux-capable Arm Cortex-A CPUs, which have hundreds of megabytes of memory. This book will not be focused on describing how to run on those platforms for the reason just mentioned, but if you're interested, there are a lot of resources and documentation available; for example, see TensorFlow Lite's mobile documentation (*https://www.tensorflow.org/lite*).

Another characteristic I care about is cost. The cheapest Raspberry Pi Zero is $5 for makers, but it is extremely difficult to buy that class of chip in large numbers at that price. Purchases of the Zero are usually restricted by quantity, and while the prices for industrial purchases aren't transparent, it's clear that $5 is definitely unusual. By contrast, the cheapest 32-bit microcontrollers cost much less than a dollar each. This low price has made it possible for manufacturers to replace traditional analog or electro-mechanical control circuits with software-defined alternatives for everything from toys to washing machines. I'm hoping we can use the ubiquity of microcontrollers in these devices to introduce artificial intelligence as a software update, without requiring a lot of changes to existing designs. It should also make it possible to get large numbers of smart sensors deployed across environments like buildings or wildlife reserves without the costs outweighing the benefits or funds available.

Embedded Devices

The definition of TinyML as having an energy cost below 1 mW does mean that we need to look to the world of embedded devices for our hardware platforms. Until a few years ago, I wasn't familiar with them myself—they were shrouded in mystery for me. Traditionally they had been 8-bit devices and used obscure and proprietary toolchains, so it seemed very intimidating to get started with any of them. A big step forward came when Arduino introduced a user-friendly integrated development environment (IDE) along with standardized hardware. Since then, 32-bit CPUs have become the standard, largely thanks to Arm's Cortex-M series of chips. When I started to prototype some ML experiments a couple of years ago, I was pleasantly surprised by how relatively straightforward the development process had become.

Embedded devices still come with some tough resource constraints, though. They often have only a few hundred kilobytes of RAM, or sometimes much less than that, and have similar amounts of flash memory for persistent program and data storage. A clock speed of just tens of megahertz is not unusual. They will definitely not have full Linux (since that requires a memory controller and at least one megabyte of RAM), and if there is an operating system, it may well not provide all or any of the POSIX or standard C library functions you expect. Many embedded systems avoid using dynamic memory allocation functions like new or malloc() because they're designed to be reliable and long-running, and it's extremely difficult to ensure that if you have a heap that can be fragmented. You might also find it tricky to use a debugger or other familiar tools from desktop development, since the interfaces you'll be using to access the chip are very specialized.

There were some nice surprises as I learned embedded development, though. Having a system with no other processes to interrupt your program can make building a mental model of what's happening very simple, and the straightforward nature of a processor without branch prediction or instruction pipelining makes manual assembly optimization a lot easier than on more complex CPUs. I also find a simple joy in seeing LEDs light up on a miniature computer that I can balance on a fingertip, knowing that it's running millions of instructions a second to understand the world around it.

Changing Landscape

It's only recently that we've been able to run ML on microcontrollers at all, and the field is very young, which means hardware, software, and research are all changing extremely quickly. This book is a based on a snapshot of the world as it existed in 2019, which in this area means some parts were out of date before we'd even finished writing the last chapter. We've tried to make sure we're relying on hardware platforms that will be available over the long term, but it's likely that devices will continue to improve and evolve. The TensorFlow Lite software framework that we use has a stable API, and we'll continue to support the examples we give in the text over time, but we also provide web links to the very latest versions of all our sample code and documentation. You can expect to see reference applications covering more use cases than we have in this book being added to the TensorFlow repository, for example. We also aim to focus on skills like debugging, model creation, and developing an understanding of how deep learning works, which will remain useful even as the infrastructure you're using changes.

We want this book to give you the foundation you need to develop embedded ML products to solve problems you care about. Hopefully we'll be able to start you along the road of building some of the exciting new applications I'm certain will be emerging over the next few years in this domain.

Pete Warden

## CHAPTER 2

Getting Started

In this chapter, we cover what you need to know to begin building and modifying machine learning applications on low-power devices. All the software is free, and the hardware development kits are available for less than $30, so the biggest challenge is likely to be the unfamiliarity of the development environment. To help with that, throughout the chapter we recommend a well-lit path of tools that we've found work well together.

Who Is This Book Aimed At?

To build a TinyML project, you will need to know a bit about both machine learning and embedded software development. Neither of these are common skills, and very few people are experts on both, so this book will start with the assumption that you have no background in either of these. The only requirements are that you have some familiarity running commands in the terminal (or Command Prompt on Windows), and are able to load a program source file into an editor, make alterations, and save it. Even if that sounds daunting, we walk you through everything we discuss step by step, like a good recipe, including screenshots (and screencasts online) in many cases, so we're hoping to make this as accessible as possible to a wide audience.

We'll show you some practical applications of machine learning on embedded devices, using projects like simple speech recognition, detecting gestures with a motion sensor, and detecting people with a camera sensor. We want to get you comfortable with building these programs yourself, and then extending them to solve problems you care about. For example, you might want to modify the speech recognition to detect barks instead of human speech, or spot dogs instead of people, and we give you ideas on how to tackle those modifications yourself. Our goal is to provide you with the tools you need to start building exciting applications you care about.

What Hardware Do You Need?

You'll need a laptop or desktop computer with a USB port. This will be your main programming environment, where you edit and compile the programs that you run on the embedded device. You'll connect this computer to the embedded device using the USB port and a specialized adapter that will depend on what development hardware you're using. The main computer can be running Windows, Linux, or macOS. For most of the examples we train our machine learning models in the cloud, using Google Colab (*https://oreil.ly/AQYDz*), so don't worry about having a specially equipped computer.

You will also need an embedded development board to test your programs on. To do something interesting you'll need a microphone, accelerometers, or a camera attached, and you want something small enough to build into a realistic prototype project, along with a battery. This was tough to find when we started this book, so we worked together with the chip manufacturer Ambiq and maker retailer SparkFun to produce the $15 SparkFun Edge board (*https://oreil.ly/-hoL-*). All of the book's examples will work with this device.

 The second revision of the SparkFun Edge board, the SparkFun Edge 2, is due to be released after this book has been published. All of the projects in this book are guaranteed to work with the new board. However, the code and the instructions for deployment will vary slightly from what is printed here. Don't worry—each project chapter links to a *README.md* that contains up-to-date instructions for deploying each example to the SparkFun Edge 2.

We also offer instructions on how to run many of the projects using the Arduino and Mbed development environments. We recommend the Arduino Nano 33 BLE Sense (*https://oreil.ly/4sER2*) board, and the STM32F746G Discovery kit (*https://oreil.ly/vKyOM*) development board for Mbed, though all of the projects should be adaptable to other devices if you can capture the sensor data in the formats needed. Table 2-1 shows which devices we've included in each project chapter.

Table 2-1. Devices written about for each project

Project name	Chapter	SparkFun Edge	Arduino Nano 33 BLE Sense	STM32F746G Discovery kit
Hello world	Chapter 5	Included	Included	Included
Wake-word detection	Chapter 7	Included	Included	Included
Person detection	Chapter 9	Included	Included	Not included
Magic wand	Chapter 11	Included	Included	Not included

None of these projects require any additional electronic components, aside from person detection, which requires a camera module. If you're using the Arduino, you'll need the Arducam Mini 2MP Plus (*https://oreil.ly/8EacT*). And you'll need SparkFun's Himax HM01B0 breakout (*https://oreil.ly/Kb0lI*) if you're using the SparkFun Edge.

What Software Do You Need?

All of the projects in this book are based around the TensorFlow Lite for Microcontrollers framework. This is a variant of the TensorFlow Lite framework designed to run on embedded devices with only a few tens of kilobytes of memory available. All of the projects are included as examples in the library, and it's open source, so you can find it on GitHub (*https://oreil.ly/TQ4CC*).

 Since the code examples in this book are part of an active open source project, they are continually changing and evolving as we add optimizations, fix bugs, and support additional devices. It's likely you'll spot some differences between the code printed in the book and the most recent code in the TensorFlow repository. That said, although the code might drift a little over time, the basic principles you'll learn here will remain the same.

You'll need some kind of editor to examine and modify your code. If you're not sure which one you should use, Microsoft's free VS Code (*https://oreil.ly/RNus3*) application is a great place to start. It works on macOS, Linux, and Windows, and has a lot of handy features like syntax highlighting and autocomplete. If you already have a favorite editor you can use that, instead; we won't be doing extensive modifications for any of our projects.

You'll also need somewhere to enter commands. On macOS and Linux this is known as the terminal, and you can find it in your Applications folder under that name. On Windows it's known as the Command Prompt, which you can find in your Start menu.

There will also be extra software that you'll need to communicate with your embedded development board, but this will depend on what device you have. If you're using either the SparkFun Edge board or an Mbed device, you'll need to have Python installed for some build scripts, and then you can use GNU Screen on Linux or macOS or Tera Term (*https://oreil.ly/oDOKn*) on Windows to access the debug logging console, showing text output from the embedded device. If you have an Arduino board, everything you need is installed as part of the IDE, so you just need to download the main software package.

What Do We Hope You'll Learn?

The goal of this book is to help more applications in this new space emerge. There is no one "killer app" for TinyML right now, and there might never be, but we know from experience that there are a lot of problems out there in the world that can be solved using the toolbox it offers. We want to familiarize you with the possible solutions. We want to take domain experts from agriculture, space exploration, medicine, consumer goods, and any other areas with addressable issues and give them an understanding of how to solve problems themselves, or at the very least communicate what problems are solvable with these techniques.

With that in mind, we're hoping that when you finish this book you'll have a good overview of what's currently possible using machine learning on embedded systems at the moment, as well as some idea of what's going to be feasible over the next few years. We want you to be able to build and modify some practical examples using time-series data like audio or input from accelerometers, and for low-power vision. We'd like you to have enough understanding of the entire system to be able to at least participate meaningfully in design discussions with specialists about new products and hopefully be able to prototype early versions yourself.

Since we want to see complete products emerge, we approach everything we're discussing from a whole-system perspective. Often hardware vendors will focus on the energy consumption of the particular component they're selling, but not consider how other necessary parts increase the power required. For example, if you have a microcontroller that consumes only 1 mW, but the only camera sensor it works with takes 10 mW to operate, any vision-based product you use it on won't be able to take advantage of the processor's low energy consumption. This means that we won't be doing many deep dives into the underlying workings of the different areas; instead, we focus on what you need to know to use and modify the components involved.

For example, we won't linger on the details of what is happening under the hood when you train a model in TensorFlow, such as how gradients and back-propagation work. Rather, we show you how to run training from scratch to create a model, what common errors you might encounter and how to handle them, and how to customize the process to build models to tackle your own problems with new datasets.

## CHAPTER 3

Getting Up to Speed on Machine Learning

There are few areas in technology with the mystique that surrounds machine learning and artificial intelligence (AI). Even if you're an experienced engineer in another domain, machine learning can seem like a dense subject with a mountain of assumed knowledge requirements. Many developers feel discouraged when they begin to read about ML and encounter explanations that invoke academic papers, obscure Python libraries, and advanced mathematics. It can feel daunting to even know where to start.

In reality, machine learning can be simple to understand and is accessible to anyone with a text editor. After you learn a few key ideas, you can easily use it in your own projects. Beneath all the mystique is a handy set of tools for solving various types of problems. It might sometimes *feel* like magic, but it's all just code, and you don't need a PhD to work with it.

This book is about using machine learning with tiny devices. In the rest of this chapter, you'll learn all the ML you need to get started. We'll cover the basic concepts, explore some tools, and train a simple machine learning model. Our focus is tiny hardware, so we won't spend long on the theory behind deep learning, or the mathematics that makes it all work. Later chapters will dig deeper into the tooling, and how to optimize models for embedded devices. But by the end of this chapter, you'll be familiar with the key terminology, have an understanding of the general workflow, and know where to go to learn more.

In this chapter, we cover the following:

- What machine learning actually is
- The types of problems it can solve

- Key terms and ideas
- The workflow for solving problems with deep learning, one of the most popular approaches to machine learning

 There are many books and courses that explain the science behind deep learning, so we won't be doing that here. That said, it's a fascinating topic and we encourage you to explore! We list some of our favorite resources in "Learning Machine Learning" on page 353. But remember, you don't need all the theory to start building useful things.

What Machine Learning Actually Is

Imagine you own a machine that manufactures widgets. Sometimes it breaks down, and it's expensive to repair. Perhaps if you collected data about the machine during operation, you might be able to predict when it is about to break down and halt operation before damage occurs. For instance, you could record its rate of production, its temperature, and how much it is vibrating. It might be that some combination of these factors indicates an impending problem. But how do you figure it out?

This is an example of the sort of problem machine learning is designed to solve. Fundamentally, machine learning is a technique for using computers to predict things based on past observations. We collect data about our factory machine's performance and then create a computer program that analyzes that data and uses it to predict future states.

Creating a machine learning program is different from the usual process of writing code. In a traditional piece of software, a programmer designs an algorithm that takes an input, applies various rules, and returns an output. The algorithm's internal operations are planned out by the programmer and implemented explicitly through lines of code. To predict breakdowns in a factory machine, the programmer would need to understand which measurements in the data indicate a problem and write code that deliberately checks for them.

This approach works fine for many problems. For example, we know that water boils at 100°C at sea level, so it's easy to write a program that can predict whether water is boiling based on its current temperature and altitude. But in many cases, it can be difficult to know the exact combination of factors that predicts a given state. To continue with our factory machine example, there might be various different combinations of production rate, temperature, and vibration level that might indicate a problem but are not immediately obvious from looking at the data.

To create a machine learning program, a programmer feeds data into a special kind of algorithm and lets the algorithm discover the rules. This means that as programmers, we can create programs that make predictions based on complex data without having to understand all of the complexity ourselves. The machine learning algorithm builds a *model* of the system based on the data we provide, through a process we call *training*. The model is a type of computer program. We run data through this model to make predictions, in a process called *inference*.

There are many different approaches to machine learning. One of the most popular is *deep learning*, which is based on a simplified idea of how the human brain might work. In deep learning, a *network* of simulated neurons (represented by arrays of numbers) is trained to model the relationships between various inputs and outputs. Different *architectures*, or arrangements of simulated neurons, are useful for different tasks. For instance, some architectures excel at extracting meaning from image data, while other architectures work best for predicting the next value in a sequence.

The examples in this book focus on deep learning, since it's a flexible and powerful tool for solving the types of problems that are well suited to microcontrollers. It might be surprising to discover that deep learning can work even on devices with limited memory and processing power. In fact, over the course of this book, you'll learn how to create deep learning models that do some really amazing things but that still fit within the constraints of tiny devices.

The next section explains the basic workflow for creating and using a deep learning model.

The Deep Learning Workflow

In the previous section, we outlined a scenario for using deep learning to predict when a factory machine is likely to break down. In this section, we introduce the work necessary to make this happen.

This process will involve the following tasks:

1. Decide on a goal
2. Collect a dataset
3. Design a model architecture
4. Train the model
5. Convert the model
6. Run inference
7. Evaluate and troubleshoot

Let's walk through them, one by one.

Decide on a Goal

When you're designing any kind of algorithm, it's important to start by establishing exactly what you want it to do. It's no different with machine learning. You need to decide what you want to predict so you can decide what data to collect and which model architecture to use.

In our example, we want to predict whether our factory machine is about to break down. We can express this as a *classification* problem. Classification is a machine learning task that takes a set of input data and returns the probability that this data fits each of a set of known *classes*. In our example, we might have two classes: "normal," meaning that our machine is operating without issue, and "abnormal," meaning that our machine is showing signs that it might soon break down.

This means that our goal is to create a model that classifies our input data as either "normal" or "abnormal."

Collect a Dataset

Our factory is likely to have a lot of available data, ranging from the operating temperature of our machine through to the type of food that was served in the cafeteria on a given day. Given the goal we've just established, we can begin to identify what data we need.

Selecting data

Deep learning models can learn to ignore noisy or irrelevant data. That said, it's best to train your model only using information that is relevant to solving the problem. Since it's unlikely that today's cafeteria food has an impact on the functioning of our machine, we can probably exclude it from our dataset. Otherwise, the model will need to learn to negate that irrelevant input, and it might be vulnerable to learning spurious associations—perhaps our machine has, coincidentally, always broken down on days that pizza is served.

You should always try to combine your domain expertise with experimentation when deciding whether to include data. You can also use statistical techniques to try to identify which data is significant. If you're still unsure about including a certain data source, you can always train two models and see which one works best!

Suppose that we've identified our most promising data as *rate of production, temperature,* and *vibration.* Our next step is to collect some data so that we can train a model.

It's really important that the data you choose will also be available when you want to make predictions. For example, since we have decided to train our model with temperature readings, we will need to provide temperature readings from the exact same physical locations when we run inference. This is because the model learns to understand how its inputs can predict its outputs. If we originally trained the model on temperature data from the insides of our machine, running the model on the current room temperature is unlikely to work.

Collecting data

It's difficult to know exactly how much data is required to train an effective model. It depends on many factors, such as the complexity of the relationships between variables, the amount of noise, and the ease with which classes can be distinguished. However, there's a rule of thumb that is always true: the more data, the better!

You should aim to collect data that represents the full range of conditions and events that can occur in the system. If our machine can fail in several different ways, we should be sure to capture data around each type of failure. If a variable changes naturally over time, it's important to collect data that represents the full range. For example, if the machine's temperature rises on warm days, you should be sure to include data from both winter and summer. This diversity will help your model represent every possible scenario, not just a select few.

The data we collect about our factory will likely be logged as a set of *time series*, meaning a sequence of readings collected on a periodic basis. For example, we might have a record of the temperature every minute, the rate of production each hour, and the level of vibration on a second-by-second basis. After we collect the data, we'll need to transform these time series into a form appropriate for our model.

Labeling data

In addition to collecting data, we need to determine which data represents "normal" and "abnormal" operation. We'll provide this information during the training process so that our model can learn how to classify inputs. The process of associating data with classes is called *labeling*, and the "normal" and "abnormal" classes are our *labels*.

This type of training, in which you instruct the algorithm what the data means during training, is called *supervised learning*. The resulting classification model will be able to process incoming data and predict to which class it is likely to belong.

To label the time-series data we've collected, we need a record of which periods of time the machine was working and which periods of time it was broken. We might assume that the period immediately prior to the machine being broken generally represents abnormal operation. However, since we can't necessarily spot abnormal operation from a superficial look at the data, getting this correct might require some experimentation!

After we've decided how to label the data, we can generate a time series that contains the labels and add this to our dataset.

Our final dataset

Table 3-1 lists the data sources that we've assembled at this point in the workflow.

Table 3-1. Data sources

Data source	Interval	Sample reading
Rate of production	Once every 2 minutes	100 units
Temperature	Once every minute	30°C
Vibration (% of typical)	Once every 10 seconds	23%
Label ("normal" or "abnormal")	Once every 10 seconds	normal

The table shows the interval of each data source. For example, the temperature is logged once per minute. We've also generated a time series that contains the labels for the data. The interval for our labels is 1 per 10 seconds, which is the same as the smallest interval for the other time series. This means that we can easily determine the label for every datapoint in our data.

Now that we've collected our data, it's time to use it to design and train a model.

Design a Model Architecture

There are many types of deep learning model architectures, designed to solve a wide range of problems. When training a model, you can choose to design your own architecture or base it on an existing architecture developed by researchers. For many common problems, you can find pretrained models available online for free.

Over the course of this book we'll introduce you to several different model architectures, but there are a huge number of possibilities beyond what is covered here. Designing a model is both an art and a science, and model architecture is a major area of research. New architectures are invented literally every day.

When deciding on an architecture, you need to think about the type of problem you are trying to solve, the type of data you have access to, and the ways you can transform that data before feeding it into a model (we discuss transforming data shortly). The fact is, because the most effective architecture varies depending on the type of data that you are working with, your data and the architecture of your model are deeply intertwined. Although we introduce them here under separate headings, they'll always be considered together.

You also need to think about the constraints of the device you will be running the model on, since microcontrollers generally have limited memory and slow processors, and larger models require more memory and take more time to run—the size of a model depends on the number of neurons it contains, and the way those neurons are connected. In addition, some devices are equipped with hardware acceleration that can speed up the execution of certain types of model architectures, so you might want to tailor your model to the strengths of the device you have in mind.

In our case, we might start by training a simple model with a few layers of neurons and then refining the architecture in an iterative process until we get a useful result. You'll see how to do that later in this book.

Deep learning models accept input and generate output in the form of *tensors*. For the purposes of this book,[1] a tensor is essentially a list that can contain either numbers or other tensors; you can think of it as similar to an array. Our hypothetical simple model will take a tensor as its input. The following subsection describes how we transform our data into this form.

Dimensions

The structure of a tensor is known as its *shape*, and they come in multiple *dimensions*. We talk about tensors throughout this book, so here is some useful terminology:

Vector
> A *vector* is a list of numbers, similar to an array. It's the name we give a tensor with a single dimension (a 1D tensor). The following is a vector of shape (5,) because it contains five numbers in a single dimension:

        [42 35 8 643 7]

Matrix
> A *matrix* is a 2D tensor, similar to a 2D array. The following matrix is of shape (3, 3) because it contains three vectors of three numbers:

        [[1 2 3]
         [4 5 6]
         [7 8 9]]

---

1 This definition of the word *tensor* is different from the mathematical and physics definitions of the word, but it has become the norm in data science.

Higher-dimensional tensors

Any shape with more than two dimensions is just referred to as a *tensor*. Here's a 3D tensor that has shape (2, 3, 3) because it contains two matrices of shape (3, 3):

```
[[[10 20 30]
  [40 50 60]
  [70 80 90]]
 [[11 21 31]
  [41 51 61]
  [71 81 91]]]
```

Scalar

A single number, known as a *scalar*, is technically a zero-dimensional tensor. For example, the number 42 is a scalar.

Generating features from data

We've established that our model will accept some type of tensor as its input. But as we discussed earlier, our data comes in the form of time series. How do we transform that time-series data into a tensor that we can pass into the model?

Our task now is to decide how to generate features from our data. In machine learning, the term *feature* refers to a particular type of information on which a model is trained. Different types of models are trained on different types of features. For example, a model might accept a single scalar value as its sole input feature.

But inputs can be much more complex than this: a model designed to process images might accept a multidimensional tensor of image data as its input, and a model designed to predict based on multiple features might accept a vector containing multiple scalar values, one for each feature.

Recall that we decided that our model should use rate of production, temperature, and vibration to make its predictions. In their raw form, as time series with different intervals, these will not be suitable to pass into the model. The following section explains why.

Windowing.   In the following diagram, each piece of data in our time series is represented by a star. The current label is included in the data, since the label is required for training. Our goal is to train a model we can use to predict whether the machine is operating normally or abnormally at any given moment based on the current conditions:

```
Production:    *                        *              (every 2 minutes)
Temperature:   *             *           *              (every minute)
Vibration:     * * * * * * * * * * * * * * * *          (every 10 seconds)
Label:         * * * * * * * * * * * * * * * *          (every 10 seconds)
```

However, since our time series each have different intervals (like once per minute, or once per 10 seconds), if we pass in only the data available at a given moment, it might not include all of the types of data we have available. For example, in the moment highlighted in the following image, only vibration is available. This would mean that our model would only have information about vibration when attempting to make its prediction:

```
Production:   *                        *      ┌─┐
Temperature:  *            *            *      │ │
Vibration:    * * * * * * * * * * * * * *│*│
Label:        * * * * * * * * * * * * * *│*│
                                             └─┘
```

One solution to this problem might be to choose a window in time, and combine all of the data in this window into a single set of values. For example, we might decide on a one-minute window and look at all the values contained within it:

```
Production:   *                   ┌───┐ *      │
Temperature:  *            *       │   │ *      │
Vibration:    * * * * * * * * * *│* * * * * *│
Label:        * * * * * * * * * *│* * * * * *│
                                 └─────────┘
```

If we average all the values in the window for each time series and take the most recent value for any that lack a datapoint in the current window, we end up with a set of single values. We can decide how to label this snapshot based on whether there are any "abnormal" labels present in the window. If there's any "abnormal" present at all, the window should be labeled "abnormal." If not, it should be labeled "normal":

```
Production:   *                   ┌───┐ *      │ Average: 102
Temperature:  *            *       │   │ *      │ Average: 34°C
Vibration:    * * * * * * * * * *│* * * * * *│ Average: 18%
Label:        * * * * * * * * * *│* * * * * *│ Label:   "normal"
                                 └─────────┘
```

The three non-label values are our features! We can pass them into our model as a vector, with one element for each time series:

```
[102 34 .18]
```

During training, we can calculate a new window for every 10 seconds of data and pass it into our model, using the label to inform the training algorithm of our desired output. During inference, whenever we want to use the model to predict abnormal behavior, we can just look at our data, calculate the most recent window, run it through the model, and receive a prediction.

This is a simplistic approach, and it might not always turn out to work in practice, but it's a good enough starting point. You'll quickly find that machine learning is all about trial and error!

Before we move on to training, let's go over one last thing about input values.

Normalization. Generally, the data you feed into a neural network will be in the form of tensors filled with *floating-point* values, or *floats*. A float is a data type used to represent numbers that have decimal points. For the training algorithm to work effectively, these floating-point values need to be similar in size to one another. In fact, it's ideal if all values are expressed as numbers in the range of 0 to 1.

Let's take another look at our input tensor from the previous section:

```
[102 34 .18]
```

These numbers are each at very different scales: the temperature is more than 100, whereas the vibration is expressed as a fraction of 1. To pass these values into our network, we need to *normalize* them so that they are all in a similar range.

One way of doing this is to calculate the mean of each feature across the dataset and subtract it from the values. This has the effect of squashing the numbers down so that they are closer to zero. Here's an example:

```
Temperature series:
[108 104 102 103 102]

Mean:
103.8

Normalized values, calculated by subtracting 103.8 from each temperature:
[ 4.2 0.2 -1.8 -0.8 -1.8 ]
```

One situation in which you'll frequently encounter normalization, implemented in a different way, is when images are fed into a neural network. Computers often store images as matrices of 8-bit integers, whose values range from 0 to 255. To normalize these values so that they are all between 0 and 1, each 8-bit value is multiplied by 1/255. Here's an example with a 3 × 3–pixel grayscale image, in which each pixel's value represents its brightness:

```
Original 8-bit values:
[[255 175 30]
 [0   45  24]
 [130 192 87]]

Normalized values:
[[1.        0.68627451 0.11764706]
 [0.        0.17647059 0.09411765]
 [0.50980392 0.75294118 0.34117647]]
```

Thinking with ML

So far, we've learned how to start thinking about solving problems with machine learning. In the context of our factory scenario, we've walked through deciding on a suitable goal, collecting and labeling the appropriate data, designing the features we are going to pass into our model, and choosing a model architecture. No matter what problem we are trying to solve, we'll use the same approach. It's important to note that this is an iterative process, and we often go back and forth through the stages of the ML workflow until we've arrived at a model that works—or decided that the task is too difficult.

For example, imagine that we're building a model to predict the weather. We'll need to decide on our goal (for instance, to predict whether it's going to rain tomorrow), collect and label a dataset (such as weather reports from the past few years), design the features that we'll feed to our model (perhaps the average conditions over the past two days), and choose a model architecture suitable for this type of data and the device that we want to run it on. We'll come up with some initial ideas, test them out, and tweak our approach until we get good results.

The next step in our workflow is training, which we explore in the following section.

Train the Model

Training is the process by which a model learns to produce the correct output for a given set of inputs. It involves feeding training data through a model and making small adjustments to it until it makes the most accurate predictions possible.

As we discussed earlier, a model is a network of simulated neurons represented by arrays of numbers arranged in layers. These numbers are known as *weights* and *biases*, or collectively as the network's *parameters*.

When data is fed into the network, it is transformed by successive mathematical operations that involve the weights and biases in each layer. The output of the model is the result of running the input through these operations. Figure 3-1 shows a simple network with two layers.

The model's weights start out with random values, and biases typically start with a value of 0. During training, *batches* of data are fed into the model, and the model's output is compared with the desired output (which in our case is the correct label, "normal" or "abnormal"). An algorithm called *backpropagation* adjusts the weights and biases incrementally so that over time, the output of the model gets closer to matching the desired value. Training, which is measured in *epochs* (meaning iterations), continues until we decide to stop.

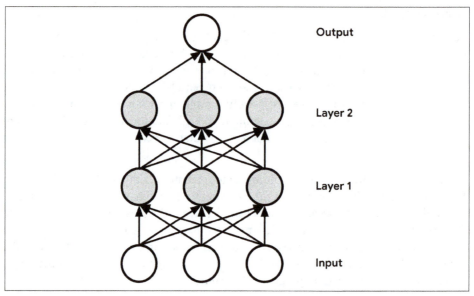

Figure 3-1. A simple deep learning network with two layers

We generally stop training when a model's performance stops improving. At the point that it begins to make accurate predictions, it is said to have *converged*. To determine whether a model has converged, we can analyze graphs of its performance during training. Two common performance metrics are *loss* and *accuracy*. The loss metric gives us a numerical estimate of how far the model is from producing the expected answers, and the *accuracy* metric tells us the percentage of the time that it chooses the correct prediction. A perfect model would have a loss of 0.0 and an accuracy of 100%, but real models are rarely perfect.

Figure 3-2 shows the loss and accuracy during training for a deep learning network. You can see how as training progresses, accuracy increases and loss is reduced, until we reach a point at which the model no longer improves.

To attempt to improve the model's performance, we can change our model architecture, and we can adjust various values used to set up the model and moderate the training process. These values are collectively known as *hyperparameters*, and they include variables such as the number of training epochs to run and the number of neurons in each layer. Each time we make a change, we can retrain the model, look at the metrics, and decide whether to optimize further. Hopefully, time and iterations will result in a model with acceptable accuracy!

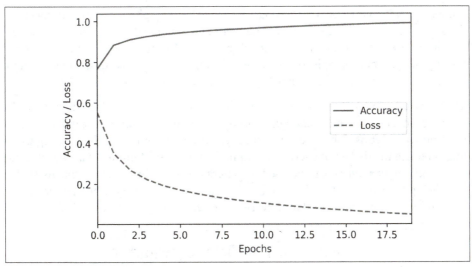

Figure 3-2. A graph showing model convergence during training

It's important to remember there's no guarantee that you'll be able to achieve good enough accuracy for the problem you are trying to solve. There isn't always enough information contained within a dataset to make accurate predictions, and some problems just can't be solved, even with state-of-the-art deep learning. That said, your model may be useful even if it is not 100% accurate. In the case of our factory example, being able to predict abnormal operation even part of the time could be a big help.

Underfitting and overfitting

The two most common reasons a model fails to converge are *underfitting* and *overfitting*.

A neural network learns to *fit* its behavior to the patterns it recognizes in data. If a model is correctly fit, it will produce the correct output for a given set of inputs. When a model is *underfit*, it has not yet been able to learn a strong enough representation of these patterns to be able to make good predictions. This can happen for a variety of reasons, most commonly that the architecture is too small to capture the complexity of the system it is supposed to model or that it has not been trained on enough data.

When a model is *overfit*, it has learned its training data too well. The model is able to exactly predict the minutiae of its training data, but it is not able to generalize its learning to data it has not previously seen. Often this happens because the model has managed to entirely memorize the training data, or it has learned to rely on a short-cut present in the training data but not in the real world.

For example, imagine you are training a model to classify photos as containing either dogs or cats. If all the dog photos in your training data are taken outdoors, and all the cat photos are taken indoors, your model may learn to cheat and use the presence of the sky in each photograph to predict which animal it is. This means that it might misclassify future dog selfies if they happen to be taken indoors.

There are many ways to fight overfitting. One possibility is to reduce the size of the model so it does not have enough capacity to learn an exact representation of its training set. A set of techniques known as *regularization* can be applied during training to reduce the degree of overfitting. To make the most of limited data, a technique called *data augmentation* can be used to generate new, artificial datapoints by slicing and dicing the existing data. But the best way to beat overfitting, when possible, is to get your hands on a larger and more varied dataset. More data always helps!

Regularization and Data Augmentation

Regularization techniques are used to make deep learning models less likely to overfit their training data. They generally involve constraining the model in some way in order to prevent it from perfectly memorizing the data that it's fed during training.

There are several methods used for regularization. Some, such as *L1* and *L2 regularization*, involve tweaking the algorithms used during training to penalize complex models that are prone to overfitting. Another, named *dropout*, involves randomly cutting the connections between neurons during training. We'll look at regularization in practice later in the book.

We'll also explore data augmentation, which is a way to artificially expand the size of a training dataset. This is done by creating multiple additional versions of every training input, each transformed in a way that preserves its meaning but varies its exact composition. In one of our examples, we train a model to recognize speech from audio samples. We augment our original training data by adding artificial background noise and shifting the samples around in time.

Training, validation, and testing

To assess the performance of a model, we can look at how it performs on its training data. However, this only tells us part of the story. During training, a model learns to fit its training data as closely as possible. As we saw earlier, in some cases the model will begin to overfit the training data, meaning that it will work well on the training data but not in real life.

To understand when this is happening, we need to *validate* the model using new data that wasn't used in training. It's common to split a dataset into three parts—*training*, *validation*, and *test*. A typical split is 60% training data, 20% validation, and 20% test. This splitting must be done so that each part contains the same distribution of information, and in a way that preserves the structure of the data. For example, since our data is a time series, we could potentially split it into three contiguous chunks of time. If our data were not a time series, we could just sample the datapoints randomly.

During training, the *training* dataset is used to train the model. Periodically, data from the *validation* dataset is fed through the model, and the loss is calculated. Because the model has not seen this data before, its loss score is a more reliable measure of how the model is performing. By comparing the training and validation loss (and accuracy, or whichever other metrics are available) over time, you can see whether the model is overfitting.

Figure 3-3 shows a model that is overfitting. You can see how as the training loss has decreased, the validation loss has gone up. This means that the model is becoming better at predicting the training data but is losing its ability to generalize to new data.

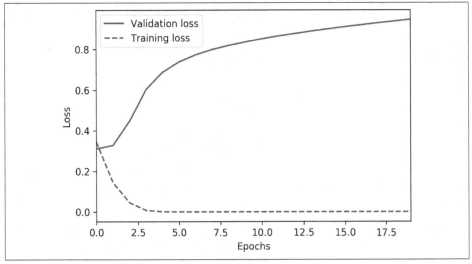

Figure 3-3. A graph showing model overfitting during training

As we tweak our models and training processes to improve performance and avoid overfitting, we will hopefully start to see our validation metrics improve.

However, this process has an unfortunate side effect. By optimizing to improve the validation metrics, we might just be nudging the model toward overfitting both the training *and* the validation data! Each adjustment we make will fit the model to the validation data slightly better, and in the end, we might have the same overfitting problem as before.

To verify that this hasn't happened, our final step when training a model is to run it on our *test* data and confirm that it performs as well as during validation. If it doesn't, we have optimized our model to overfit both our training and validation data. In this case, we might need to go back to the drawing board and come up with a new model architecture, since if we continue to tweak to improve performance on our test data, we'll just overfit to that, too.

After we have a model that performs acceptably well with training, validation, and test data, the training part of this process is over. Next, we get our model ready to run on-device!

Convert the Model

Throughout this book, we use TensorFlow to build and train models. A TensorFlow model is essentially a set of instructions that tell an *interpreter* how to transform data in order to produce an output. When we want to use our model, we just load it into memory and execute it using the TensorFlow interpreter.

However, TensorFlow's interpreter is designed to run models on powerful desktop computers and servers. Since we'll be running our models on tiny microcontrollers, we need a different interpreter that's designed for our use case. Fortunately, Tensor-Flow provides an interpreter and accompanying tools to run models on small, low-powered devices. This set of tools is called TensorFlow Lite.

Before TensorFlow Lite can run a model, it first must be converted into the Tensor-Flow Lite format and then saved to disk as a file. We do this using a tool named the *TensorFlow Lite Converter*. The converter can also apply special optimizations aimed at reducing the size of the model and helping it run faster, often without sacrificing performance.

In Chapter 13, we dive into the details of TensorFlow Lite and how it helps us run models on tiny devices. For now, all you need to know is that you'll need to convert your models, and that the conversion process is quick and easy.

Run Inference

After the model has been converted, it's ready to deploy! We'll now use the Tensor-Flow Lite for Microcontrollers C++ library to load the model and make predictions.

Since this is the part where our model meets our application code, we need to write some code that takes raw input data from our sensors and transforms it into the same form that our model was trained on. We then pass this transformed data into our model and run inference.

This will result in output data containing predictions. In the case of our classifier model, the output will be a score for each of our classes, "normal" and "abnormal."

For models that classify data, typically the scores for all of the classes will sum to 1, and the class with the highest score will be the prediction. The higher the difference between the scores, the higher the confidence in the prediction. Table 3-2 lists some example outputs.

Table 3-2. Example outputs

Normal score	Abnormal score	Explanation
0.1	0.9	High confidence in an abnormal state
0.9	0.1	High confidence in a normal state
0.7	0.3	Slight confidence in a normal state
0.49	0.51	Inconclusive result, since neither state is significantly ahead

In our factory machine example, each individual inference takes into account only a snapshot of the data—it tells us the probability of an abnormal state within the last 10 seconds, based on various sensor readings. Since real-world data is often messy and machine learning models aren't perfect, it's possible that a temporary glitch might result in an incorrect classification. For example, we might see a spike in a temperature value due to a temporary sensor malfunction. This transient, unreliable input might result in an output classification that momentarily doesn't reflect reality.

To prevent these momentary glitches from causing problems, we could potentially take the average of all of our model's outputs across a period of time. For example, we could run our model on the current data window every 10 seconds, and take the averages of the last 6 outputs to give a smoothed score for each class. This would mean that transient issues are ignored, and we only act upon consistent behavior. We use this technique to help with wake-word detection in Chapter 7.

After we have a score for each class, it's up to our application code to decide what to do. Perhaps if an abnormal state is detected consistently for one minute, our code will send a signal to shut down our machine and alert the maintenance team.

Evaluate and Troubleshoot

After we've deployed our model and have it running on-device, we'll start to see whether its real-world performance approaches what we hoped. Even though we've already proved that our model makes accurate predictions on its test data, performance on the actual problem might be different.

There are many reasons why this might happen. For example, the data used in training might not be exactly representative of the data available in real operation. Perhaps due to local climate, our machine's temperature is generally cooler than the one from which our dataset was collected. This might affect the predictions made by our model, such that they are no longer as accurate as expected.

Another possibility is that our model might have overfit our dataset without us realizing. In "Train the Model" on page 21, we learned how this can happen by accident when the dataset happens to contain additional signals that a model can learn to recognize in place of those we expect.

If our model isn't working in production, we'll need to do some troubleshooting. First, we rule out any hardware problems (like faulty sensors or unexpected noise) that might be affecting the data that gets to our model. Second, we capture some data from the device where the model is deployed and compare it with our original dataset to make sure that it is in the same ballpark. If not, perhaps there's a difference in environmental conditions or sensor characteristics that we weren't expecting. If the data checks out, it might be that overfitting is the problem.

After we've ruled out hardware issues, the best fix for overfitting is often to train with more data. We can capture additional data from our deployed hardware, combine it with our original dataset, and retrain our model. In the process, we can apply regularization and data augmentation techniques to help make the most of the data we have.

Reaching good real-world performance can sometimes take some iteration on your model, your hardware, and the accompanying software. If you run into a problem, treat it like any other technology issue. Take a scientific approach to troubleshooting, eliminating possible factors, and analyze your data to figure out what is going wrong.

Wrapping Up

Now that you're familiar with the basic workflow used by machine learning practitioners, we're ready to take the next steps in our TinyML adventure.

In Chapter 4, we'll build our first model and deploy it to some tiny hardware!

The "Hello World" of TinyML: Building and Training a Model

In Chapter 3, we learned the basic concepts of machine learning and the general workflow that machine learning projects follow. In this chapter and the next, we'll start putting our knowledge into practice. We're going to build and train a model from scratch and then integrate it into a simple microcontroller program.

In the process, you'll get your hands dirty with some powerful developer tools that are used every day by cutting-edge machine learning practitioners. You'll also learn how to integrate a machine learning model into a C++ program and deploy it to a microcontroller to control current flowing in a circuit. This might be your first taste of mixing hardware and ML, and it should be fun!

You can test the code that we write in these chapters on your Mac, Linux, or Windows machine, but for the full experience, you'll need one of the embedded devices mentioned in "What Hardware Do You Need?" on page 6:

- Arduino Nano 33 BLE Sense (*https://oreil.ly/6qlMD*)
- SparkFun Edge (*https://oreil.ly/-hoL-*)
- ST Microelectronics STM32F746G Discovery kit (*https://oreil.ly/cvm4J*)

To create our machine learning model, we'll use Python, TensorFlow, and Google's Colaboratory, which is a cloud-based interactive notebook for experimenting with Python code. These are some of the most important tools for real-world machine learning engineers, and they're all free to use.

Wondering about the title of this chapter? It's a tradition in programming that new technologies are introduced with example code that demonstrates how to do something very simple. Often, the simple task is to make a program output the words, "Hello, world." (*https://oreil.ly/zK06G*) There's no clear equivalent in ML, but we're using the term "hello world" to refer to a simple, easy-to-read example of an end-to-end TinyML application.

Over the course of this chapter, we will do the following:

1. Obtain a simple dataset.

2. Train a deep learning model.

3. Evaluate the model's performance.

4. Convert the model to run on-device.

5. Write code to perform on-device inference.

6. Build the code into a binary.

7. Deploy the binary to a microcontroller.

All the code that we will use is available in TensorFlow's GitHub repository (*https://oreil.ly/TQ4CC*).

We recommend that you walk through each part of this chapter and then try running the code. There are instructions on how to do this along the way. But before we start, let's discuss exactly what we're going to build.

What We're Building

In Chapter 3, we discussed how deep learning networks learn to model patterns in their training data so they can make predictions. We're now going to train a network to model some very simple data. You've probably heard of the sine (*https://oreil.ly/jxAmF*) function. It's used in trigonometry to help describe the properties of right-angled triangles. The data we'll be training with is a sine wave (*https://oreil.ly/XDvJu*), which is the graph obtained by plotting the result of the sine function over time (see Figure 4-1).

Our goal is to train a model that can take a value, x, and predict its sine, y. In a real-world application, if you needed the sine of x, you could just calculate it directly. However, by training a model to approximate the result, we can demonstrate the basics of machine learning.

The second part of our project will be to run this model on a hardware device. Visually, the sine wave is a pleasant curve that runs smoothly from –1 to 1 and back. This makes it perfect for controlling a visually pleasing light show! We'll be using the output of our model to control the timing of either some flashing LEDs or a graphical animation, depending on the capabilities of the device.

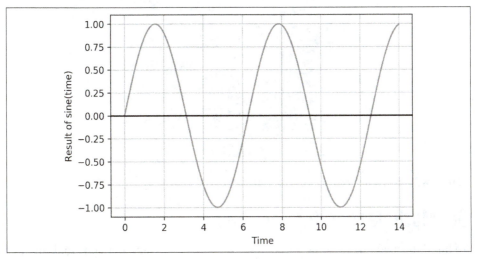

Figure 4-1. A sine wave

Online, you can see an animated GIF (*https://oreil.ly/XhqG9*) of this code flashing the LEDs of a SparkFun Edge. Figure 4-2 is a still from this animation, showing a couple of the device's LEDs lit. This may not be a particularly useful application of machine learning, but in the spirit of a "hello world" example, it's simple, fun, and will help demonstrate the basic principles you need to know.

After we get our basic code working, we'll be deploying it to three different devices: the SparkFun Edge, an Arduino Nano 33 BLE Sense, and an ST Microelectronics STM32F746G Discovery kit.

> Since TensorFlow is an actively developed open source project that is continually evolving, you might notice some slight differences between the code printed here and the code hosted online. Don't worry—even if a few lines of code change, the basic principles remain the same.

Figure 4-2. The code running on a SparkFun Edge

Our Machine Learning Toolchain

To build the machine learning parts of this project, we're using the same tools used by real-world machine learning practitioners. This section introduces them to you.

Python and Jupyter Notebooks

Python is the favorite programming language of machine learning scientists and engineers. It's easy to learn, works well for many different applications, and has a ton of libraries for useful tasks involving data and mathematics. The vast majority of deep learning research is done using Python, and researchers often release the Python source code for the models they create.

Python is especially great when combined with something called *Jupyter Notebooks* (*https://jupyter.org/*). This is a special document format that allows you to mix writing, graphics, and code that can be run at the click of a button. Jupyter notebooks are widely used as a way to describe, explain, and explore machine learning code and problems.

We'll be creating our model inside of a Jupyter notebook, which permits us to do awesome things to visualize our data during development. This includes displaying graphs that show our model's accuracy and convergence.

If you have some programming experience, Python is easy to read and learn. You should be able to follow this tutorial without any trouble.

Google Colaboratory

To run our notebook we'll use a tool called Colaboratory (*https://oreil.ly/ZV7NK*), or *Colab* for short. Colab is made by Google, and it provides an online environment for running Jupyter notebooks. It's provided for free as a tool to encourage research and development in machine learning.

Traditionally, you needed to create a notebook on your own computer. This required installing a lot of dependencies, such as Python libraries, which can be a headache. It was also difficult to share the resulting notebook with other people, since they might have different versions of the dependencies, meaning the notebook might not run as expected. In addition, machine learning can be computationally intensive, so training models might be slow on your development computer.

Colab allows you to run notebooks on Google's powerful hardware, at zero cost. You can edit and view your notebooks from any web browser, and you can share them with other people, who are guaranteed to get the same results when they run them. You can even configure Colab to run your code on specially accelerated hardware that can perform training more quickly than a normal computer.

TensorFlow and Keras

TensorFlow (*https://tensorflow.org*) is a set of tools for building, training, evaluating, and deploying machine learning models. Originally developed at Google, TensorFlow is now an open source project built and maintained by thousands of contributors across the world. It is the most popular and widely used framework for machine learning. Most developers interact with TensorFlow via its Python library.

TensorFlow does many different things. In this chapter we'll use Keras (*https://oreil.ly/ JgNtS*), TensorFlow's high-level API that makes it easy to build and train deep learning networks. We'll also use TensorFlow Lite (*https://oreil.ly/LbDBK*), a set of tools for deploying TensorFlow models to mobile and embedded devices, to run our model on-device.

Chapter 13 will cover TensorFlow in much more detail. For now, just know that it is an extremely powerful and industry-standard tool that will continue to serve your needs as you go from beginner to deep learning expert.

Building Our Model

We're now going to walk through the process of building, training, and converting our model. We include all of the code in this chapter, but you can also follow along in Colab and run the code as you go.

First, load the notebook (*https://oreil.ly/NN6Mj*). After the page loads, at the top, click the "Run in Google Colab" button, as shown in Figure 4-3. This copies the notebook from GitHub into Colab, allowing you to run it and make edits.

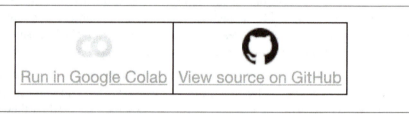

Figure 4-3. The "Run in Google Colab" button

Problems Loading the Notebook

As of this writing, there's a known issue with GitHub (*https://oreil.ly/1jLJG*) that results in intermittent error messages when displaying Jupyter notebooks. If you see the message "Sorry, something went wrong. Reload?" when trying to access the notebook, you can open it directly in Colab by using the following process. Copy the part of the notebook's GitHub URL that appears after *https://github.com*:

```
tensorflow/tensorflow/blob/master/tensorflow/lite/micro/examples/
    hello_world/create_sine_model.ipynb
```

And prepend it with *https://colab.research.google.com/github*. This will result in a full URL:

```
https://colab.research.google.com/github/tensorflow/tensorflow/blob/master/
    tensorflow/lite/micro/examples/hello_world/train/
    train_hello_world_model.ipynb
```

Navigate to that URL in your browser to open the notebook directly in Colab.

By default, in addition to the code, the notebook contains a sample of the output you should expect to see when the code is run. Since we'll be running through the code in this chapter, let's clear this output so the notebook is in a pristine state. To do this, in Colab's menu, click Edit and then select "Clear all outputs," as shown in Figure 4-4.

The menu shows:

File Edit View Insert Runtime Tools Hel

+ Code +

Table of cont

Select all cells	⌘/Ctrl+Shift+A
Cut selection	
Copy selection	
Paste	
Delete selected cells	⌘/Ctrl+M D
Find and replace...	⌘/Ctrl+H
Find next	⌘/Ctrl+G
Find previous	⌘/Ctrl+Shift+G
Notebook settings	
Show/hide code	
Clear all outputs	

○ create_sine_model.ipynb

Licensed und
(the "License"

Create and cc

Import de

Generate

Add som

Split our c

Design a

Train the

Figure 4-4. The "Clear all outputs" option

Nice work. Our notebook is now ready to go!

> If you're already familiar with machine learning, TensorFlow, and Keras, you might want to skip ahead to the part where we convert our model to use with TensorFlow Lite. In the book, jump to "Converting the Model for TensorFlow Lite" on page 60. In Colab, scroll down to the heading "Convert to TensorFlow Lite."

Importing Dependencies

Our first task is to import the dependencies we need. In Jupyter notebooks, code and text are arranged in *cells*. There are *code* cells, which contain executable Python code, and *text* cells, which contain formatted text.

Our first code cell is located under "Import dependencies." It sets up all of the libraries that we need to train and convert our model. Here's the code:

```
# TensorFlow is an open source machine learning library
!pip install tensorflow==2.0
import tensorflow as tf
# NumPy is a math library
import numpy as np
# Matplotlib is a graphing library
```

```
import matplotlib.pyplot as plt
# math is Python's math library
import math
```

In Python, the `import` statement loads a library so that it can be used from our code. You can see from the code and comments that this cell does the following:

- Installs the TensorFlow 2.0 library using `pip`, a package manager for Python
- Imports TensorFlow, NumPy, Matplotlib, and Python's `math` library

When we import a library, we can give it an alias so that it's easy to refer to later. For example, in the preceding code, we use `import numpy as np` to import NumPy and give it the alias `np`. When we use it in our code, we can refer to it as `np`.

The code in code cells can be run by clicking the button that appears at the upper left when the cell is selected. In the "Import dependencies" section, click anywhere in the first code cell so that it becomes selected. Figure 4-5 shows what a selected cell looks like.

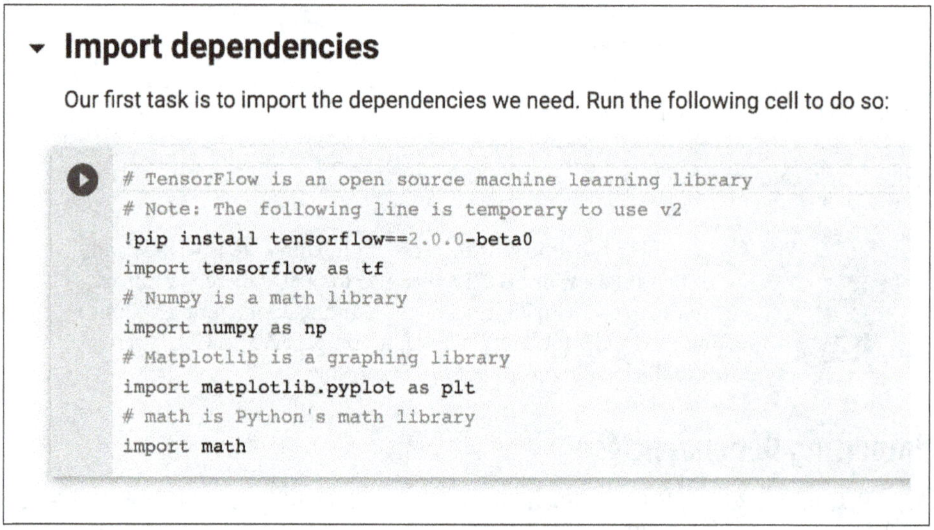

▾ **Import dependencies**

Our first task is to import the dependencies we need. Run the following cell to do so:

```
# TensorFlow is an open source machine learning library
# Note: The following line is temporary to use v2
!pip install tensorflow==2.0.0-beta0
import tensorflow as tf
# Numpy is a math library
import numpy as np
# Matplotlib is a graphing library
import matplotlib.pyplot as plt
# math is Python's math library
import math
```

Figure 4-5. The "Import dependencies" cell in its selected state

To run the code, click the button that appears in the upper left. As the code is being run, the button will animate with a circle as depicted in Figure 4-6.

The dependencies will begin to be installed, and you'll see some output appearing. You should eventually see the following line, meaning that the library was installed successfully:

```
Successfully installed tensorboard-2.0.0 tensorflow-2.0.0 tensorflow-
estimator-2.0.0
```

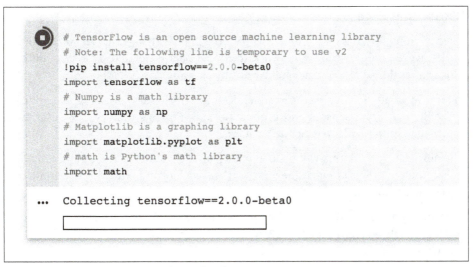

```
# TensorFlow is an open source machine learning library
# Note: The following line is temporary to use v2
!pip install tensorflow==2.0.0-beta0
import tensorflow as tf
# Numpy is a math library
import numpy as np
# Matplotlib is a graphing library
import matplotlib.pyplot as plt
# math is Python's math library
import math
```

... Collecting tensorflow==2.0.0-beta0

Figure 4-6. The "Import dependencies" cell in its running state

After a cell has been run in Colab, you'll see that a 1 is now displayed in the upper-left corner when it is no longer selected, as illustrated in Figure 4-7. This number is a counter that is incremented each time the cell is run.

```
[1]  # TensorFlow is an open source machine learning library
     # Note: The following line is temporary to use v2
     !pip install tensorflow==2.0.0-beta0
     import tensorflow as tf
     # Numpy is a math library
     import numpy as np
     # Matplotlib is a graphing library
     import matplotlib.pyplot as plt
     # math is Python's math library
     import math
```

Figure 4-7. The cell run counter in the upper-left corner

You can use this to understand which cells have been run, and how many times.

Generating Data

Deep learning networks learn to model patterns in underlying data. As we mentioned earlier, we're going to train a network to model data generated by a sine function. This will result in a model that can take a value, x, and predict its sine, y.

Before we go any further, we need some data. In a real-world situation, we might be collecting data from sensors and production logs. For this example, however, we're using some simple code to generate a dataset.

The next cell is where this will happen. Our plan is to generate 1,000 values that represent random points along a sine wave. Let's take a look at Figure 4-8 to remind ourselves what a sine wave looks like.

Each full cycle of a wave is called its *period*. From the graph, we can see that a full cycle is completed approximately every six units on the x-axis. In fact, the period of a sine wave is $2 \times \pi$, or 2π.

So that we have a full sine wave worth of data to train on, our code will generate random x values from 0 to 2π. It will then calculate the sine for each of these values.

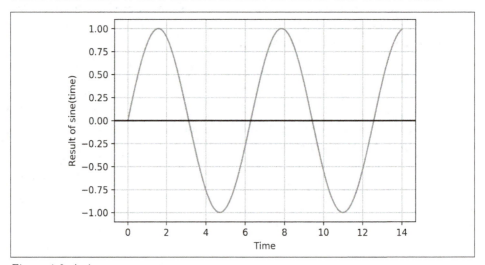

Figure 4-8. A sine wave

Here's the full code for this cell, which uses NumPy (np, which we imported earlier) to generate random numbers and calculate their sine:

```
# We'll generate this many sample datapoints
SAMPLES = 1000

# Set a "seed" value, so we get the same random numbers each time we run this
# notebook. Any number can be used here.
SEED = 1337
```

```
np.random.seed(SEED)
tf.random.set_seed(SEED)

# Generate a uniformly distributed set of random numbers in the range from
# 0 to 2n, which covers a complete sine wave oscillation
x_values = np.random.uniform(low=0, high=2*math.pi, size=SAMPLES)

# Shuffle the values to guarantee they're not in order
np.random.shuffle(x_values)

# Calculate the corresponding sine values
y_values = np.sin(x_values)

# Plot our data. The 'b.' argument tells the library to print blue dots.
plt.plot(x_values, y_values, 'b.')
plt.show()
```

In addition to what we discussed earlier, there are a few things worth pointing out in this code. First, you'll see that we use `np.random.uniform()` to generate our x values. This method returns an array of random numbers in the specified range. NumPy contains a lot of useful methods that operate on entire arrays of values, which is very convenient when dealing with data.

Second, after generating the data, we shuffle it. This is important because the training process used in deep learning depends on data being fed to it in a truly random order. If the data were in order, the resulting model would be less accurate.

Next, notice that we use NumPy's `sin()` method to calculate our sine values. NumPy can do this for all of our x values at once, returning an array. NumPy is great!

Finally, you'll see some mysterious code invoking `plt`, which is our alias for Matplotlib:

```
# Plot our data. The 'b.' argument tells the library to print blue dots.
plt.plot(x_values, y_values, 'b.')
plt.show()
```

What does this code do? It plots a graph of our data. One of the best things about Jupyter notebooks is their ability to display graphics that are output by the code you run. Matplotlib is an excellent tool for creating graphs from data. Since visualizing data is a crucial part of the machine learning workflow, this will be incredibly helpful as we train our model.

To generate the data and render it as a graph, run the code in the cell. After the code cell finishes running, you should see a beautiful graph appear underneath, like the one shown in Figure 4-9.

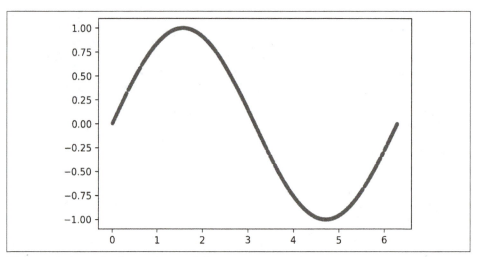

Figure 4-9. A graph of our generated data

This is our data! It is a selection of random points along a nice, smooth sine curve. We could use this to train our model. However, this would be too easy. One of the exciting things about deep learning networks is their ability to sift patterns from noise. This allows them to make predictions even when trained on messy, real-world data. To show this off, let's add some random noise to our datapoints and draw another graph:

```
# Add a small random number to each y value
y_values += 0.1 * np.random.randn(*y_values.shape)

# Plot our data
plt.plot(x_values, y_values, 'b.')
plt.show()
```

Run this cell and take a look at the results, as shown in Figure 4-10.

Much better! Our points are now randomized, so they represent a distribution around a sine wave instead of a smooth, perfect curve. This is much more reflective of a real-world situation, in which data is generally quite messy.

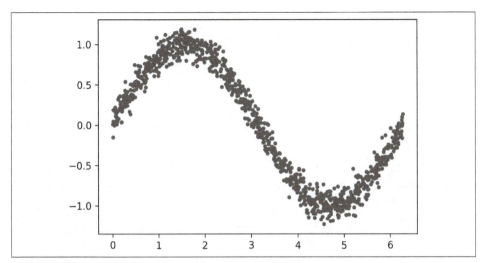

Figure 4-10. A graph of our data with noise added

Splitting the Data

From the previous chapter, you might remember that a dataset is often split into three parts: *training*, *validation*, and *test*. To evaluate the accuracy of the model we train, we need to compare its predictions to real data and check how well they match up.

This evaluation happens during training (where it is referred to as validation) and after training (referred to as testing). It's important in each case that we use fresh data that was not already used to train the model.

To ensure that we have data to use for evaluation, we'll set some aside before we begin training. Let's reserve 20% of our data for validation, and another 20% for testing. We'll use the remaining 60% to train the model. This is a typical split used when training models.

The following code splits our data and then plots each set as a different color:

```
# We'll use 60% of our data for training and 20% for testing. The remaining 20%
# will be used for validation. Calculate the indices of each section.
TRAIN_SPLIT =  int(0.6 * SAMPLES)
TEST_SPLIT = int(0.2 * SAMPLES + TRAIN_SPLIT)

# Use np.split to chop our data into three parts.
# The second argument to np.split is an array of indices where the data will be
# split. We provide two indices, so the data will be divided into three chunks.
x_train, x_validate, x_test = np.split(x_values, [TRAIN_SPLIT, TEST_SPLIT])
y_train, y_validate, y_test = np.split(y_values, [TRAIN_SPLIT, TEST_SPLIT])

# Double check that our splits add up correctly
assert (x_train.size + x_validate.size + x_test.size) ==  SAMPLES
```

```
# Plot the data in each partition in different colors:
plt.plot(x_train, y_train, 'b.', label="Train")
plt.plot(x_validate, y_validate, 'y.', label="Validate")
plt.plot(x_test, y_test, 'r.', label="Test")
plt.legend()
plt.show()
```

To split our data, we use another handy NumPy method: `split()`. This method takes an array of data and an array of indices and then chops the data into parts at the indices provided.

Run this cell to see the results of our split. Each type of data will be represented by a different color (or shade, if you're reading the print version of this book), as demonstrated in Figure 4-11.

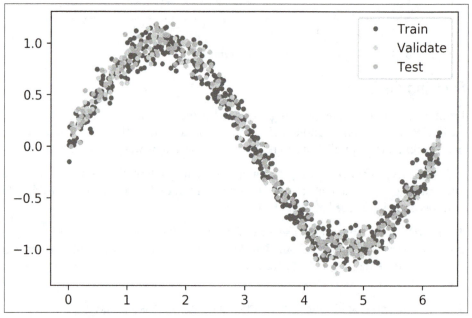

Figure 4-11. A graph of our data split into training, validation, and test sets

Defining a Basic Model

Now that we have our data, it's time to create the model that we'll train to fit it.

We're going to build a model that will take an input value (in this case, x) and use it to predict a numeric output value (the sine of x). This type of problem is called a *regression*. We can use regression models for all sorts of tasks that require a numeric output. For example, a regression model could attempt to predict a person's running speed in miles per hour based on data from an accelerometer.

To create our model, we're going to design a simple neural network. It uses layers of neurons to attempt to learn any patterns underlying the training data so that it can make predictions.

The code to do this is actually quite straightforward. It uses *Keras* (*https://oreil.ly/ IpFqC*), TensorFlow's high-level API for creating deep learning networks:

```
# We'll use Keras to create a simple model architecture
from tf.keras import layers
model_1 = tf.keras.Sequential()

# First layer takes a scalar input and feeds it through 16 "neurons." The
# neurons decide whether to activate based on the 'relu' activation function.
model_1.add(layers.Dense(16, activation='relu', input_shape=(1,)))

# Final layer is a single neuron, since we want to output a single value
model_1.add(layers.Dense(1))

# Compile the model using a standard optimizer and loss function for regression
model_1.compile(optimizer='rmsprop', loss='mse', metrics=['mae'])

# Print a summary of the model's architecture
model_1.summary()
```

First, we create a `Sequential` model using Keras, which just means a model in which each layer of neurons is stacked on top of the next, as we saw in Figure 3-1. We then define two layers. Here's where the first layer is defined:

```
model_1.add(layers.Dense(16, activation='relu', input_shape=(1,)))
```

The first layer has a single input—our x value—and 16 neurons. It's a `Dense` layer (also known as a *fully connected* layer), meaning the input will be fed into every single one of its neurons during inference, when we're making predictions. Each neuron will then become *activated* to a certain degree. The amount of activation for each neuron is based on both its *weight* and *bias* values, learned during training, and its *activation function*. The neuron's activation is output as a number.

Activation is calculated by a simple formula, shown in Python. We won't ever need to code this ourselves, since it is handled by Keras and TensorFlow, but it will be helpful to know as we go further into deep learning:

```
activation = activation_function((input * weight) + bias)
```

To calculate the neuron's activation, its input is multiplied by the weight, and the bias is added to the result. The calculated value is passed into the activation function. The resulting number is the neuron's activation.

The activation function is a mathematical function used to shape the output of the neuron. In our network, we're using an activation function called *rectified linear unit*, or *ReLU* for short. This is specified in Keras by the argument `activation=relu`.

ReLU is a simple function, shown here in Python:

```python
def relu(input):
    return max(0.0, input)
```

ReLU returns whichever is the larger value: its input, or zero. If its input value is negative, ReLU returns zero. If its input value is above zero, ReLU returns it unchanged.

Figure 4-12 shows the output of ReLU for a range of input values.

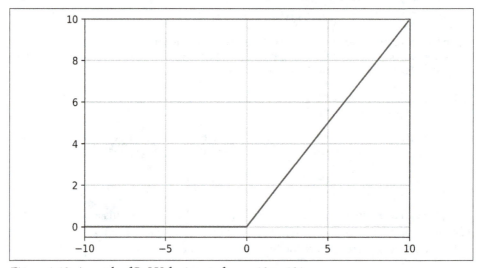

Figure 4-12. A graph of ReLU for inputs from –10 to 10

Without an activation function, the neuron's output would always be a linear function of its input. This would mean that the network could model only linear relationships in which the ratio between x and y remains the same across the entire range of values. This would prevent a network from modeling our sine wave, because a sine wave is nonlinear.

Since ReLU is nonlinear, it allows multiple layers of neurons to join forces and model complex nonlinear relationships, in which the y value doesn't increase by the same amount for every increment of x.

There are other activation functions, but ReLU is the most commonly used. You can see some of the other options in the Wikipedia article on activation functions (*https://oreil.ly/Yxe-N*). Each activation function has different trade-offs, and machine learning engineers experiment to find which options work best for a given architecture.

The activation numbers from our first layer will be fed as inputs to our second layer, which is defined in the following line:

```
model_1.add(layers.Dense(1))
```

Because this layer is a single neuron, it will receive 16 inputs, one for each of the neurons in the previous layer. Its purpose is to combine all of the activations from the previous layer into a single output value. Since this is our output layer, we don't specify an activation function—we just want the raw result.

Because this neuron has multiple inputs, it has a corresponding weight value for each. The neuron's output is calculated by the following formula, shown in Python:

```
# Here, `inputs` and `weights` are both NumPy arrays with 16 elements each
output = sum((inputs * weights)) + bias
```

The output value is obtained by multiplying each input with its corresponding weight, summing the results, and then adding the neuron's bias.

The network's weights and biases are learned during training. The compile() step in the code shown earlier in the chapter configures some important arguments used in the training process, and prepares the model to be trained:

```
model_1.compile(optimizer='rmsprop', loss='mse', metrics=['mae'])
```

The optimizer argument specifies the algorithm that will adjust the network to model its input during training. There are several choices, and finding the best one often comes down to experimentation. You can read about the options in the Keras documentation (*https://oreil.ly/oT-pU*).

The loss argument specifies the method used during training to calculate how far the network's predictions are from reality. This method is called a *loss function*. Here, we're using mse, or *mean squared error*. This loss function is used in the case of regression problems, for which we're trying to predict a number. There are various loss functions available in Keras. You can see some of the options listed in the Keras docs (*https://keras.io/losses*).

The metrics argument allows us to specify some additional functions that are used to judge the performance of our model. We specify mae, or *mean absolute error*, which is a helpful function for measuring the performance of a regression model. This metric will be measured during training, and we'll have access to the results after training is done.

After we compile our model, we can use the following line to print some summary information about its architecture:

```
# Print a summary of the model's architecture
model_1.summary()
```

Run the cell in Colab to define the model. You'll see the following output printed:

```
Model: "sequential"

_____
Layer (type)                 Output Shape              Param #
=================================================================
dense (Dense)                (None, 16)                32
_____
dense_1 (Dense)              (None, 1)                 17
=================================================================
Total params: 49
Trainable params: 49
Non-trainable params: 0
_____
```

This table shows the layers of the network, their output shapes, and their numbers of *parameters*. The size of a network—how much memory it takes up—depends mostly on its number of parameters, meaning its total number of weights and biases. This can be a useful metric when discussing model size and complexity.

For simple models like ours, the number of weights can be determined by calculating the number of connections between neurons in the model, given that each connection has a weight.

The network we've just designed consists of two layers. Our first layer has 16 connections—one between its input and each of its neurons. Our second layer has a single neuron, which also has 16 connections—one to each neuron in the first layer. This makes the total number of connections 32.

Since every neuron has a bias, the network has 17 biases, meaning it has a total of 32 + 17 = 49 parameters.

We've now walked through the code that defines our model. Next, we'll begin the training process.

Training Our Model

After we define our model, it's time to train it and then evaluate its performance to see how well it works. When we see the metrics, we can decide if it's good enough, or if we should make changes to our design and train it again.

To train a model in Keras we just call its `fit()` method, passing all of our data and some other important arguments. The code in the next cell shows how:

```
history_1 = model_1.fit(x_train, y_train, epochs=1000, batch_size=16,
                        validation_data=(x_validate, y_validate))
```

Run the code in the cell to begin training. You'll see some logs start to appear:

```
Train on 600 samples, validate on 200 samples
Epoch 1/1000
600/600 [==============================] - 1s 1ms/sample - loss: 0.7887 - mae:
0.7848 - val_loss: 0.5824 - val_mae: 0.6867
Epoch 2/1000
600/600 [==============================] - 0s 155us/sample - loss: 0.4883 -
mae: 0.6194 - val_loss: 0.4742 - val_mae: 0.6056
```

Our model is now training. This will take a little while, so while we wait let's walk through the details of our call to fit():

```
history_1 = model_1.fit(x_train, y_train, epochs=1000, batch_size=16,
                        validation_data=(x_validate, y_validate))
```

First, you'll notice that we assign the return value of our fit() call to a variable named history_1. This variable contains a ton of information about our training run, and we'll use it later to investigate how things went.

Next, let's take a look at the fit() function's arguments:

x_train, y_train

> The first two arguments to fit() are the x and y values of our training data. Remember that parts of our data are kept aside for validation and testing, so only the training set is used to train the network.

epochs

> The next argument specifies how many times our entire training set will be run through the network during training. The more epochs, the more training will occur. You might think that the more training happens, the better the network will be. However, some networks will start to overfit their training data after a certain number of epochs, so we might want to limit the amount of training we do.

> In addition, even if there's no overfitting, a network will stop improving after a certain amount of training. Since training costs time and computational resources, it's best not to train if the network isn't getting better!

> We're starting out with 1,000 epochs of training. When training is complete, we can dig into our metrics to discover whether this is the correct number.

batch_size

> The batch_size argument specifies how many pieces of training data to feed into the network before measuring its accuracy and updating its weights and biases. If we wanted, we could specify a batch_size of 1, meaning we'd run inference on a single datapoint, measure the loss of the network's prediction, update the weights and biases to make the prediction more accurate next time, and then continue this cycle for the rest of the data.

Because we have 600 datapoints, each epoch would result in 600 updates to the network. This is a lot of computation, so our training would take ages! An alternative might be to select and run inference on multiple datapoints, measure the loss in aggregate, and then updating the network accordingly.

If we set `batch_size` to 600, each batch would include all of our training data. We'd now have to make only one update to the network every epoch—much quicker. The problem is, this results in less accurate models. Research has shown that models trained with large batch sizes have less ability to generalize to new data—they are more likely to overfit.

The compromise is to use a batch size that is somewhere in the middle. In our training code, we use a batch size of 16. This means that we'll choose 16 datapoints at random, run inference on them, calculate the loss in aggregate, and update the network once per batch. If we have 600 points of training data, the network will be updated around 38 times per epoch, which is far better than 600.

When choosing a batch size, we're making a compromise between training efficiency and model accuracy. The ideal batch size will vary from model to model. It's a good idea to start with a batch size of 16 or 32 and experiment to see what works best.

`validation_data`
> This is where we specify our validation dataset. Data from this dataset will be run through the network throughout the training process, and the network's predictions will be compared with the expected values. We'll see the results of validation in the logs and as part of the `history_1` object.

Training Metrics

Hopefully, by now, training has finished. If not, wait a few moments for it to complete.

We're now going to check various metrics to see how well our network has learned. To begin, let's look at the logs written during training. This will show how the network has improved during training from its random initial state.

Here are the logs for our first and last epochs:

```
Epoch 1/1000
600/600 [==============================] - 1s 1ms/sample - loss: 0.7887 - mae:
0.7848 - val_loss: 0.5824 - val_mae: 0.6867

Epoch 1000/1000
600/600 [==============================] - 0s 124us/sample - loss: 0.1524 -
mae: 0.3039 - val_loss: 0.1737 - val_mae: 0.3249
```

The `loss`, `mae`, `val_loss`, and `val_mae` tell us various things:

loss

> This is the output of our loss function. We're using mean squared error, which is expressed as a positive number. Generally, the smaller the loss value, the better, so this is a good thing to watch as we evaluate our network.
>
> Comparing the first and last epochs, the network has clearly improved during training, going from a loss of ~0.7 to a smaller value of ~0.15. Let's look at the other numbers to see whether this improvement is enough!

mae

> This is the mean absolute error of our training data. It shows the average difference between the network's predictions and the expected y values from the training data.
>
> We can expect our initial error to be pretty dismal, given that it's based on an untrained network. This is certainly the case: the network's predictions are off by an average of ~0.78, which is a large number when the range of acceptable values is only from –1 to 1!
>
> However, even after training, our mean absolute error is ~0.30. This means that our predictions are off by an average of ~0.30, which is still quite awful.

val_loss

> This is the output of our loss function on our validation data. In our final epoch, the training loss (~0.15) is slightly lower than the validation loss (~0.17). This is a hint that our network might be overfitting, because it is performing worse on data it has not seen before.

val_mae

> This is the mean absolute error for our validation data. With a value of ~0.32, it's worse than the mean absolute error on our training set, which is another sign that the network might be overfitting.

Graphing the History

So far, it's clear that our model is not doing a great job of making accurate predictions. Our task now is to figure out why. To do so, let's make use of the data collected in our `history_1` object.

The next cell extracts the training and validation loss data from the history object and plots it on a chart:

```
loss = history_1.history['loss']
val_loss = history_1.history['val_loss']
```

```
epochs = range(1, len(loss) + 1)

plt.plot(epochs, loss, 'g.', label='Training loss')
plt.plot(epochs, val_loss, 'b', label='Validation loss')
plt.title('Training and validation loss')
plt.xlabel('Epochs')
plt.ylabel('Loss')
plt.legend()
plt.show()
```

The history_1 object contains an attribute called, history_1.history, which is a dictionary recording metric values during training and validation. We use this to collect the data we're going to plot. For our x-axis we use the epoch number, which we determine by looking at the number of loss datapoints. Run the cell and you'll see the graph in Figure 4-13.

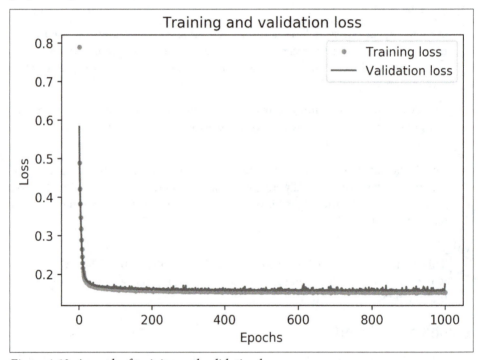

Figure 4-13. A graph of training and validation loss

As you can see, the amount of loss rapidly decreases over the first 50 epochs, before flattening out. This means that the model is improving and producing more accurate predictions.

Our goal is to stop training when either the model is no longer improving or the training loss is less than the validation loss, which would mean that the model has learned to predict the training data so well that it can no longer generalize to new data.

The loss drops precipitously in the first few epochs, which makes the rest of the graph quite difficult to read. Let's skip the first 100 epochs by running the next cell:

```
# Exclude the first few epochs so the graph is easier to read
SKIP = 100

plt.plot(epochs[SKIP:], loss[SKIP:], 'g.', label='Training loss')
plt.plot(epochs[SKIP:], val_loss[SKIP:], 'b.', label='Validation loss')
plt.title('Training and validation loss')
plt.xlabel('Epochs')
plt.ylabel('Loss')
plt.legend()
plt.show()
```

Figure 4-14 presents the graph produced by this cell.

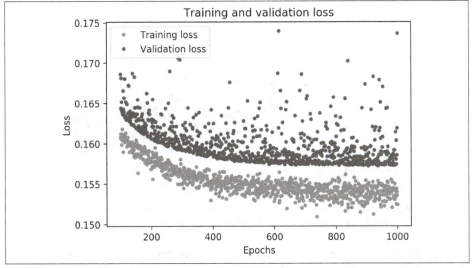

Figure 4-14. A graph of training and validation loss, skipping the first 100 epochs

Now that we've zoomed in, you can see that loss continues to reduce until around 600 epochs, at which point it is mostly stable. This means that there's probably no need to train our network for so long.

However, you can also see that the lowest loss value is still around 0.15. This seems relatively high. In addition, the validation loss values are consistently even higher.

To gain more insight into our model's performance we can plot some more data. This time, let's plot the mean absolute error. Run the next cell to do so:

```
# Draw a graph of mean absolute error, which is another way of
# measuring the amount of error in the prediction.
mae = history_1.history['mae']
val_mae = history_1.history['val_mae']

plt.plot(epochs[SKIP:], mae[SKIP:], 'g.', label='Training MAE')
plt.plot(epochs[SKIP:], val_mae[SKIP:], 'b.', label='Validation MAE')
plt.title('Training and validation mean absolute error')
plt.xlabel('Epochs')
plt.ylabel('MAE')
plt.legend()
plt.show()
```

Figure 4-15 shows the resulting graph.

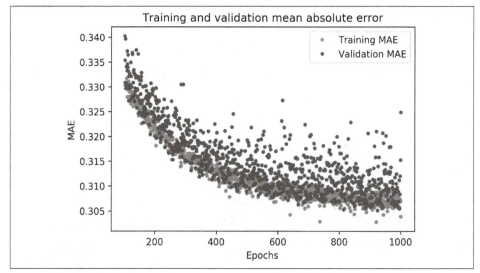

Figure 4-15. A graph of mean absolute error during training and validation

This graph of mean absolute error gives us some further clues. We can see that on average, the training data shows lower error than the validation data, which means that the network might have overfit, or learned the training data so rigidly that it can't make effective predictions about new data.

In addition, the mean absolute error values are quite high, around ~0.31, which means that some of the model's predictions are wrong by at least 0.31. Since our expected values only range in size from –1 to +1, an error of 0.31 means we are very far from accurately modeling the sine wave.

To get more insight into what is happening, we can plot our network's predictions for the training data against the expected values.

This happens in the following cell:

```
# Use the model to make predictions from our validation data
predictions = model_1.predict(x_train)

# Plot the predictions along with the test data
plt.clf()
plt.title('Training data predicted vs actual values')
plt.plot(x_test, y_test, 'b.', label='Actual')
plt.plot(x_train, predictions, 'r.', label='Predicted')
plt.legend()
plt.show()
```

By calling `model_1.predict(x_train)`, we run inference on all of the x values from the training data. The method returns an array of predictions. Let's plot this on the graph alongside the actual y values from our training set. Run the cell to see the graph in Figure 4-16.

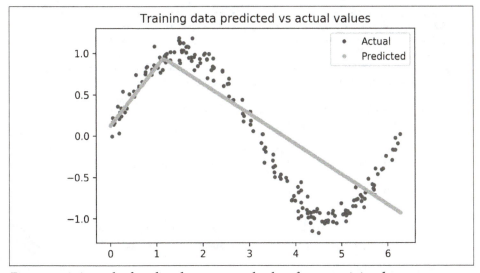

Figure 4-16. A graph of predicted versus actual values for our training data

Oh, dear! The graph makes it clear that our network has learned to approximate the sine function in a very limited way. The predictions are highly linear, and only very roughly fit the data.

The rigidity of this fit suggests that the model does not have enough capacity to learn the full complexity of the sine wave function, so it's able to approximate it only in an overly simplistic way. By making our model bigger, we should be able to improve its performance.

Improving Our Model

Armed with the knowledge that our original model was too small to learn the complexity of our data, we can try to make it better. This is a normal part of the machine learning workflow: design a model, evaluate its performance, and make changes in the hope of seeing improvement.

An easy way to make the network bigger is to add another layer of neurons. Each layer of neurons represents a transformation of the input that will hopefully get it closer to the expected output. The more layers of neurons a network has, the more complex these transformations can be.

Run the following cell to redefine our model in the same way as earlier, but with an additional layer of 16 neurons in the middle:

```
model_2 = tf.keras.Sequential()

# First layer takes a scalar input and feeds it through 16 "neurons." The
# neurons decide whether to activate based on the 'relu' activation function.
model_2.add(layers.Dense(16, activation='relu', input_shape=(1,)))

# The new second layer may help the network learn more complex representations
model_2.add(layers.Dense(16, activation='relu'))

# Final layer is a single neuron, since we want to output a single value
model_2.add(layers.Dense(1))

# Compile the model using a standard optimizer and loss function for regression
model_2.compile(optimizer='rmsprop', loss='mse', metrics=['mae'])

# Show a summary of the model
model_2.summary()
```

As you can see, the code is basically the same as for our first model, but with an additional Dense layer. Let's run the cell to see the summary() results:

```
Model: "sequential_1"
```

Layer (type)	Output Shape	Param #
dense_2 (Dense)	(None, 16)	32
dense_3 (Dense)	(None, 16)	272
dense_4 (Dense)	(None, 1)	17

```
Total params: 321
Trainable params: 321
Non-trainable params: 0
```

With two layers of 16 neurons, our new model is a lot larger. It has (1 * 16) + (16 * 16) + (16 * 1) = 288 weights, plus 16 + 16 + 1 = 33 biases, for a total of 288 + 33 = 321 parameters. Our original model had only 49 total parameters, so this is a 555% increase in model size. Hopefully, this extra capacity will help represent the complexity of our data.

The following cell will train our new model. Since our first model stopped improving so quickly, let's train for fewer epochs this time—only 600. Run this cell to begin training:

```
history_2 = model_2.fit(x_train, y_train, epochs=600, batch_size=16,
                        validation_data=(x_validate, y_validate))
```

When training is complete, we can take a look at the final log to get a quick feel for whether things have improved:

```
Epoch 600/600
600/600 [==============================] - 0s 150us/sample - loss: 0.0115 -
mae: 0.0859 - val_loss: 0.0104 - val_mae: 0.0806
```

Wow! You can see that we've already achieved a huge improvement—validation loss has dropped from 0.17 to 0.01, and validation mean absolute error has dropped from 0.32 to 0.08. This looks very promising.

To see how things are going, let's run the next cell. It's set up to generate the same graphs we used last time. First, we draw a graph of the loss:

```
# Draw a graph of the loss, which is the distance between
# the predicted and actual values during training and validation.
loss = history_2.history['loss']
val_loss = history_2.history['val_loss']

epochs = range(1, len(loss) + 1)

plt.plot(epochs, loss, 'g.', label='Training loss')
plt.plot(epochs, val_loss, 'b', label='Validation loss')
plt.title('Training and validation loss')
plt.xlabel('Epochs')
plt.ylabel('Loss')
plt.legend()
plt.show()
```

Figure 4-17 shows the result.

Next, we draw the same loss graph but with the first 100 epochs skipped so that we can better see the detail:

```
# Exclude the first few epochs so the graph is easier to read
SKIP = 100

plt.clf()
```

```
plt.plot(epochs[SKIP:], loss[SKIP:], 'g.', label='Training loss')
plt.plot(epochs[SKIP:], val_loss[SKIP:], 'b.', label='Validation loss')
plt.title('Training and validation loss')
plt.xlabel('Epochs')
plt.ylabel('Loss')
plt.legend()
plt.show()
```

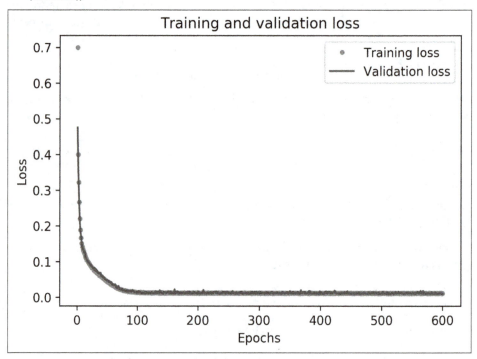

Figure 4-17. A graph of training and validation loss

Figure 4-18 presents the output.

Finally, we plot the mean absolute error for the same set of epochs:

```
plt.clf()

# Draw a graph of mean absolute error, which is another way of
# measuring the amount of error in the prediction.
mae = history_2.history['mae']
val_mae = history_2.history['val_mae']

plt.plot(epochs[SKIP:], mae[SKIP:], 'g.', label='Training MAE')
plt.plot(epochs[SKIP:], val_mae[SKIP:], 'b.', label='Validation MAE')
plt.title('Training and validation mean absolute error')
plt.xlabel('Epochs')
plt.ylabel('MAE')
```

```
plt.legend()
plt.show()
```

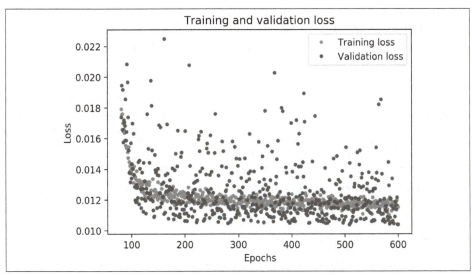

Figure 4-18. A graph of training and validation loss, skipping the first 100 epochs

Figure 4-19 depicts the graph.

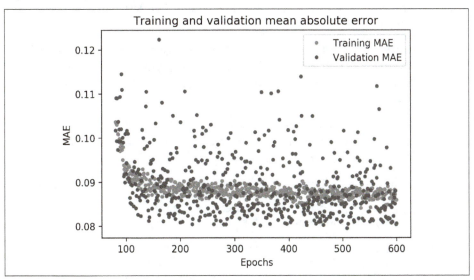

Figure 4-19. A graph of mean absolute error during training and validation

Great results! From these graphs, we can see two exciting things:

- The metrics are broadly better for validation than training, which means the network is not overfitting.
- The overall loss and mean absolute error are much better than in our previous network.

You might be wondering why the metrics for validation are better than those for training, and not merely identical. The reason is that validation metrics are calculated at the end of each epoch, meanwhile training metrics are calculated while the epoch of training is still in progress. This means validation happens on a model that has been trained for slightly longer.

Based on our validation data, our model seems to be performing great. However, to be sure of this, we need to run one final test.

Testing

Earlier, we set aside 20% of our data to use for testing. As we discussed, it's very important to have separate validation and test data. Since we fine-tune our network based on its validation performance, there's a risk that we might accidentally tune the model to overfit its validation set and that it might not be able to generalize to new data. By retaining some fresh data and using it for a final test of our model, we can make sure that this has not happened.

After we've used our test data, we need to resist the urge to tune our model further. If we did make changes with the goal of improving test performance, we might cause it to overfit our test set. If we did this, we wouldn't be able to know, because we'd have no fresh data left to test with.

This means that if our model performs badly on our test data, it's time to go back to the drawing board. We'll need to stop optimizing the current model and come up with a brand new architecture.

With that in mind, the following cell will evaluate our model against our test data:

```
# Calculate and print the loss on our test dataset
loss = model_2.evaluate(x_test, y_test)

# Make predictions based on our test dataset
predictions = model_2.predict(x_test)

# Graph the predictions against the actual values
plt.clf()
plt.title('Comparison of predictions and actual values')
plt.plot(x_test, y_test, 'b.', label='Actual')
plt.plot(x_test, predictions, 'r.', label='Predicted')
```

```
plt.legend()
plt.show()
```

First, we call the model's `evaluate()` method with the test data. This will calculate and print the loss and mean absolute error metrics, informing us as to how far the model's predictions deviate from the actual values. Next, we make a set of predictions and plot them on a graph alongside the actual values.

Now we can run the cell to learn how our model is performing! First, let's see the results of `evaluate()`:

```
200/200 [==============================] - 0s 71us/sample - loss: 0.0103 - mae:
0.0718
```

This shows that 200 datapoints were evaluated, which is our entire test set. The model took 71 microseconds to make each prediction. The loss metric was 0.0103, which is excellent, and very close to our validation loss of 0.0104. Our mean absolute error, 0.0718, is also very small and fairly close to its equivalent in validation, 0.0806.

This means that our model is working great, and it isn't overfitting! If the model had overfit our validation data, we could expect that the metrics on our test set would be significantly worse than those resulting from validation.

The graph of our predictions against our actual values, shown in Figure 4-20, makes it clear how well our model is performing.

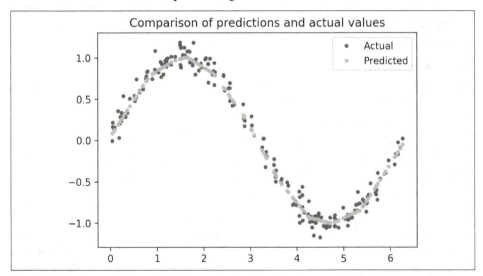

Figure 4-20. A graph of predicted versus actual values for our test data

You can see that, for the most part, the dots representing *predicted* values form a smooth curve along the center of the distribution of *actual* values. Our network has learned to approximate a sine curve, even though the dataset was noisy!

If you look closely, however, you'll see that there are some imperfections. The peak and trough of our predicted sine wave are not perfectly smooth, like a real sine wave would be. Variations in our training data, which is randomly distributed, have been learned by our model. This is a mild case of overfitting: instead of learning the smooth sine function, our model has learned to replicate the exact shape of our data.

For our purposes, this overfitting isn't a major problem. Our goal is for this model to gently fade an LED on and off, and it doesn't need to be perfectly smooth to achieve this. If we thought the level of overfitting was problematic, we could attempt to address it through regularization techniques or by obtaining more training data.

Now that we're happy with our model, let's get it ready to deploy on-device!

Converting the Model for TensorFlow Lite

At the beginning of this chapter we briefly touched on TensorFlow Lite, which is a set of tools for running TensorFlow models on "edge devices"—meaning everything from mobile phones down to microcontroller boards.

Chapter 13 goes into detail on TensorFlow Lite for Microcontrollers. For now, we can think of it as having two main components:

TensorFlow Lite Converter
> This converts TensorFlow models into a special, space-efficient format for use on memory-constrained devices, and it can apply optimizations that further reduce the model size and make it run faster on small devices.

TensorFlow Lite Interpreter
> This runs an appropriately converted TensorFlow Lite model using the most efficient operations for a given device.

Before we use our model with TensorFlow Lite, we need to convert it. We use the TensorFlow Lite Converter's Python API to do this. It takes our Keras model and writes it to disk in the form of a *FlatBuffer*, which is a special file format designed to be space-efficient. Because we're deploying to devices with limited memory, this will come in handy! We'll look at FlatBuffers in more detail in Chapter 12.

In addition to creating a FlatBuffer, the TensorFlow Lite Converter can also apply optimizations to the model. These optimizations generally reduce the size of the model, the time it takes to run, or both. This can come at the cost of a reduction in accuracy, but the reduction is often small enough that it's worthwhile. You can read more about optimizations in Chapter 13.

One of the most useful optimizations is *quantization*. By default, the weights and biases in a model are stored as 32-bit floating-point numbers so that high-precision calculations can occur during training. Quantization allows you to reduce the precision of these numbers so that they fit into 8-bit integers—a four times reduction in size. Even better, because it's easier for a CPU to perform math with integers than with floats, a quantized model will run faster.

The coolest thing about quantization is that it often results in minimal loss in accuracy. This means that when deploying to low-memory devices, it is nearly always worthwhile.

In the following cell, we use the converter to create and save two new versions of our model. The first is converted to the TensorFlow Lite FlatBuffer format, but without any optimizations. The second is quantized.

Run the cell to convert the model into these two variants:

```
# Convert the model to the TensorFlow Lite format without quantization
converter = tf.lite.TFLiteConverter.from_keras_model(model_2)
tflite_model = converter.convert()

# Save the model to disk
open("sine_model.tflite", "wb").write(tflite_model)

# Convert the model to the TensorFlow Lite format with quantization
converter = tf.lite.TFLiteConverter.from_keras_model(model_2)
# Indicate that we want to perform the default optimizations,
# which include quantization
converter.optimizations = [tf.lite.Optimize.DEFAULT]
# Define a generator function that provides our test data's x values
# as a representative dataset, and tell the converter to use it
def representative_dataset_generator():
  for value in x_test:
    # Each scalar value must be inside of a 2D array that is wrapped in a list
    yield [np.array(value, dtype=np.float32, ndmin=2)]
converter.representative_dataset = representative_dataset_generator
# Convert the model
tflite_model = converter.convert()

# Save the model to disk
open("sine_model_quantized.tflite", "wb").write(tflite_model)
```

To create a quantized model that runs as efficiently as possible, we need to provide a *representative dataset*—a set of numbers that represent the full range of input values of the dataset on which the model was trained.

In the preceding cell, we can use our test dataset's x values as a representative dataset. We define a function, `representative_dataset_generator()`, that uses the `yield` operator to return them one by one.

To prove these models are still accurate after conversion and quantization, we use both of them to make predictions and compare these against our test results. Given that these are TensorFlow Lite models, we need to use the TensorFlow Lite interpreter to do so.

Because it's designed primarily for efficiency, the TensorFlow Lite interpreter is slightly more complicated to use than the Keras API. To make predictions with our Keras model, we could just call the `predict()` method, passing an array of inputs. With TensorFlow Lite, we need to do the following:

1. Instantiate an `Interpreter` object.
2. Call some methods that allocate memory for the model.
3. Write the input to the input tensor.
4. Invoke the model.
5. Read the output from the output tensor.

This sounds like a lot, but don't worry about it too much for now; we'll walk through it in detail in Chapter 5. For now, run the following cell to make predictions with both models and plot them on a graph, alongside the results from our original, unconverted model:

```
# Instantiate an interpreter for each model
sine_model = tf.lite.Interpreter('sine_model.tflite')
sine_model_quantized = tf.lite.Interpreter('sine_model_quantized.tflite')

# Allocate memory for each model
sine_model.allocate_tensors()
sine_model_quantized.allocate_tensors()

# Get indexes of the input and output tensors
sine_model_input_index = sine_model.get_input_details()[0]["index"]
sine_model_output_index = sine_model.get_output_details()[0]["index"]
sine_model_quantized_input_index = sine_model_quantized.get_input_details()[0]
["index"]
sine_model_quantized_output_index = \
  sine_model_quantized.get_output_details()[0]["index"]

# Create arrays to store the results
sine_model_predictions = []
sine_model_quantized_predictions = []

# Run each model's interpreter for each value and store the results in arrays
for x_value in x_test:
  # Create a 2D tensor wrapping the current x value
  x_value_tensor = tf.convert_to_tensor([[x_value]], dtype=np.float32)
  # Write the value to the input tensor
  sine_model.set_tensor(sine_model_input_index, x_value_tensor)
  # Run inference
  sine_model.invoke()
  # Read the prediction from the output tensor
```

```
sine_model_predictions.append(
    sine_model.get_tensor(sine_model_output_index)[0])
# Do the same for the quantized model
sine_model_quantized.set_tensor\
(sine_model_quantized_input_index, x_value_tensor)
sine_model_quantized.invoke()
sine_model_quantized_predictions.append(
    sine_model_quantized.get_tensor(sine_model_quantized_output_index)[0])


# See how they line up with the data
plt.clf()
plt.title('Comparison of various models against actual values')
plt.plot(x_test, y_test, 'bo', label='Actual')
plt.plot(x_test, predictions, 'ro', label='Original predictions')
plt.plot(x_test, sine_model_predictions, 'bx', label='Lite predictions')
plt.plot(x_test, sine_model_quantized_predictions, 'gx', \
  label='Lite quantized predictions')
plt.legend()
plt.show()
```

Running this cell yields the graph in Figure 4-21.

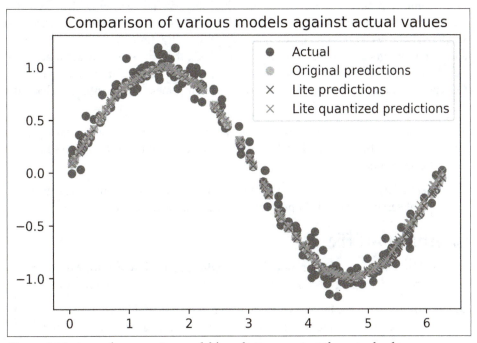

Figure 4-21. A graph comparing models' predictions against the actual values

We can see from the graph that the predictions for the original model, the converted model, and the quantized model are all close enough to be indistinguishable. Things are looking good!

Since quantization makes models smaller, let's compare both converted models to see the difference in size. Run the following cell to calculate their sizes and compare them:

```
import os
basic_model_size = os.path.getsize("sine_model.tflite")
print("Basic model is %d bytes" % basic_model_size)
quantized_model_size = os.path.getsize("sine_model_quantized.tflite")
print("Quantized model is %d bytes" % quantized_model_size)
difference = basic_model_size - quantized_model_size
print("Difference is %d bytes" % difference)
```

You should see the following output:

```
Basic model is 2736 bytes
Quantized model is 2512 bytes
Difference is 224 bytes
```

Our quantized model is 224 bytes smaller than the original version, which is great— but it's only a minor reduction in size. At around 2.4 KB, this model is already so small that the weights and biases make up only a fraction of the overall size. In addition to weights, the model contains all the logic that makes up the architecture of our deep learning network, known as its *computation graph*. For truly tiny models, this can add up to more size than the model's weights, meaning quantization has little effect.

More complex models have many more weights, meaning the space saving from quantization will be much higher. It can be expected to approach four times for most sophisticated models.

Regardless of its exact size, our quantized model will take less time to execute than the original version, which is important on a tiny microcontroller.

Converting to a C File

The final step in preparing our model for use with TensorFlow Lite for Microcontrollers is to convert it into a C source file that can be included in our application.

So far during this chapter, we've been using TensorFlow Lite's Python API. This means that we've been able to use the `Interpreter` constructor to load our model files from disk.

However, most microcontrollers don't have a filesystem, and even if they did, the extra code required to load a model from disk would be wasteful given our limited space. Instead, as an elegant solution, we provide the model in a C source file that can be included in our binary and loaded directly into memory.

In the file, the model is defined as an array of bytes. Fortunately, there's a convenient Unix tool named xxd that is able to convert a given file into the required format.

The following cell runs xxd on our quantized model, writes the output to a file called *sine_model_quantized.cc*, and prints it to the screen:

```
# Install xxd if it is not available
!apt-get -qq install xxd
# Save the file as a C source file
!xxd -i sine_model_quantized.tflite > sine_model_quantized.cc
# Print the source file
!cat sine_model_quantized.cc
```

The output is very long, so we won't reproduce it all here, but here's a snippet that includes just the beginning and end:

```
unsigned char sine_model_quantized_tflite[] = {
  0x1c, 0x00, 0x00, 0x00, 0x54, 0x46, 0x4c, 0x33, 0x00, 0x00, 0x12, 0x00,
  0x1c, 0x00, 0x04, 0x00, 0x08, 0x00, 0x0c, 0x00, 0x10, 0x00, 0x14, 0x00,
  // ...
  0x00, 0x00, 0x08, 0x00, 0x0a, 0x00, 0x00, 0x00, 0x00, 0x00, 0x00, 0x09,
  0x04, 0x00, 0x00, 0x00
};
unsigned int sine_model_quantized_tflite_len = 2512;
```

To use this model in a project, you could either copy and paste the source or download the file from the notebook.

Wrapping Up

And with that, we're done building our model. We've trained, evaluated, and converted a TensorFlow deep learning network that can take a number between 0 and 2π and output a good-enough approximation of its sine.

This was our first taste of using Keras to train a tiny model. In future projects, we'll be training models that are still tiny, but *far* more sophisticated.

For now, let's move on to Chapter 5, where we'll write code to run our model on microcontrollers.

The "Hello World" of TinyML: Building an Application

A model is just one part of a machine learning application. Alone, it's just a blob of information; it can't do much at all. To use our model, we need to wrap it in code that sets up the necessary environment for it to run, provides it with inputs, and uses its outputs to generate behavior. Figure 5-1 shows how the model, on the right hand side, fits into a basic TinyML application.

In this chapter, we will build an embedded application that uses our sine model to create a tiny light show. We'll set up a continuous loop that feeds an x value into the model, runs inference, and uses the result to switch an LED on and off, or to control an animation if our device has an LCD display.

This application (*https://oreil.ly/mqkw3*) has already been written. It's a C++ 11 program whose code is designed to show the smallest possible implementation of a full TinyML application, avoiding any complex logic. This simplicity makes it a helpful tool for learning how to use TensorFlow Lite for Microcontrollers, since you can see exactly what code is necessary and very little else. It also makes it a useful template. After reading this chapter, you'll understand the general structure of a TensorFlow Lite for Microcontrollers program, and you can reuse the same structure in your own projects.

This chapter walks through the application code and explains how it works. The next chapter will provide detailed instructions for building and deploying it to several devices. If you're not familiar with C++, don't panic. The code is relatively simple, and we explain everything in detail. By the time we're done, you should feel comfortable with all the code that's required to run a model, and you might even learn a little C++ along the way.

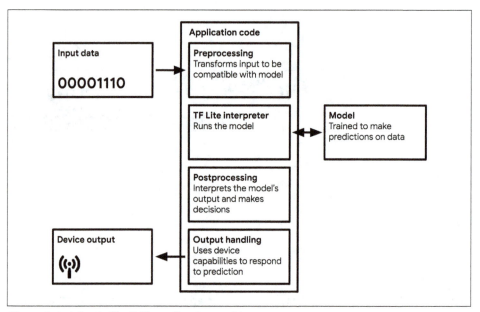

Figure 5-1. A basic TinyML application architecture

Remember, since TensorFlow is an actively developed open source project, there might be some minor differences between the code printed here and the code online. Don't worry—even if a few lines of code change, the basic principles remain the same.

Walking Through the Tests

Before getting our hands dirty with application code, it's often a good idea to write some tests. Tests are short snippets of code that demonstrate a particular piece of logic. Since they are made of working code, we can run them to prove that the code does what it's supposed to. After we have written them, tests are often run automatically as a way to continually verify that a project is still doing what we expect despite any changes we might make to its code. They're also very useful as working examples of how to do things.

The hello_world example has a test, defined in *hello_world_test.cc* (*https://oreil.ly/QW0SS*), that loads our model and uses it to run inference, checking that its predictions are what we expect. It contains the exact code needed to do this, and nothing else, so it will be a great place to start learning TensorFlow Lite for Microcontrollers. In this section, we walk through the test and explain what each and every part of it does. After we're done reading the code, we can run the test to prove that it's correct.

Let's now walk through it, section by section. If you're at a computer, it might be helpful to open up *hello_world_test.cc* (*https://oreil.ly/s0f6Q*) and follow along.

Including Dependencies

The first part, below the license header (which specifies that anybody can use or share this code under the Apache 2.0 (*https://oreil.ly/Xa5_x*) open source license), looks like this:

```
#include "tensorflow/lite/micro/examples/hello_world/sine_model_data.h"
#include "tensorflow/lite/micro/kernels/all_ops_resolver.h"
#include "tensorflow/lite/micro/micro_error_reporter.h"
#include "tensorflow/lite/micro/micro_interpreter.h"
#include "tensorflow/lite/micro/testing/micro_test.h"
#include "tensorflow/lite/schema/schema_generated.h"
#include "tensorflow/lite/version.h"
```

The `#include` directive is a way for C++ code to specify other code that it depends on. When a code file is referenced with an `#include`, any logic or variables it defines will be available for us to use. In this section, we use `#include` to import the following items:

tensorflow/lite/micro/examples/hello_world/sine_model_data.h
> The sine model we trained, converted, and transformed into C++ using xxd

tensorflow/lite/micro/kernels/all_ops_resolver.h
> A class that allows the interpreter to load the operations used by our model

tensorflow/lite/micro/micro_error_reporter.h
> A class that can log errors and output to help with debugging

tensorflow/lite/micro/micro_interpreter.h
> The TensorFlow Lite for Microcontrollers interpreter, which will run our model

tensorflow/lite/micro/testing/micro_test.h
> A lightweight framework for writing tests, which allows us to run this file as a test

tensorflow/lite/schema/schema_generated.h
> The schema that defines the structure of TensorFlow Lite FlatBuffer data, used to make sense of the model data in *sine_model_data.h*

tensorflow/lite/version.h
> The current version number of the schema, so we can check that the model was defined with a compatible version

We'll talk more about some of these dependencies as we dig into the code.

By convention, C++ code designed to be used with #include directives is written as two files: a *.cc* file, known as the *source file*, and a *.h* file, known as the *header file*. Header files define the interface that allows the code to connect to other parts of the program. They contain things like variable and class declarations, but very little logic. Source files implement the actual logic that performs computation and makes things happen. When we #include a dependency, we specify its header file. For example, the test we're walking through includes *micro_interpreter.h* (*https://oreil.ly/60uYt*). If we look at that file, we can see that it defines a class but doesn't contain much logic. Instead, its logic is contained within *micro_interpreter.cc* (*https://oreil.ly/twN7J*).

Setting Up the Test

The next part of the code is used by the TensorFlow Lite for Microcontrollers testing framework. It looks like this:

```
TF_LITE_MICRO_TESTS_BEGIN

TF_LITE_MICRO_TEST(LoadModelAndPerformInference) {
```

In C++, you can define specially named chunks of code that can be reused by including their names elsewhere. These chunks of code are called *macros*. The two statements here, TF_LITE_MICRO_TESTS_BEGIN and TF_LITE_MICRO_TEST, are the names of macros. They are defined in the file *micro_test.h* (*https://oreil.ly/NoGm4*).

These macros wrap the rest of our code in the necessary apparatus for it to be executed by the TensorFlow Lite for Microcontrollers testing framework. We don't need to worry about how exactly this works; we just know that we can use these macros as shortcuts to set up a test.

The second macro, named TF_LITE_MICRO_TEST, accepts an argument. In this case, the argument being passed in is LoadModelAndPerformInference. This argument is the test name, and when the tests are run, it will be output along with the test results so that we can see whether the test passed or failed.

Getting Ready to Log Data

The remaining code in the file is the actual logic of our test. Let's take a look at the first portion:

```
// Set up logging
tflite::MicroErrorReporter micro_error_reporter;
tflite::ErrorReporter* error_reporter = &micro_error_reporter;
```

In the first line, we define a `MicroErrorReporter` instance. The `MicroErrorReporter` class is defined in *micro_error_reporter.h* (*https://oreil.ly/AkZrm*). It provides a mechanism for logging debug information during inference. We'll be calling it to print debug information, and the TensorFlow Lite for Microcontrollers interpreter will use it to print any errors it encounters.

 You've probably noticed the `tflite::` prefix before each of the type names, such as `tflite::MicroErrorReporter`. This is a *namespace*, which is just a way to help organize C++ code. TensorFlow Lite defines all of its useful stuff under the namespace `tflite`, which means that if another library happens to implement classes with the same name, they won't conflict with those that TensorFlow Lite provides.

The first declaration seems straightforward, but what about the funky-looking second line, with the * and & characters? Why are we declaring an `ErrorReporter` when we already have a `MicroErrorReporter`?

```
tflite::ErrorReporter* error_reporter = &micro_error_reporter;
```

To explain what is happening here, we need to know a little background information.

`MicroErrorReporter` is a subclass of the `ErrorReporter` class, which provides a template for how this sort of debug logging mechanism should work in TensorFlow Lite. `MicroErrorReporter` overrides one of `ErrorReporter`'s methods, replacing it with logic that is specifically written for use on microcontrollers.

In the preceding code line, we create a variable called `error_reporter`, which has the type `ErrorReporter`. It's also a pointer, indicated by the * used in its declaration.

A pointer is a special type of variable that, instead of holding a value, holds a reference to a location in memory where a value can be found. In C++, a pointer of a certain class (such as `ErrorReporter`) can point to a value that is one of its child classes (such as `MicroErrorReporter`).

As we mentioned earlier, `MicroErrorReporter` overrides one of the methods of `ErrorReporter`. Without going into too much detail, the process of overriding this method has the side effect of obscuring some of its other methods.

To still have access to the non overridden methods of `ErrorReporter`, we need to treat our `MicroErrorReporter` instance as if it were actually an `ErrorReporter`. We achieve this by creating an `ErrorReporter` pointer and pointing it at the `micro_error_reporter` variable. The ampersand (&) in front of `micro_error_reporter` in the assignment means that we are assigning its pointer, not its value.

Phew! This sounds complicated. Don't panic if you found it difficult to follow; C++ can be a little unwieldy. For our purposes, all we need to know is that that we should use error_reporter to print debug information, and that it's a pointer.

Mapping Our Model

The reason we immediately set up a mechanism for printing debug information is so that we can log any problems that occur in the rest of the code. We rely on this in the next piece of code:

```
// Map the model into a usable data structure. This doesn't involve any
// copying or parsing, it's a very lightweight operation.
const tflite::Model* model = ::tflite::GetModel(g_sine_model_data);
if (model->version() != TFLITE_SCHEMA_VERSION) {
error_reporter->Report(
    "Model provided is schema version %d not equal "
    "to supported version %d.\n",
    model->version(), TFLITE_SCHEMA_VERSION);
    return 1;
}
```

In the first line, we take our model data array (defined in the file *sine_model_data.h* (*https://oreil.ly/m68Wj*)) and pass it into a method named GetModel(). This method returns a Model pointer, which is assigned to a variable named model. As you might have anticipated, this variable represents our model.

The type Model is a *struct*, which in C++ is very similar to class. It's defined in *schema_generated.h* (*https://oreil.ly/SGNtU*), and it holds our model's data and allows us to query information about it.

Data Alignment

If you inspect our model's source file in *sine_model_data.cc* (*https://oreil.ly/FCmuw*), you'll see that the definition of g_sine_model_data references a macro, DATA_ALIGN_ATTRIBUTE:

```
const unsigned char g_sine_model_data[] DATA_ALIGN_ATTRIBUTE = {
```

Processors can read data most efficiently when it is *aligned* in memory, meaning data structures are stored so that they don't overlap the boundaries of what the processor can read in a single operation. By specifying this macro we make sure that, when possible, our model data is correctly aligned for optimal read performance. If you're curious, you can read about alignment in the Wikipedia article (*https://oreil.ly/Ej5ga*).

As soon as `model` is ready, we call a method that retrieves the model's version number:

```
if (model->version() != TFLITE_SCHEMA_VERSION) {
```

We then compare the model's version number to `TFLITE_SCHEMA_VERSION`, which indicates the version of the TensorFlow Lite library we are currently using. If the numbers match, our model was converted with a compatible version of the Tensor-Flow Lite Converter. It's good practice to check the model version, because a mismatch might result in strange behavior that is tricky to debug.

In the preceding line of code, `version()` is a method that belongs to `model`. Notice the arrow (`->`) that points from `model` to `version()`. This is C++'s *arrow operator*, and it's used whenever we want to access the members of an object to which we have a pointer. If we had the object itself (and not just a pointer), we would use a dot (`.`) to access its members.

If the version numbers don't match, we'll carry on anyway, but we'll log a warning using our `error_reporter`:

```
error_reporter->Report(
    "Model provided is schema version %d not equal "
    "to supported version %d.\n",
    model->version(), TFLITE_SCHEMA_VERSION);
```

We call the `Report()` method of `error_reporter` to log this warning. Since `error_reporter` is also a pointer, we use the `->` operator to access `Report()`.

The `Report()` method is designed to behave similarly to a commonly used C++ method, `printf()`, which is used to log text. As its first parameter, we pass in a string that we want to log. This string contains two `%d` format specifiers, which act as placeholders where variables will be inserted when the message is logged. The next two parameters we pass in are the model version and the TensorFlow Lite schema version. These will be inserted into the string, in order, to replace the `%d` characters.

The `Report()` method supports different format specifiers that work as placeholders for different types of variables. `%d` should be used as a placeholder for integers, `%f` should be used as a placeholder for floating-point numbers, and `%s` should be used as a placeholder for strings.

Creating an AllOpsResolver

So far so good! Our code can log errors, and we've loaded our model into a handy struct and checked that it is a compatible version. We've been moving a little slowly, given that we're reviewing some C++ concepts along the way, but things are starting to make sense. Next up, we create an instance of `AllOpsResolver`:

```
// This pulls in all the operation implementations we need
tflite::ops::micro::AllOpsResolver resolver;
```

This class, defined in *all_ops_resolver.h* (*https://oreil.ly/O0qgy*), is what allows the TensorFlow Lite for Microcontrollers interpreter to access *operations*.

In Chapter 3, you learned that a machine learning model is composed of various mathematical operations that are run successively to transform input into output. The `AllOpsResolver` class knows all of the operations that are available to Tensor-Flow Lite for Microcontrollers and is able to provide them to the interpreter.

Defining a Tensor Arena

We almost have all the ingredients ready to create an interpreter. The final thing we need to do is allocate an area of working memory that our model will need while it runs:

```
// Create an area of memory to use for input, output, and intermediate arrays.
// Finding the minimum value for your model may require some trial and error.
const int tensor_arena_size = 2 × 1024;
uint8_t tensor_arena[tensor_arena_size];
```

As the comment says, this area of memory will be used to store the model's input, output, and intermediate tensors. We call it our *tensor arena*. In our case, we've allocated an array that is 2,048 bytes in size. We specify this with the expression 2×1024.

So, how large should our tensor arena be? That's a good question. Unfortunately, there's not a simple answer. Different model architectures have different sizes and numbers of input, output, and intermediate tensors, so it's difficult to know how much memory we'll need. The number doesn't need to be exact—we can reserve more memory than we need—but since microcontrollers have limited RAM, we should keep it as small as possible so there's space for the rest of our program.

We can do this through trial and error. That's why we express the array size as $n \times 1024$: so that it's easy to scale the number up and down (by changing n) while keeping it a multiple of eight. To find the correct array size, start fairly high so that you can be sure it works. The highest number used in this book's examples is 70×1024. Then, reduce the number until your model no longer runs. The last number that worked is the correct one!

Creating an Interpreter

Now that we've declared `tensor_arena`, we're ready to set up the interpreter. Here's how that looks:

```
// Build an interpreter to run the model with
tflite::MicroInterpreter interpreter(model, resolver, tensor_arena,
                                     tensor_arena_size, error_reporter);

// Allocate memory from the tensor_arena for the model's tensors
interpreter.AllocateTensors();
```

First, we declare a `MicroInterpreter` named `interpreter`. This class is the heart of TensorFlow Lite for Microcontrollers: a magical piece of code that will execute our model on the data we provide. We pass in most of the objects we've created so far to its constructor, and then make a call to `AllocateTensors()`.

In the previous section, we set aside an area of memory by defining an array called `tensor_arena`. The `AllocateTensors()` method walks through all of the tensors defined by the model and assigns memory from the `tensor_arena` to each of them. It's critical that we call `AllocateTensors()` before attempting to run inference, because otherwise inference will fail.

Inspecting the Input Tensor

After we've created an interpreter, we need to provide some input for our model. To do this, we write our input data to the model's input tensor:

```
// Obtain a pointer to the model's input tensor
TfLiteTensor* input = interpreter.input(0);
```

To grab a pointer to an input tensor, we call the interpreter's `input()` method. Since a model can have multiple input tensors, we need to pass an index to the `input()` method that specifies which tensor we want. In this case, our model has only one input tensor, so its index is 0.

In TensorFlow Lite, tensors are represented by the `TfLiteTensor` struct, which is defined in *c_api_internal.h* (*https://oreil.ly/Qvhre*). This struct provides an API for interacting with and learning about tensors. In the next chunk of code, we use this functionality to verify that our tensor looks and feels correct. Because we'll be using tensors a lot, let's walk through this code to become familiar with how the `TfLiteTen sor` struct works:

```
// Make sure the input has the properties we expect
TF_LITE_MICRO_EXPECT_NE(nullptr, input);
// The property "dims" tells us the tensor's shape. It has one element for
// each dimension. Our input is a 2D tensor containing 1 element, so "dims"
// should have size 2.
TF_LITE_MICRO_EXPECT_EQ(2, input->dims->size);
```

```
// The value of each element gives the length of the corresponding tensor.
// We should expect two single element tensors (one is contained within the
// other).
TF_LITE_MICRO_EXPECT_EQ(1, input->dims->data[0]);
TF_LITE_MICRO_EXPECT_EQ(1, input->dims->data[1]);
// The input is a 32 bit floating point value
TF_LITE_MICRO_EXPECT_EQ(kTfLiteFloat32, input->type);
```

The first thing you'll notice is a couple of macros: TFLITE_MICRO_EXPECT_NE and
TFLITE_MICRO_EXPECT_EQ. These macros are part of the TensorFlow Lite for Microcontrollers testing framework, and they allow us to make *assertions* about the values
of variables, proving that they have certain expected values.

For example, the macro TF_LITE_MICRO_EXPECT_NE is designed to assert that the two
variables it is called with are not equal (hence the _NE part of its name, which stands
for Not Equal). If the variables are not equal, the code will continue to execute. If they
are equal, an error will be logged, and the test will be marked as having failed.

More Assertions

The macros for assertions are defined in *micro_test.h* (*https://oreil.ly/d69rG*), and you
can read the file to see how they work. Here are the available assertions:

TF_LITE_MICRO_EXPECT(*x*)
: Asserts that *x* evaluates to true.

TF_LITE_MICRO_EXPECT_EQ(*x*, *y*)
: Asserts that *x* is equal to *y*.

TF_LITE_MICRO_EXPECT_NE(*x*, *y*)
: Asserts that *x* is not equal to *y*.

TF_LITE_MICRO_EXPECT_NEAR(*x*, *y*, *epsilon*)
: For numeric values, asserts that the difference between *x* and *y* is less than or
equal to *epsilon*. For example, TF_LITE_MICRO_EXPECT_NEAR(5, 7, 3) would
pass, because the difference between 5 and 7 is 2.

TF_LITE_MICRO_EXPECT_GT(*x*, *y*)
: For numeric values, asserts that *x* is greater than *y*.

TF_LITE_MICRO_EXPECT_LT(*x*, *y*)
: For numeric values, asserts that *x* is less than *y*.

TF_LITE_MICRO_EXPECT_GE(*x*, *y*)
: For numeric values, asserts that *x* greater than or equal to *y*.

TF_LITE_MICRO_EXPECT_LE(*x*, *y*)
: For numeric values, asserts that *x* is less than or equal to *y*.

The first thing we check is that our input tensor actually exists. To do this, we assert that it is *not equal* to a `nullptr`, which is a special C++ value representing a pointer that is not actually pointing at any data:

```
TF_LITE_MICRO_EXPECT_NE(nullptr, input);
```

The next thing we check is the *shape* of our input tensor. As discussed in Chapter 3, all tensors have a shape, which is a way of describing their dimensionality. The input to our model is a scalar value (meaning a single number). However, due to the way Keras layers accept input (*https://oreil.ly/SFiRV*), this value must be provided inside of a 2D tensor containing one number. For an input of 0, it should look like this:

```
[[0]]
```

Note how the input scalar, 0, is wrapped inside of two vectors, making this a 2D tensor.

The `TfLiteTensor` struct contains a `dims` member that describes the dimensions of the tensor. The member is a struct of type `TfLiteIntArray`, also defined in *c_api_internal.h*. Its `size` member represents the number of dimensions that the tensor has. Since the input tensor should be 2D, we can assert that the value of `size` is 2:

```
TF_LITE_MICRO_EXPECT_EQ(2, input->dims->size);
```

We can further inspect the `dims` struct to ensure the tensor's structure is what we expect. Its `data` variable is an array with one element for each dimension. Each element is an integer representing the size of that dimension. Because we are expecting a 2D tensor containing one element in each dimension, we can assert that both dimensions contain a single element:

```
TF_LITE_MICRO_EXPECT_EQ(1, input->dims->data[0]);
TF_LITE_MICRO_EXPECT_EQ(1, input->dims->data[1]);
```

We can now be confident that our input tensor has the correct shape. Finally, since tensors can consist of a variety of different types of data (think integers, floating-point numbers, and Boolean values), we should make sure that our input tensor has the correct type.

The tensor struct's `type` variable informs us of the data type of the tensor. We'll be providing a 32-bit floating-point number, represented by the constant `kTfLiteFloat32`, and we can easily assert that the type is correct:

```
TF_LITE_MICRO_EXPECT_EQ(kTfLiteFloat32, input->type);
```

Perfect—our input tensor is now guaranteed to be the correct size and shape for our input data, which will be a single floating-point value. We're ready to run inference!

Running Inference on an Input

To run inference, we need to add a value to our input tensor and then instruct the interpreter to invoke the model. Afterward, we will check whether the model successfully ran. Here's how that looks:

```
// Provide an input value
input->data.f[0] = 0.;

// Run the model on this input and check that it succeeds
TfLiteStatus invoke_status = interpreter.Invoke();
if (invoke_status != kTfLiteOk) {
 error_reporter->Report("Invoke failed\n");
}
TF_LITE_MICRO_EXPECT_EQ(kTfLiteOk, invoke_status);
```

TensorFlow Lite's TfLiteTensor struct has a data variable that we can use to set the contents of our input tensor. You can see this being used here:

```
input->data.f[0] = 0.;
```

The data variable is a TfLitePtrUnion—it's a *union*, which is a special C++ data type that allows you to store different data types at the same location in memory. Since a given tensor can contain one of many different types of data (for example, floating-point numbers, integers, or Booleans), a union is the perfect type to help us store it.

The TfLitePtrUnion union is declared in *c_api_internal.h* (*https://oreil.ly/v4h7K*). Here's what it looks like:

```
// A union of pointers that points to memory for a given tensor.
typedef union {
    int32_t* i32;
    int64_t* i64;
    float* f;
    TfLiteFloat16* f16;
    char* raw;
    const char* raw_const;
    uint8_t* uint8;
    bool* b;
    int16_t* i16;
    TfLiteComplex64* c64;
    int8_t* int8;
} TfLitePtrUnion;
```

You can see that there are a bunch of members, each representing a certain type. Each member is a pointer, which can point at a place in memory where the data should be stored. When we call interpreter.AllocateTensors(), like we did earlier, the appropriate pointer is set to point at the block of memory that was allocated for the tensor to store its data. Because each tensor has a specific data type, only the pointer for the corresponding type will be set.

This means that to store data, we can use whichever is the appropriate pointer in our `TfLitePtrUnion`. For example, if our tensor is of type `kTfLiteFloat32`, we'll use `data.f`.

Since the pointer points at a block of memory, we can use square brackets (`[]`) after the pointer name to instruct our program where to store the data. In our example, we do the following:

```
input->data.f[0] = 0.;
```

The value we're assigning is written as `0.`, which is shorthand for `0.0`. By specifying the decimal point, we make it clear to the C++ compiler that this value should be a floating-point number, not an integer.

You can see that we assign this value to `data.f[0]`. This means that we're assigning it as the first item in our block of allocated memory. Given that there's only one value, this is all we need to do.

More Complex Inputs

In the example we're walking through, our model accepts a scalar input, so we have to assign only one value (`input->data.f[0] = 0.`). If our model's input was a vector consisting of several values, we would add them to subsequent memory locations.

Here's an example of a vector containing the numbers 1, 2, and 3:

```
[1 2 3]
```

And here's how we might set these values in a `TfLiteTensor`:

```
// Vector with 6 elements
input->data.f[0] = 1.;
input->data.f[1] = 2.;
input->data.f[2] = 3.;
```

But what about matrices, which consist of multiple vectors? Here's an example:

```
[[1 2 3]
 [4 5 6]]
```

To set this in a `TfLiteTensor`, we just assign the values in order, from left to right and top to bottom. This is called *flattening*, because we squash the structure from two to one dimension:

```
// Vector with 3 elements
input->data.f[0] = 1.;
input->data.f[1] = 2.;
input->data.f[2] = 3.;
input->data.f[3] = 4.;
input->data.f[4] = 5.;
input->data.f[5] = 6.;
```

Because the `TfLiteTensor` struct has a record of its actual dimensions, it knows which locations in memory correspond to which elements in its multidimensional shape, even though the memory has a flat structure. We make use of 2D input tensors in the later chapters to feed in images and other 2D data.

After we've set up the input tensor, it's time to run inference. This is a one-liner:

```
TfLiteStatus invoke_status = interpreter.Invoke();
```

When we call `Invoke()` on the `interpreter`, the TensorFlow Lite interpreter runs the model. The model consists of a graph of mathematical operations which the interpreter executes to transform the input data into an output. This output is stored in the model's output tensors, which we'll dig into later.

The `Invoke()` method returns a `TfLiteStatus` object, which lets us know whether inference was successful or there was a problem. Its value can either be `kTfLiteOk` or `kTfLiteError`. We check for an error and report it if there is one:

```
if (invoke_status != kTfLiteOk) {
    error_reporter->Report("Invoke failed\n");
}
```

Finally, we assert that the status must be `kTfLiteOk` in order for our test to pass:

```
TF_LITE_MICRO_EXPECT_EQ(kTfLiteOk, invoke_status);
```

That's it—inference has been run! Next up, we grab the output and make sure it looks good.

Reading the Output

Like the input, our model's output is accessed through a `TfLiteTensor`, and getting a pointer to it is just as simple:

```
TfLiteTensor* output = interpreter.output(0);
```

The output is, like the input, a floating-point scalar value nestled inside a 2D tensor. For the sake of our test, we double-check that the output tensor has the expected size, dimensions, and type:

```
TF_LITE_MICRO_EXPECT_EQ(2, output->dims->size);
TF_LITE_MICRO_EXPECT_EQ(1, input->dims->data[0]);
TF_LITE_MICRO_EXPECT_EQ(1, input->dims->data[1]);
TF_LITE_MICRO_EXPECT_EQ(kTfLiteFloat32, output->type);
```

Yep, it all looks good. Now, we grab the output value and inspect it to make sure that it meets our high standards. First we assign it to a `float` variable:

```
// Obtain the output value from the tensor
float value = output->data.f[0];
```

Each time inference is run, the output tensor will be overwritten with new values. This means that if you want to keep an output value around in your program while continuing to run inference, you'll need to copy it from the output tensor, like we just did.

Next, we use `TF_LITE_MICRO_EXPECT_NEAR` to prove that the value is close to the value we're expecting:

```
// Check that the output value is within 0.05 of the expected value
TF_LITE_MICRO_EXPECT_NEAR(0., value, 0.05);
```

As we saw earlier, `TF_LITE_MICRO_EXPECT_NEAR` asserts that the difference between its first argument and its second argument is less than the value of its third argument. In this statement, we're testing that the output is within 0.05 of 0, which is the mathematical sine of the input, 0.

There are two reasons why we expect a number that is *near* to what we want, but not an exact value. The first is that our model only *approximates* the real sine value, so we know that it will not be exactly correct. The second is because floating-point calculations on computers have a margin of error. The error can vary from computer to computer: for example, a laptop's CPU might come up with slightly different results to an Arduino. By having flexible expectations, we make it more likely that our test will pass on any platform.

If this test passes, things are looking good. The remaining tests run inference a few more times, just to further prove that our model is working. To run inference again, all we need to do is assign a new value to our input tensor, call `interpreter.Invoke()`, and read the output from our output tensor:

```
// Run inference on several more values and confirm the expected outputs
input->data.f[0] = 1.;
interpreter.Invoke();
value = output->data.f[0];
TF_LITE_MICRO_EXPECT_NEAR(0.841, value, 0.05);

input->data.f[0] = 3.;
interpreter.Invoke();
value = output->data.f[0];
TF_LITE_MICRO_EXPECT_NEAR(0.141, value, 0.05);

input->data.f[0] = 5.;
interpreter.Invoke();
value = output->data.f[0];
TF_LITE_MICRO_EXPECT_NEAR(-0.959, value, 0.05);
```

Note how we're reusing the same `input` and `output` tensor pointer. Because we already have the pointers, we don't need to call `interpreter.input(0)` or `interpreter.output(0)` again.

At this point in our tests we've proven that TensorFlow Lite for Microcontrollers can successfully load our model, allocate the appropriate input and output tensors, run inference, and return the expected results. The final thing to do is indicate the end of the tests by using a macro:

```
}
```

```
TF_LITE_MICRO_TESTS_END
```

And with that, we're done walking through the tests. Next, let's run them!

Running the Tests

Even though this code is eventually destined to run on microcontrollers, we can still build and run our tests on our development machine. This makes it much easier to write and debug code. Compared with microcontrollers, a personal computer has far more convenient tools for logging output and stepping through code, which makes it a lot simpler to figure out any bugs. In addition, deploying code to a device takes time, so it's a lot quicker to just run our code locally.

A good workflow for building embedded applications (or, honestly, any kind of software) is to write as much of the logic as you can in tests that can be run on a normal development machine. There'll always be some parts that require the actual hardware to run, but the more you can test locally, the easier your life will be.

Practically, this means that we should try to write the code that preprocesses inputs, runs inference with the model, and processes any outputs in a set of tests before trying to get it working on-device. In Chapter 7, we walk through a speech recognition application that is much more complex than this example. You'll see how we've written detailed unit tests for each of its components.

Grabbing the code

Until now, between Colab and GitHub, we've been doing everything in the cloud. To run our tests, we need to pull down the code to our development computer and compile it.

To do all this, we need the following software tools:

- A terminal emulator, such as Terminal in macOS
- A bash shell (the default in macOS prior to Catalina and most Linux distributions)

- Git (*https://git-scm.com/*) (installed by default in macOS and most Linux distributions)
- Make, version 3.82 or later

Git and Make

Git and Make are often preinstalled on modern operating systems. To check whether they are installed on your system, open a terminal and do the following:

For Git

> Any version of Git will work. To confirm Git is installed, enter `git` at the command line. You should see usage instructions being printed.

For Make

> To check the version of Make installed, enter `make --version` at the command line. You need a version greater than 3.82.

If you are missing either tool, you should search the web for instructions on installing them for your specific operating system.

After you have all the tools, open up a terminal and enter the command that follows to download the TensorFlow source code, which includes the example code we're working with. It will create a directory containing the source code in whatever location you run it:

```
git clone https://github.com/tensorflow/tensorflow.git
```

Next, change into the *tensorflow* directory that was just created:

```
cd tensorflow
```

Great stuff—we're now ready to run some code!

Using Make to run the tests

As you saw from our list of tools, we use a program called *Make* to run the tests. Make is a tool for automating build tasks in software. It's been in use since 1976, which in computing terms is almost forever. Developers use a special language, written in files called *Makefiles*, to instruct Make how to build and run code. TensorFlow Lite for Microcontrollers has a Makefile defined in *micro/tools/make/Makefile* (*https://oreil.ly/6Kvx5*); there's more information about it in Chapter 13.

To run our tests using Make, we can issue the following command, making sure we're running it from the root of the *tensorflow* directory we downloaded with Git. We first specify the Makefile to use, followed by the *target*, which is the component that we want to build:

```
make -f tensorflow/lite/micro/tools/make/Makefile test_hello_world_test
```

The Makefile is set up so that in order to run tests, we provide a target with the prefix test_ followed by the name of the component that we want to build. In our case, that component is *hello_world_test*, so the full target name is *test_hello_world_test*.

Try running this command. You should start to see a ton of output fly past! First, some necessary libraries and tools will be downloaded. Next, our test file, along with all of its dependencies, will be built. Our Makefile has instructed the C++ compiler to build the code and create a binary, which it will then run.

You'll need to wait a few moments for the process to complete. When the text stops zooming past, the last few lines should look like this:

```
Testing LoadModelAndPerformInference
1/1 tests passed
~~~ALL TESTS PASSED~~~
```

Nice! This output shows that our test passed as expected. You can see the name of the test, LoadModelAndPerformInference, as defined at the top of its source file. Even if it's not on a microcontroller yet, our code is successfully running inference.

To see what happens when tests fail, let's introduce an error. Open up the test file, *hello_world_test.cc*. It will be at this path, relative to the root of the directory:

```
tensorflow/lite/micro/examples/hello_world/hello_world_test.cc
```

To make the test fail, let's provide a different input to the model. This will cause the model's output to change, so the assertion that checks the value of our output will fail. Find the following line:

```
input->data.f[0] = 0.;
```

Change the assigned value, like so:

```
input->data.f[0] = 1.;
```

Now save the file, and use the following command to run the test again (remember to do this from the root of the *tensorflow* directory):

```
make -f tensorflow/lite/micro/tools/make/Makefile test_hello_world_test
```

The code will be rebuilt, and the test will run. The final output you see should look like this:

```
Testing LoadModelAndPerformInference
0.0486171 near value failed at tensorflow/lite/micro/examples/hello_world/\
  hello_world_test.cc:94
0/1 tests passed
~~~SOME TESTS FAILED~~~
```

The output contains some useful information about why the test failed, including the file and line number where the failure took place (`hello_world_test.cc:94`). If this were caused by a real bug, this output would be helpful in tracking down the issue.

Project File Structure

With the help of our test, you've learned how to use the TensorFlow Lite for Microcontrollers library to run inference in C++. Next, we're going to walk through the source code of an actual application.

As discussed earlier, the program we're building consists of a continuous loop that feeds an x value into the model, runs inference, and uses the result to produce some sort of visible output (like a pattern of flashing LEDs), depending on the platform.

Because the application is complex and spans multiple files, let's take a look at its structure and how it all fits together.

The root of the application is in *tensorflow/lite/micro/examples/hello_world*. It contains the following files:

BUILD
: A file that lists the various things that can be built using the application's source code, including the main application binary and the tests we walked through earlier. We don't need to worry too much about it at this point.

Makefile.inc
: A Makefile that contains information about the build targets within our application, including *hello_world_test*, which is the test we ran earlier, and *hello_world*, the main application binary. It defines which source files are part of them.

README.md
: A readme file containing instructions on building and running the application.

constants.h, constants.cc
: A pair of files containing various *constants* (variables that don't change during the lifetime of a program) that are important for defining the program's behavior.

create_sine_model.ipynb
: The Jupyter notebook used in the previous chapter.

hello_world_test.cc
: A test that runs inference using our model.

main.cc
: The entry point of the program, which runs first when the application is deployed to a device.

main_functions.h, main_functions.cc

A pair of files that define a `setup()` function, which performs all the initialization required by our program, and a `loop()` function, which contains the program's core logic and is designed to be called repeatedly in a loop. These functions are called by *main.cc* when the program starts.

output_handler.h, output_handler.cc

A pair of files that define a function we can use to display an output each time inference is run. The default implementation, in *output_handler.cc*, prints the result to the screen. We can override this implementation so that it does different things on different devices.

output_handler_test.cc

A test that proves that the code in *output_handler.h* and *output_handler.cc* is working correctly.

sine_model_data.h, sine_model_data.cc

A pair of files that define an array of data representing our model, as exported using xxd in the first part of this chapter.

In addition to these files, the directory contains the following subdirectories (and perhaps more):

- *arduino/*
- *disco_f76ng/*
- *sparkfun_edge/*

Because different microcontroller platforms have different capabilities and APIs, our project structure allows us to provide device-specific versions of source files that will be used instead of the defaults if the application is built for that device. For example, the *arduino* directory contains custom versions of *main.cc*, *constants.cc*, and *output_handler.cc* that tailor the application to work with Arduino. We dig into these custom implementations later.

Walking Through the Source

Now that we know how the application's source is structured, let's dig into the code. We'll begin with *main_functions.cc* (*https://oreil.ly/BYS5k*), where most of the magic happens, and branch out into the other files from there.

A lot of this code will look very familiar from our earlier adventures in *hello_world_test.cc*. If we've covered something already, we won't go into depth on how it works; we'd rather focus mainly on the things you haven't seen before.

Starting with main_functions.cc

This file contains the core logic of our program. It begins like this, with some familiar #include statements and some new ones:

```
#include "tensorflow/lite/micro/examples/hello_world/main_functions.h"
#include "tensorflow/lite/micro/examples/hello_world/constants.h"
#include "tensorflow/lite/micro/examples/hello_world/output_handler.h"
#include "tensorflow/lite/micro/examples/hello_world/sine_model_data.h"
#include "tensorflow/lite/micro/kernels/all_ops_resolver.h"
#include "tensorflow/lite/micro/micro_error_reporter.h"
#include "tensorflow/lite/micro/micro_interpreter.h"
#include "tensorflow/lite/schema/schema_generated.h"
#include "tensorflow/lite/version.h"
```

We saw a lot of these in *hello_world_test.cc*. New to the scene are *constants.h* and output_handler.h, which we learned about in the list of files earlier.

The next part of the file sets up the global variables that will be used within *main_functions.cc*:

```
namespace {
tflite::ErrorReporter* error_reporter = nullptr;
const tflite::Model* model = nullptr;
tflite::MicroInterpreter* interpreter = nullptr;
TfLiteTensor* input = nullptr;
TfLiteTensor* output = nullptr;
int inference_count = 0;

// Create an area of memory to use for input, output, and intermediate arrays.
// Finding the minimum value for your model may require some trial and error.
constexpr int kTensorArenaSize = 2 × 1024;
uint8_t tensor_arena[kTensorArenaSize];
} // namespace
```

You'll notice that these variables are wrapped in a namespace. This means that even though they will be accessible from anywhere within *main_functions.cc*, they won't be accessible from any other files within the project. This helps prevent problems if two different files happen to define variables with the same name.

All of these variables should look familiar from the tests. We set up variables to hold all of our familiar TensorFlow objects, along with a tensor_arena. The only new thing is an int that holds inference_count, which will keep track of how many inferences our program has performed.

The next part of the file declares a function named setup(). This function will be called when the program first starts, but never again after that. We use it to do all of the one-time housekeeping work that needs to happen before we start running inference.

The first part of `setup()` is almost exactly the same as in our tests. We set up logging, load our model, set up the interpreter, and allocate memory:

```
void setup() {
  // Set up logging.
  static tflite::MicroErrorReporter micro_error_reporter;
  error_reporter = &micro_error_reporter;

  // Map the model into a usable data structure. This doesn't involve any
  // copying or parsing, it's a very lightweight operation.
  model = tflite::GetModel(g_sine_model_data);
  if (model->version() != TFLITE_SCHEMA_VERSION) {
    error_reporter->Report(
        "Model provided is schema version %d not equal "
        "to supported version %d.",
        model->version(), TFLITE_SCHEMA_VERSION);
    return;
  }

  // This pulls in all the operation implementations we need.
  static tflite::ops::micro::AllOpsResolver resolver;

  // Build an interpreter to run the model with.
  static tflite::MicroInterpreter static_interpreter(
      model, resolver, tensor_arena, kTensorArenaSize, error_reporter);
  interpreter = &static_interpreter;

  // Allocate memory from the tensor_arena for the model's tensors.
  TfLiteStatus allocate_status = interpreter->AllocateTensors();
  if (allocate_status != kTfLiteOk) {
    error_reporter->Report("AllocateTensors() failed");
    return;
  }
```

Familiar territory so far. After this point, though, things get a little different. First, we grab pointers to both the input *and* output tensors:

```
  // Obtain pointers to the model's input and output tensors.
  input = interpreter->input(0);
  output = interpreter->output(0);
```

You might be wondering how we can interact with the output before inference has been run. Well, remember that `TfLiteTensor` is just a struct that has a member, `data`, pointing to an area of memory that has been allocated to store the output. Even though no output has been written yet, the struct and its `data` member still exist.

Finally, to end the `setup()` function, we set our `inference_count` variable to 0:

```
  // Keep track of how many inferences we have performed.
  inference_count = 0;
}
```

At this point, all of our machine learning infrastructure is set up and ready to go. We have all the tools required to run inference and get the results. The next thing to define is our application logic. What is the program actually going to *do*?

Our model was trained to predict the sine of any number from 0 to 2π, which represents the full cycle of a sine wave. To demonstrate our model, we could just feed in numbers in this range, predict their sines, and then output the values somehow. We could do this in a sequence so that we show the model working across the entire range. This sounds like a good plan!

To do this, we need to write some code that runs in a loop. First, we declare a function called `loop()`, which is what we'll be walking through next. The code we place in this function will be run repeatedly, over and over again:

```
void loop() {
```

First in our `loop()` function, we must determine what value to pass into the model (let's call it our x value). We determine this using two constants: `kXrange`, which specifies the maximum possible x value as 2π, and `kInferencesPerCycle`, which defines the number of inferences that we want to perform as we step from 0 to 2π. The next few lines of code calculate the x value:

```
// Calculate an x value to feed into the model. We compare the current
// inference_count to the number of inferences per cycle to determine
// our position within the range of possible x values the model was
// trained on, and use this to calculate a value.
float position = static_cast<float>(inference_count) /
                 static_cast<float>(kInferencesPerCycle);
float x_val = position * kXrange;
```

The first two lines of code just divide `inference_count` (which is the number of inferences we've done so far) by `kInferencesPerCycle` to obtain our current "position" within the range. The next line multiplies that value by `kXrange`, which represents the maximum value in the range (2π). The result, `x_val`, is the value we'll be passing into our model.

 `static_cast<float>()` is used to convert `inference_count` and `kInferencesPerCycle`, which are both integer values, into floating-point numbers. We do this so that we can correctly perform division. In C++, if you divide two integers, the result is an integer; any fractional part of the result is dropped. Because we want our x value to be a floating-point number that includes the fractional part, we need to convert the numbers being divided into floating points.

The two constants we use, kInferencesPerCycle and kXrange, are defined in the files *constants.h* and *constants.cc*. It's a C++ convention to prefix the names of constants with a k, so they're easily identifiable as constants when using them in code. It can be useful to define constants in a separate file so they can be included and used in any place that they are needed.

The next part of our code should look nice and familiar; we write our x value to the model's input tensor, run inference, and then grab the result (let's call it our y value) from the output tensor:

```
// Place our calculated x value in the model's input tensor
input->data.f[0] = x_val;

// Run inference, and report any error
TfLiteStatus invoke_status = interpreter->Invoke();
if (invoke_status != kTfLiteOk) {
  error_reporter->Report("Invoke failed on x_val: %f\n",
                         static_cast<double>(x_val));
  return;
}

// Read the predicted y value from the model's output tensor
float y_val = output->data.f[0];
```

We now have a sine value. Since it takes a small amount of time to run inference on each number, and this code is running in a loop, we'll be generating a sequence of sine values over time. This will be perfect for controlling some blinking LEDs or an animation. Our next job is to output it somehow.

The following line calls the HandleOutput() function, defined in *output_handler.cc*:

```
// Output the results. A custom HandleOutput function can be implemented
// for each supported hardware target.
HandleOutput(error_reporter, x_val, y_val);
```

We pass in our x and y values, along with our ErrorReporter instance, which we can use to log things. To see what happens next, let's explore *output_handler.cc*.

Handling Output with output_handler.cc

The file *output_handler.cc* defines our HandleOutput() function. Its implementation is very simple:

```
void HandleOutput(tflite::ErrorReporter* error_reporter, float x_value,
                  float y_value) {
  // Log the current X and Y values
  error_reporter->Report("x_value: %f, y_value: %f\n", x_value, y_value);
}
```

All this function does is use the `ErrorReporter` instance to log the x and y values. This is just a bare-minimum implementation that we can use to test the basic functionality of our application, for example by running it on our development computer.

Our goal, though, is to deploy this application to several different microcontroller platforms, using each platform's specialized hardware to display the output. For each individual platform we're planning to deploy to, such as Arduino, we provide a custom replacement for *output_handler.cc* that uses the platform's APIs to control output—for example, by lighting some LEDs.

As mentioned earlier, these replacement files are located in subdirectories with the name of each platform: *arduino/*, *disco_f76ng/*, and *sparkfun_edge/*. We'll dive into the platform-specific implementations later. For now, let's jump back into *main_functions.cc*.

Wrapping Up main_functions.cc

The last thing we do in our `loop()` function is increment our `inference_count` counter. If it has reached the maximum number of inferences per cycle defined in `kInferencesPerCycle`, we reset it to 0:

```
// Increment the inference_counter, and reset it if we have reached
// the total number per cycle
inference_count += 1;
if (inference_count     >= kInferencesPerCycle) inference_count = 0;
```

The next time our loop iterates, this will have the effect of either moving our x value along by a step or wrapping it around back to 0 if it has reached the end of the range.

We've now reached the end of our `loop()` function. Each time it runs, a new x value is calculated, inference is run, and the result is output by `HandleOutput()`. If `loop()` is continually called, it will run inference for a progression of x values in the range 0 to 2π and then repeat.

But what is it that makes the `loop()` function run over and over again? The answer lies in the file *main.cc*.

Understanding main.cc

The C++ standard (*https://oreil.ly/BfmkW*) specifies that every C++ program contain a global function named `main()`, which will be run when the program starts. In our program, this function is defined in the file *main.cc*. The existence of this `main()` function is the reason *main.cc* represents the entry point of our program. The code in `main()` will be run any time the microcontroller starts up.

The file *main.cc* is very short and sweet. First, it contains an `#include` statement for *main_functions.h*, which will bring in the `setup()` and `loop()` functions defined there:

```
#include "tensorflow/lite/micro/examples/hello_world/main_functions.h"
```

Next, it declares the `main()` function itself:

```
int main(int argc, char* argv[]) {
  setup();
  while (true) {
    loop();
  }
}
```

When `main()` runs, it first calls our `setup()` function. It will do this only once. After that, it enters a `while` loop that will continually call the `loop()` function, over and over again.

This loop will keep running indefinitely. Yikes! If you're from a server or web programming background, this might not sound like a great idea. The loop will block our single thread of execution, and there's no way to exit the program.

However, when writing software for microcontrollers, this type of endless loop is actually pretty common. Because there's no multitasking, and only one application will ever run, it doesn't really matter that the loop goes on and on. We just continue making inferences and outputting data for as long as the microcontroller is connected to power.

We've now walked through our entire microcontroller application. In the next section, we'll try out the application code by running it on our development machine.

Running Our Application

To give our application code a test run, we first need to build it. Enter the following Make command to create an executable binary for our program:

```
make -f tensorflow/lite/micro/tools/make/Makefile hello_world
```

When the build completes, you can run the application binary by using the following command, depending on your operating system:

```
# macOS:
tensorflow/lite/micro/tools/make/gen/osx_x86_64/bin/hello_world

# Linux:
tensorflow/lite/micro/tools/make/gen/linux_x86_64/bin/hello_world

# Windows
tensorflow/lite/micro/tools/make/gen/windows_x86_64/bin/hello_world
```

If you can't find the correct path, list the directories in *tensorflow/lite/micro/tools/make/gen/*.

After you run the binary, you should hopefully see a bunch of output scrolling past, looking something like this:

```
x_value: 1.4137159*2^1, y_value: 1.374213*2^-2

x_value: 1.5707957*2^1, y_value: -1.4249528*2^-5

x_value: 1.7278753*2^1, y_value: -1.4295994*2^-2

x_value: 1.8849551*2^1, y_value: -1.2867725*2^-1

x_value: 1.210171*2^2, y_value: -1.7542461*2^-1
```

Very exciting! These are the logs written by the `HandleOutput()` function in *output_handler.cc*. There's one log per inference, and the `x_value` gradually increments until it reaches 2π, at which point it goes back to 0 and starts again.

As soon as you've had enough excitement, you can press Ctrl-C to terminate the program.

 You'll notice that the numbers are output as values with power-of-two exponents, like `1.4137159*2^1`. This is an efficient way to log floating-point numbers on microcontrollers, which often don't have hardware support for floating-point operations.

To get the original value, just pull out your calculator: for example, `1.4137159*2^1` evaluates to `2.8274318`. If you're curious, the code that prints these numbers is in *debug_log_numbers.cc* (*https://oreil.ly/sb06c*).

Wrapping Up

We've now confirmed the program works on our development machine. In the next chapter, we'll get it running on some microcontrollers!

## CHAPTER 6

The "Hello World" of TinyML: Deploying to Microcontrollers

Now it's time to get our hands dirty. Over the course of this chapter, we will deploy the code to three different devices:

- Arduino Nano 33 BLE Sense (*https://oreil.ly/6qlMD*)
- SparkFun Edge (*https://oreil.ly/-hoL-*)
- ST Microelectronics STM32F746G Discovery kit (*https://oreil.ly/cvm4J*)

We'll walk through the build and deployment process for each one.

 TensorFlow Lite regularly adds support for new devices, so if the device you'd like to use isn't listed here, it's worth checking the example's *README.md* (*https://oreil.ly/ez0ef*).

You can also check there for updated deployment instructions if you run into trouble following these steps.

Every device has its own unique output capabilities, ranging from a bank of LEDs to a full LCD display, so the example contains a custom implementation of `HandleOut put()` for each one. We'll also walk through each of these and talk about how its logic works. Even if you don't have all of the devices, reading through this code should be interesting, so we strongly recommend taking a look.

What Exactly Is a Microcontroller?

Depending on your past experience, you might not be familiar with how microcontrollers interact with other electronic components. Because we're about to start playing with hardware, it's worth introducing some ideas before we move along.

On a microcontroller board like the Arduino, SparkFun Edge, or STM32F746G Discovery kit, the actual microcontroller is just one of many electronic components attached to the circuit board. Figure 6-1 shows the microcontroller on the SparkFun Edge.

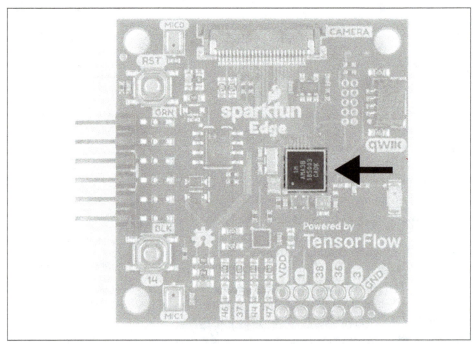

Figure 6-1. The SparkFun Edge board with its microcontroller highlighted

The microcontroller is connected to the circuit board it lives on using *pins*. A typical microcontroller has dozens of pins, and they serve all sorts of purposes. Some provide power to the microcontroller; others connect it to various important components. Some pins are set aside for the input and output of digital signals by programs running on the microcontroller. These are called *GPIO* pins, which stands for general-purpose input/output. They can act as inputs, determining whether a voltage is being applied to them, or outputs, sourcing current that can power or communicate with other components.

GPIO pins are digital. This means that in output mode, they are like switches that can either be fully on, or fully off. In input mode, they can detect whether the voltage applied to them by another component is either above or below a certain threshold.

In addition to GPIOs, some microcontrollers have analog input pins, which can measure the exact level of voltage that is being applied to them.

By calling special functions, the program running on a microcontroller can control whether a given pin is in input or output mode. Other functions are used to switch an output pin on or off, or to read the current state of an input pin.

Now that you know a bit more about microcontrollers, let's take a closer look at our first device: the Arduino.

Arduino

There are a huge variety of Arduino (*https://www.arduino.cc/*) boards, all with different capabilities. Not all of them will run TensorFlow Lite for Microcontrollers. The board we recommend for this book is the Arduino Nano 33 BLE Sense (*https://oreil.ly/9g1bJ*). In addition to being compatible with TensorFlow Lite, it also includes a microphone and an accelerometer (which we use in later chapters). We recommend buying the version of the board with headers, which makes it easier to connect other components without soldering.

Most Arduino boards come with a built-in LED, and this is what we'll be using to visually output our sine values. Figure 6-2 shows an Arduino Nano 33 BLE Sense board with the LED highlighted.

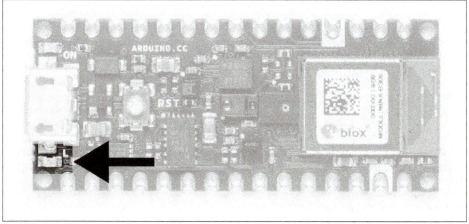

Figure 6-2. The Arduino Nano 33 BLE Sense board with the LED highlighted

Handling Output on Arduino

Because we have only one LED to work with, we need to think creatively. One option is to vary the brightness of the LED based on the most recently predicted sine value. Given that the value ranges from –1 to 1, we could represent 0 with an LED that is fully off, –1 and 1 with a fully lit LED, and any intermediate values with a partially dimmed LED. As the program runs inferences in a loop, the LED will fade repeatedly on and off.

We can vary the number of inferences we perform across a full sine wave cycle using the kInferencesPerCycle constant. Because one inference takes a set amount of time, tweaking kInferencesPerCycle, defined in *constants.cc*, will adjust how fast the LED fades.

There's an Arduino-specific version of this file in *hello_world/arduino/constants.cc* (*https://oreil.ly/YNsvq*). The file has been given the same name as *hello_world/ constants.cc*, so it will be used instead of the original implementation when the application is built for Arduino.

To dim our built-in LED, we can use a technique called *pulse width modulation* (PWM). If we switch an output pin on and off extremely rapidly, the pin's output voltage becomes a factor of the ratio between time spent in the off and on states. If the pin spends 50% of the time in each state, its output voltage will be 50% of its maximum. If it spends 75% in the on state and 25% in the off state, its voltage will be 75% of its maximum.

PWM is only available on certain pins of certain Arduino devices, but it's very easy to use: we just call a function that sets our desired output level for the pin.

The code that implements output handling for Arduino is in *hello_world/arduino/ output_handler.cc* (*https://oreil.ly/OpLMB*), which is used instead of the original file, *hello_world/output_handler.cc*.

Let's walk through the source:

```
#include "tensorflow/lite/micro/examples/hello_world/output_handler.h"
#include "Arduino.h"
#include "tensorflow/lite/micro/examples/hello_world/constants.h"
```

First, we include some header files. Our *output_handler.h* specifies the interface for this file. *Arduino.h* provides the interface for the Arduino platform; we use this to control the board. Because we need access to kInferencesPerCycle, we also include *constants.h*.

Next, we define the function and instruct it what to do the first time it runs:

```
// Adjusts brightness of an LED to represent the current y value
void HandleOutput(tflite::ErrorReporter* error_reporter, float x_value,
                  float y_value) {
```

```
// Track whether the function has run at least once
static bool is_initialized = false;

// Do this only once
if (!is_initialized) {
  // Set the LED pin to output
  pinMode(LED_BUILTIN, OUTPUT);
  is_initialized = true;
}
```

In C++, a variable declared as static within a function will hold its value across multiple runs of the function. Here, we use the is_initialized variable to track whether the code in the following if (!is_initialized) block has ever been run before.

The initialization block calls Arduino's pinMode() (*https://oreil.ly/6Kxep*) function, which indicates to the microcontroller whether a given pin should be in input or output mode. This is necessary before using a pin. The function is called with two constants defined by the Arduino platform: LED_BUILTIN and OUTPUT. LED_BUILTIN represents the pin connected to the board's built-in LED, and OUTPUT represents output mode.

After configuring the built-in LED's pin to output mode, set is_initialized to true so that this block code will not run again.

Next up, we calculate the desired brightness of the LED:

```
// Calculate the brightness of the LED such that y=-1 is fully off
// and y=1 is fully on. The LED's brightness can range from 0-255.
int brightness = (int)(127.5f * (y_value + 1));
```

The Arduino allows us to set the level of a PWM output as a number from 0 to 255, where 0 means fully off and 255 means fully on. Our y_value is a number between –1 and 1. The preceding code maps y_value to the range 0 to 255 so that when y = -1 the LED is fully off, when y = 0 the LED is half lit, and when y = 1 the LED is fully lit.

The next step is to actually set the LED's brightness:

```
// Set the brightness of the LED. If the specified pin does not support PWM,
// this will result in the LED being on when y > 127, off otherwise.
analogWrite(LED_BUILTIN, brightness);
```

The Arduino platform's analogWrite() (*https://oreil.ly/nNseR*) function takes a pin number (we provide LED_BUILTIN) and a value between 0 and 255. We provide our brightness, calculated in the previous line. When this function is called, the LED will be lit at that level.

Unfortunately, on some models of Arduino boards, the pin that the built-in LED is connected to is not capable of PWM. This means our calls to `analogWrite()` won't vary its brightness. Instead, the LED will be switched on if the value passed into `analogWrite()` is above 127, and switched off if it is 126 or below. This means the LED will flash on and off instead of fading. Not quite as cool, but it still demonstrates our sine wave prediction.

Finally, we use the `ErrorReporter` instance to log the brightness value:

```
// Log the current brightness value for display in the Arduino plotter
error_reporter->Report("%d\n", brightness);
```

On the Arduino platform, the `ErrorReporter` is set up to log data via a serial port. Serial is a very common way for microcontrollers to communicate with host computers, and it's often used for debugging. It's a communication protocol in which data is communicated one bit at a time by switching an output pin on and off. We can use it to send and receive anything, from raw binary data to text and numbers.

The Arduino IDE contains tools for capturing and displaying data received through a serial port. One of the tools, the Serial Plotter, can display a graph of values it receives via serial. By outputting a stream of brightness values from our code, we'll be able to see them graphed. Figure 6-3 shows this in action.

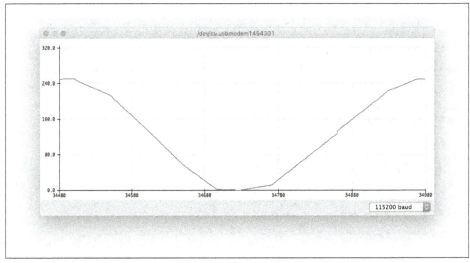

Figure 6-3. The Arduino IDE's Serial Plotter

We provide instructions on how to use the Serial Plotter later in this section.

You might be wondering how the ErrorReporter is able to output data via Arduino's serial interface. You can find the code implementation in *micro/arduino/debug_log.cc* (*https://oreil.ly/fkF8H*). It replaces the original implementation at *micro/debug_log.cc* (*https://oreil.ly/nxXgJ*). Just like how *output_handler.cc* is overwritten, we can provide platform-specific implementations of any source file in TensorFlow Lite for Microcontrollers by adding them to a directory with the platform's name.

Running the Example

Our next task is to build the project for Arduino and deploy it to a device.

 There's always a chance that the build process might have changed since this book was written, so check *README.md* (*https://oreil.ly/s2mj1*) for the latest instructions.

Here's everything that we'll need:

- A supported Arduino board (we recommend the Arduino Nano 33 BLE Sense)
- The appropriate USB cable
- The Arduino IDE (*https://oreil.ly/c-rv6*) (you'll need to download and install this before continuing)

The projects in this book are available as example code in the TensorFlow Lite Arduino library, which you can easily install via the Arduino IDE and select Manage Libraries from the Tools menu. In the window that appears, search for and install the library named *Arduino_TensorFlowLite*. You should be able to use the latest version, but if you run into issues, the version that was tested with this book is 1.14-ALPHA.

 You can also install the library from a *.zip* file, which you can either download (*https://oreil.ly/blgB8*) from the TensorFlow Lite team or generate yourself using the TensorFlow Lite for Microcontrollers Makefile. If you'd prefer to do this, see Appendix A.

After you've installed the library, the hello_world example will show up in the File menu under Examples→Arduino_TensorFlowLite, as shown in Figure 6-4.

Click "hello_world" to load the example. It will appear as a new window, with a tab for each of the source files. The file in the first tab, *hello_world*, is equivalent to the *main_functions.cc* we walked through earlier.

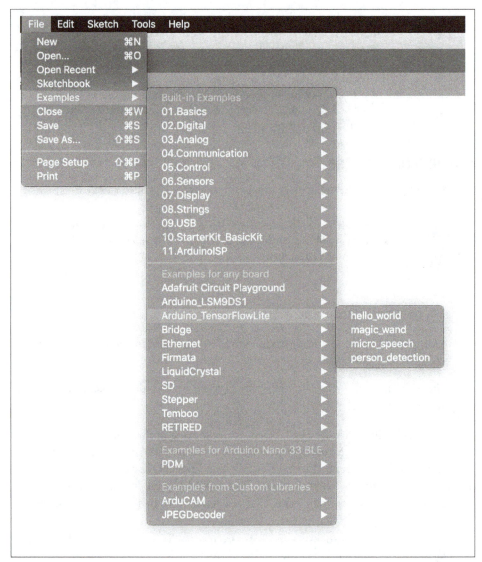

Figure 6-4. The Examples menu

Differences in the Arduino Example Code

When the Arduino library is generated, some minor changes are made to the code so that it works nicely with the Arduino IDE. This means that there are some subtle differences between the code in our Arduino example and in the TensorFlow GitHub repository. For example, in the *hello_world* file, the setup() and loop() functions are called automatically by the Arduino environment, so the *main.cc* file and its main() function aren't needed.

The Arduino IDE also expects the source files to have the *.cpp* extension, instead of *.cc*. In addition, since the Arduino IDE doesn't support subfolders, each filename in the Arduino example is prefixed with its original subfolder name. For example, *arduino_constants.cpp* is equivalent to the file originally named *arduino/constants.cc*.

Beyond a few minor differences, however, the code remains mostly unchanged.

To run the example, plug in your Arduino device via USB. Make sure the correct device type is selected from the Board drop-down list in the Tools menu, as shown in Figure 6-5.

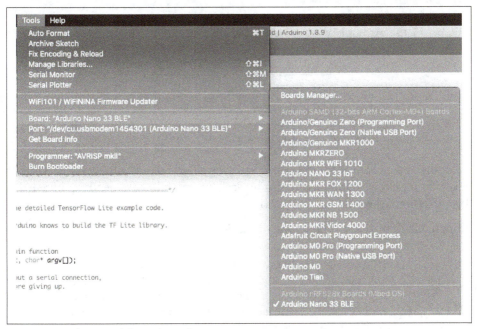

Figure 6-5. The Board drop-down list

If your device's name doesn't appear in the list, you'll need to install its support package. To do this, click Boards Manager. In the window that appears, search for your device and install the latest version of the corresponding support package.

Next, make sure the device's port is selected in the Port drop-down list, also in the Tools menu, as shown in Figure 6-6.

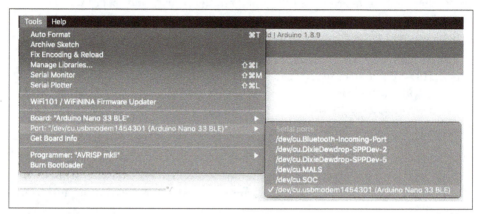

Figure 6-6. The Port drop-down list

Finally, in the Arduino window, click the upload button (highlighted in white in Figure 6-7) to compile and upload the code to your Arduino device.

Figure 6-7. The upload button, a right-facing arrow

After the upload has successfully completed you should see the LED on your Arduino board begin either fading in and out or flashing on and off, depending on whether the pin it is attached to supports PWM.

Congratulations: you're running ML on-device!

 Different models of Arduino boards have different hardware, and will run inference at varying speeds. If your LED is either flickering or stays fully on, you might need to increase the number of inferences per cycle. You can do this via the kInferencesPerCycle constant in *arduino_constants.cpp*.

"Making Your Own Changes" on page 106 shows you how to edit the example's code.

You can also view the brightness value plotted on a graph. To do this, open the Arduino IDE's Serial Plotter by selecting it in the Tools menu, as shown in Figure 6-8.

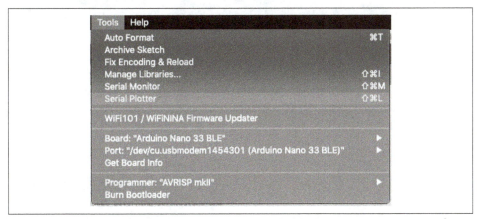

Figure 6-8. The Serial Plotter menu option

The plotter shows the value as it changes over time, as demonstrated in Figure 6-9.

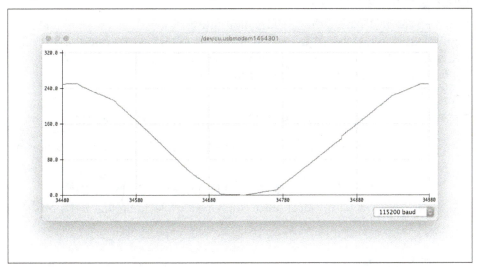

Figure 6-9. The Serial Plotter graphing the value

To view the raw data that is received from the Arduino's serial port, open the Serial Monitor from the Tools menu. You'll see a stream of numbers flying past, like in Figure 6-10.

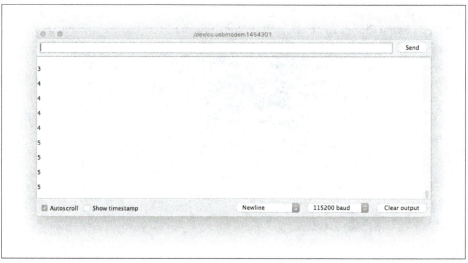

Figure 6-10. The Serial Monitor displaying raw data

Making Your Own Changes

Now that you've deployed the application, it might be fun to play around and make some changes to the code. You can edit the source files in the Arduino IDE. When you save, you'll be prompted to resave the example in a new location. When you're done making changes, you can click the upload button in the Arduino IDE to build and deploy.

To get started making changes, here are a few experiments you could try:

- Make the LED blink slower or faster by adjusting the number of inferences per cycle.
- Modify *output_handler.cc* to log a text-based animation to the serial port.
- Use the sine wave to control other components, like additional LEDs or sound generators.

SparkFun Edge

The SparkFun Edge (*https://oreil.ly/-hoL-*) development board was designed specifically as a platform for experimenting with machine learning on tiny devices. It has a power-efficient Ambiq Apollo 3 microcontroller with an Arm Cortex M4 processor core.

It features a bank of four LEDs, as shown in Figure 6-11. We use these to visually output our sine values.

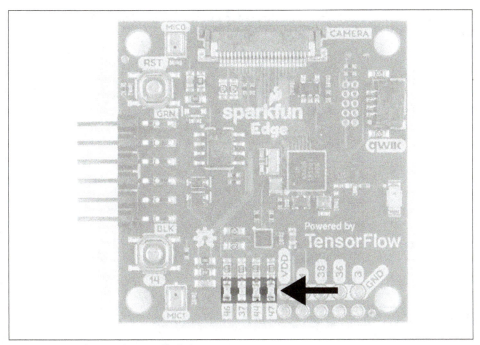

Figure 6-11. The SparkFun Edge's four LEDs

Handling Output on SparkFun Edge

We can use the board's bank of LEDs to make a simple animation, because nothing says cutting-edge AI like blinkenlights (*https://oreil.ly/T90fy*).

The LEDs (red, green, blue, and yellow) are physically lined up in the following order:

```
[ R G B Y ]
```

The following table represents how we will light the LEDs for different y values:

Range	LEDs lit
0.75 <= y <= 1	[0 0 1 1]
0 < y < 0.75	[0 0 1 0]
y = 0	[0 0 0 0]
-0.75 < y < 0	[0 1 0 0]
-1 <= y <= 0.75	[1 1 0 0]

Each inference takes a certain amount of time, so tweaking `kInferencesPerCycle`, defined in *constants.cc*, will adjust how fast the LEDs cycle.

Figure 6-12 shows a still from an animated *.gif* (*https://oreil.ly/cXdPY*) of the program running.

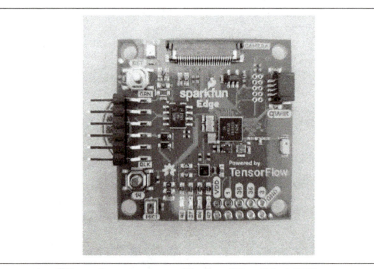

Figure 6-12. A still from the animation of the SparkFun Edge's LEDs

The code that implements output handling for the SparkFun Edge is in *hello_world/sparkfun_edge/output_handler.cc* (*https://oreil.ly/tegLK*), which is used instead of the original file, *hello_world/output_handler.cc*.

Let's start walking through it:

```
#include "tensorflow/lite/micro/examples/hello_world/output_handler.h"
#include "am_bsp.h"
```

First, we include some header files. Our *output_handler.h* specifies the interface for this file. The other file, *am_bsp.h,* comes from something called the *Ambiq Apollo3 SDK*. Ambiq is the manufacturer of the SparkFun Edge's microcontroller, which is called the Apollo3. The SDK (short for *software development kit*) is a collection of source files that define constants and functions that can be used to control the microcontroller's features.

Because we are planning to control the board's LEDs, we need to be able to switch the microcontroller's pins on and off. This is what we use the SDK for.

> The Makefile will automatically download the SDK when we eventually build the project. If you're curious, you can read more about it or download the code to explore on SparkFun's website (*https://oreil.ly/RHHqI*).

Next, we define the `HandleOutput()` function and indicate what to do on its first run:

```
void HandleOutput(tflite::ErrorReporter* error_reporter, float x_value,
                  float y_value) {
  // The first time this method runs, set up our LEDs correctly
  static bool is_initialized = false;
  if (!is_initialized) {
    // Set up LEDs as outputs
    am_hal_gpio_pinconfig(AM_BSP_GPIO_LED_RED, g_AM_HAL_GPIO_OUTPUT_12);
    am_hal_gpio_pinconfig(AM_BSP_GPIO_LED_BLUE, g_AM_HAL_GPIO_OUTPUT_12);
    am_hal_gpio_pinconfig(AM_BSP_GPIO_LED_GREEN, g_AM_HAL_GPIO_OUTPUT_12);
    am_hal_gpio_pinconfig(AM_BSP_GPIO_LED_YELLOW, g_AM_HAL_GPIO_OUTPUT_12);
    // Ensure all pins are cleared
    am_hal_gpio_output_clear(AM_BSP_GPIO_LED_RED);
    am_hal_gpio_output_clear(AM_BSP_GPIO_LED_BLUE);
    am_hal_gpio_output_clear(AM_BSP_GPIO_LED_GREEN);
    am_hal_gpio_output_clear(AM_BSP_GPIO_LED_YELLOW);
    is_initialized = true;
  }
```

Phew, that's a lot of setup! We're using the `am_hal_gpio_pinconfig()` function, provided by *am_bsp.h*, to configure the pins connected to the board's built-in LEDs, putting them into output mode (represented by the `g_AM_HAL_GPIO_OUTPUT_12` constant). The pin number of each LED is represented by a constant, such as `AM_BSP_GPIO_LED_RED`.

We then clear all of the outputs using `am_hal_gpio_output_clear()`, so the LEDs are all switched off. As in the Arduino implementation, we use a `static` variable named `is_initialized` to ensure the code in this block is run only once. Next, we determine which LEDs should be lit if the y value is negative:

```
  // Set the LEDs to represent negative values
  if (y_value < 0) {
    // Clear unnecessary LEDs
    am_hal_gpio_output_clear(AM_BSP_GPIO_LED_GREEN);
    am_hal_gpio_output_clear(AM_BSP_GPIO_LED_YELLOW);
    // The blue LED is lit for all negative values
    am_hal_gpio_output_set(AM_BSP_GPIO_LED_BLUE);
    // The red LED is lit in only some cases
    if (y_value <= -0.75) {
      am_hal_gpio_output_set(AM_BSP_GPIO_LED_RED);
    } else {
      am_hal_gpio_output_clear(AM_BSP_GPIO_LED_RED);
    }
```

First, in case the y value only just became negative, we clear the two LEDs that are used to indicate positive values. Next, we call `am_hal_gpio_output_set()` to switch on the blue LED, which will always be lit if the value is negative. Finally, if the value is less than –0.75, we switch on the red LED. Otherwise, we switch it off.

Next up, we do the same thing but for positive values of y:

```
  // Set the LEDs to represent positive values
} else if (y_value > 0) {
  // Clear unnecessary LEDs
  am_hal_gpio_output_clear(AM_BSP_GPIO_LED_RED);
  am_hal_gpio_output_clear(AM_BSP_GPIO_LED_BLUE);
  // The green LED is lit for all positive values
  am_hal_gpio_output_set(AM_BSP_GPIO_LED_GREEN);
  // The yellow LED is lit in only some cases
  if (y_value >= 0.75) {
    am_hal_gpio_output_set(AM_BSP_GPIO_LED_YELLOW);
  } else {
    am_hal_gpio_output_clear(AM_BSP_GPIO_LED_YELLOW);
  }
}
```

That's just about it for the LEDs. The last thing we do is log the current output values to anyone who is listening on the serial port:

```
// Log the current X and Y values
error_reporter->Report("x_value: %f, y_value: %f\n", x_value, y_value);
```

 Our ErrorReporter is able to output data via the SparkFun Edge's serial interface due to a custom implementation of *micro/spark-fun_edge/debug_log.cc* (*https://oreil.ly/ufEv9*) that replaces the original implementation at *mmicro/debug_log.cc* (*https://oreil.ly/ACaFt*).

Running the Example

Now we can build the sample code and deploy it to the SparkFun Edge.

 There's always a chance that the build process might have changed since this book was written, so check *README.md* (*https://oreil.ly/EcPZ8*) for the latest instructions.

To build and deploy our code, we'll need the following:

- A SparkFun Edge board
- A USB programmer (we recommend the SparkFun Serial Basic Breakout, which is available in micro-B USB (*https://oreil.ly/A6oDw*) and USB-C (*https://oreil.ly/3REjg*) variants)
- A matching USB cable
- Python 3 and some dependencies

Python and Dependencies

This process involves running some Python scripts. Before continuing, you should make sure that you have Python 3 installed. To check whether it's present on your system, open a terminal and enter the following:

```
python --version
```

If you have Python 3 installed, you will see the following output (where x and y are minor version numbers; the exact ones don't matter):

```
Python 3.x.y
```

If this worked, you can use the command `python` to run Python scripts later in this section.

If you saw a different output, try the following command:

```
python3 --version
```

You should hopefully see the same output we were looking for earlier:

```
Python 3.x.y
```

If you do, this means that you can use the command `python3` to run Python scripts when needed.

If not, you'll need to install Python 3 on your system. Search the web for instructions on installing it for your specific operating system.

After you've installed Python 3, you'll have to install some dependencies. Run the following command to do so (if your Python command is `python3`, you should use the command `pip3` instead of `pip`):

```
pip install pycrypto pyserial --user
```

After you've installed the dependencies, you're ready to go.

To begin, open a terminal, clone the TensorFlow repository, and then change into its directory:

```
git clone https://github.com/tensorflow/tensorflow.git
cd tensorflow
```

Next, we're going to build the binary and run some commands that get it ready for downloading to the device. To avoid some typing, you can copy and paste these commands from *README.md* (*https://oreil.ly/PYmUu*).

Build the binary

The following command downloads all the required dependencies and then compiles a binary for the SparkFun Edge:

```
make -f tensorflow/lite/micro/tools/make/Makefile \
  TARGET=sparkfun_edge hello_world_bin
```

 A binary is a file that contains the program in a form that can be run directly by the SparkFun Edge hardware.

The binary will be created as a *.bin* file, in the following location:

```
tensorflow/lite/micro/tools/make/gen/ \
  sparkfun_edge_cortex-m4/bin/hello_world.bin
```

To check that the file exists, you can use the following command:

```
test -f tensorflow/lite/micro/tools/make/gen/ \
  sparkfun_edge_cortex-m4/bin/hello_world.bin \
  && echo "Binary was successfully created" || echo "Binary is missing"
```

If you run that command, you should see `Binary was successfully created` printed to the console.

If you see `Binary is missing`, there was a problem with the build process. If so, it's likely that you can find some clues to what went wrong in the output of the `make` command.

Sign the binary

The binary must be signed with cryptographic keys to be deployed to the device. Let's now run some commands that will sign the binary so it can be flashed to the Spark-Fun Edge. The scripts used here come from the Ambiq SDK, which is downloaded when the Makefile is run.

Enter the following command to set up some dummy cryptographic keys that you can use for development:

```
cp tensorflow/lite/micro/tools/make/downloads/AmbiqSuite-Rel2.0.0/ \
  tools/apollo3_scripts/keys_info0.py \
  tensorflow/lite/micro/tools/make/downloads/AmbiqSuite-Rel2.0.0/ \
  tools/apollo3_scripts/keys_info.py
```

Next, run the following command to create a signed binary. Substitute `python3` with `python` if necessary:

```
python3 tensorflow/lite/micro/tools/make/downloads/ \
  AmbiqSuite-Rel2.0.0/tools/apollo3_scripts/create_cust_image_blob.py \
  --bin tensorflow/lite/micro/tools/make/gen/ \
  sparkfun_edge_cortex-m4/bin/hello_world.bin \
  --load-address 0xC000 \
  --magic-num 0xCB -o main_nonsecure_ota \
  --version 0x0
```

This creates the file *main_nonsecure_ota.bin*. Now run this command to create a final version of the file that you can use to flash your device with the script you will use in the next step:

```
python3 tensorflow/lite/micro/tools/make/downloads/ \
  AmbiqSuite-Rel2.0.0/tools/apollo3_scripts/create_cust_wireupdate_blob.py \
  --load-address 0x20000 \
  --bin main_nonsecure_ota.bin \
  -i 6 \
  -o main_nonsecure_wire \
  --options 0x1
```

You should now have a file called *main_nonsecure_wire.bin* in the directory where you ran the commands. This is the file you'll be flashing to the device.

Flash the binary

The SparkFun Edge stores the program it is currently running in its 1 megabyte of flash memory. If you want the board to run a new program, you need to send it to the board, which will store it in flash memory, overwriting any program that was previously saved.

This process is called *flashing*. Let's walk through the steps.

Attach the programmer to the board.   To download new programs to the board, you'll use the SparkFun USB-C Serial Basic serial programmer. This device allows your computer to communicate with the microcontroller via USB.

To attach this device to your board, perform the following steps:

1. On the side of the SparkFun Edge, locate the six-pin header.
2. Plug the SparkFun USB-C Serial Basic into these pins, ensuring that the pins labeled BLK and GRN on each device are lined up correctly.

You can see the correct arrangement in Figure 6-13.

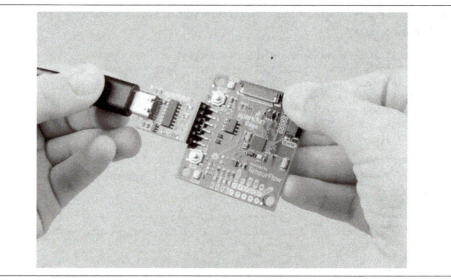

Figure 6-13. Connecting the SparkFun Edge and USB-C Serial Basic (courtesy of SparkFun)

Attach the programmer to your computer.   Next, connect the board to your computer via USB. To program the board, you need to determine the name that your computer gives the device. The best way of doing this is to list all of the computer's devices before and after attaching it and then look to see which device is new.

 Some people have reported issues with their operating system's default drivers for the programmer, so we strongly recommend installing the driver (*https://oreil.ly/Wkxaf*) before you continue.

Before attaching the device via USB, run the following command:

```
# macOS:
ls /dev/cu*

# Linux:
ls /dev/tty*
```

This should output a list of attached devices that looks something like the following:

```
/dev/cu.Bluetooth-Incoming-Port
/dev/cu.MALS
/dev/cu.SOC
```

Now, connect the programmer to your computer's USB port and run the command again:

```
# macOS:
ls /dev/cu*

# Linux:
ls /dev/tty*
```

You should see an extra item in the output, as in the example that follows. Your new item might have a different name. This new item is the name of the device:

```
/dev/cu.Bluetooth-Incoming-Port
/dev/cu.MALS
/dev/cu.SOC
/dev/cu.wchusbserial-1450
```

This name will be used to refer to the device. However, it can change depending on which USB port the programmer is attached to, so if you disconnect the board from your computer and then reattach it, you might need to look up its name again.

 Some users have reported two devices appearing in the list. If you see two devices, the correct one to use begins with the letters "wch"; for example, "/dev/wchusbserial-14410."

After you've identified the device name, put it in a shell variable for later use:

```
export DEVICENAME=<your device name here>
```

This is a variable that you can use when running commands that require the device name, later in the process.

Run the script to flash your board.   To flash the board, you need to put it into a special "bootloader" state that prepares it to receive the new binary. You can then run a script to send the binary to the board.

First create an environment variable to specify the baud rate, which is the speed at which data will be sent to the device:

```
export BAUD_RATE=921600
```

Now paste the command that follows into your terminal—but *do not press Enter yet!*. The ${DEVICENAME} and ${BAUD_RATE} in the command will be replaced with the values you set in the previous sections. Remember to substitute python3 with python if necessary:

```
python3 tensorflow/lite/micro/tools/make/downloads/ \
  AmbiqSuite-Rel2.0.0/tools/apollo3_scripts/ \
  uart_wired_update.py -b ${BAUD_RATE} \
  ${DEVICENAME} -r 1 -f main_nonsecure_wire.bin -i 6
```

Next, you'll reset the board into its bootloader state and flash the board. On the board, locate the buttons marked RST and 14, as shown in Figure 6-14.

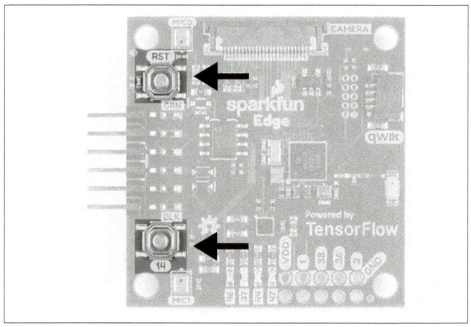

Figure 6-14. The SparkFun Edge's buttons

Perform the following steps:

1. Ensure that your board is connected to the programmer and that the entire thing is connected to your computer via USB.

2. On the board, press and hold the button marked 14. *Continue holding it.*

3. While still holding the button marked 14, press the button marked RST to reset the board.

4. Press Enter on your computer to run the script. *Continue holding button 14.*

You should now see something like the following appearing on your screen:

```
Connecting with Corvette over serial port /dev/cu.usbserial-1440...
Sending Hello.
Received response for Hello
Received Status
length =  0x58
version =  0x3
Max Storage =  0x4ffa0
Status =  0x2
State =  0x7
```

```
AMInfo =
0x1
0xff2da3ff
0x55fff
0x1
0x49f40003
0xffffffff
[...lots more 0xffffffff...]
Sending OTA Descriptor = 0xfe000
Sending Update Command.
number of updates needed = 1
Sending block of size  0x158b0  from  0x0  to  0x158b0
Sending Data Packet of length  8180
Sending Data Packet of length  8180
[...lots more Sending Data Packet of length  8180...]
```

Keep holding button 14 until you see `Sending Data Packet of length 8180`. You can release the button after seeing this (but it's okay if you keep holding it).

The program will continue to print lines on the terminal. Eventually you will see something like the following:

```
[...lots more Sending Data Packet of length  8180...]
Sending Data Packet of length  8180
Sending Data Packet of length  6440
Sending Reset Command.
Done.
```

This indicates a successful flashing.

 If the program output ends with an error, check whether `Sending Reset Command.` was printed. If so, flashing was likely successful despite the error. Otherwise, flashing might have failed. Try running through these steps again (you can skip over setting the environment variables).

Testing the Program

The binary should now be deployed to the device. Press the button marked `RST` to reboot the board. You should see the device's four LEDs flashing in sequence. Nice work!

Viewing Debug Data

Debug information is logged by the board while the program is running. To view it, we can monitor the board's serial port output using a baud rate of 115200. On macOS and Linux, the following command should work:

```
screen ${DEVICENAME} 115200
```

You will see a lot of output flying past! To stop the scrolling, press Ctrl-A, immediately followed by Esc. You can then use the arrow keys to explore the output, which will contain the results of running inference on various x values:

```
x_value: 1.1843798*2^2, y_value: -1.9542645*2^-1
```

To stop viewing the debug output with `screen`, press Ctrl-A, immediately followed by the K key, and then press the Y key.

The program `screen` is a helpful utility program for connecting to other computers. In this case, we're using it to listen to the data the SparkFun Edge board is logging via its serial port. If you're using Windows, you could try using the program `CoolTerm` (*https://oreil.ly/sPWQP*) to do the same thing.

Making Your Own Changes

Now that you've deployed the basic application, try playing around and making some changes. You can find the application's code in the *tensorflow/lite/micro/examples/hello_world* folder. Just edit and save, and then repeat the previous instructions to deploy your modified code to the device.

Here are a few things you could try:

- Make the LED blink slower or faster by adjusting the number of inferences per cycle.
- Modify *output_handler.cc* to log a text-based animation to the serial port.
- Use the sine wave to control other components, like additional LEDs or sound generators.

ST Microelectronics STM32F746G Discovery Kit

The STM32F746G (*https://oreil.ly/cvm4J*) is a microcontroller development board with a relatively powerful Arm Cortex-M7 processor core.

This board runs Arm's Mbed OS (*https://os.mbed.com*), an embedded operating system designed to make it easier to build and deploy embedded applications. This means that we can use many of the instructions in this section to build for other Mbed devices.

The STM32F746G comes with an attached LCD screen, which will allow us to build a much more elaborate visual display.

Handling Output on STM32F746G

Now that we have an entire LCD to play with, we can draw a nice animation. Let's use the *x*-axis of the screen to represent number of inferences, and the *y*-axis to represent the current value of our prediction.

We'll draw a dot where this value should be, and it will move around the screen as we loop through the input range of 0 to 2π. Figure 6-15 presents a wireframe of this.

Each inference takes a certain amount of time, so tweaking `kInferencesPerCycle`, defined in *constants.cc*, will adjust the speed and smoothness of the dot's motion.

Figure 6-16 shows a still from an animated *.gif* (*https://oreil.ly/1EM7C*) of the program running.

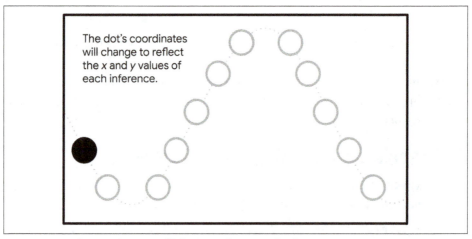

The dot's coordinates will change to reflect the x and y values of each inference.

Figure 6-15. The animation we'll draw on the LCD display

Figure 6-16 shows a still from an animated *.gif* (*https://oreil.ly/1EM7C*) of the program running.

Figure 6-16. The code running on an STM32F746G Discovery kit, which has an LCD display

The code that implements output handling for the STM32F746G is in *hello_world/disco_f746ng/output_handler.cc* (*https://oreil.ly/bj4iL*), which is used instead of the original file, *hello_world/output_handler.cc*.

Let's walk through it:

```
#include "tensorflow/lite/micro/examples/hello_world/output_handler.h"
#include "LCD_DISCO_F746NG.h"
#include "tensorflow/lite/micro/examples/hello_world/constants.h"
```

First, we have some header files. Our *output_handler.h* specifies the interface for this file. *LCD_DISCO_F74NG.h*, supplied by the board's manufacturer, declares the interface we will use to control its LCD screen. We also include *constants.h*, since we need access to kInferencesPerCycle and kXrange.

Next, we set up a ton of variables. First comes an instance of LCD_DISCO_F746NG, which is defined in *LCD_DISCO_F74NG.h* and provides methods that we can use to control the LCD:

```
// The LCD driver
LCD_DISCO_F746NG lcd;
```

Details on the LCD_DISCO_F746NG classes are available on the Mbed site (*https://oreil.ly/yiPHS*).

Next, we define some constants that control the look and feel of our visuals:

```
// The colors we'll draw
const uint32_t background_color = 0xFFF4B400;  // Yellow
const uint32_t foreground_color = 0xFFDB4437;  // Red
// The size of the dot we'll draw
const int dot_radius = 10;
```

The colors are provided as hex values, like 0xFFF4B400. They are in the format AARRGGBB, where AA represents the alpha value (or opacity, with FF being fully opaque), and RR, GG, and BB represent the amounts of red, green, and blue.

With some practice, you can learn to read the color from the hex value. 0xFFF4B400 is fully opaque and has a lot of red and a fair amount of green, which makes it a nice orange-yellow.

You can also look up the values with a quick Google search.

We then declare a few more variables that define the shape and size of our animation:

```
// Size of the drawable area
int width;
int height;
// Midpoint of the y axis
int midpoint;
```

```
// Pixels per unit of x_value
int x_increment;
```

After the variables, we define the `HandleOutput()` function and tell it what to do on its first run:

```
// Animates a dot across the screen to represent the current x and y values
void HandleOutput(tflite::ErrorReporter* error_reporter, float x_value,
                  float y_value) {
  // Track whether the function has run at least once
  static bool is_initialized = false;

  // Do this only once
  if (!is_initialized) {
    // Set the background and foreground colors
    lcd.Clear(background_color);
    lcd.SetTextColor(foreground_color);
    // Calculate the drawable area to avoid drawing off the edges
    width = lcd.GetXSize() - (dot_radius * 2);
    height = lcd.GetYSize() - (dot_radius * 2);
    // Calculate the y axis midpoint
    midpoint = height / 2;
    // Calculate fractional pixels per unit of x_value
    x_increment = static_cast<float>(width) / kXrange;
    is_initialized = true;
  }
```

There's a lot in there! First, we use methods belonging to `lcd` to set a background and foreground color. The oddly named `lcd.SetTextColor()` sets the color of anything we draw, not just text:

```
// Set the background and foreground colors
lcd.Clear(background_color);
lcd.SetTextColor(foreground_color);
```

Next, we calculate how much of the screen we can actually draw to, so that we know where to plot our circle. If we got this wrong, we might try to draw past the edge of the screen, with unexpected results:

```
width = lcd.GetXSize() - (dot_radius * 2);
height = lcd.GetYSize() - (dot_radius * 2);
```

After that, we determine the location of the middle of the screen, below which our negative y values will be drawn. We also calculate how many pixels of screen width represent one unit of our x value. Note how we use `static_cast` to ensure that we get a floating-point result:

```
// Calculate the y axis midpoint
midpoint = height / 2;
// Calculate fractional pixels per unit of x_value
x_increment = static_cast<float>(width) / kXrange;
```

As we did before, use a `static` variable named `is_initialized` to ensure that the code in this block is run only once.

After initialization is complete, we can start with our output. First, we clear any previous drawing:

```
// Clear the previous drawing
lcd.Clear(background_color);
```

Next, we use `x_value` to calculate where along the display's *x*-axis we should draw our dot:

```
// Calculate x position, ensuring the dot is not partially offscreen,
// which causes artifacts and crashes
int x_pos = dot_radius + static_cast<int>(x_value * x_increment);
```

We then do the same for our y value. This is a little more complex because we want to plot positive values above the `midpoint` and negative values below:

```
// Calculate y position, ensuring the dot is not partially offscreen
int y_pos;
if (y_value >= 0) {
  // Since the display's y runs from the top down, invert y_value
  y_pos = dot_radius + static_cast<int>(midpoint * (1.f - y_value));
} else {
  // For any negative y_value, start drawing from the midpoint
  y_pos =
      dot_radius + midpoint + static_cast<int>(midpoint * (0.f - y_value));
}
```

As soon as we've determined its position, we can go ahead and draw the dot:

```
// Draw the dot
lcd.FillCircle(x_pos, y_pos, dot_radius);
```

Finally, we use our `ErrorReporter` to log the x and y values to the serial port:

```
// Log the current X and Y values
error_reporter->Report("x_value: %f, y_value: %f\n", x_value, y_value);
```

The `ErrorReporter` can output data via the STM32F746G's serial interface due to a custom implementation, *micro/disco_f746ng/debug_log.cc* (*https://oreil.ly/eL1ft*), that replaces the original implementation at *micro/debug_log.cc* (*https://oreil.ly/HpJ-t*).

Running the Example

Next up, let's build the project! The STM32F746G runs Arm's Mbed OS, so we'll be using the Mbed toolchain to deploy our application to the device.

 There's always a chance that the build process might have changed since this book was written, so check *README.md* (*https://oreil.ly/ WuhIz*) for the latest instructions.

Before we begin, we'll need the following:

- An STM32F746G Discovery kit board
- A mini-USB cable
- The Arm Mbed CLI (follow the Mbed setup guide (*https://oreil.ly/TkRwd*))
- Python 3 and `pip`

Like the Arduino IDE, Mbed requires source files to be structured in a certain way. The TensorFlow Lite for Microcontrollers Makefile knows how to do this for us, and can generate a directory suitable for Mbed.

To do so, run the following command:

```
make -f tensorflow/lite/micro/tools/make/Makefile \
    TARGET=mbed TAGS="CMSIS disco_f746ng" generate_hello_world_mbed_project
```

This results in the creation of a new directory:

```
tensorflow/lite/micro/tools/make/gen/mbed_cortex-m4/prj/ \
    hello_world/mbed
```

This directory contains all of the example's dependencies structured in the correct way for Mbed to be able to build it.

First, change into the directory so that your can run some commands in there:

```
cd tensorflow/lite/micro/tools/make/gen/mbed_cortex-m4/prj/ \
    hello_world/mbed
```

Now you'll use Mbed to download the dependencies and build the project.

To get started, use the following command to specify to Mbed that the current directory is the root of an Mbed project:

```
mbed config root .
```

Next, instruct Mbed to download the dependencies and prepare to build:

```
mbed deploy
```

By default, Mbed will build the project using C++98. However, TensorFlow Lite requires C++11. Run the following Python snippet to modify the Mbed configuration files so that it uses C++11. You can just type or paste it into the command line:

```
python -c 'import fileinput, glob;
for filename in glob.glob("mbed-os/tools/profiles/*.json"):
  for line in fileinput.input(filename, inplace=True):
    print(line.replace("\"-std=gnu++98\"","\"-std=c++11\", \"-fpermissive\""))'
```

Finally, run the following command to compile:

```
mbed compile -m DISCO_F746NG -t GCC_ARM
```

This should result in a binary at the following path:

```
cp ./BUILD/DISCO_F746NG/GCC_ARM/mbed.bin
```

One of the nice things about using Mbed-enabled boards like the STM32F746G is that deployment is really easy. To deploy, just plug in your STM board and copy the file to it. On macOS, you can do this with the following command:

```
cp ./BUILD/DISCO_F746NG/GCC_ARM/mbed.bin /Volumes/DIS_F746NG/
```

Alternately, just find the `DIS_F746NG` volume in your file browser and drag the file over. Copying the file will initiate the flashing process. When this is complete, you should see an animation on the device's screen.

In addition to this animation, debug information is logged by the board while the program is running. To view it, establish a serial connection to the board using a baud rate of 9600.

On macOS and Linux, the device should be listed when you issue the following command:

```
ls /dev/tty*
```

It will look something like the following:

```
/dev/tty.usbmodem1454203
```

After you've identified the device, use the following command to connect to it, replacing *</dev/tty.devicename>* with the name of your device as it appears in */dev*:

```
screen /<dev/tty.devicename> 9600
```

You will see a lot of output flying past. To stop the scrolling, press Ctrl-A, immediately followed by Esc. You can then use the arrow keys to explore the output, which will contain the results of running inference on various x values:

```
x_value: 1.1843798*2^2, y_value: -1.9542645*2^-1
```

To stop viewing the debug output with `screen`, press Ctrl-A, immediately followed by the K key, then hit the Y key.

Making Your Own Changes

Now that you've deployed the application, it could be fun to play around and make some changes! You can find the application's code in the *tensorflow/lite/micro/tools/ make/gen/mbed_cortex-m4/prj/hello_world/mbed* folder. Just edit and save, and then repeat the previous instructions to deploy your modified code to the device.

Here are a few things you could try:

- Make the dot move slower or faster by adjusting the number of inferences per cycle.
- Modify *output_handler.cc* to log a text-based animation to the serial port.
- Use the sine wave to control other components, like LEDs or sound generators.

Wrapping Up

Over the past three chapters, we've gone through the full end-to-end journey of training a model, converting it for TensorFlow Lite, writing an application around it, and deploying it to a tiny device. In the coming chapters, we'll explore some more sophisticated and exciting examples that put embedded machine learning to work.

First up, we'll build an application that recognizes spoken commands using a tiny, 18 KB model.

## CHAPTER 7

Wake-Word Detection: Building an Application

TinyML might be a new phenomenon, but its most widespread application is perhaps already at work in your home, in your car, or even in your pocket. Can you guess what it is?

The past few years have seen the rise of digital assistants. These products provide a voice user interface (UI) designed to give instant access to information without the need for a screen or keyboard. Between Google Assistant, Apple's Siri, and Amazon Alexa, these digital assistants are nearly ubiquitous. Some variant is built into almost every mobile phone, from flagship models to voice-first devices designed for emerging markets. They're also in smart speakers, computers, and vehicles.

In most cases, the heavy lifting of speech recognition, natural language processing, and generating responses to users' queries is done in the cloud, on powerful servers running large ML models. When a user asks a question, it's sent to the server as a stream of audio. The server figures out what it means, looks up any required information, and sends the appropriate response back.

But part of an assistants' appeal is that they're always on, ready to help you out. By saying "Hey Google," or "Alexa," you can wake up your assistant and tell it what you need without ever having to press a button. This means they must be listening for your voice 24/7, whether you're sitting in your living room, driving down the freeway, or in the great outdoors with a phone in your hand.

Although it's easy to do speech recognition on a server, it's just not feasible to send a constant stream of audio from a device to a data center. From a privacy perspective, sending every second of audio captured to a remote server would be an absolute disaster. Even if that were somehow okay, it would require vast amounts of bandwidth and chew through mobile data plans in hours. In addition, network communication uses energy, and sending a constant stream of data would quickly drain the device's battery. What's more, with every request going to a server and back, the assistant would feel laggy and slow to respond.

The only audio the assistant really needs is what immediately follows the wake word (e.g., "Hey Google"). What if we could detect that word without sending data, but start streaming when we heard it? We'd protect user privacy, save battery life and bandwidth, and wake up the assistant without waiting for the network.

And this is where TinyML comes in. We can train a tiny model that listens for a wake word, and run it on a low-powered chip. If we embed this in a phone, it can listen for wake words all the time. When it hears the magic word, it informs the phone's operating system (OS), which can begin to capture audio and send it to the server.

Wake-word detection is the perfect application for TinyML. It's ideally suited to delivering privacy, efficiency, speed, and offline inference. This approach, in which a tiny, efficient model "wakes up" a larger, more resource-hungry model, is called *cascading*.

In this chapter, we examine how we can use a pretrained speech detection model to provide always-on wake-word detection using a tiny microcontroller. In Chapter 8, we'll explore how the model is trained, and how to create our own.

What We're Building

We're going to build an embedded application that uses an 18 KB model, trained on a dataset of speech commands, to classify spoken audio. The model is trained to recognize the words "yes" and "no," and is also capable of distinguishing between unknown words and silence or background noise.

Our application will listen to its surroundings with a microphone and indicate when it has detected a word by lighting an LED or displaying data on a screen, depending on the capabilities of the device. Understanding this code will give you the ability to control any electronics project with voice commands.

 Like with Chapter 5, the source code for this application is available in the TensorFlow GitHub repository (*https://oreil.ly/Bql0J*).

We'll follow a similar pattern to Chapter 5, walking through the tests, then the application code, followed by the logic that makes the sample work on various devices.

We provide instructions for deploying the application to the following devices:

- Arduino Nano 33 BLE Sense (*https://oreil.ly/6qlMD*)
- SparkFun Edge (*https://oreil.ly/-hoL-*)
- ST Microelectronics STM32F746G Discovery kit (*https://oreil.ly/cvm4J*)

 TensorFlow Lite regularly adds support for new devices, so if the device you'd like to use isn't listed here, check the example's *README.md* (*https://oreil.ly/OE3Pn*). You can also check there for updated deployment instructions if you run into trouble following these steps.

This is a significantly more complex application than the "hello world" example, so let's begin by walking through its structure.

Application Architecture

Over the previous few chapters, you've learned that a machine learning application does the following sequence of things:

1. Obtains an input
2. Preprocesses the input to extract features suitable to feed into a model
3. Runs inference on the processed input
4. Postprocesses the model's output to make sense of it
5. Uses the resulting information to make things happen

The "hello world" example followed these steps in a very straightforward manner. It took a single floating-point number as input, generated by a simple counter. Its output was another floating-point number that we used directly to control visual output.

Our wake-word application will be more complicated for the following reasons:

- It takes audio data as an input. As you'll see, this requires heavy processing before it can be fed into a model.
- Its model is a classifier, outputting class probabilities. We'll need to parse and make sense of this output.
- It's designed to perform inference continually, on live data. We'll need to write code to make sense of a stream of inferences.

- The model is larger and more complex. We'll be pushing our hardware to the limits of its capabilities.

Because much of this complexity results from the model we'll be using, let's learn a little more about it.

Introducing Our Model

As we mentioned earlier, the model we use in this chapter is trained to recognize the words "yes" and "no," and is also capable of distinguishing between unknown words and silence or background noise.

The model was trained on a dataset called the Speech Commands dataset (*https://oreil.ly/qtOSI*). This consists of 65,000 one-second-long utterances of 30 short words, crowdsourced online.

Although the dataset contains 30 different words, the model was trained to distinguish between only four categories: the words "yes" and "no," "unknown" words (meaning the other 28 words in the dataset), and silence.

The model takes in one second's worth of data at a time. It outputs four probability scores, one for each of these four classes, predicting how likely it is that the data represented one of them.

However, the model doesn't take in raw audio sample data. Instead, it works with *spectrograms*, which are two-dimensional arrays that are made up of slices of frequency information, each taken from a different time window.

Figure 7-1 is a visual representation of a spectrogram generated from a one-second audio clip of someone saying "yes." Figure 7-2 shows the same thing for the word "no."

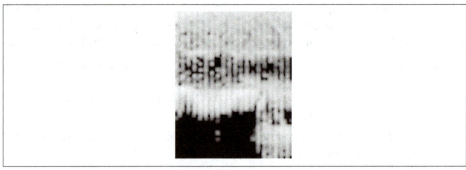

Figure 7-1. Spectrogram for "yes"

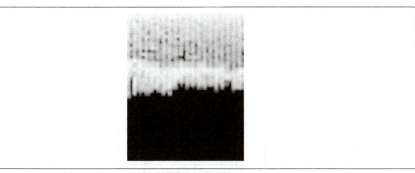

Figure 7-2. Spectrogram for "no"

By isolating the frequency information during preprocessing, we make the model's life easier. During training, it doesn't need to learn how to interpret raw audio data; instead, it gets to work with a higher-layer abstraction that distills the most useful information.

We'll look at how the spectrogram is generated later in this chapter. For now, we just need to know that the model takes a spectrogram as input. Because a spectrogram is a two-dimensional array, we feed it into the model as a 2D tensor.

There's a type of neural network architecture that is specifically designed to work well with multidimensional tensors in which information is contained in the relationships between groups of adjacent values. It's called a *convolutional neural network* (CNN).

The most common example of this type of data is images, for which a group of adjacent pixels might represent a shape, pattern, or texture. During training, a CNN is able to identify these features and learn what they represent.

It can learn how simple image features (like lines or edges) fit together into more complex features (like an eye or an ear), and in turn how those features might be combined to form an input image, such as a photo of a human face. This means that a CNN can learn to distinguish between different classes of input image, such as between a photo of a person and a photo of a dog.

Although they're often applied to images, which are 2D grids of pixels, CNNs can be used with any multidimensional vector input. It turns out they're very well suited to working with spectrogram data.

In Chapter 8, we'll look at how this model was trained. Until then, let's get back to discussing the architecture of our application.

All the Moving Parts

As mentioned earlier, our wake-word application is a more complicated than the "hello world" example. Figure 7-3 shows the components that comprise it.

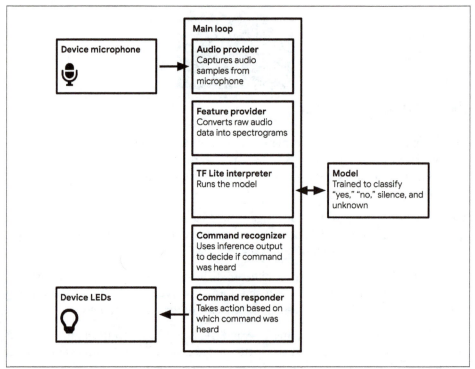

Figure 7-3. The components of our wake-word application

Let's investigate what each of these pieces do:

Main loop

Like the "hello world" example, our application runs in a continuous loop. All of the subsequent processes are contained within it, and they execute continually, as fast as the microcontroller can run them, which is multiple times per second.

Audio provider

The audio provider captures raw audio data from the microphone. Because the methods for capturing audio vary from device to device, this component can be overridden and customized.

Feature provider

The feature provider converts raw audio data into the spectrogram format that our model requires. It does so on a rolling basis as part of the main loop, providing the interpreter with a sequence of overlapping one-second windows.

TF Lite interpreter

The interpreter runs the TensorFlow Lite model, transforming the input spectrogram into a set of probabilities.

Model

The model is included as a data array and run by the interpreter. The array is located in *tiny_conv_micro_features_model_data.cc (https://oreil.ly/XIUz9)*.

Command recognizer

Because inference is run multiple times per second, the `RecognizeCommands` class aggregates the results and determines whether, on average, a known word was heard.

Command responder

If a command was heard, the command responder uses the device's output capabilities to let the user know. Depending on the device, this could mean flashing an LED or showing data on an LCD display. It can be overridden for different device types.

The example's files on GitHub contain tests for each of these components. We'll walk through them next to learn how they work.

Walking Through the Tests

As in Chapter 5, we can use tests to learn how the application works. We've already covered a lot of C++ and TensorFlow Lite basics, so we won't need to explain every single line. Instead, let's focus on the most important parts of each test and explain what's going on.

We'll explore the following tests, which you can find in the GitHub repository (*https://oreil.ly/YiSbu*):

micro_speech_test.cc (https://oreil.ly/FiBEN)

Shows how to run inference on spectrogram data and interpret the results

audio_provider_test.cc (https://oreil.ly/bQOKd)

Shows how to use the audio provider

feature_provider_mock_test.cc (https://oreil.ly/V9rK8)

Shows how to use the feature provider, using a *mock* (fake) implementation of the audio provider to pass in fake data

recognize_commands_test.cc (https://oreil.ly/P9pCG)

Shows how to interpret the model's output to decide whether a command was found

command_responder_test.cc (https://oreil.ly/OqftF)
    Shows how to call the command responder to trigger an output

There are many more tests in the example, but exploring these few will give us an understanding of the key moving parts.

The Basic Flow

The test *micro_speech_test.cc* follows the same basic flow we're familiar with from the "hello world" example: we load the model, set up the interpreter, and allocate tensors.

However, there's a notable difference. In the "hello world" example, we used the AllOpsResolver to pull in all of the deep learning operations that might be necessary to run the model. This is a reliable approach, but it's wasteful because a given model probably doesn't use all of the dozens of available operations. When deployed to a device, these unnecessary operations will take up valuable memory, so it's best if we include only those we need.

To do this, we first define the ops that our model will need, at the top of the test file:

```
namespace tflite {
namespace ops {
namespace micro {
TfLiteRegistration* Register_DEPTHWISE_CONV_2D();
TfLiteRegistration* Register_FULLY_CONNECTED();
TfLiteRegistration* Register_SOFTMAX();
}  // namespace micro
}  // namespace ops
}  // namespace tflite
```

Next, we set up logging and load our model, as normal:

```
// Set up logging.
tflite::MicroErrorReporter micro_error_reporter;
tflite::ErrorReporter* error_reporter = &micro_error_reporter;
// Map the model into a usable data structure. This doesn't involve any
// copying or parsing, it's a very lightweight operation.
const tflite::Model* model =
    ::tflite::GetModel(g_tiny_conv_micro_features_model_data);
if (model->version() != TFLITE_SCHEMA_VERSION) {
  error_reporter->Report(
      "Model provided is schema version %d not equal "
      "to supported version %d.\n",
      model->version(), TFLITE_SCHEMA_VERSION);
}
```

After our model is loaded, we declare a MicroMutableOpResolver and use its method AddBuiltin() to add the ops we listed earlier:

```
tflite::MicroMutableOpResolver micro_mutable_op_resolver;
micro_mutable_op_resolver.AddBuiltin(
```

```
        tflite::BuiltinOperator_DEPTHWISE_CONV_2D,
        tflite::ops::micro::Register_DEPTHWISE_CONV_2D());
micro_mutable_op_resolver.AddBuiltin(
        tflite::BuiltinOperator_FULLY_CONNECTED,
        tflite::ops::micro::Register_FULLY_CONNECTED());
micro_mutable_op_resolver.AddBuiltin(tflite::BuiltinOperator_SOFTMAX,
                                     tflite::ops::micro::Register_SOFTMAX());
```

You're probably wondering how we know which ops to include for a given model. One way is to try running the model using a `MicroMutableOpResolver`, but without calling `AddBuiltin()` at all. Inference will fail, and the accompanying error messages will inform us which ops are missing and need to be added.

 The `MicroMutableOpResolver` is defined in *tensorflow/lite/micro/ micro_mutable_op_resolver.h* (*https://oreil.ly/TGVZz*), which you'll need to add to your `include` statements.

After the `MicroMutableOpResolver` is set up, we just carry on as usual, setting up our interpreter and its working memory:

```
// Create an area of memory to use for input, output, and intermediate arrays.
const int tensor_arena_size = 10 * 1024;
uint8_t tensor_arena[tensor_arena_size];
// Build an interpreter to run the model with.
tflite::MicroInterpreter interpreter(model, micro_mutable_op_resolver, ten
sor_arena,
                                     tensor_arena_size, error_reporter);
interpreter.AllocateTensors();
```

In our "hello world" application we allocated only 2 * 1,024 bytes for the `tensor_arena`, given that the model was so small. Our speech model is a lot bigger, and it deals with more complex input and output, so it needs more space (10 1,024). This was determined by trial and error.

Next, we check the input tensor size. However, it's a little different this time around:

```
// Get information about the memory area to use for the model's input.
TfLiteTensor* input = interpreter.input(0);
// Make sure the input has the properties we expect.
TF_LITE_MICRO_EXPECT_NE(nullptr, input);
TF_LITE_MICRO_EXPECT_EQ(4, input->dims->size);
TF_LITE_MICRO_EXPECT_EQ(1, input->dims->data[0]);
TF_LITE_MICRO_EXPECT_EQ(49, input->dims->data[1]);
TF_LITE_MICRO_EXPECT_EQ(40, input->dims->data[2]);
TF_LITE_MICRO_EXPECT_EQ(1, input->dims->data[3]);
TF_LITE_MICRO_EXPECT_EQ(kTfLiteUInt8, input->type);
```

Because we're dealing with a spectrogram as our input, the input tensor has more dimensions—four, in total. The first dimension is just a wrapper containing a single element. The second and third represent the "rows" and "columns" of our spectrogram, which happens to have 49 rows and 40 columns. The fourth, innermost dimension of the input tensor, which has size 1, holds each individual "pixel" of the spectrogram. We'll look more at the spectrogram's structure later on.

Next, we grab a sample spectrogram for a "yes," stored in the constant g_yes_micro_f2e59fea_nohash_1_data. The constant is defined in the file *micro_features/yes_micro_features_data.cc* (*https://oreil.ly/rVn8O*), which was included by this test. The spectrogram exists as a 1D array, and we just iterate through it to copy it into the input tensor:

```
// Copy a spectrogram created from a .wav audio file of someone saying "Yes"
// into the memory area used for the input.
const uint8_t* yes_features_data = g_yes_micro_f2e59fea_nohash_1_data;
for (int i = 0; i < input->bytes; ++i) {
  input->data.uint8[i] = yes_features_data[i];
}
```

After the input has been assigned, we run inference and inspect the output tensor's size and shape:

```
// Run the model on this input and make sure it succeeds.
TfLiteStatus invoke_status = interpreter.Invoke();
if (invoke_status != kTfLiteOk) {
  error_reporter->Report("Invoke failed\n");
}
TF_LITE_MICRO_EXPECT_EQ(kTfLiteOk, invoke_status);

// Get the output from the model, and make sure it's the expected size and
// type.
TfLiteTensor* output = interpreter.output(0);
TF_LITE_MICRO_EXPECT_EQ(2, output->dims->size);
TF_LITE_MICRO_EXPECT_EQ(1, output->dims->data[0]);
TF_LITE_MICRO_EXPECT_EQ(4, output->dims->data[1]);
TF_LITE_MICRO_EXPECT_EQ(kTfLiteUInt8, output->type);
```

Our output has two dimensions. The first is just a wrapper. The second has four elements. This is the structure that holds the probabilities that each of our four classes (silence, unknown, "yes," and "no") were matched.

The next chunk of code checks whether the probabilities were as expected. A given element of the output tensor always represents a certain class, so we know which index to check for each one. The order is defined during training:

```
// There are four possible classes in the output, each with a score.
const int kSilenceIndex = 0;
const int kUnknownIndex = 1;
const int kYesIndex = 2;
const int kNoIndex = 3;

// Make sure that the expected "Yes" score is higher than the other classes.
```

```
uint8_t silence_score = output->data.uint8[kSilenceIndex];
uint8_t unknown_score = output->data.uint8[kUnknownIndex];
uint8_t yes_score = output->data.uint8[kYesIndex];
uint8_t no_score = output->data.uint8[kNoIndex];
TF_LITE_MICRO_EXPECT_GT(yes_score, silence_score);
TF_LITE_MICRO_EXPECT_GT(yes_score, unknown_score);
TF_LITE_MICRO_EXPECT_GT(yes_score, no_score);
```

We passed in a "yes" spectrogram, so we expect that the variable yes_score contains a higher probability than silence_score, unknown_score, and no_score.

When we're satisfied with "yes," we do the same thing with a "no" spectrogram. First, we copy in an input and run inference:

```
// Now test with a different input, from a recording of "No".
const uint8_t* no_features_data = g_no_micro_f9643d42_nohash_4_data;
for (int i = 0; i < input->bytes; ++i) {
  input->data.uint8[i] = no_features_data[i];
}
// Run the model on this "No" input.
invoke_status = interpreter.Invoke();
if (invoke_status != kTfLiteOk) {
  error_reporter->Report("Invoke failed\n");
}
TF_LITE_MICRO_EXPECT_EQ(kTfLiteOk, invoke_status);
```

After inference is done, we confirm that "no" achieved the highest score:

```
// Make sure that the expected "No" score is higher than the other classes.
silence_score = output->data.uint8[kSilenceIndex];
unknown_score = output->data.uint8[kUnknownIndex];
yes_score = output->data.uint8[kYesIndex];
no_score = output->data.uint8[kNoIndex];
TF_LITE_MICRO_EXPECT_GT(no_score, silence_score);
TF_LITE_MICRO_EXPECT_GT(no_score, unknown_score);
TF_LITE_MICRO_EXPECT_GT(no_score, yes_score);
```

And we're done!

To run this test, issue the following command from the root of the TensorFlow repository:

```
make -f tensorflow/lite/micro/tools/make/Makefile \
  test_micro_speech_test
```

Next up, let's look at the source of all our audio data: the audio provider.

The Audio Provider

The audio provider is what connects a device's microphone hardware to our code. Every device has a different mechanism for capturing audio. As a result, *audio_provider.h* (*https://oreil.ly/89FGG*) defines an interface for requesting audio data, and developers can write their own implementations for any platforms that they want to support.

 The example includes audio provider implementations for Arduino, STM32F746G, SparkFun Edge, and macOS. If you'd like this example to support a new device, you can read the existing implementations to learn how to do it.

The core part of the audio provider is a function named GetAudioSamples(), defined in *audio_provider.h*. It looks like this:

```
TfLiteStatus GetAudioSamples(tflite::ErrorReporter* error_reporter,
                             int start_ms, int duration_ms,
                             int* audio_samples_size, int16_t** audio_samples);
```

As described in *audio_provider.h*, the function is expected to return an array of 16-bit pulse code modulated (PCM) audio data. This is a very common format for digital audio.

The function is called with an ErrorReporter instance, a start time (start_ms), a duration (duration_ms), and two pointers.

These pointers are a mechanism for GetAudioSamples() to provide data. The caller declares variables of the appropriate type and then passes pointers to them when it calls the function. Inside the function's implementation, the pointers are dereferenced and the variables' values are set.

The first pointer, audio_samples_size, will receive the total number of 16-bit samples in the audio data. The second pointer, audio_samples, will receive an array containing the audio data itself.

By looking at the tests, we can see this in action. There are two tests in *audio_provider_test.cc* (*https://oreil.ly/9XgFg*), but we need to look only at the first to learn how to use the audio provider:

```
TF_LITE_MICRO_TEST(TestAudioProvider) {
  tflite::MicroErrorReporter micro_error_reporter;
  tflite::ErrorReporter* error_reporter = &micro_error_reporter;

  int audio_samples_size = 0;
  int16_t* audio_samples = nullptr;
  TfLiteStatus get_status =
      GetAudioSamples(error_reporter, 0, kFeatureSliceDurationMs,
```

```
                        &audio_samples_size, &audio_samples);
  TF_LITE_MICRO_EXPECT_EQ(kTfLiteOk, get_status);
  TF_LITE_MICRO_EXPECT_LE(audio_samples_size, kMaxAudioSampleSize);
  TF_LITE_MICRO_EXPECT_NE(audio_samples, nullptr);

  // Make sure we can read all of the returned memory locations.
  int total = 0;
  for (int i = 0; i < audio_samples_size; ++i) {
    total += audio_samples[i];
  }
}
```

The test shows how `GetAudioSamples()` is called with some values and some pointers. The test confirms that the pointers are assigned correctly after the function is
called.

 You'll notice the use of some constants, `kFeatureSliceDurationMs`
and `kMaxAudioSampleSize`. These are values that were chosen
when the model was trained, and you can find them in *micro_fea-
tures/micro_model_settings.h* (*https://oreil.ly/WLuug*).

The default implementation of *audio_provider.cc* just returns an empty array. To
prove that it's the right size, the test simply loops through it for the expected number
of samples.

In addition to `GetAudioSamples()`, the audio provider contains a function called
`LatestAudioTimestamp()`. This is intended to return the time that audio data was last
captured, in milliseconds. This information is needed by the feature provider to
determine what audio data to fetch.

To run the audio provider tests, use the following command:

```
make -f tensorflow/lite/micro/tools/make/Makefile \
  test_audio_provider_test
```

The audio provider is used by the feature provider as a source of fresh audio samples,
so let's take a look at that next.

The Feature Provider

The feature provider converts raw audio, obtained from the audio provider, into spectrograms that can be fed into our model. It is called during the main loop.

Its interface is defined in *feature_provider.h* (*https://oreil.ly/59uTO*), and looks like
this:

```
class FeatureProvider {
 public:
  // Create the provider, and bind it to an area of memory. This memory should
```

```
  // remain accessible for the lifetime of the provider object, since subsequent
  // calls will fill it with feature data. The provider does no memory
  // management of this data.
  FeatureProvider(int feature_size, uint8_t* feature_data);
  ~FeatureProvider();

  // Fills the feature data with information from audio inputs, and returns how
  // many feature slices were updated.
  TfLiteStatus PopulateFeatureData(tflite::ErrorReporter* error_reporter,
                                   int32_t last_time_in_ms, int32_t time_in_ms,
                                   int* how_many_new_slices);

 private:
  int feature_size_;
  uint8_t* feature_data_;
  // Make sure we don't try to use cached information if this is the first call
  // into the provider.
  bool is_first_run_;
};
```

To see how it's used, we can take a look at the tests in *feature_provider_mock_test.cc* (*https://oreil.ly/N3YPu*).

For there to be audio data for the feature provider to work with, these tests use a special fake version of the audio provider, known as a mock, that is set up to provide audio data. It is defined in *audio_provider_mock.cc* (*https://oreil.ly/aQSP8*).

 The mock audio provider is substituted for the real thing in the build instructions for the test, which you can find in *Makefile.inc* (*https://oreil.ly/51m0b*) under FEATURE_PROVIDER_MOCK_TEST_SRCS.

The file *feature_provider_mock_test.cc* contains two tests. Here's the first one:

```
TF_LITE_MICRO_TEST(TestFeatureProviderMockYes) {
  tflite::MicroErrorReporter micro_error_reporter;
  tflite::ErrorReporter* error_reporter = &micro_error_reporter;

  uint8_t feature_data[kFeatureElementCount];
  FeatureProvider feature_provider(kFeatureElementCount, feature_data);

  int how_many_new_slices = 0;
  TfLiteStatus populate_status = feature_provider.PopulateFeatureData(
      error_reporter, /* last_time_in_ms= */ 0, /* time_in_ms= */ 970,
      &how_many_new_slices);
  TF_LITE_MICRO_EXPECT_EQ(kTfLiteOk, populate_status);
  TF_LITE_MICRO_EXPECT_EQ(kFeatureSliceCount, how_many_new_slices);

  for (int i = 0; i < kFeatureElementCount; ++i) {
    TF_LITE_MICRO_EXPECT_EQ(g_yes_micro_f2e59fea_nohash_1_data[i],
```

```
                        feature_data[i]);
    }
  }
```

To create a `FeatureProvider`, we call its constructor, passing in `feature_size` and `feature_data` arguments:

```
FeatureProvider feature_provider(kFeatureElementCount, feature_data);
```

The first argument indicates how many total data elements should be in the spectrogram. The second argument is a pointer to an array that we want to be populated with the spectrogram data.

The number of elements in the spectrogram was decided when the model was trained and is defined as `kFeatureElementCount` in *micro_features/micro_model_settings.h* (*https://oreil.ly/FdUCq*).

To obtain features for the past second of audio, `feature_provider.PopulateFeature Data()` is called:

```
TfLiteStatus populate_status = feature_provider.PopulateFeatureData(
        error_reporter, /* last_time_in_ms= */ 0, /* time_in_ms= */ 970,
        &how_many_new_slices);
```

We supply an `ErrorReporter` instance, an integer representing the last time this method was called (`last_time_in_ms`), the current time (`time_in_ms`), and a pointer to an integer that will be updated with how many new *feature slices* we receive (`how_many_new_slices`). A slice is just one row of the spectrogram, representing a chunk of time.

Because we always want the last second of audio, the feature provider will compare when it was last called (`last_time_in_ms`) with the current time (`time_in_ms`), create spectrogram data from the audio captured during that time, and then update the `feature_data` array to add any additional slices and drop any that are older than one second.

When `PopulateFeatureData()` runs, it will request audio from the mock audio provider. The mock will give it audio representing a "yes," and the feature provider will process it and provide the result.

After calling `PopulateFeatureData()`, we check whether its result is what we expect. We compare the data it generated to a known spectrogram that is correct for the "yes" input given by the mock audio provider:

```
TF_LITE_MICRO_EXPECT_EQ(kTfLiteOk, populate_status);
TF_LITE_MICRO_EXPECT_EQ(kFeatureSliceCount, how_many_new_slices);
for (int i = 0; i < kFeatureElementCount; ++i) {
  TF_LITE_MICRO_EXPECT_EQ(g_yes_micro_f2e59fea_nohash_1_data[i],
                          feature_data[i]);
}
```

The mock audio provider can provide audio for a "yes" or a "no" depending on which start and end times are passed into it. The second test in *feature_provider_mock_test.cc* does exactly the same thing as the first, but for audio representing "no."

To run the tests, use the following command:

```
make -f tensorflow/lite/micro/tools/make/Makefile \
    test_feature_provider_mock_test
```

How the feature provider converts audio to a spectrogram

The feature provider is implemented in *feature_provider.cc* (*https://oreil.ly/xzLzE*). Let's talk through how it works.

As we've discussed, its job is to populate an array that represents a spectrogram of one second of audio. It's designed to be called in a loop, so to avoid unnecessary work, it will generate new features only for the time between now and when it was last called. If it were called less than a second ago, it would keep some of its previous output and generate only the missing parts.

In our code, each spectrogram is represented as a 2D array, with 40 columns and 49 rows, where each row represents a 30-millisecond (ms) sample of audio split into 43 frequency buckets.

To create each row, we run a 30-ms slice of audio input through a *fast Fourier transform* (FFT) algorithm. This technique analyzes the frequency distribution of audio in the sample and creates an array of 256 frequency buckets, each with a value from 0 to 255. These are averaged together into groups of six, leaving us with 43 buckets.

The code that does this is in the file *micro_features/micro_features_generator.cc* (*https://oreil.ly/HVU2G*), and is called by the feature provider.

To build the entire 2D array, we combine the results of running the FFT on 49 consecutive 30-ms slices of audio, with each slice overlapping the last by 10 ms. Figure 7-4 shows how this happens.

You can see how the 30-ms sample window is moved forward by 20 ms each time until it has covered the full one-second sample. The resulting spectrogram is ready to pass into our model.

We can understand how this process happens in *feature_provider.cc*. First, it determines which slices it actually needs to generate based on the time `PopulateFeature Data()` was last called:

```
// Quantize the time into steps as long as each window stride, so we can
// figure out which audio data we need to fetch.
const int last_step = (last_time_in_ms / kFeatureSliceStrideMs);
const int current_step = (time_in_ms / kFeatureSliceStrideMs);

int slices_needed = current_step - last_step;
```

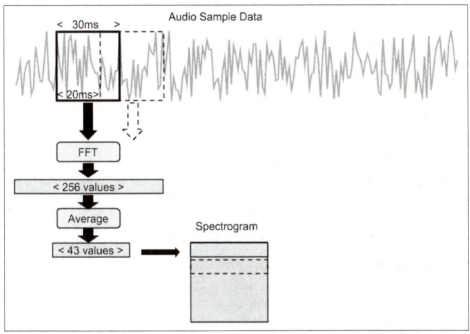

Figure 7-4. Diagram of audio samples being processed

If it hasn't run before, or it ran more than one second ago, it will generate the maximum number of slices:

```
if (is_first_run_) {
  TfLiteStatus init_status = InitializeMicroFeatures(error_reporter);
  if (init_status != kTfLiteOk) {
    return init_status;
  }
  is_first_run_ = false;
  slices_needed = kFeatureSliceCount;
}
if (slices_needed > kFeatureSliceCount) {
  slices_needed = kFeatureSliceCount;
}
*how_many_new_slices = slices_needed;
```

The resulting number is written to how_many_new_slices.

Next, it calculates how many of any existing slices it should keep, and shifts data in the array around to make room for any new ones:

```
const int slices_to_keep = kFeatureSliceCount - slices_needed;
const int slices_to_drop = kFeatureSliceCount - slices_to_keep;
// If we can avoid recalculating some slices, just move the existing data
// up in the spectrogram, to perform something like this:
// last time = 80ms            current time = 120ms
// +-----------+                +-----------+
// | data@20ms |          --> | data@60ms |
// +-----------+        --      +-----------+
// | data@40ms |     --  --> | data@80ms |
// +-----------+   --  --      +-----------+
// | data@60ms | --  --        | <empty>   |
// +-----------+      --        +-----------+
// | data@80ms | --            | <empty>   |
// +-----------+                +-----------+
if (slices_to_keep > 0) {
  for (int dest_slice = 0; dest_slice < slices_to_keep; ++dest_slice) {
    uint8_t* dest_slice_data =
        feature_data_ + (dest_slice * kFeatureSliceSize);
    const int src_slice = dest_slice + slices_to_drop;
    const uint8_t* src_slice_data =
        feature_data_ + (src_slice * kFeatureSliceSize);
    for (int i = 0; i < kFeatureSliceSize; ++i) {
      dest_slice_data[i] = src_slice_data[i];
    }
  }
}
```

 If you're a seasoned C++ author, you might wonder why we don't use standard libraries to do things like copying data around. The reason is that we're trying to avoid unnecessary dependencies, in an effort to keep our binary size small. Because embedded platforms have very little memory, a smaller application binary means that we have space for a larger and more accurate deep learning model.

After moving data around, it begins a loop that iterates once for each new slice that it needs. In this loop, it first requests audio for that slice from the audio provider using GetAudioSamples():

```
for (int new_slice = slices_to_keep; new_slice < kFeatureSliceCount;
    ++new_slice) {
  const int new_step = (current_step - kFeatureSliceCount + 1) + new_slice;
  const int32_t slice_start_ms = (new_step * kFeatureSliceStrideMs);
  int16_t* audio_samples = nullptr;
  int audio_samples_size = 0;
  GetAudioSamples(error_reporter, slice_start_ms, kFeatureSliceDurationMs,
                  &audio_samples_size, &audio_samples);
  if (audio_samples_size < kMaxAudioSampleSize) {
```

```
    error_reporter->Report("Audio data size %d too small, want %d",
                           audio_samples_size, kMaxAudioSampleSize);
    return kTfLiteError;
}
```

To complete the loop iteration, it passes that data into GenerateMicroFeatures(), defined in *micro_features/micro_features_generator.h*. This is the function that performs the FFT and returns the audio frequency information.

It also passes a pointer, new_slice_data, which points at the memory location where the new data should be written:

```
uint8_t* new_slice_data = feature_data_ + (new_slice * kFeatureSliceSize);
size_t num_samples_read;
TfLiteStatus generate_status = GenerateMicroFeatures(
    error_reporter, audio_samples, audio_samples_size, kFeatureSliceSize,
    new_slice_data, &num_samples_read);
if (generate_status != kTfLiteOk) {
  return generate_status;
}
}
```

After this process has happened for each slice, we have an entire second's worth of up-to-date spectrogram.

> The function that generates the FFT is GenerateMicroFeatures(). If you're interested, you can read its definition in *micro_features/ micro_features_generator.cc* (*https://oreil.ly/L0juB*).
>
> If you're building your own application that uses spectrograms, you can reuse this code as is. You'll need to use the same code to pre-process data into spectrograms when training your model.

Once we have a spectrogram, we can run inference on it using the model. After this happens, we need to interpret the results. That task belongs to the class we explore next, RecognizeCommands.

The Command Recognizer

After our model outputs a set of probabilities that a known word was spoken in the last second of audio, it's the job of the RecognizeCommands class to determine whether this indicates a successful detection.

It seems like this would be simple: if the probability in a given category is more than a certain threshold, the word was spoken. However, in the real world, things become a bit more complicated.

As we established earlier, we're running multiple inferences per second, each on a one-second window of data. This means that we'll run inference on any given word multiple times, in multiple windows.

In Figure 7-5, you can see a waveform of the word "noted" being spoken, surrounded by a box representing a one-second window being captured.

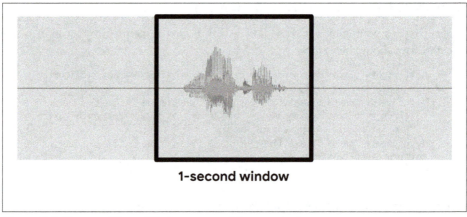

Figure 7-5. The word "noted" being captured in our window

Our model is trained to detect the word "no," and it understands that the word "noted" is not the same thing. If we run inference on this one-second window, it will (hopefully) output a low probability for the word "no." However, what if the window came slightly earlier in the audio stream, as in Figure 7-6?

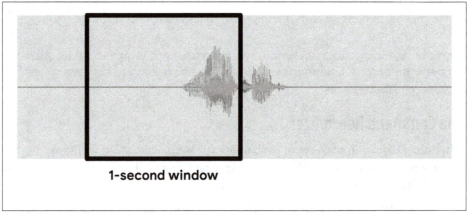

Figure 7-6. Part of the word "noted" being captured in our window

In this case, the only part of the word "noted" that appears within the window is its first syllable. Because the first syllable of "noted" sounds like "no," it's likely that the model will interpret this as having a high probability of being a "no."

This problem, along with others, means that we can't rely on a single inference to tell us whether a word was spoken. This is where RecognizeCommands comes in!

The recognizer calculates the average score for each word over the past few inferences, and decides whether it's high enough to count as a detection. To do this, we feed it each inference result as they roll in.

You can see its interface in *recognize_commands.h* (*https://oreil.ly/5W3Ea*), partially reproduced here:

```
class RecognizeCommands {
 public:
  explicit RecognizeCommands(tflite::ErrorReporter* error_reporter,
                             int32_t average_window_duration_ms = 1000,
                             uint8_t detection_threshold = 200,
                             int32_t suppression_ms = 1500,
                             int32_t minimum_count = 3);

  // Call this with the results of running a model on sample data.
  TfLiteStatus ProcessLatestResults(const TfLiteTensor* latest_results,
                                    const int32_t current_time_ms,
                                    const char** found_command, uint8_t* score,
                                    bool* is_new_command);
```

The class RecognizeCommands is defined, along with a constructor that defines default values for a few things:

- The length of the averaging window (average_window_duration_ms)
- The minimum average score that counts as a detection (detection_threshold)
- The amount of time we'll wait after hearing a command before recognizing a second one (suppression_ms)
- The minimum number of inferences required in the window for a result to count (3)

The class has one method, ProcessLatestResults(). It accepts a pointer to a TfLite Tensor containing the model's output (latest_results), and it must be called with the current time (current_time_ms).

In addition, it takes three pointers that it uses for output. First, it gives us the name of any word that was detected (found_command). It also provides the average score of the command (score) and whether the command is new or has been heard in previous inferences within a certain timespan (is_new_command).

Averaging the results of multiple inferences is a useful and common technique when dealing with time-series data. In the next few pages, we'll walk through the code in *recognize_commands.cc* (*https://oreil.ly/lAh-0*) and learn a bit about how it works. You don't need to understand every line, but it's helpful to get some insight into what might be a helpful tool in your own projects.

First, we make sure the input tensor is the right shape and type:

```
TfLiteStatus RecognizeCommands::ProcessLatestResults(
    const TfLiteTensor* latest_results, const int32_t current_time_ms,
    const char** found_command, uint8_t* score, bool* is_new_command) {
  if ((latest_results->dims->size != 2) ||
      (latest_results->dims->data[0] != 1) ||
      (latest_results->dims->data[1] != kCategoryCount)) {
    error_reporter_->Report(
        "The results for recognition should contain %d elements, but there are "
        "%d in an %d-dimensional shape",
        kCategoryCount, latest_results->dims->data[1],
        latest_results->dims->size);
    return kTfLiteError;
  }

  if (latest_results->type != kTfLiteUInt8) {
    error_reporter_->Report(
        "The results for recognition should be uint8 elements, but are %d",
        latest_results->type);
    return kTfLiteError;
  }
```

Next, we check `current_time_ms` to verify that it is after the most recent result in our averaging window:

```
  if ((!previous_results_.empty()) &&
      (current_time_ms < previous_results_.front().time_)) {
    error_reporter_->Report(
        "Results must be fed in increasing time order, but received a "
        "timestamp of %d that was earlier than the previous one of %d",
        current_time_ms, previous_results_.front().time_);
    return kTfLiteError;
  }
```

After that, we add the latest result to a list of results we'll be averaging:

```
  // Add the latest results to the head of the queue.
  previous_results_.push_back({current_time_ms, latest_results->data.uint8});
  // Prune any earlier results that are too old for the averaging window.
  const int64_t time_limit = current_time_ms - average_window_duration_ms_;
  while ((!previous_results_.empty()) &&
          previous_results_.front().time_ < time_limit) {
    previous_results_.pop_front();
```

If there are fewer results in our averaging window than the minimum number (defined by `minimum_count_`, which is 3 by default), we can't provide a valid average. In this case, we set the output pointers to indicate that `found_command` is the most recent top command, that the score is 0, and that the command is not a new one:

```
// If there are too few results, assume the result will be unreliable and
// bail.
const int64_t how_many_results = previous_results_.size();
const int64_t earliest_time = previous_results_.front().time_;
const int64_t samples_duration = current_time_ms - earliest_time;
if ((how_many_results < minimum_count_) ||
    (samples_duration < (average_window_duration_ms_ / 4))) {
  *found_command = previous_top_label_;
  *score = 0;
  *is_new_command = false;
  return kTfLiteOk;
}
```

Otherwise, we continue by averaging all of the scores in the window:

```
// Calculate the average score across all the results in the window.
int32_t average_scores[kCategoryCount];
for (int offset = 0; offset < previous_results_.size(); ++offset) {
  PreviousResultsQueue::Result previous_result =
      previous_results_.from_front(offset);
  const uint8_t* scores = previous_result.scores_;
  for (int i = 0; i < kCategoryCount; ++i) {
    if (offset == 0) {
      average_scores[i] = scores[i];
    } else {
      average_scores[i] += scores[i];
    }
  }
}
for (int i = 0; i < kCategoryCount; ++i) {
  average_scores[i] /= how_many_results;
}
```

We now have enough information to identify which category is our winner. Establishing this is a simple process:

```
// Find the current highest scoring category.
int current_top_index = 0;
int32_t current_top_score = 0;
for (int i = 0; i < kCategoryCount; ++i) {
  if (average_scores[i] > current_top_score) {
    current_top_score = average_scores[i];
    current_top_index = i;
  }
}
const char* current_top_label = kCategoryLabels[current_top_index];
```

The final piece of logic determines whether the result was a valid detection. To do this, it ensures that its score is above the detection threshold (200 by default), and that it didn't happen too quickly after the last valid detection, which can be an indication of a faulty result:

```
// If we've recently had another label trigger, assume one that occurs too
// soon afterwards is a bad result.
int64_t time_since_last_top;
if ((previous_top_label_ == kCategoryLabels[0]) ||
    (previous_top_label_time_ == std::numeric_limits<int32_t>::min())) {
  time_since_last_top = std::numeric_limits<int32_t>::max();
} else {
  time_since_last_top = current_time_ms - previous_top_label_time_;
}
if ((current_top_score > detection_threshold_) &&
    ((current_top_label != previous_top_label_) ||
     (time_since_last_top > suppression_ms_))) {
  previous_top_label_ = current_top_label;
  previous_top_label_time_ = current_time_ms;
  *is_new_command = true;
} else {
  *is_new_command = false;
}
*found_command = current_top_label;
*score = current_top_score;
```

If the result was valid, is_new_command is set to true. This is what the caller can use to determine whether a word was genuinely detected.

The tests (in *recognize_commands_test.cc* (*https://oreil.ly/rOkMb*)) exercise various different combinations of inputs and results that are stored in the averaging window.

Let's walk through one of the tests, RecognizeCommandsTestBasic, which demonstrates how RecognizeCommands is used. First, we just create an instance of the class:

```
TF_LITE_MICRO_TEST(RecognizeCommandsTestBasic) {
  tflite::MicroErrorReporter micro_error_reporter;
  tflite::ErrorReporter* error_reporter = &micro_error_reporter;

  RecognizeCommands recognize_commands(error_reporter);
```

Next, we create a tensor containing some fake inference results, which will be used by ProcessLatestResults() to decide whether a command was heard:

```
TfLiteTensor results = tflite::testing::CreateQuantizedTensor(
    {255, 0, 0, 0}, tflite::testing::IntArrayFromInitializer({2, 1, 4}),
    "input_tensor", 0.0f, 128.0f);
```

Then, we set up some variables that will be set with the output of ProcessLatestResults():

```
const char* found_command;
uint8_t score;
bool is_new_command;
```

Finally, we call ProcessLatestResults(), providing pointers to these variables along with the tensor containing the results. We assert that the function will return kTfLiteOk, indicating that the input was processed successfully:

```
TF_LITE_MICRO_EXPECT_EQ(
    kTfLiteOk, recognize_commands.ProcessLatestResults(
                    &results, 0, &found_command, &score, &is_new_command));
```

The other tests in the file perform some more exhaustive checks to make sure the function is performing correctly. You can read through them to learn more.

To run all of the tests, use the following command:

```
make -f tensorflow/lite/micro/tools/make/Makefile \
    test_recognize_commands_test
```

As soon as we've determined whether a command was detected, it's time to share our results with the world (or at least our on-board LEDs). The command responder is what makes this happen.

The Command Responder

The final piece in our puzzle, the command responder, is what produces an output to let us know that a word was detected.

The command responder is designed to be overridden for each type of device. We explore the device-specific implementations later in this chapter.

For now, let's look at its very simple reference implementation, which just logs detection results as text. You can find it in the file *command_responder.cc* (*https://oreil.ly/kMjg2*):

```
void RespondToCommand(tflite::ErrorReporter* error_reporter,
                      int32_t current_time, const char* found_command,
                      uint8_t score, bool is_new_command) {
  if (is_new_command) {
    error_reporter->Report("Heard %s (%d) @%dms", found_command, score,
                           current_time);
  }
}
```

That's it! The file implements just one function: RespondToCommand(). As parameters, it expects an error_reporter, the current time (current_time), the command that was last detected (found_command), the score it received (score), and whether the command was newly heard (is_new_command).

It's important to note that in our program's main loop, this function will be called every time inference is performed, even if a command was not detected. This means that we should check is_new_command to determine whether anything needs to be done.

The test for this function, in *command_responder_test.cc* (*https://oreil.ly/loLZo*), is equally simple. It just calls the function, given that there's no way for it to test that it generates the correct output:

```
TF_LITE_MICRO_TEST(TestCallability) {
  tflite::MicroErrorReporter micro_error_reporter;
  tflite::ErrorReporter* error_reporter = &micro_error_reporter;

  // This will have external side-effects (like printing to the debug console
  // or lighting an LED) that are hard to observe, so the most we can do is
  // make sure the call doesn't crash.
  RespondToCommand(error_reporter, 0, "foo", 0, true);
}
```

To run this test, enter this in your terminal:

```
make -f tensorflow/lite/micro/tools/make/Makefile \
  test_command_responder_test
```

And that's it! We've walked through all of the components of the application. Now, let's see how they come together in the program itself.

Listening for Wake Words

You can find the following code in *main_functions.cc* (*https://oreil.ly/n2eD1*), which defines the setup() and loop() functions that are the core of our program. Let's read through it together!

Because you're now a seasoned TensorFlow Lite expert, a lot of this code will look familiar to you. So let's try to focus on the new bits.

First, we list the ops that we want to use:

```
namespace tflite {
namespace ops {
namespace micro {
TfLiteRegistration* Register_DEPTHWISE_CONV_2D();
TfLiteRegistration* Register_FULLY_CONNECTED();
TfLiteRegistration* Register_SOFTMAX();
}  // namespace micro
}  // namespace ops
}  // namespace tflite
```

Next, we set up our global variables:

```
namespace {
tflite::ErrorReporter* error_reporter = nullptr;
const tflite::Model* model = nullptr;
tflite::MicroInterpreter* interpreter = nullptr;
TfLiteTensor* model_input = nullptr;
FeatureProvider* feature_provider = nullptr;
RecognizeCommands* recognizer = nullptr;
int32_t previous_time = 0;

// Create an area of memory to use for input, output, and intermediate arrays.
// The size of this will depend on the model you're using, and may need to be
// determined by experimentation.
```

```
constexpr int kTensorArenaSize = 10 * 1024;
uint8_t tensor_arena[kTensorArenaSize];
}  // namespace
```

Notice how we declare a `FeatureProvider` and a `RecognizeCommands` in addition to the usual TensorFlow suspects. We also declare a variable named `g_previous_time`, which keeps track of the most recent time we received new audio samples.

Next up, in the `setup()` function, we load the model, set up our interpreter, add ops, and allocate tensors:

```
void setup() {
  // Set up logging.
  static tflite::MicroErrorReporter micro_error_reporter;
  error_reporter = &micro_error_reporter;

  // Map the model into a usable data structure. This doesn't involve any
  // copying or parsing, it's a very lightweight operation.
  model = tflite::GetModel(g_tiny_conv_micro_features_model_data);
  if (model->version() != TFLITE_SCHEMA_VERSION) {
    error_reporter->Report(
        "Model provided is schema version %d not equal "
        "to supported version %d.",
        model->version(), TFLITE_SCHEMA_VERSION);
    return;
  }

  // Pull in only the operation implementations we need.
  static tflite::MicroMutableOpResolver micro_mutable_op_resolver;
  micro_mutable_op_resolver.AddBuiltin(
      tflite::BuiltinOperator_DEPTHWISE_CONV_2D,
      tflite::ops::micro::Register_DEPTHWISE_CONV_2D());
  micro_mutable_op_resolver.AddBuiltin(
      tflite::BuiltinOperator_FULLY_CONNECTED,
      tflite::ops::micro::Register_FULLY_CONNECTED());
  micro_mutable_op_resolver.AddBuiltin(tflite::BuiltinOperator_SOFTMAX,
                                       tflite::ops::micro::Register_SOFTMAX());

  // Build an interpreter to run the model with.
  static tflite::MicroInterpreter static_interpreter(
      model, micro_mutable_op_resolver, tensor_arena, kTensorArenaSize,
      error_reporter);
  interpreter = &static_interpreter;

  // Allocate memory from the tensor_arena for the model's tensors.
  TfLiteStatus allocate_status = interpreter->AllocateTensors();
  if (allocate_status != kTfLiteOk) {
    error_reporter->Report("AllocateTensors() failed");
    return;
  }
```

After allocating tensors, we check that the input tensor is the correct shape and type:

```
// Get information about the memory area to use for the model's input.
model_input = interpreter->input(0);
if ((model_input->dims->size != 4) || (model_input->dims->data[0] != 1) ||
    (model_input->dims->data[1] != kFeatureSliceCount) ||
    (model_input->dims->data[2] != kFeatureSliceSize) ||
    (model_input->type != kTfLiteUInt8)) {
  error_reporter->Report("Bad input tensor parameters in model");
  return;
}
```

Next comes the interesting stuff. First, we instantiate a FeatureProvider, pointing it at our input tensor:

```
// Prepare to access the audio spectrograms from a microphone or other source
// that will provide the inputs to the neural network.
static FeatureProvider static_feature_provider(kFeatureElementCount,
                                               model_input->data.uint8);
feature_provider = &static_feature_provider;
```

We then create a RecognizeCommands instance and initialize our previous_time variable:

```
static RecognizeCommands static_recognizer(error_reporter);
recognizer = &static_recognizer;

previous_time = 0;
}
```

Up next, it's time for our loop() function. Like in the previous example, this function will be called over and over again, indefinitely. In the loop, we first use the feature provider to create a spectrogram:

```
void loop() {
  // Fetch the spectrogram for the current time.
  const int32_t current_time = LatestAudioTimestamp();
  int how_many_new_slices = 0;
  TfLiteStatus feature_status = feature_provider->PopulateFeatureData(
      error_reporter, previous_time, current_time, &how_many_new_slices);
  if (feature_status != kTfLiteOk) {
    error_reporter->Report("Feature generation failed");
    return;
  }
  previous_time = current_time;
  // If no new audio samples have been received since last time, don't bother
  // running the network model.
  if (how_many_new_slices == 0) {
    return;
  }
```

If there's no new data since the last iteration, we don't bother running inference.

After we have our input, we just invoke the interpreter:

```
// Run the model on the spectrogram input and make sure it succeeds.
TfLiteStatus invoke_status = interpreter->Invoke();
if (invoke_status != kTfLiteOk) {
  error_reporter->Report("Invoke failed");
  return;
}
```

The model's output tensor is now filled with the probabilities for each category. To interpret them, we use our RecognizeCommands instance. We obtain a pointer to the output tensor, then set up a few variables to receive the ProcessLatestResults() output:

```
// Obtain a pointer to the output tensor
TfLiteTensor* output = interpreter->output(0);
// Determine whether a command was recognized based on the output of inference
const char* found_command = nullptr;
uint8_t score = 0;
bool is_new_command = false;
TfLiteStatus process_status = recognizer->ProcessLatestResults(
    output, current_time, &found_command, &score, &is_new_command);
if (process_status != kTfLiteOk) {
  error_reporter->Report("RecognizeCommands::ProcessLatestResults() failed");
  return;
}
```

Finally, we call the command responder's RespondToCommand() method so that it can notify users if a word was detected:

```
// Do something based on the recognized command. The default implementation
// just prints to the error console, but you should replace this with your
// own function for a real application.
RespondToCommand(error_reporter, current_time, found_command, score,
                 is_new_command);
}
```

And that's it! The call to RespondToCommand() is the final thing in our loop. Everything from feature generation onward will repeat endlessly, checking the audio for known words and producing some output if one is confirmed.

The setup() and loop() functions are called by our main() function, defined in *main.cc*, which begins the loop when the application starts:

```
int main(int argc, char* argv[]) {
  setup();
  while (true) {
    loop();
  }
}
```

Running Our Application

The example contains an audio provider compatible with macOS. If you have access to a Mac, you can run the example on your development machine. First, use the following command to build it:

```
make -f tensorflow/lite/micro/tools/make/Makefile micro_speech
```

After the build completes, you can run the example with the following command:

```
tensorflow/lite/micro/tools/make/gen/osx_x86_64/bin/micro_speech
```

You might see a pop-up asking for microphone access. If so, grant it, and the program will start.

Try saying "yes" and "no." You should see output that looks like the following:

```
Heard yes (201) @4056ms
Heard no (205) @6448ms
Heard unknown (201) @13696ms
Heard yes (205) @15000ms
Heard yes (205) @16856ms
Heard unknown (204) @18704ms
Heard no (206) @21000ms
```

The number after each detected word is its score. By default, the command recognizer component considers matches as valid only if their score is more than 200, so all of the scores you see will be at least 200.

The number after the score is the number of milliseconds since the program was started.

If you don't see any output, make sure your Mac's internal microphone is selected in the Mac's Sound menu and that its input volume is turned up high enough.

We've established that the program works on a Mac. Now, let's get it running on some embedded hardware.

Deploying to Microcontrollers

In this section, we deploy the code to three different devices:

- Arduino Nano 33 BLE Sense (*https://oreil.ly/ztU5E*)
- SparkFun Edge (*https://oreil.ly/-hoL-*)
- ST Microelectronics STM32F746G Discovery kit (*https://oreil.ly/cvm4J*)

For each one, we'll walk through the build and deployment process.

Because every device has its own mechanism for capturing audio, there's a separate implementation of *audio_provider.cc* for each one. The same is true for output, so each has a variant of *command_responder.cc*, too.

The *audio_provider.cc* implementations are complex and device-specific, and not directly related to machine learning. Consequently, we won't walk through them in this chapter. However, there's a walkthrough of the Arduino variant in Appendix B. If you need to capture audio in your own project, you're welcome to reuse these implementations in your own code.

Alongside deployment instructions, we're also going to walk through the *command_responder.cc* implementation for each device. First up, it's time for Arduino.

Arduino

As of this writing, the only Arduino board with a built-in microphone is the Arduino Nano 33 BLE Sense (*https://oreil.ly/hjOzL*), so that's what we'll be using for this section. If you're using a different Arduino board and attaching your own microphone, you'll need to implement your own *audio_provider.cc*.

The Arduino Nano 33 BLE Sense also has a built-in LED, which is what we use to indicate that a word has been recognized.

Figure 7-7 shows a picture of the board with its LED highlighted.

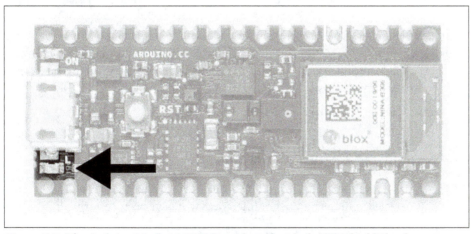

Figure 7-7. The Arduino Nano 33 BLE Sense board with the LED highlighted

Now let's look at how we use this LED to indicate that a word has been detected.

Responding to commands on Arduino

Every Arduino board has a built-in LED, and there's a convenient constant called LED_BUILTIN that we can use to obtain its pin number, which varies across boards. To keep this code portable, we'll constrain ourselves to using this single LED for output.

Here's what we're going to do. To show that inference is running, we'll flash the LED by toggling it on or off with each inference. However, when we hear the word "yes," we'll switch on the LED for a few seconds.

What about the word "no"? Well, because this is just a demonstration, we won't worry about it too much. We do, however, log all of the detected commands to the serial port, so we can connect to the device and see every match.

The replacement command responder for Arduino is located in *arduino/command_responder.cc* (*https://oreil.ly/URkYi*). Let's walk through its source. First, we include the command responder header file and the Arduino platform's library header file:

```
#include "tensorflow/lite/micro/examples/micro_speech/command_responder.h"
#include "Arduino.h"
```

Next, we begin our function implementation:

```
// Toggles the LED every inference, and keeps it on for 3 seconds if a "yes"
// was heard
void RespondToCommand(tflite::ErrorReporter* error_reporter,
                      int32_t current_time, const char* found_command,
                      uint8_t score, bool is_new_command) {
```

Our next step is to place the built-in LED's pin into output mode so that we can switch it on and off. We do this inside an if statement that runs only once, thanks to a static bool called is_initialized. Remember, static variables preserve their state between function calls:

```
static bool is_initialized = false;
if (!is_initialized) {
  pinMode(LED_BUILTIN, OUTPUT);
  is_initialized = true;
}
```

Next, we set up another couple of static variables to keep track of the last time a "yes" was detected, and the number of inferences that have been performed:

```
static int32_t last_yes_time = 0;
static int count = 0;
```

Now comes the fun stuff. If the is_new_command argument is true, we know we've heard something, so we log it with the ErrorReporter instance. But if it's a "yes" we heard—which we determine by checking the first character of the found_command character array—we store the current time and switch on the LED:

```
if (is_new_command) {
  error_reporter->Report("Heard %s (%d) @%dms", found_command, score,
                         current_time);
  // If we heard a "yes", switch on an LED and store the time.
  if (found_command[0] == 'y') {
    last_yes_time = current_time;
    digitalWrite(LED_BUILTIN, HIGH);
  }
}
```

Next, we implement the behavior that switches off the LED after a few seconds—three, to be precise:

```
// If last_yes_time is non-zero but was >3 seconds ago, zero it
// and switch off the LED.
if (last_yes_time != 0) {
  if (last_yes_time < (current_time - 3000)) {
    last_yes_time = 0;
    digitalWrite(LED_BUILTIN, LOW);
  }
  // If it is non-zero but <3 seconds ago, do nothing.
  return;
}
```

When the LED is switched off, we also set last_yet_time to 0, so we won't enter this if statement until the next time a "yes" is heard. The return statement is important: it's what prevents any further output code from running if we recently heard a "yes," so the LED stays solidly lit.

So far, our implementation will switch on the LED for around three seconds when a "yes" is heard. The next part will toggle the LED on and off with each inference—except for while we're in "yes" mode, when we're prevented from reaching this point by the aforementioned return statement.

Here's the final chunk of code:

```
// Otherwise, toggle the LED every time an inference is performed.
++count;
if (count & 1) {
  digitalWrite(LED_BUILTIN, HIGH);
} else {
  digitalWrite(LED_BUILTIN, LOW);
}
```

By incrementing the count variable for each inference, we keep track of the total number of inferences that we've performed. Inside the if conditional, we use the & operator to do a binary AND operation with the count variable and the number 1.

By performing an AND on count with 1, we filter out all of count's bits except the smallest. If the smallest bit is a 0, meaning count is an odd number, the result will be a 0. In a C++ if statement, this evaluates to false.

Otherwise, the result will be a 1, indicating an even number. Because a 1 evaluates to true, our LED will switch on with even values and off with odd values. This is what makes it toggle.

And that's it! We've now implemented our command responder for Arduino. Let's get it running so that we can see it in action.

Running the example

To deploy this example, here's what we'll need:

- An Arduino Nano 33 BLE Sense board
- A micro-USB cable
- The Arduino IDE

 There's always a chance that the build process might have changed since this book was written, so check *README.md* (*https://oreil.ly/ 7VozJ*) for the latest instructions.

The projects in this book are available as example code in the TensorFlow Lite Arduino library. If you haven't already installed the library, open the Arduino IDE and select Manage Libraries from the Tools menu. In the window that appears, search for and install the library named *Arduino_TensorFlowLite*. You should be able to use the latest version, but if you run into issues, the version that was tested with this book is 1.14-ALPHA.

 You can also install the library from a *.zip* file, which you can either download (*https://oreil.ly/blgB8*) from the TensorFlow Lite team or generate yourself using the TensorFlow Lite for Microcontrollers Makefile. If you'd prefer to do the latter, see Appendix A.

After you've installed the library, the micro_speech example will show up in the File menu under Examples→Arduino_TensorFlowLite, as shown in Figure 7-8.

Click "micro_speech" to load the example. It will appear as a new window, with a tab for each of the source files. The file in the first tab, *micro_speech*, is equivalent to the *main_functions.cc* we walked through earlier.

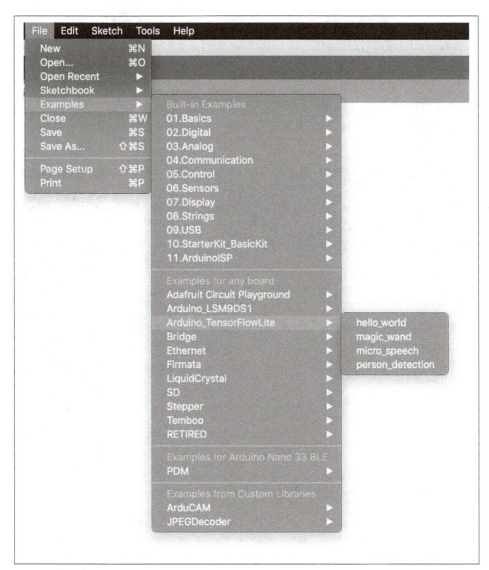

Figure 7-8. The Examples menu

"Running the Example" on page 101 already explained the structure of the Arduino example, so we won't cover it again here.

To run the example, plug in your Arduino device via USB. Make sure the correct device type is selected from the Board drop-down list in the Tools menu, as shown in Figure 7-9.

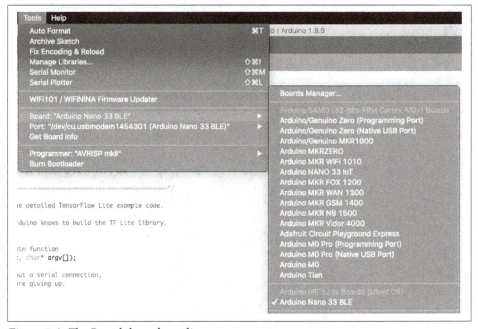

Figure 7-9. The Board drop-down list

If your device's name doesn't appear in the list, you'll need to install its support package. To do this, click Boards Manager. In the window that appears, search for your device, and then install the latest version of the corresponding support package. Next, make sure the device's port is selected in the Port drop-down list, also in the Tools menu, as demonstrated in Figure 7-10.

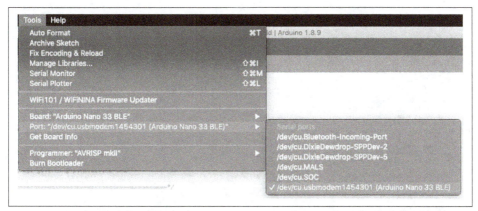

Figure 7-10. The Port drop-down list

Finally, in the Arduino window, click the upload button (highlighted in white in Figure 7-11) to compile and upload the code to your Arduino device.

Figure 7-11. The upload button, a right-facing arrow

After the upload has successfully completed you should see the LED on your Arduino board begin to flash.

To test the program, try saying "yes." When it detects a "yes," the LED will remain lit solidly for around three seconds.

If you can't get the program to recognize your "yes," try saying it a few times in a row.

You can also see the results of inference via the Arduino Serial Monitor. To do this, open the Serial Monitor from the Tools menu. Now, try saying "yes," "no," and other words. You should see something like Figure 7-12.

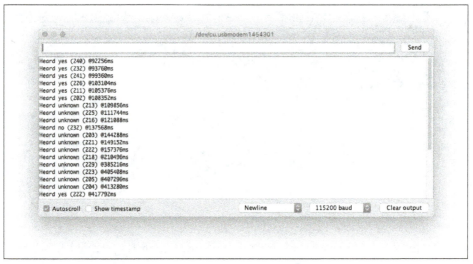

```
●  ●  ●                        /dev/cu.usbmodem1454301
[                                                              ]  Send
Heard yes (240) @92256ms
Heard yes (232) @93760ms
Heard yes (241) @99360ms
Heard yes (226) @103104ms
Heard yes (211) @105376ms
Heard yes (202) @108352ms
Heard unknown (213) @109856ms
Heard unknown (225) @111744ms
Heard unknown (216) @121088ms
Heard no (232) @137568ms
Heard unknown (203) @144288ms
Heard unknown (221) @149152ms
Heard unknown (222) @157376ms
Heard unknown (218) @210496ms
Heard unknown (229) @385216ms
Heard unknown (223) @405408ms
Heard unknown (205) @407296ms
Heard unknown (204) @413280ms
Heard yes (222) @417792ms
☑ Autoscroll  ◯ Show timestamp      Newline  ⬍   115200 baud  ⬍   Clear output
```

Figure 7-12. The Serial Monitor displaying some matches

 The model we're using is small and imperfect, and you'll probably notice that it's better at detecting "yes" than "no." This is an example of how optimizing for a tiny model size can result in issues with accuracy. We cover this topic in Chapter 8.

Making your own changes

Now that you've deployed the application, try playing around with the code! You can edit the source files in the Arduino IDE. When you save, you'll be prompted to re-save the example in a new location. After you've made your changes, you can click the upload button in the Arduino IDE to build and deploy.

Here are a few ideas you could try:

- Switch the example to light the LED when "no" is spoken, instead of "yes,"
- Make the application respond to a specific sequence of "yes" and "no" commands, like a secret code phrase.
- Use the "yes" and "no" commands to control other components, like additional LEDs or servos.

SparkFun Edge

The SparkFun Edge has both a microphone and a row of four colored LEDs—red, blue, green, and yellow—which will make displaying results easy. Figure 7-13 shows the SparkFun Edge with its LEDs highlighted.

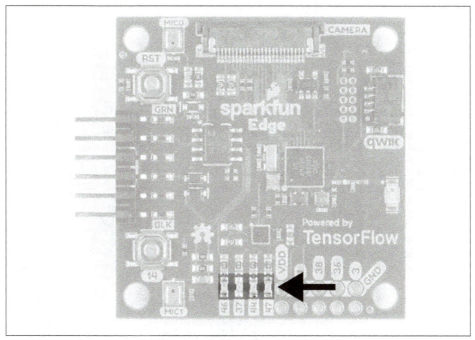

Figure 7-13. The SparkFun Edge's four LEDs

Responding to commands on SparkFun Edge

To make it clear that our program is running, let's toggle the blue LED on and off with each inference. We'll switch on the yellow LED when a "yes" is heard, the red LED when a "no" is heard, and the green LED when an unknown command is heard.

The command responder for SparkFun Edge is implemented in *sparkfun_edge/command_responder.cc* (*https://oreil.ly/i-3eJ*). The file begins with some includes:

```
#include "tensorflow/lite/micro/examples/micro_speech/command_responder.h"
#include "am_bsp.h"
```

The *command_responder.h* include is this file's corresponding header. *am_bsp.h* is the Ambiq Apollo3 SDK, which you saw in the last chapter.

Inside the function definition, the first thing we do is set up the pins connected to the LEDs as outputs:

```
// This implementation will light up the LEDs on the board in response to
// different commands.
void RespondToCommand(tflite::ErrorReporter* error_reporter,
                      int32_t current_time, const char* found_command,
                      uint8_t score, bool is_new_command) {
  static bool is_initialized = false;
  if (!is_initialized) {
    am_hal_gpio_pinconfig(AM_BSP_GPIO_LED_RED, g_AM_HAL_GPIO_OUTPUT_12);
    am_hal_gpio_pinconfig(AM_BSP_GPIO_LED_BLUE, g_AM_HAL_GPIO_OUTPUT_12);
    am_hal_gpio_pinconfig(AM_BSP_GPIO_LED_GREEN, g_AM_HAL_GPIO_OUTPUT_12);
    am_hal_gpio_pinconfig(AM_BSP_GPIO_LED_YELLOW, g_AM_HAL_GPIO_OUTPUT_12);
    is_initialized = true;
  }
```

We call the `am_hal_gpio_pinconfig()` function from the Apollo3 SDK to set all four
LED pins to output mode, represented by the constant `g_AM_HAL_GPIO_OUTPUT_12`.
We use the `is_initialized` `static` variable to ensure that we do this only once!

Next comes the code that will toggle the blue LED on and off. We do this using a
count variable, in the same way as in the Arduino implementation:

```
static int count = 0;
// Toggle the blue LED every time an inference is performed.
++count;
if (count & 1) {
  am_hal_gpio_output_set(AM_BSP_GPIO_LED_BLUE);
} else {
  am_hal_gpio_output_clear(AM_BSP_GPIO_LED_BLUE);
}
```

This code uses the `am_hal_gpio_output_set()` and `am_hal_gpio_output_clear()`
functions to switch the blue LED's pin either on or off.

By incrementing the count variable at each inference, we keep track of the total number of inferences we've performed. Inside the `if` conditional, we use the & operator to
do a binary AND operation with the count variable and the number 1.

By performing an AND on count with 1, we filter out all of count's bits except the
smallest. If the smallest bit is a 0, meaning count is an odd number, the result will be
a 0. In a C++ `if` statement, this evaluates to `false`.

Otherwise, the result will be a 1, indicating an even number. Because a 1 evaluates to
`true`, our LED will switch on with even values and off with odd values. This is what
makes it toggle.

Next, we light the appropriate LED depending on which word was just heard. By
default, we clear all of the LEDs, so if a word was not recently heard the LEDs will all
be unlit:

```
am_hal_gpio_output_clear(AM_BSP_GPIO_LED_RED);
am_hal_gpio_output_clear(AM_BSP_GPIO_LED_YELLOW);
am_hal_gpio_output_clear(AM_BSP_GPIO_LED_GREEN);
```

We then use some simple `if` statements to switch on the appropriate LED depending on which command was heard:

```
if (is_new_command) {
  error_reporter->Report("Heard %s (%d) @%dms", found_command, score,
                         current_time);
  if (found_command[0] == 'y') {
    am_hal_gpio_output_set(AM_BSP_GPIO_LED_YELLOW);
  }
  if (found_command[0] == 'n') {
    am_hal_gpio_output_set(AM_BSP_GPIO_LED_RED);
  }
  if (found_command[0] == 'u') {
    am_hal_gpio_output_set(AM_BSP_GPIO_LED_GREEN);
  }
}
```

As we saw earlier, `is_new_command` is `true` only if `RespondToCommand()` was called with a genuinely new command, so if a new command wasn't heard the LEDs will remain off. Otherwise, we use the `am_hal_gpio_output_set()` function to switch on the appropriate LED.

Running the example

We've now walked through how our example code lights up LEDs on the SparkFun Edge. Next, let's get the example up and running.

There's always a chance that the build process might have changed since this book was written, so check *README.md* (*https://oreil.ly/ U3Cgo*) for the latest instructions.

To build and deploy our code, we'll need the following:

- A SparkFun Edge board
- A USB programmer (we recommend the SparkFun Serial Basic Breakout, which is available in micro-B USB (*https://oreil.ly/2GMNf*) and USB-C (*https://oreil.ly/ lp39T*) variants)
- A matching USB cable
- Python 3 and some dependencies

Chapter 6 shows how to confirm whether you have the correct version of Python installed. If you already did this, great. If not, it's worth flipping back to "Running the Example" on page 110 to take a look.

In your terminal, clone the TensorFlow repository and then change into its directory:

```
git clone https://github.com/tensorflow/tensorflow.git
cd tensorflow
```

Next, we're going to build the binary and run some commands that get it ready for downloading to the device. To avoid some typing, you can copy and paste these commands from *README.md* (*https://oreil.ly/xY-Rj*).

Build the binary.   The following command downloads all of the required dependencies and then compiles a binary for the SparkFun Edge:

```
make -f tensorflow/lite/micro/tools/make/Makefile \
    TARGET=sparkfun_edge TAGS=cmsis-nn micro_speech_bin
```

The binary is created as a *.bin* file, in the following location:

```
tensorflow/lite/micro/tools/make/gen/ \
    sparkfun_edge_cortex-m4/bin/micro_speech.bin
```

To check whether the file exists, you can use the following command:

```
test -f tensorflow/lite/micro/tools/make/gen/ \
    sparkfun_edge_cortex-m4/bin/micro_speech.bin \
    && echo "Binary was successfully created" || echo "Binary is missing"
```

If you run that command, you should see `Binary was successfully created` printed to the console. If you see `Binary is missing`, there was a problem with the build process. If so, it's likely that there are some clues to what went wrong in the output of the `make` command.

Sign the binary.   The binary must be signed with cryptographic keys to be deployed to the device. Let's now run some commands that will sign the binary so it can be flashed to the SparkFun Edge. The scripts used here come from the Ambiq SDK, which is downloaded when the Makefile is run.

Enter the following command to set up some dummy cryptographic keys that you can use for development:

```
cp tensorflow/lite/micro/tools/make/downloads/AmbiqSuite-Rel2.0.0/ \
    tools/apollo3_scripts/keys_info0.py \
    tensorflow/lite/micro/tools/make/downloads/AmbiqSuite-Rel2.0.0/ \
    tools/apollo3_scripts/keys_info.py
```

Next, run the following command to create a signed binary. Substitute `python3` with `python` if necessary:

```
python3 tensorflow/lite/micro/tools/make/downloads/ \
  AmbiqSuite-Rel2.0.0/tools/apollo3_scripts/create_cust_image_blob.py \
  --bin tensorflow/lite/micro/tools/make/gen/ \
  sparkfun_edge_cortex-m4/bin/micro_speech.bin \
  --load-address 0xC000 \
  --magic-num 0xCB -o main_nonsecure_ota \
  --version 0x0
```

This creates the file *main_nonsecure_ota.bin*. Now run this command to create a final version of the file that can be used to flash your device with the script you will use in the next step:

```
python3 tensorflow/lite/micro/tools/make/downloads/ \
  AmbiqSuite-Rel2.0.0/tools/apollo3_scripts/create_cust_wireupdate_blob.py \
  --load-address 0x20000 \
  --bin main_nonsecure_ota.bin \
  -i 6 -o main_nonsecure_wire \
  --options 0x1
```

You should now have a file called *main_nonsecure_wire.bin* in the directory where you ran the commands. This is the file you'll be flashing to the device.

Flash the binary.   The SparkFun Edge stores the program it is currently running in its 1 megabyte of flash memory. If you want the board to run a new program, you need to send it to the board, which will store it in flash memory, overwriting any program that was previously saved.

Attach the programmer to the board.   To download new programs to the board, you'll use the SparkFun USB-C Serial Basic serial programmer. This device allows your computer to communicate with the microcontroller via USB.

To attach this device to your board, perform the following steps:

1. On the side of the SparkFun Edge, locate the six-pin header.

2. Plug the SparkFun USB-C Serial Basic into these pins, ensuring the pins labeled BLK and GRN on each device are lined up correctly, as illustrated in Figure 7-14.

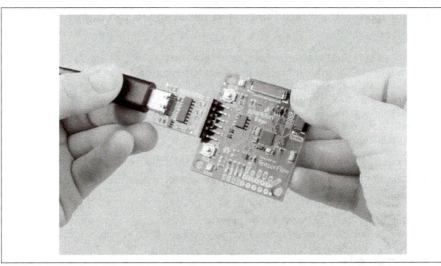

Figure 7-14. Connecting the SparkFun Edge and USB-C Serial Basic (courtesy of SparkFun)

Attach the programmer to your computer. You connect the board to your computer via USB. To program the board, you need to find out the name that your computer gives the device. The best way of doing this is to list all the computer's devices before and after attaching it, and look to see which device is new.

 Some people have reported issues with their operating system's default drivers for the programmer, so we strongly recommend installing the driver (*https://oreil.ly/kohTX*) before you continue.

Before attaching the device via USB, run the following command:

```
# macOS:
ls /dev/cu*

# Linux:
ls /dev/tty*
```

This should output a list of attached devices that looks something like the following:

```
/dev/cu.Bluetooth-Incoming-Port
/dev/cu.MALS
/dev/cu.SOC
```

Now, connect the programmer to your computer's USB port and run the command again:

```
# macOS:
ls /dev/cu*

# Linux:
ls /dev/tty*
```

You should see an extra item in the output, as shown in the example that follows. Your new item might have a different name. This new item is the name of the device:

```
/dev/cu.Bluetooth-Incoming-Port
/dev/cu.MALS
/dev/cu.SOC
/dev/cu.wchusbserial-1450
```

This name will be used to refer to the device. However, it can change depending on which USB port the programmer is attached to, so if you disconnect the board from your computer and then reattach it, you might need to look up its name again.

 Some users have reported two devices appearing in the list. If you see two devices, the correct one to use begins with the letters "wch"; for example, "/dev/wchusbserial-14410."

After you've identified the device name, put it in a shell variable for later use:

```
export DEVICENAME=<your device name here>
```

This is a variable that you can use when running commands that require the device name, later in the process.

Run the script to flash your board.   To flash the board, you must put it into a special "bootloader" state that prepares it to receive the new binary. You'll then run a script to send the binary to the board.

First create an environment variable to specify the baud rate, which is the speed at which data will be sent to the device:

```
export BAUD_RATE=921600
```

Now paste the command that follows into your terminal—but *do not press Enter yet*! The ${DEVICENAME} and ${BAUD_RATE} in the command will be replaced with the values you set in the previous sections. Remember to substitute python3 with python if necessary:

```
python3 tensorflow/lite/micro/tools/make/downloads/ \
  AmbiqSuite-Rel2.0.0/tools/apollo3_scripts/uart_wired_update.py \
  -b ${BAUD_RATE} ${DEVICENAME} \
```

```
-r 1 -f main_nonsecure_wire.bin \
-i 6
```

Next, you'll reset the board into its bootloader state and flash the board. On the board, locate the buttons marked RST and 14, as shown in Figure 7-15. Perform the following steps:

1. Ensure that your board is connected to the programmer and the entire thing is connected to your computer via USB.

2. On the board, press and hold the button marked 14. *Continue holding it.*

3. While still holding the button marked 14, press the button marked RST to reset the board.

4. Press Enter on your computer to run the script. *Continue holding button 14.*

You should now see something like the following appearing on your screen:

```
Connecting with Corvette over serial port /dev/cu.usbserial-1440...
Sending Hello.
Received response for Hello
Received Status
length =  0x58
version =  0x3
Max Storage =  0x4ffa0
Status =  0x2
State =  0x7
AMInfo =
0x1
0xff2da3ff
0x55fff
0x1
0x49f40003
0xffffffff
[...lots more 0xffffffff...]
Sending OTA Descriptor =  0xfe000
Sending Update Command.
number of updates needed =  1
Sending block of size  0x158b0  from  0x0  to  0x158b0
Sending Data Packet of length  8180
Sending Data Packet of length  8180
[...lots more Sending Data Packet of length  8180...]
```

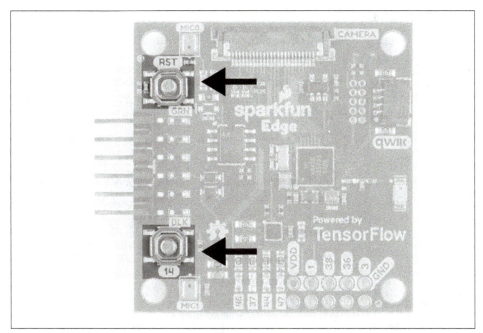

Figure 7-15. The SparkFun Edge's buttons

Keep holding button 14 until you see `Sending Data Packet of length 8180`. You can release the button after seeing this (but it's okay if you keep holding it). The program will continue to print lines on the terminal. Eventually, you'll see something like the following:

```
[...lots more Sending Data Packet of length  8180...]
Sending Data Packet of length  8180
Sending Data Packet of length  6440
Sending Reset Command.
Done.
```

This indicates a successful flashing.

 If the program output ends with an error, check whether `Sending Reset Command.` was printed. If so, flashing was likely successful despite the error. Otherwise, flashing might have failed. Try running through these steps again (you can skip over setting the environment variables).

Testing the program

To make sure the program is running, press the RST button. You should now see the blue LED flashing.

To test the program, try saying "yes." When it detects a "yes," the orange LED will flash. The model is also trained to recognize "no," and when unknown words are spoken. The red LED should flash for "no," and the green for unknown.

If you can't get the program to recognize your "yes," try saying it a few times in a row: "yes, yes, yes."

The model we're using is small and imperfect, and you'll probably notice that it's better at detecting "yes" than "no," which it often recognizes as "unknown." This is an example of how optimizing for a tiny model size can result in issues with accuracy. We cover this topic in Chapter 8.

What If It Didn't Work?

Here are some possible issues and how to debug them:

Problem: When flashing, the script hangs for a while at Sending Hello. and then prints an error.

Solution: You need to hold down the button marked 14 while running the script. Hold down button 14, press the RST button, and then run the script, while holding the button marked 14 the entire time.

Problem: After flashing, none of the LEDs are coming on.

Solution: Try pressing the RST button, or disconnecting the board from the programmer and then reconnecting it. If neither of these works, try flashing the board again.

Viewing debug data

The program will also log successful recognitions to the serial port. To view this data, we can monitor the board's serial port output using a baud rate of 115200. On macOS and Linux, the following command should work:

```
screen ${DEVICENAME} 115200
```

You should initially see output that looks something like the following:

```
Apollo3 Burst Mode is Available

                         Apollo3 operating in Burst Mode (96MHz)
```

Try issuing some commands by saying "yes" or "no." You should see the board printing debug information for each command:

```
Heard yes (202) @65536ms
```

To stop viewing the debug output with `screen`, press Ctrl-A immediately followed by the K key, and then press the Y key.

Making your own changes

Now that you've deployed the basic application, try playing around and making some changes. You can find the application's code in the *tensorflow/lite/micro/examples/micro_speech* folder. Just edit and save and then repeat the preceding instructions to deploy your modified code to the device.

Here are a few things that you could try:

- `RespondToCommand()`'s `score` argument shows the prediction score. Use the LEDs as a meter to show the strength of the match.
- Make the application respond to a specific sequence of "yes" and "no" commands, like a secret code phrase.
- Use the "yes" and "no" commands to control other components, like additional LEDs or servos.

ST Microelectronics STM32F746G Discovery Kit

Because the STM32F746G comes with a fancy LCD display, we can use this to show off whichever wake words are detected, as depicted in Figure 7-16.

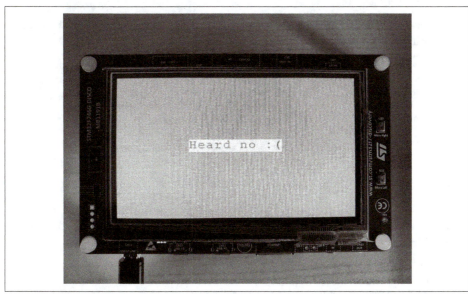

Figure 7-16. STM32F746G displaying a "no"

Responding to commands on STM32F746G

The STM32F746G's LCD driver gives us methods that we can use to write text to the display. In this exercise, we'll use these to show one of the following messages, depending on which command was heard:

- "Heard yes!"
- "Heard no :("
- "Heard unknown"
- "Heard silence"

We'll also set the background color differently depending on which command was heard.

To begin, we include some header files:

```
#include "tensorflow/lite/micro/examples/micro_speech/command_responder.h"
#include "LCD_DISCO_F746NG.h"
```

The first, *command_responder.h*, just declares the interface for this file. The second, *LCD_DISCO_F74NG.h*, gives us an interface to control the device's LCD display. You can read more about it on the Mbed site (*https://oreil.ly/6oirs*).

Next, we instantiate an `LCD_DISCO_F746NG` object, which holds the methods we use to control the LCD:

```
LCD_DISCO_F746NG lcd;
```

In the next few lines, the `RespondToCommand()` function is declared, and we check whether it has been called with a new command:

```
// When a command is detected, write it to the display and log it to the
// serial port.
void RespondToCommand(tflite::ErrorReporter *error_reporter,
                      int32_t current_time, const char *found_command,
                      uint8_t score, bool is_new_command) {
  if (is_new_command) {
    error_reporter->Report("Heard %s (%d) @%dms", found_command, score,
                           current_time);
```

When we know this is a new command, we use the `error_reporter` to log it to the serial port.

Next, we use a big `if` statement to determine what happens when each command is found. First comes "yes":

```
if (*found_command == 'y') {
  lcd.Clear(0xFF0F9D58);
  lcd.DisplayStringAt(0, LINE(5), (uint8_t *)"Heard yes!", CENTER_MODE);
```

We use lcd.Clear() to both clear any previous content from the screen and set a new background color, like a fresh coat of paint. The color 0xFF0F9D58 is a nice, rich green.

On our green background, we use lcd.DisplayStringAt() to draw some text. The first argument specifies an *x* coordinate, the second specifies a *y*. To position our text roughly in the middle of the display, we use a helper function, LINE(), to determine the *y* coordinate that would correspond to the fifth line of text on the screen.

The third argument is the string of text we'll be displaying, and the fourth argument determines the alignment of the text; here, we use the constant CENTER_MODE to specify that the text is center-aligned.

We continue the if statement to cover the remaining three possibilities, "no," "unknown," and "silence" (which is captured by the else block):

```
} else if (*found_command == 'n') {
  lcd.Clear(0xFFDB4437);
  lcd.DisplayStringAt(0, LINE(5), (uint8_t *)"Heard no :(", CENTER_MODE);
} else if (*found_command == 'u') {
  lcd.Clear(0xFFF4B400);
  lcd.DisplayStringAt(0, LINE(5), (uint8_t *)"Heard unknown", CENTER_MODE);
} else {
  lcd.Clear(0xFF4285F4);
  lcd.DisplayStringAt(0, LINE(5), (uint8_t *)"Heard silence", CENTER_MODE);
}
```

And that's it! Because the LCD library gives us such easy high-level control over the display, it doesn't take much code to output our results. Let's deploy the example to see this all in action.

Running the example

Now we can use the Mbed toolchain to deploy our application to the device.

> There's always a chance that the build process might have changed since this book was written, so check *README.md* (*https://oreil.ly/1INIO*) for the latest instructions.

Before we begin, we'll need the following:

- An STM32F746G Discovery kit board
- A mini-USB cable
- The Arm Mbed CLI (follow the Mbed setup guide (*https://oreil.ly/tR57j*))

- Python 3 and pip

Like the Arduino IDE, Mbed requires source files to be structured in a certain way. The TensorFlow Lite for Microcontrollers Makefile knows how to do this for us and can generate a directory suitable for Mbed.

To do so, run the following command:

```
make -f tensorflow/lite/micro/tools/make/Makefile \
  TARGET=mbed TAGS="cmsis-nn disco_f746ng" generate_micro_speech_mbed_project
```

This results in the creation of a new directory:

```
tensorflow/lite/micro/tools/make/gen/mbed_cortex-m4/prj/ \
  micro_speech/mbed
```

This directory contains all of the example's dependencies structured in the correct way for Mbed to be able to build it.

First, change into the directory so that you can run some commands within it:

```
cd tensorflow/lite/micro/tools/make/gen/mbed_cortex-m4/prj/micro_speech/mbed
```

Next, you'll use Mbed to download the dependencies and build the project.

To begin, use the following command to inform Mbed that the current directory is the root of an Mbed project:

```
mbed config root .
```

Next, instruct Mbed to download the dependencies and prepare to build:

```
mbed deploy
```

By default, Mbed builds the project using C++98. However, TensorFlow Lite requires C++11. Run the following Python snippet to modify the Mbed configuration files so that it uses C++11. You can just type or paste it into the command line:

```
python -c 'import fileinput, glob;
for filename in glob.glob("mbed-os/tools/profiles/*.json"):
  for line in fileinput.input(filename, inplace=True):
    print(line.replace("\"-std=gnu++98\"","\"-std=c++11\", \"-fpermissive\""))'
```

Finally, run the following command to compile:

```
mbed compile -m DISCO_F746NG -t GCC_ARM
```

This should result in a binary at the following path:

```
./BUILD/DISCO_F746NG/GCC_ARM/mbed.bin
```

One of the nice things about the STM32F746G board is that deployment is really easy. To deploy, just plug in your STM board and copy the file to it. On macOS, you can do this by using the following command:

```
cp ./BUILD/DISCO_F746NG/GCC_ARM/mbed.bin /Volumes/DIS_F746NG/
```

Alternately, just find the `DIS_F746NG` volume in your file browser and drag the file over.

Copying the file initiates the flashing process.

Testing the program

When this is complete, try saying "yes." You should see the appropriate text appear on the display and the background color change.

If you can't get the program to recognize your "yes," try saying it a few times in a row, like "yes, yes, yes."

The model we're using is small and imperfect, and you'll probably notice that it's better at detecting "yes" than "no," which it often recognizes as "unknown." This is an example of how optimizing for a tiny model size can result in issues with accuracy. We cover this topic in Chapter 8.

Viewing debug data

The program also logs successful recognitions to the serial port. To view the output, establish a serial connection to the board using a baud rate of 9600.

On macOS and Linux, the device should be listed when you issue the following command:

```
ls /dev/tty*
```

It will look something like the following:

```
/dev/tty.usbmodem1454203
```

After you've identified the device, use the following command to connect to it, replacing *</dev/tty.devicename>* with the name of your device as it appears in */dev*:

```
screen /dev/<tty.devicename 9600>
```

Try issuing some commands by saying "yes" or "no." You should see the board printing debug information for each command:

```
Heard yes (202) @65536ms
```

To stop viewing the debug output with `screen`, press Ctrl-A, immediately followed by the K key, and then press the Y key.

 If you're not sure how to make a serial connection on your platform, you could try CoolTerm (*https://oreil.ly/FP7gK*), which works on Windows, macOS, and Linux. The board should show up in CoolTerm's Port drop-down list. Make sure you set the baud rate to 9600.

Making your own changes

Now that you've deployed the application, it could be fun to play around and make some changes. You can find the application's code in the *tensorflow/lite/micro/tools/make/gen/mbed_cortex-m4/prj/micro_speech/mbed* folder. Just edit and save and then repeat the preceding instructions to deploy your modified code to the device.

Here are a few things you could try:

- RespondToCommand()'s score argument shows the prediction score. Create a visual indicator of the score on the LCD display.
- Make the application respond to a specific sequence of "yes" and "no" commands, like a secret code phrase.
- Use the "yes" and "no" commands to control other components, like additional LEDs or servos.

Wrapping Up

The application code we've walked through has been mostly concerned with capturing data from the hardware and then extracting features that are suitable for inference. The part that actually feeds data into the model and runs inference is relatively small, and it's very similar to the example covered in Chapter 6.

This is fairly typical of machine learning projects. The model is already trained, thus our job is just to keep it fed with the appropriate sort of data. As an embedded developer working with TensorFlow Lite, you'll be spending most of your programming time on capturing sensor data, processing it into features, and responding to the output of your model. The inference part itself is quick and easy.

But the embedded application is only part of the package—the really fun part is the model. In Chapter 8, you'll learn how to train your own speech model to listen for different words. You'll also learn more about how it works.

Wake-Word Detection: Training a Model

In Chapter 7, we built an application around a model trained to recognize "yes" and "no." In this chapter, we will train a *new* model that can recognize different words.

Our application code is fairly general. All it does is capture and process audio, feed it into a TensorFlow Lite model, and do something based on the output. It mostly doesn't care which words the model is looking for. This means that if we train a new model, we can just drop it into our application and it should work right away.

Here are the things we need to consider when training a new model:

Input
> The new model must be trained on input data that is the same shape and format, with the same preprocessing as our application code.

Output
> The output of the new model must be in the same format: a tensor of probabilities, one for each class.

Training data
> Whichever new words we pick, we'll need many recordings of people saying them so that we can train our new model.

Optimization
> The model must be optimized to run efficiently on a microcontroller with limited memory.

Fortunately for us, our existing model was trained using a publicly available script that was published by the TensorFlow team, and we can use this script to train a new model. We also have access to a free dataset of spoken audio that we can use as training data.

In the next section, we'll walk through the process of training a model with this script. Then, in "Using the Model in Our Project" on page 197, we'll incorporate the new model into our existing application code. After that, in "How the Model Works" on page 202, you'll learn how the model actually works. Finally, in "Training with Your Own Data" on page 214, you'll see how to train a model using your own dataset.

Training Our New Model

The model we are using was trained with the TensorFlow Simple Audio Recognition (*https://oreil.ly/E292V*) script, an example script designed to demonstrate how to build and train a model for audio recognition using TensorFlow.

The script makes it very easy to train an audio recognition model. Among other things, it allows us to do the following:

- Download a dataset with audio featuring 20 spoken words.
- Choose which subset of words to train the model on.
- Specify what type of preprocessing to use on the audio.
- Choose from several different types of model architecture.
- Optimize the model for microcontrollers using quantization.

When we run the script, it downloads the dataset, trains a model, and outputs a file representing the trained model. We then use some other tools to convert this file into the correct form for TensorFlow Lite.

 It's common for model authors to create these types of training scripts. It allows them to easily experiment with different variants of model architectures and hyperparameters, and to share their work with others.

The easiest way to run the training script is within a Colaboratory (Colab) notebook, which we do in the following section.

Training in Colab

Google Colab is a great place to train models. It provides access to powerful computing resources in the cloud, and it comes set up with tools that we can use to monitor the training process. It's also completely free.

Over the course of this section, we will use a Colab notebook to train our new model. The notebook we use is available in the TensorFlow repository.

Open the notebook (*https://oreil.ly/0Z2ra*) and click the "Run in Google Colab" button, as shown in Figure 8-1.

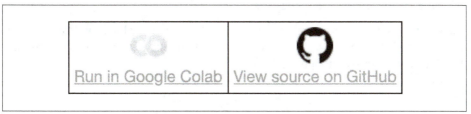

Figure 8-1. The "Run in Google Colab" button

 As of this writing, there's a bug in GitHub that results in intermittent error messages when displaying Jupyter notebooks. If you see the message "Sorry, something went wrong. Reload?" when trying to access the notebook, follow the instructions in "Building Our Model" on page 34.

This notebook will guide us through the process of training a model. It runs through the following steps:

- Configuring parameters
- Installing the correct dependencies
- Monitoring training using something called TensorBoard
- Running the training script
- Converting the training output into a model we can use

Enable GPU training

In Chapter 4, we trained a very simple model on a small amount of data. The model we are training now is a lot more sophisticated, has a much larger dataset, and will take a lot longer to train. On an average modern computer CPU, training it would take three or four hours.

To reduce the time it takes to train the model, we can use something called *GPU acceleration*. A *GPU*, or graphics processing unit. It's a piece of hardware designed to help computers process image data quickly, allowing them to smoothly render things like user interfaces and video games. Most computers have one.

Image processing involves running a lot of tasks in parallel, and so does training a deep learning network. This means that it's possible to use GPU hardware to accelerate deep learning training. It's common for training to be 5 to 10 times faster when run on a GPU as opposed to a CPU.

The audio preprocessing required in our training process means that we won't see quite such a massive speed-up, but our model will still train a lot faster on a GPU—it will take around one to two hours, total.

Luckily for us, Colab supports training via GPU. It's not enabled by default, but it's easy to switch on. To do so, go to Colab's Runtime menu, then click "Change runtime type," as demonstrated in Figure 8-2.

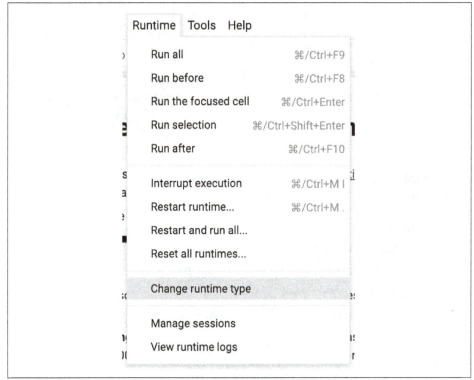

Figure 8-2. The "Change runtime type" option in Colab

When you select this option, the "Notebook settings" box shown in Figure 8-3 opens.

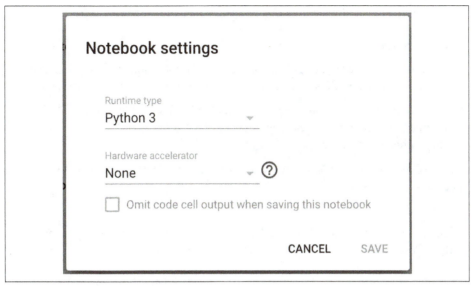

Figure 8-3. The "Notebook settings" box

Select GPU from the "Hardware accelerator" drop-down list, as in Figure 8-4, and then click SAVE.

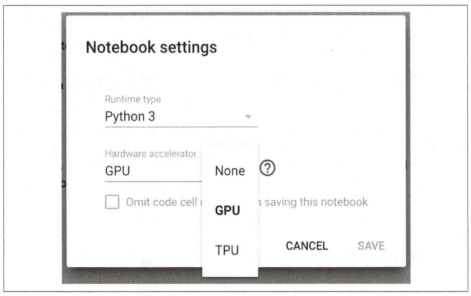

Figure 8-4. The "Hardware accelerator" drop-down list

Colab will now run its Python on a backend computer (referred to as a *runtime*) that has a GPU.

The next step is to configure the notebook with the words we'd like to train.

Configure training

The training scripts are configured via a bunch of command-line flags that control everything from the model's architecture to the words it will be trained to classify.

To make it easier to run the scripts, the notebook's first cell stores some important values in environment variables. These will be substituted into the scripts' command-line flags when they are run.

The first one, WANTED_WORDS, allows us to select the words on which to train the model:

```
os.environ["WANTED_WORDS"] = "yes,no"
```

By default the selected words are "yes" and "no," but we can provide any combination of the following words, all of which appear in our dataset:

- Common commands: *yes, no, up, down, left, right, on, off, stop, go, backward, forward, follow, learn*
- Digits zero through nine: *zero, one, two, three, four, five, six, seven, eight, nine*
- Random words: *bed, bird, cat, dog, happy, house, Marvin, Sheila, tree, wow*

To select words, we can just include them in a comma-separated list. Let's choose the words "on" and "off" to train our new model:

```
os.environ["WANTED_WORDS"] = "on,off"
```

Any words not included in the list will be grouped under the "unknown" category when the model is trained.

It's fine to choose more than two words here; we would just need to tweak the application code slightly. We provide instructions on doing this in "Using the Model in Our Project" on page 197.

Notice also the TRAINING_STEPS and LEARNING_RATE variables:

```
os.environ["TRAINING_STEPS"]="15000,3000"
os.environ["LEARNING_RATE"]="0.001,0.0001"
```

In Chapter 3, we learned that a model's weights and biases are incrementally adjusted so that over time, the output of the model gets closer to matching the desired value. TRAINING_STEPS refers to the number of times a batch of training data will be run through the network and its weights and biases updated. LEARNING_RATE sets the rate of adjustment.

With a high learning rate, the weights and biases are adjusted more with each iteration, meaning convergence happens fast. However, these big jumps mean that it's more difficult to get to the ideal values because we might keep jumping past them. With a lower learning rate, the jumps are smaller. It takes more steps to converge, but the final result might be better. The best learning rate for a given model is determined through trial and error.

In the aforementioned variables, the training steps and learning rate are defined as comma-separated lists that define the learning rate for each stage of training. With the values we just looked at, the model will train for 15,000 steps with a learning rate of 0.001, and then 3,000 steps with a learning rate of 0.0001. The total number of steps will be 18,000.

This means we'll do a bunch of iterations with a high learning rate, allowing the network to quickly converge. We'll then do a smaller number of iterations with a low learning rate, fine-tuning the weights and biases.

For now, we'll leave these values as they are, but it's good to know what they are for. Run the cell. You'll see the following output printed:

```
Training these words: on,off
Training steps in each stage: 15000,3000
Learning rate in each stage: 0.001,0.0001
Total number of training steps: 18000
```

This gives a summary of how our model will be trained.

Install dependencies

Next up, we grab some dependencies that are necessary for running the scripts.

Run the next two cells to do the following:

- Install a specific version of the TensorFlow pip package that includes the ops required for training.
- Clone a corresponding version of the TensorFlow GitHub repository so that we can access the training scripts.

Load TensorBoard

To monitor the training process, we use TensorBoard (*https://oreil.ly/wginD*). It's a user interface that can show us graphs, statistics, and other insight into how training is going.

When training has completed, it will look something like the screenshot in Figure 8-5. You'll learn what all of these graphs mean later in this chapter.

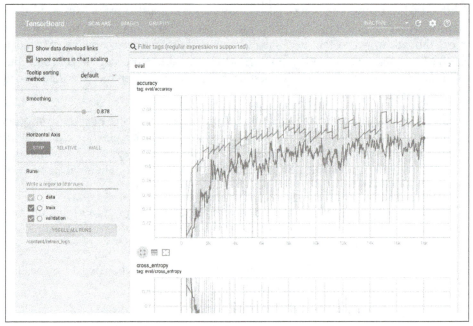

Figure 8-5. A screenshot of TensorBoard after training is complete

Run the next cell to load TensorBoard. It will appear in Colab, but it won't show anything interesting until we begin training.

Begin training

The following cell runs the script that begins training. You can see that it has a lot of command-line arguments:

```
!python tensorflow/tensorflow/examples/speech_commands/train.py \
--model_architecture=tiny_conv --window_stride=20 --preprocess=micro \
--wanted_words=${WANTED_WORDS} --silence_percentage=25 --unknown_percentage=25 \
--quantize=1 --verbosity=WARN --how_many_training_steps=${TRAINING_STEPS} \
--learning_rate=${LEARNING_RATE} --summaries_dir=/content/retrain_logs \
--data_dir=/content/speech_dataset --train_dir=/content/speech_commands_train
```

Some of these, like `--wanted_words=${WANTED_WORDS}`, use the environment variables we defined earlier to configure the model we're creating. Others set up the output of the script, such as `--train_dir=/content/speech_commands_train`, which defines where the trained model will be saved.

Leave the arguments as they are, and run the cell. You'll begin to see some output stream past. It will pause for a few moments while the Speech Commands dataset is downloaded:

```
>> Downloading speech_commands_v0.02.tar.gz 18.1%
```

When this is done, some more output will appear. There might be some warnings, which you can ignore as long as the cell continues running. At this point, you should scroll back up to TensorBoard, which should hopefully look something like Figure 8-6. If you don't see any graphs, click the SCALARS tab.

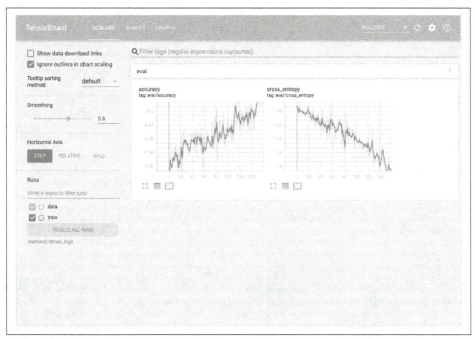

Figure 8-6. A screenshot of TensorBoard at the beginning of training

Hooray! This means that training has begun. The cell you've just run will continue to execute for the duration of training, which will take up to two hours to complete. The cell won't output any more logs, but data about the training run will appear in TensorBoard.

You can see that TensorBoard shows two graphs, "accuracy" and "cross_entropy," as shown in Figure 8-7. Both graphs show the current steps on the x-axis. The "accuracy" graph shows the model's accuracy on its y-axis, which signals how much of the time it is able to detect a word correctly. The "cross_entropy" graph shows the model's loss, which quantifies how far from the correct values the model's predictions are.

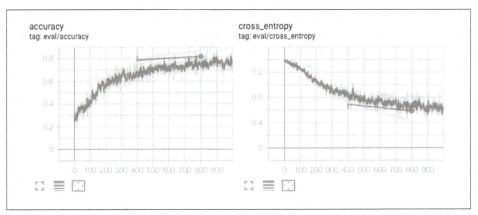

Figure 8-7. The "accuracy" and "cross_entropy" graphs

 Cross entropy is a common way of measuring loss in machine learning models that perform classification, for which the goal is to predict which category an input belongs to.

The jagged lines on the graph correspond to performance on the training dataset, whereas the straight lines reflect performance on the validation dataset. Validation occurs periodically, so there are fewer validation datapoints on the graph.

New data will arrive in the graphs over time, but to show it, you need to adjust their scales to fit. You can do this by clicking the rightmost button under each graph, as shown in Figure 8-8.

Figure 8-8. Click this button to adjust the graph's scale to fit all available data

You can also click the button shown in Figure 8-9 to make each graph larger.

Figure 8-9. Click this button to enlarge the graph

In addition to graphs, TensorBoard can show the inputs being fed into the model. Click the IMAGES tab, which displays a view similar to Figure 8-10. This is an example of a spectrogram that is being input to the model during training.

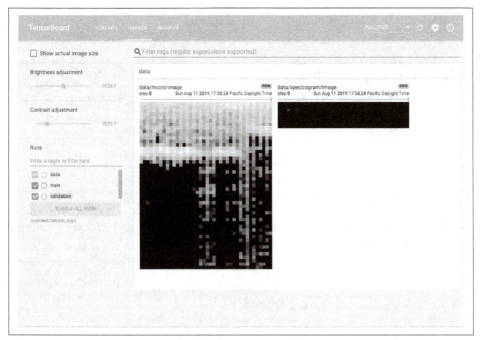

Figure 8-10. The IMAGES tab of TensorBoard

Wait for training to complete

Training the model will take between one and two hours, so our job now is to be patient. Fortunately for us, we have TensorBoard's pretty graphs to keep us entertained.

As training progresses, you'll notice that the metrics tend to jump around within a range. This is normal, but it makes the graphs appear fuzzy and difficult to read. To make it easier to see how training is going, we can use TensorFlow's Smoothing feature.

Figure 8-11 shows graphs with the default amount of smoothing applied; notice how fuzzy they are.

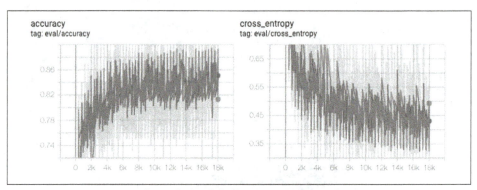

Figure 8-11. Training graphs with the default amount of smoothing

By adjusting the Smoothing slider, shown in Figure 8-12, we can increase the amount of smoothing, making the trends more obvious.

Figure 8-12. TensorBoard's Smoothing slider

Figure 8-13 shows the same graphs with a higher level of smoothing. The original data is visible in lighter colors, underneath.

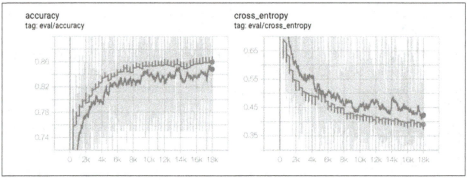

Figure 8-13. Training graphs with increased smoothing

Keeping Colab running. To prevent abandoned projects from consuming resources, Colab will shut down your runtime if it isn't actively being used. Because our training will take a while, we need to prevent this from happening. There are a couple of things we need to think about.

First, if we're not actively interacting with the Colab browser tab, the web user interface will disconnect from the backend runtime where the training scripts are being executed. This will happen after a few minutes, and will cause your TensorBoard graphs to stop updating with the latest training metrics. There's no need to panic if this happens—your training is still running in the background.

If your runtime has disconnected, you'll see a Reconnect button appear in Colab's user interface, as shown in Figure 8-14. Click this button to reconnect your runtime.

Reconnect ▾

Figure 8-14. Colab's Reconnect button

A disconnected runtime is no big deal, but Colab's next timeout deserves some attention. *If you don't interact with Colab for 90 consecutive minutes, your runtime instance will be recycled.* This is a problem: you will lose all of your training progress, along with any data stored in the instance!

To avoid this happening, you just need to interact with Colab at least once every 90 minutes. Open the tab, make sure the runtime is connected, and take a look at your beautiful graphs. As long as you do this before 90 minutes have elapsed, the connection will stay open.

> Even if your Colab tab is closed, the runtime will continue running in the background for up to 90 minutes. As long as you open the original URL in your browser, you can reconnect to the runtime and continue as before.
>
> However, TensorBoard will disappear when the tab is closed. If training is still running when the tab is reopened, you will not be able to view TensorBoard again until training is complete.

Finally, *a Colab runtime has a maximum lifespan of 12 hours.* If your training takes longer than 12 hours, you're out of luck—Colab will shut down and reset your instance before training has a chance to complete. If your training is likely to run this long, you should avoid Colab and use one of the alternative solutions described in "Other Ways to Run the Scripts" on page 201. Luckily, training our wake-word model won't take anywhere near that long.

When your graphs show data for 18,000 steps, training is complete! We now must run a few more commands to prepare our model for deployment. Don't worry—this part is *much* quicker.

Freeze the graph

As you learned earlier in this book, training is the process of iteratively tweaking a model's weights and biases until it produces useful predictions. The training script writes these weights and biases to *checkpoint* files. A checkpoint is written once every hundred steps. This means that if training fails partway through, it can be restarted from the most recent checkpoint without losing progress.

The *train.py* script is called with an argument, `--train_dir`, which specifies where these checkpoint files will be written. In our Colab, it's set to */content/speech_commands_train*.

You can see the checkpoint files by opening Colab's lefthand panel, which has a file browser. To do so, click the button shown in Figure 8-15.

Figure 8-15. The button that opens Colab's sidebar

In this panel, click the Files tab to see the runtime's filesystem. If you open the *speech_commands_train/* directory you'll see the checkpoint files, as in Figure 8-16. The number in each filename indicates the step at which the checkpoint was saved.

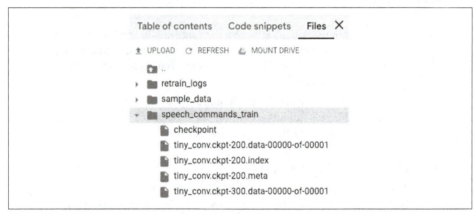

Figure 8-16. Colab's file browser showing a list of checkpoint files

A TensorFlow model consists of two main things:

- The weights and biases resulting from training
- A graph of operations that combine the model's input with these weights and biases to produce the model's output

---

At this juncture, our model's operations are defined in the Python scripts, and its trained weights and biases are in the most recent checkpoint file. We need to unite the two into a single model file with a specific format, which we can use to run inference. The process of creating this model file is called *freezing*—we're creating a static representation of the graph with the weights *frozen* into it.

To freeze our model, we run a script. You'll find it in the next cell, in the "Freeze the graph" section. The script is called as follows:

```
!python tensorflow/tensorflow/examples/speech_commands/freeze.py \
    --model_architecture=tiny_conv --window_stride=20 --preprocess=micro \
    --wanted_words=${WANTED_WORDS} --quantize=1 \
    --output_file=/content/tiny_conv.pb \
    --start_checkpoint=/content/speech_commands_train/tiny_conv. \
    ckpt-${TOTAL_STEPS}
```

To point the script toward the correct graph of operations to freeze, we pass some of the same arguments we used in training. We also pass a path to the final checkpoint file, which is the one whose filename ends with the total number of training steps.

Run this cell to freeze the graph. The frozen graph will be output to a file named *tiny_conv.pb*.

This file is the fully trained TensorFlow model. It can be loaded by TensorFlow and used to run inference. That's great, but it's still in the format used by regular TensorFlow, not TensorFlow Lite. Our next step is to convert the model into the TensorFlow Lite format.

Convert to TensorFlow Lite

Conversion is another easy step: we just need to run a single command. Now that we have a frozen graph file to work with, we'll be using `toco`, the command-line interface for the TensorFlow Lite converter.

In the "Convert the model" section, run the first cell:

```
!toco
    --graph_def_file=/content/tiny_conv.pb --output_file= \
    /content/tiny_conv.tflite \
    --input_shapes=1,49,40,1 --input_arrays=Reshape_2
    --output_arrays='labels_softmax' \
    --inference_type=QUANTIZED_UINT8 --mean_values=0 --std_dev_values=9.8077
```

In the arguments, we specify the model that we want to convert, the output location for the TensorFlow Lite model file, and some other values that depend on the model architecture. Because the model was quantized during training, we also provide some arguments (`inference_type`, `mean_values`, and `std_dev_values`) that instruct the converter how to map its low-precision values into real numbers.

You might be wondering why the `input_shape` argument has a leading 1 before the width, height, and channels parameters. This is the batch size; for efficiency during training, we send a lot of inputs in together, but when we're running in a real-time application we'll be working on only one sample at a time, which is why the batch size is fixed as 1.

The converted model will be written to *tiny_conv.tflite*. Congratulations; this a fully formed TensorFlow Lite model!

To see how tiny this model is, in the next cell, run the code:

```
import os
model_size = os.path.getsize("/content/tiny_conv.tflite")
print("Model is %d bytes" % model_size)
```

The output shows that the model is super small: `Model is 18208 bytes`.

Our next step is to get this model into a form that we can deploy to microcontrollers.

Create a C array

Back in "Converting to a C File" on page 64, we used the xxd command to convert a TensorFlow Lite model into a C array. We'll do the same thing in the next cell:

```
# Install xxd if it is not available
!apt-get -qq install xxd
# Save the file as a C source file
!xxd -i /content/tiny_conv.tflite > /content/tiny_conv.cc
# Print the source file
!cat /content/tiny_conv.cc
```

The final part of the output will be the file's contents, which are a C array and an integer holding its length, as follows (the exact values you see might be slightly different):

```
unsigned char _content_tiny_conv_tflite[] = {
  0x1c, 0x00, 0x00, 0x00, 0x54, 0x46, 0x4c, 0x33, 0x00, 0x00, 0x00, 0x00,
  0x00, 0x00, 0x0e, 0x00, 0x18, 0x00, 0x04, 0x00, 0x08, 0x00, 0x0c, 0x00,
  // ...
  0x00, 0x09, 0x06, 0x00, 0x08, 0x00, 0x07, 0x00, 0x06, 0x00, 0x00, 0x00,
  0x00, 0x00, 0x00, 0x04
};
unsigned int _content_tiny_conv_tflite_len = 18208;
```

This code is also written to a file, *tiny_conv.cc*, which you can download using Colab's file browser. Because your Colab runtime will expire after 12 hours, it's a good idea to download this file to your computer now.

Next, we'll integrate this newly trained model with the `micro_speech` project so that we can deploy it to some hardware.

Using the Model in Our Project

To use our new model, we need to do three things:

1. In *micro_features/tiny_conv_micro_features_model_data.cc* (*https://oreil.ly/ EAR0U*), replace the original model data with our new model.

2. Update the label names in *micro_features/micro_model_settings.cc* (*https://oreil.ly/ bqw67*) with our new "on" and "off" labels.

3. Update the device-specific *command_responder.cc* to take the actions we want for the new labels.

Replacing the Model

To replace the model, open *micro_features/tiny_conv_micro_features_model_data.cc* in your text editor.

 If you're working with the Arduino example, the file will appear as a tab in the Arduino IDE. Its name will be *micro_features_tiny_conv_micro_features_model_data.cpp*. If you're working with the SparkFun Edge, you can edit the files directly in your local copy of the TensorFlow repository. If you're working with the STM32F746G, you should edit the files in your Mbed project directory.

The *tiny_conv_micro_features_model_data.cc* file contains an array declaration that looks like this:

```
const unsigned char
    g_tiny_conv_micro_features_model_data[] DATA_ALIGN_ATTRIBUTE = {
        0x18, 0x00, 0x00, 0x00, 0x54, 0x46, 0x4c, 0x33, 0x00, 0x00, 0x0e, 0x00,
        0x18, 0x00, 0x04, 0x00, 0x08, 0x00, 0x0c, 0x00, 0x10, 0x00, 0x14, 0x00,
        //...
        0x00, 0x09, 0x06, 0x00, 0x08, 0x00, 0x07, 0x00, 0x06, 0x00, 0x00, 0x00,
        0x00, 0x00, 0x00, 0x04};
const int g_tiny_conv_micro_features_model_data_len = 18208;
```

You'll need to replace the contents of the array as well as the value of the constant `g_tiny_conv_micro_features_model_data_len`, if it has changed.

To do so, open the *tiny_conv.cc* file that you downloaded at the end of the previous section. Copy and paste the contents of the array, but not its definition, into the array defined in *tiny_conv_micro_features_model_data.cc*. Make sure you are overwriting the array's contents, but not its declaration.

At the bottom of *tiny_conv.cc* you'll find `_content_tiny_conv_tflite_len`, a variable whose value represents the length of the array. Back in *tiny_conv_micro_features_model_data.cc*, replace the value of `g_tiny_conv_micro_features_model_data_len` with the value of this variable. Then save the file; you're done updating it.

Updating the Labels

Next, open *micro_features/micro_model_settings.cc*. This file contains an array of class labels:

```
const char* kCategoryLabels[kCategoryCount] = {
    "silence",
    "unknown",
    "yes",
    "no",
};
```

To adjust this for our new model, we can just swap the "yes" and "no" for "on" and "off." We match labels with the model's output tensor elements by order, so it's important to list these in the same order in which they were provided to the training script.

Here's the expected code:

```
const char* kCategoryLabels[kCategoryCount] = {
    "silence",
    "unknown",
    "on",
    "off",
};
```

If you trained a model with more than two labels, just add them all to the list.

We're now done switching over the model. The only remaining step is to update any output code that uses the labels.

Updating command_responder.cc

The project contains a different device-specific implementation of *command_responder.cc* for the Arduino, SparkFun Edge, and STM32F746G. We show how to update each of these in the following sections.

Arduino

The Arduino command responder, located in *arduino/command_responder.cc*, lights an LED for 3 seconds when it hears the word "yes." Let's update it to light the LED when it hears either "on" or "off." In the file, locate the following if statement:

```
// If we heard a "yes", switch on an LED and store the time.
if (found_command[0] == 'y') {
```

```
    last_yes_time = current_time;
    digitalWrite(LED_BUILTIN, HIGH);
  }
```

The `if` statement tests whether the first letter of the command is "y," for "yes." If we change this "y" to an "o," the LED will be lit for either "on" or "off," because they both begin with "o":

```
if (found_command[0] == 'o') {
    last_yes_time = current_time;
    digitalWrite(LED_BUILTIN, HIGH);
  }
```

Project Idea

Switching an LED on by saying "off" doesn't make much sense. Try changing the code so that you can turn the LED on by saying "on" and off by saying "off."

You can use the second letter of each command, accessed via `found_command[1]`, to disambiguate between "on" and "off":

```
if (found_command[0] == 'o' && found_command[1] == 'n') {
```

After you've made these code changes, deploy to your device and give it a try.

SparkFun Edge

The SparkFun Edge command responder, located in *sparkfun_edge/command_responder.cc*, lights up a different LED depending on whether it heard "yes" or "no." In the file, locate the following `if` statements:

```
if (found_command[0] == 'y') {
  am_hal_gpio_output_set(AM_BSP_GPIO_LED_YELLOW);
}
if (found_command[0] == 'n') {
  am_hal_gpio_output_set(AM_BSP_GPIO_LED_RED);
}
if (found_command[0] == 'u') {
  am_hal_gpio_output_set(AM_BSP_GPIO_LED_GREEN);
}
```

It's simple to update these so that "on" and "off" each turn on different LEDs:

```
if (found_command[0] == 'o' && found_command[1] == 'n') {
  am_hal_gpio_output_set(AM_BSP_GPIO_LED_YELLOW);
}
if (found_command[0] == 'o' && found_command[1] == 'f') {
  am_hal_gpio_output_set(AM_BSP_GPIO_LED_RED);
}
if (found_command[0] == 'u') {
```

```
    am_hal_gpio_output_set(AM_BSP_GPIO_LED_GREEN);
  }
```

Because both commands begin with the same letter, we need to look at their second letters to disambiguate them. Now, the yellow LED will light when "on" is spoken, and the red will light for "off."

Project Idea

Try changing the code so that you can turn on an LED continuously by saying "on," and turn it off by saying "off."

When you're finished making the changes, deploy and run the code using the same process you followed in "Running the example" on page 167.

STM32F746G

The STM32F746G command responder, located in *disco_f746ng/command_responder.cc*, displays a different word depending on which command it heard. In the file, locate the following if statement:

```
if (*found_command == 'y') {
  lcd.Clear(0xFF0F9D58);
  lcd.DisplayStringAt(0, LINE(5), (uint8_t *)"Heard yes!", CENTER_MODE);
} else if (*found_command == 'n') {
  lcd.Clear(0xFFDB4437);
  lcd.DisplayStringAt(0, LINE(5), (uint8_t *)"Heard no :(", CENTER_MODE);
} else if (*found_command == 'u') {
  lcd.Clear(0xFFF4B400);
  lcd.DisplayStringAt(0, LINE(5), (uint8_t *)"Heard unknown", CENTER_MODE);
} else {
  lcd.Clear(0xFF4285F4);
  lcd.DisplayStringAt(0, LINE(5), (uint8_t *)"Heard silence", CENTER_MODE);
}
```

It's easy to update this so that it responds to "on" and "off," instead:

```
if (found_command[0] == 'o' && found_command[1] == 'n') {
  lcd.Clear(0xFF0F9D58);
  lcd.DisplayStringAt(0, LINE(5), (uint8_t *)"Heard on!", CENTER_MODE);
} else if (found_command[0] == 'o' && found_command[1] == 'f') {
  lcd.Clear(0xFFDB4437);
  lcd.DisplayStringAt(0, LINE(5), (uint8_t *)"Heard off", CENTER_MODE);
} else if (*found_command == 'u') {
  lcd.Clear(0xFFF4B400);
  lcd.DisplayStringAt(0, LINE(5), (uint8_t *)"Heard unknown", CENTER_MODE);
} else {
  lcd.Clear(0xFF4285F4);
  lcd.DisplayStringAt(0, LINE(5), (uint8_t *)"Heard silence", CENTER_MODE);
}
```

Again, because both commands begin with the same letter, we look at their second letters to disambiguate them. Now we display the appropriate text for each command.

Project Idea

Try changing the code so that you can display a secret message by saying "on," and hide it by saying "off."

Other Ways to Run the Scripts

If you're not able to use Colab, there are two other recommended ways to train the model:

- In a cloud virtual machine (VM) with a GPU
- On your local workstation

The drivers necessary for GPU-based training are available only on Linux. Without Linux, training will take around four hours. For this reason, it's recommended to use either a cloud VM with a GPU, or a similarly equipped Linux workstation.

Setting up your VM or workstation is beyond the scope of this book. However, we do have some recommendations. If you're using a VM, you can launch a Google Cloud Deep Learning VM Image (*https://oreil.ly/PVRtP*), which is preconfigured with all of the dependencies you'll need for GPU training. If you're using a Linux workstation, the TensorFlow GPU Docker image (*https://oreil.ly/PFYVr*) has everything you'll need.

To train the model, you need to install a nightly build of TensorFlow. To uninstall any existing version and replace it with one that is confirmed to work, use the following commands:

```
pip uninstall -y tensorflow tensorflow_estimator
pip install -q tf-estimator-nightly==1.14.0.dev2019072901 \
  tf-nightly-gpu==1.15.0.dev20190729
```

Next, open a command line and change to a directory you use to store code. Use the following commands to clone TensorFlow and open a specific commit that is confirmed to work:

```
git clone -q https://github.com/tensorflow/tensorflow
git -c advice.detachedHead=false -C tensorflow checkout 17ce384df70
```

Now you can run the *train.py* script to train the model. This will train a model to recognize "yes" and "no," and output the checkpoint files to */tmp*:

```
python tensorflow/tensorflow/examples/speech_commands/train.py \
  --model_architecture=tiny_conv --window_stride=20 --preprocess=micro \
```

```
--wanted_words="on,off" --silence_percentage=25 --unknown_percentage=25 \
--quantize=1 --verbosity=INFO --how_many_training_steps="15000,3000" \
--learning_rate="0.001,0.0001" --summaries_dir=/tmp/retrain_logs \
--data_dir=/tmp/speech_dataset --train_dir=/tmp/speech_commands_train
```

After training, run the following script to freeze the model:

```
python tensorflow/tensorflow/examples/speech_commands/freeze.py \
--model_architecture=tiny_conv --window_stride=20 --preprocess=micro \
--wanted_words="on,off" --quantize=1 --output_file=/tmp/tiny_conv.pb \
--start_checkpoint=/tmp/speech_commands_train/tiny_conv.ckpt-18000
```

Next, convert the model to the TensorFlow Lite format:

```
toco
--graph_def_file=/tmp/tiny_conv.pb --output_file=/tmp/tiny_conv.tflite \
--input_shapes=1,49,40,1 --input_arrays=Reshape_2 \
--output_arrays='labels_softmax' \
--inference_type=QUANTIZED_UINT8 --mean_values=0 --std_dev_values=9.8077
```

Finally, convert the file into a C source file that you can compile into an embedded system:

```
xxd -i /tmp/tiny_conv.tflite > /tmp/tiny_conv_micro_features_model_data.cc
```

How the Model Works

Now that you know how to train your own model, let's explore how it works. So far, we've treated the machine learning model as a black box—something that we feed training data into, and eventually it figures out how to predict results. It's not essential to understand what's happening under the hood to use the model, but it can be helpful for debugging problems, and it's interesting in its own right. This section gives you some insights into how the model comes up with its predictions.

Visualizing the Inputs

Figure 8-17 illustrates what is actually being fed into the neural network. This is a 2D array with a single channel, so we can visualize it as a monochrome image. We're working with 16 KHz audio sample data, so how do we get to this representation from that source? The process is an example of what's known as "feature generation" in machine learning, and the goal is to turn an input format that's more difficult to work with (in this case 16,000 numerical values representing a second of audio) into something that's easier for a machine learning model to make sense of. You might not have encountered this if you've previously studied machine vision use cases for deep learning, because it happens that images are usually comparatively easy for a network to take as inputs without much preprocessing; but in a lot of other domains, like audio and natural language processing, it's still common to transform the input before feeding it into a model.

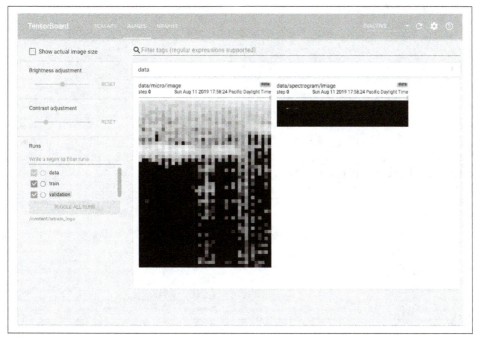

Figure 8-17. The IMAGES tab of TensorBoard

To develop an intuition for why it's easier for our model to deal with preprocessed input, let's look at the original raw representations of some audio recordings, as presented in Figures 8-18 through 8-21.

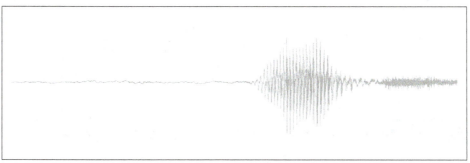

Figure 8-18. Waveform of an audio recording of someone saying "yes"

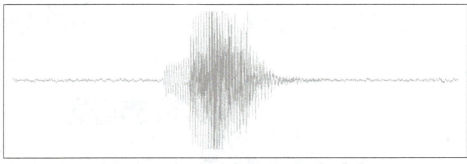

Figure 8-19. Waveform of an audio recording of someone saying "no"

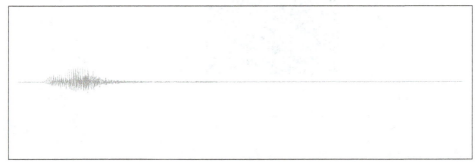

Figure 8-20. Another waveform of an audio recording of someone saying "yes"

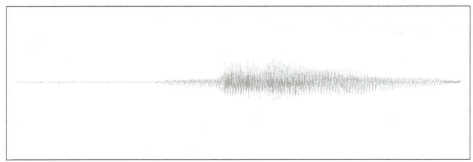

Figure 8-21. Another waveform of an audio recording of someone saying "no"

Without the labels, you'd have trouble distinguishing which pairs of waveforms represented the same words. Now look at Figures 8-22 through 8-25, which shows the result of running those same one-second recordings through feature generation.

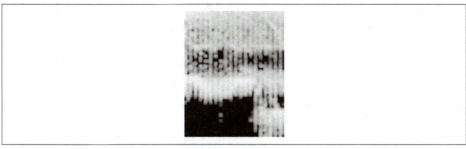

Figure 8-22. Spectrogram of an audio recording of someone saying "yes"

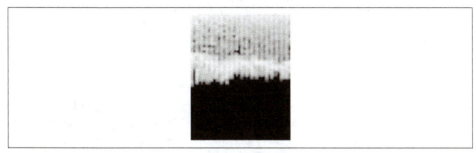

Figure 8-23. Spectrogram of an audio recording of someone saying "no"

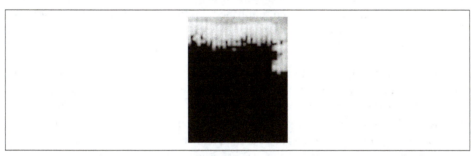

Figure 8-24. Another spectrogram of an audio recording of someone saying "yes"

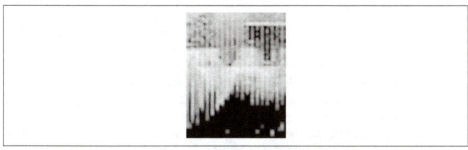

Figure 8-25. Another spectrogram of an audio recording of someone saying "no"

These still aren't simple to interpret, but hopefully you can see that both of the "yes" spectrograms have a shape a bit like an inverted L, and the "no" features show a different shape. We can discern the difference between spectrograms more easily than raw waveforms, and hopefully it's intuitive that it is easier for models to do the same.

Another aspect to this is that the generated spectrograms are a lot smaller than the sample data. Each spectrogram consist of 1,960 numeric values, whereas the waveform has 16,000. They are a summary of the audio data, which reduces the amount of work that the neural network must do. It is in fact possible for a specifically designed model, like DeepMind's WaveNet (*https://oreil.ly/IH9J3*), to take raw sample data as its input instead, but the resulting models tend to involve more computation than the combination of a neural network fed with hand-engineered features that we're using, so for resource-constrained environments like embedded systems, we prefer the approach used here.

How Does Feature Generation Work?

If you've had experience working with audio processing, you might be familiar with approaches like mel-frequency cepstral coefficients (MFCCs) (*https://oreil.ly/HTAev*). This is a common approach to generating the kind of spectrograms we're working with, but our example actually uses a related but different approach. It's the same method used in production across Google, which means that it has had a lot of practical validation, but it hasn't been published in the research literature. Here, we describe roughly how it works, but for the details the best reference is the code itself (*https://oreil.ly/NeOnW*).

The process begins by generating a Fourier transform, (also known as a fast Fourier transform or FFT) for a given time slice—in our case 30 ms of audio data. This FFT is generated on data that's been filtered with a Hann window (*https://oreil.ly/jhn8c*), a bell-shaped function that reduces the influence of samples at either end of the 30-ms window. A Fourier transform produces complex numbers with real and imaginary components for every frequency, but all we care about is the overall energy, so we sum the squares of the two components and then apply a square root to get a magnitude for each frequency bucket.

Given N samples, a Fourier transform produces information on $N/2$ frequencies. 30 ms at a rate of 16,000 samples per second requires 480 samples, and because our FFT algorithm needs a power of two input, we pad that with zeros to 512 samples, giving us 256 frequency buckets. This is larger than we need, so to shrink it down we average adjacent frequencies into 40 downsampled buckets. This downsampling isn't linear, though; instead, it uses the human perception–based mel frequency scale to give more weight to lower frequencies so that there are more buckets available for them, and higher frequencies are merged into broader buckets. Figure 8-26 presents a diagram of that process.

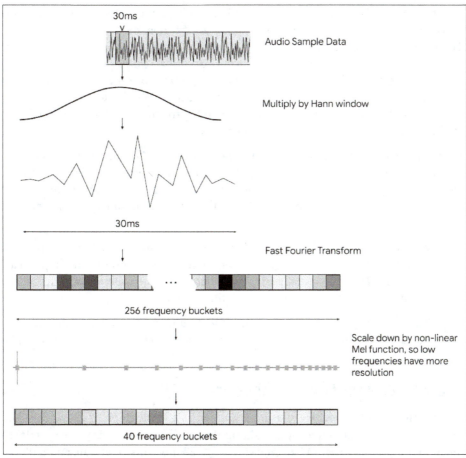

Figure 8-26. Diagram of the feature-generation process

One unusual aspect of this feature generator is that it then includes a noise reduction step. This works by keeping a running average of the value in each frequency bucket and then subtracting this average from the current value. The idea is that background noise will be fairly constant over time and show up in particular frequencies. By subtracting the running average, we have a good chance of removing some of the effect of that noise and leaving the more rapidly changing speech that we're interested in intact. The tricky part is that the feature generator does retain state to track the running averages for each bucket, so if you're trying to reproduce the same spectrogram output for a given input—like we try to for testing (*https://oreil.ly/HtPve*)—you will need to reset that state to the correct values.

Another part of the noise reduction that initially surprised us was its use of different coefficients for the odd and even frequency buckets. This results in the distinctive comb-tooth patterns that you can see in the final generated feature images (Figures

8-22 through 8-25). Initially we thought this was a bug, but on talking to the original implementors, we learned that it was actually added deliberately to help performance. There's an extended discussion of this approach in section 4.3 of the "Trainable Frontend for Robust and Far-Field Keyword Spotting" (*https://oreil.ly/QZ4Yb*), by Yuxuan Wang et al. which also includes the background to some of the other design decisions that went into this feature generation pipeline. We also tested it empirically with our model, and removing the difference in the treatment of odd and even buckets did noticeably reduce accuracy in evaluations.

We then use per-channel amplitude normalization (PCAN) auto-gain to boost the signal based on the running average noise. Finally, we apply a log scale to all the bucket values, so that relatively loud frequencies don't drown out quieter portions of the spectrum—a normalization that helps the subsequent model work with the features.

This process is repeated 49 times in total, with a 30-ms window that's moved forward 20 ms each time between iterations, to cover the full one second of audio input data. This produces a 2D array of values that's 40 elements wide (one for each frequency bucket) and 49 rows high (one row for each time slice).

If this all sounds very complicated to implement, don't worry. Because the code that implements it is all open source, you're welcome to reuse it in your own audio projects.

Understanding the Model Architecture

The neural network model we're using is defined as a small graph of operations. You can find the code that defines it at training time in the `create_tiny_conv_model()` function (*https://oreil.ly/fMARv*), and Figure 8-27 presents a visualization of the result.

This model consists of a convolutional layer, followed by a fully connected layer, and then a softmax layer at the end. In the figure the convolutional layer is labeled as "DepthwiseConv2D," but this is just a quirk of the TensorFlow Lite converter (it turns out that a convolutional layer with a single-channel input image can also be expressed as a depthwise convolution). You'll also see a layer labeled "Reshape_1," but this is just an input placeholder rather than a real operation.

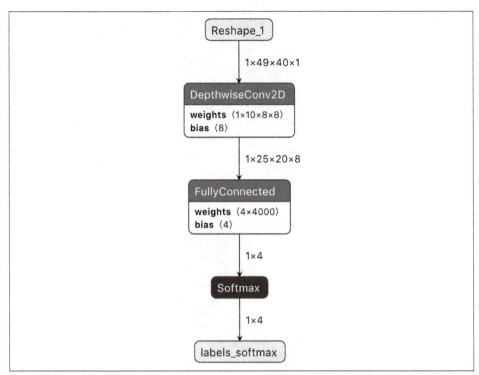

Figure 8-27. Graph visualization of the speech recognition model, courtesy of the Netron tool (https://oreil.ly/UiuXU)

Convolutional layers are used for spotting 2D patterns in input images. Each filter is a rectangular array of values that is moved as a sliding window across the input, and the output image is a representation of how closely the input and filter match at every point. You can think of the convolution operation as moving a series of rectangular filters across the image, with the result at each pixel for each filter corresponding to how similar the filter is to that patch in the image. In our case, each filter is 8 pixels wide and 10 high, and there are 8 of them in total. Figures 8-28 through 8-35 show what they look like.

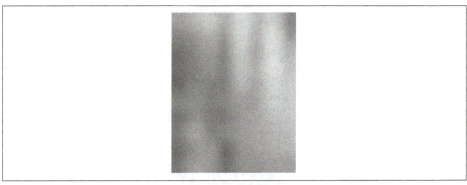

Figure 8-28. First filter image

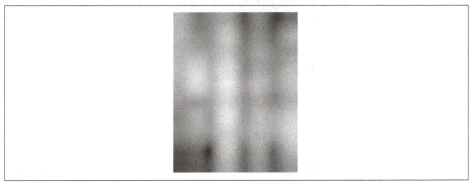

Figure 8-29. Second filter image

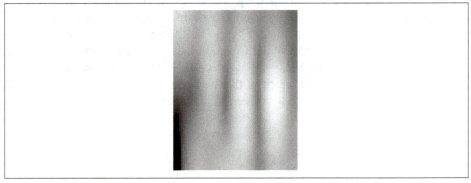

Figure 8-30. Third filter image

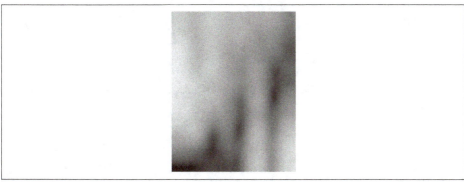

Figure 8-31. Fourth filter image

Figure 8-32. Fifth filter image

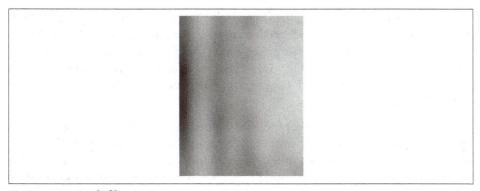

Figure 8-33. Sixth filter image

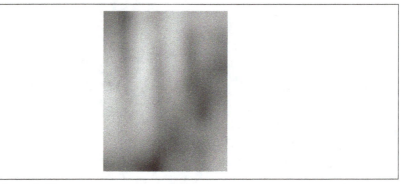

Figure 8-34. Seventh filter image

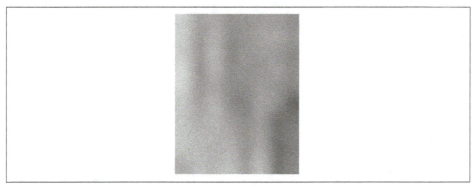

Figure 8-35. Eighth filter image

You can think of each of these filters as a small patch of the input image. The operation is trying to match this small patch to parts of the input image that look similar. Where the image is similar to the patch, a high value will be written into the corresponding part of the output image. Intuitively, each filter is a pattern that the model has learned to look for in the training inputs to help it distinguish between the different classes that it has to deal with.

Because we have eight filters, there will be eight different output images, each corresponding to the respective filter's match value as it's slid across the input. These filter outputs are actually combined into a single output image with eight channels. We have set the stride to be two in both directions, which means we slide each filter by two pixels each time, rather than just by one. Because we're skipping every other position, this means our output image is half the size of the input.

You can see in the visualization that the input image is 49 pixels high and 40 wide, with a single channel, which is what we'd expect given the feature spectrograms we discussed in the previous section. Because we're skipping every other pixel in the horizontal and vertical directions when we slide the convolutional filters across the input, the output of the convolution is half the size, or 25 pixels high and 20 wide. There are eight filters though, so the image becomes eight channels deep.

The next operation is a fully connected layer. This is a different kind of pattern matching process. Instead of sliding a small window across the input, there's a weight for every value in the input tensor. The result is an indication of how closely the input matches the weights, after comparing every value. You can think of this as a global pattern match, where you have an ideal result that you'd expect to get as an input, and the output is how close that ideal (held in the weights) is to the actual input. Each class in our model has its own weights, so there's an ideal pattern for "silence," "unknown," "yes," and "no," and four output values are generated. There are 4,000 values in the input (25 * 20 * 8), so each class is represented by 4,000 weights.

The last layer is a softmax. This effectively helps increase the difference between the highest output and its nearest competitors, which doesn't change their relative order (whichever class produced the largest value from the fully connected layer will remain the highest) but does help produce a more useful score. This score is often informally referred to as a *probability*, but strictly speaking you can't reliably use it like that without more calibration on what the mix of input data actually is. For example, if you had more words in the detector, it's likely that an uncommon one like "antidisestablishmentarianism" would be less likely to show up than something like "okay," but depending on the distribution of the training data that might not be reflected in the raw scores.

As well as these major layers, there are biases that are added on to the results of the fully connected and convolutional layers to help tweak their outputs, and a rectified linear unit (ReLU) activation function after each. The ReLU just makes sure that no output is less than zero, setting any negative results to a minimum of zero. This type of activation function was one of the breakthroughs that enabled deep learning to become much more effective: it helps the training process converge much more quickly than the network would otherwise.

Understanding the Model Output

The end result of the model is the output of the softmax layer. This is four numbers, one for each of "silence," "unknown," "yes," and "no." These values are the scores for each category, and the one with the highest score is the model's prediction, with the score representing the confidence the model has in its prediction. As an example, if the model output is [10, 4, 231, 80], it's predicting that the third category, "yes," is the most likely result with a score of 231. (We're giving these values in their quantized forms, between 0 and 255, but because these are just relative scores it's not usually necessary to convert them back to their real-valued equivalents.)

One thing that's tricky is that this result is based on analyzing the entire last second of audio. If we run it only once per second, we might end up with an utterance that is half in the previous second, and half in the current. It's not possible for any model to do a good job recognizing a word when it hears only a part of it, so in that case the word spotting would fail. To overcome this, we need to run the model more often than once per second to give us as high a chance as possible of catching an entire word in our one-second window. In practice, we've found we have to run it 10 or 15 times per second to achieve good results.

If we're getting all of these results coming in so fast, how do we decide when a score is high enough? We implement a postprocessing class that averages the scores over time and triggers a recognition only when we've had several high scores for the same word in a short amount of time. You can see the implementation of this in the `Recognize` `Commands class` (*https://oreil.ly/FuYfL*). This is fed the raw results from the model, and then it uses an accumulation and averaging algorithm to determine whether any of the categories have crossed the threshold. These postprocessed results are then fed to the `CommandResponder` (*https://oreil.ly/b8ArK*) to take an action, depending on the platform's output capabilities.

The model parameters are all learned from the training data, but the algorithm used by the command recognizer was manually created, so all of the thresholds (*https://oreil.ly/tfNfr*)—like the score value required to trigger a recognition, or the time window of positive results needed—have been hand-picked. This means that there's no guarantee they are optimal, so if you're seeing poor results in your own application, you might want to try tweaking them yourself.

More sophisticated speech recognition models typically use a model that's able to take in streaming data (like a recursive neural network) rather than the single-layer convolutional network we show in this chapter. Having the streaming baked into the model design means that you don't need to do the postprocessing to get accurate results, though it does make the training significantly more complicated.

Training with Your Own Data

It's not very likely that the product you want to build only needs to respond to "yes" and "no," so you'll want to train a model that is sensitive to the audio you care about. The training script we used earlier has been designed to let you create custom models using your own data. The toughest part of the process is usually gathering a large enough dataset, and ensuring that it's appropriate for your problem. We discuss general approaches to data gathering and cleaning in Chapter 16, but this section covers some of the ways in which you can train your own audio model.

The Speech Commands Dataset

The *train.py* script downloads the Speech Commands dataset by default. This is an open source collection of more than 100,000 one-second WAV files, covering a variety of short words from a lot of different speakers. It's distributed by Google, but the utterances have been collected from volunteers around the world. "Visual Wake Words Dataset" (*https://oreil.ly/EC6nd*) by Aakanksha Chowdhery et al. provides more details.

As well as *yes* and *no*, the dataset includes eight other command words (*on*, *off*, *up*, *down*, *left*, *right*, *stop* and *go*), and the 10 digits from *zero* through *nine*. There are several thousand examples of each of these words. There are also other words, like *Marvin*, that have a lot fewer examples each. The command words are intended to have enough utterances that you can train a reasonable model to recognize them. The other words are intended to be used to populate an *unknown* category, so a model can spot when a word it's not been trained on is uttered, instead of mistaking it for a command.

Because the training script uses this dataset, you can easily train a model on a combination of some of the command words that have lots of examples. If you update the `--wanted_words` argument with a comma-separated list of words present in the training set and run training from scratch, you should find you can create a useful model. The main things to watch out for are that you are restricting yourself to the 10 command words and/or digits, or you won't have enough examples to train accurately, and that you adjust the `--silence_percentage` and `--unknown_percentage` values down if you have more than two wanted words. These last two arguments control how many silent and unknown samples are mixed in during training. The *silent* examples aren't actually complete silence; instead, they're randomly selected one-second snippets of recorded background noise, pulled from the WAVs in the *background* folder of the dataset. The *unknown* samples are utterances picked from any of the words that are in the training set, but aren't in the `wanted_words` list. This is why we have a selection of miscellaneous words in the dataset with comparatively few utterances each; it gives us the chance to recognize that a lot of different words aren't actually the ones we're looking for. This is a particular problem with speech and audio recognition, because our products often need to operate in environments in which there are a lot of words and noises we might never have encountered in training. There are many thousands of different words that could show up just in common English, and to be useful, a model must be able to ignore those on which it hasn't been trained. That's why the *unknown* category is so important in practice.

Here is an example of training on different words using the existing dataset:

```
python tensorflow/examples/speech_commands/train.py \
  --model_architecture=tiny_conv --window_stride=20 --preprocess=micro \
```

```
--wanted_words="up,down,left,right" --silence_percentage=15 \
--unknown_percentage=15 --quantize=1
```

Training on Your Own Dataset

The default for the training script is to use Speech Commands, but if you have your own dataset, you can use the `--data_dir` argument to use it, instead. The directory you're pointing to should be organized like Speech Commands, with one subfolder per class that you want to recognize, each containing a set of WAV files. You should also have a special *background* subfolder that contains longer WAV recordings of the kind of background noise you expect your application to encounter. You'll also need to pick a recognition duration if the default of one second doesn't work for your use case, and specify it through the `--sample_duration_ms` argument. Then you can set the classes that you want to recognize using the `--wanted_words` argument. Despite the name, these classes can be any kind of audio event, from breaking glass to laughter; as long as you have enough WAVs of each class the training process should work just as it does for speech.

If you had folders of WAVs named *glass* and *laughter* inside a root */tmp/my_wavs* directory, here's how you could train your own model:

```
python tensorflow/examples/speech_commands/train.py \
  --model_architecture=tiny_conv --window_stride=20 --preprocess=micro \
  --data_url="" --data_dir=/tmp/my_wavs/ --wanted_words="laughter,glass" \
  --silence_percentage=25 --unknown_percentage=25 --quantize=1
```

The most difficult part often is finding enough data. As an example, it turns out that the real sound of breaking glass is very different from the sound effects we're used to hearing in movies. This means that you need to either find existing recordings, or arrange to record some yourself. Because the training process can require many thousand examples of each class, and they need to cover all of the variations that are likely to occur in a real application, this data-gathering process can be frustrating, expensive, and time-consuming.

A common solution for this with image models is to use *transfer learning*, where you take a model that's been trained on a large public dataset and fine-tune its weights on different classes using other data. This approach doesn't require nearly as many examples in the secondary dataset as you would need if you were training from scratch with it, and it often produces high-accuracy results. Unfortunately transfer learning for speech models is still being researched, but watch this space.

How to Record Your Own Audio

If you need to capture audio of words you care about, it's a lot easier if you have a tool that prompts speakers and splits the result into labeled files. The Speech Commands dataset was recorded using the Open Speech Recording app (*https://oreil.ly/UWsG3*), a hosted app that lets users record utterances through most common web browsers. As a user, you'll see a web page that first asks you to agree to being recorded, with a default Google agreement, that's easily changeable (*https://oreil.ly/z5vka*). After you have agreed, you're sent to a new page that has recording controls. When you press the record button, words will appear as prompts, and the audio you say for each word is recorded. When all of the requested words have been recorded, you'll be asked to submit the results to the server.

There are instructions in the README for running it on Google Cloud, but it's a Flask app written in Python, so you should be able to port it to other environments. If you are using Google Cloud, you'll need to update the *app.yaml* (*https://oreil.ly/dV2kv*) file to point to your own storage bucket and supply your own random session key (this is used just for hashing, so it can be any value). To customize which words are recorded, you'll need to edit a couple of arrays in the client-side JavaScript (*https://oreil.ly/XcJIe*): one for the frequently repeated main words, and one for the secondary fillers.

The recorded files are stored as OGG compressed audio in the Google Cloud bucket, but training requires WAVs, so you need to convert them. It's also likely that some of your recordings contain errors, like people forgetting to say the word or saying it too quietly, so it's helpful to automatically filter out those mistakes where possible. If you have set up your bucket name in a BUCKET_NAME variable, you can begin by copying your files to a local machine by using these bash commands:

```
mkdir oggs
gsutil -m cp gs://${BUCKET_NAME}/* oggs/
```

One nice property of the compressed OGG format is that quiet or silent audio results in very small files, so a good first step is removing any that are particularly tiny, like so:

```
find ${BASEDIR}/oggs -iname "*.ogg" -size -5k -delete
```

The easiest way we've found to convert OGGs to WAVs is using the FFmpeg project (*https://ffmpeg.org/*), which offers a command-line tool. Here are a set of commands that can convert an entire directory of OGG files into the format we need:

```
mkdir -p ${BASEDIR}/wavs
find ${BASEDIR}/oggs -iname "*.ogg" -print0 | \
  xargs -0 basename -s .ogg | \
  xargs -I {} ffmpeg -i ${BASEDIR}/oggs/{}.ogg -ar 16000 ${BASEDIR}/wavs/{}.wav
```

The Open Speech Recording application records more than one second for each word. This ensures that the user's utterance is captured even if their timing is a bit earlier or later than we expect. The training requires one-second recordings, and it works best if the word is centered in the middle of each recording. We've created a small open source utility to look at the volume of each recording over time to try to get the centering right and trim the audio so that it is just one second. Enter the following commands in your terminal to use it:

```
git clone https://github.com/petewarden/extract_loudest_section \
    /tmp/extract_loudest_section_github
pushd /tmp/extract_loudest_section_github
make
popd
mkdir -p ${BASEDIR}/trimmed_wavs
/tmp/extract_loudest_section/gen/bin/extract_loudest_section \
    ${BASEDIR}'/wavs/*.wav' ${BASEDIR}/trimmed_wavs/
```

This will give you a folder full of files in the correct format and of the required length, but the training process needs the WAVs organized into subfolders by labels. The label is encoded in the name of each file, so we have an example Python script (*https://oreil.ly/BpQBJ*) that uses those filenames to sort them into the appropriate folders.

Data Augmentation

Data augmentation is another method to effectively enlarge your training data and improve accuracy. In practice, this means taking recorded utterances and applying audio transformations to them before they're used for training. These transforms can include altering the volume, mixing in background noise, or trimming the start or end of the clips slightly. The training script applies all of these transformations by default, but you can adjust how often they're used and how strongly they're applied using command-line arguments.

This kind of augmentation does help make a small dataset go further, but it can't work miracles. If you apply transformations too strongly, you can end up distorting the training inputs so much that they'd no longer be recognizable by a person, which can cause the model to mistakenly start triggering on sounds that bear no resemblance to the intended categories.

Here's how you can use some of those command-line arguments to control the augmentation:

```
python tensorflow/examples/speech_commands/train.py \
    --model_architecture=tiny_conv --window_stride=20 --preprocess=micro \
    --wanted_words="yes,no" --silence_percentage=25 --unknown_percentage=25 \
    --quantize=1 --background_volume=0.2 --background_frequency=0.7 \
    --time_shift_ms=200
```

Model Architectures

The "yes"/"no" model we trained earlier was designed to be small and fast. It's only 18 KB, and requires 400,000 arithmetic operations to execute once. To fit within those constraints, it trades off accuracy. If you're designing your own application, you might want to make different trade-offs, especially if you're trying to recognize more than two categories. You can specify your own model architectures by modifying the *models.py* file and then using the `--model_architecture` argument. You'll need to write your own model creation function, like `create_tiny_conv_model0` but with the layers you want in your model specified instead. Then, you can update the `if` statement in `create_model0` to give your architecture a name, and call your new creation function when it's passed in as the architecture argument on the command line. You can look at some of the existing creation functions for inspiration, including how to handle dropout. If you have added your own model code, here's how you can call it:

```
python tensorflow/examples/speech_commands/train.py \
  --model_architecture=my_model_name --window_stride=20 --preprocess=micro \
  --wanted_words="yes,no" --silence_percentage=25 \--unknown_percentage=25 \
  --quantize=1
```

Wrapping Up

Recognizing spoken words with a small memory footprint is a tricky real-world problem, and tackling it requires us to work with many more components than we need to for a simpler example. Most production machine learning applications require thinking about issues like feature generation, model architecture choices, data augmentation, finding the best-suited training data, and how to turn the results of a model into actionable information.

There are a lot of trade-offs to consider depending on the actual requirements of your product, and hopefully you now understand some of the options you have as you try to move from training into deployment.

In the next chapter, we explore how to run inference with a different type of data that, although *seemingly* more complex than audio, is surprisingly easy to work with.

## CHAPTER 9

Person Detection: Building an Application

If you asked people which of their senses has the biggest impact on their day-to-day lives, many would answer vision.[1]

Vision is a profoundly useful sense. It allows countless natural organisms to navigate their environments, find sources of food, and avoid running into danger. As humans, vision helps us recognize our friends, interpret symbolic information, and understand the world around us—without having to get too close.

Until quite recently, the power of vision was not available to machines. Most of our robots merely poked around the world with touch and proximity sensors, gleaning knowledge of its structure from a series of collisions. At a glance, a person can describe to you the shape, properties, and purpose of an object, without having to interact with it at all. A robot would have no such luck. Visual information was just too messy, unstructured, and difficult to interpret.

With the evolution of convolutional neural networks, it's become easy to build programs that can *see*. Inspired by the structure of the mammalian visual cortex, CNNs learn to make sense of our visual world, filtering an overwhelmingly complex input into a map of known patterns and shapes. The precise combination of these pieces can tell us the entities that are present in a given digital image.

Today, vision models are used for many different tasks. Autonomous vehicles use vision to spot hazards on the road. Factory robots use cameras to catch defective parts. Researchers have trained models that can diagnose disease from medical images. And there's a fair chance your smartphone spots faces in photographs, to make sure they're perfectly in focus.

---

1 In a 2018 YouGov poll (*https://oreil.ly/KvzGk*), 70% of respondents said that they would miss sight the most if they lost it.

Machines with sight could help transform our homes and cities, automating chores that were previously out of reach. But vision is an intimate sense. Most of us don't like the thought of our actions being recorded, or our lives being streamed to the cloud, which is traditionally where ML inference is done.

Imagine a household appliance that can "see" with a built-in camera. It could be a security system that can spot intruders, a stove that knows it's been left unattended, or a television that shuts off when there's no one in the room. In each of these cases, privacy is critical. Even if no human being ever watches the footage, the security implications of internet-connected cameras embedded in always-on devices make them unappealing to most consumers.

But all this changes with TinyML. Picture a smart stove that shuts off its burners if it's left unattended for too long. If it can "see" there's a cook nearby using a tiny microcontroller, without any connection to the internet, we get all of the benefits of a smart device without any of the privacy trade-offs.

Even more, tiny devices with vision can go where no sight-enabled machines have dared to go before. With its miniscule power consumption, a microcontroller-based vision system could run for months or years on a tiny battery. Planted in the jungle, or a coral reef, these devices could keep count of endangered animals without the need to be online.

The same technology makes it possible to build a vision sensor as a self-contained electronic component. The sensor outputs a 1 if a certain object is in view and a 0 if it is not, but it never shares any of the image data collected by its camera. This type of sensor could be embedded in all kinds of products—from smart home systems to personal vehicles. Your bicycle could flash a light when a car is behind you. Your air conditioner could know when someone's home. And because the image data never leaves the self-contained sensor, it's guaranteed secure, even if the product is connected to the internet.

The application we explore in this chapter uses a pretrained person-detection model, running on a microcontroller with a camera attached, to know when a human being is in view. In Chapter 10, you will learn how this model works, and how to train your own models that detect whatever you want.

After reading this chapter, you'll understand how to work with camera data on a microcontroller and how to run inference with a vision model and interpret the output. You might be surprised how easy it actually is!

What We're Building

We're going to build an embedded application that uses a model to classify images captured by a camera. The model is trained to recognize when a person is present in the camera input. This means that our application will be able to detect the presence or absence of a person and produce an output accordingly.

This is, essentially, the smart vision sensor we described a little earlier. When a person is detected, our example code will light an LED—but you can extend it to control all sorts of projects.

As with the application we worked on in Chapter 7, you can find the source code for this application in the TensorFlow GitHub repository (*https://oreil.ly/9aLhs*).

Like in the previous chapters, we first walk through the tests and the application code, followed by the logic that makes the sample work on various devices.

We provide instructions for deploying the application to the following microcontroller platforms:

- Arduino Nano 33 BLE Sense (*https://oreil.ly/6qlMD*)
- SparkFun Edge (*https://oreil.ly/-hoL-*)

TensorFlow Lite regularly adds support for new devices, so if the device you'd like to use isn't listed here, it's worth checking the example's *README.md* (*https://oreil.ly/6gRlo*). You can also check there for updated deployment instructions if you run into trouble following these steps.

Unlike with the previous chapters, you'll need some additional hardware to run this application. Because neither of these boards have an integrated camera, we recommend buying a *camera module*. You'll find this information in each device's section.

Camera Modules

Camera modules are electronic components based on *image sensors*, which capture image data digitally. The image sensor is combined with a lens and control electronics and the module is manufactured in a form that is easy to attach to an electronics project.

Let's begin by walking through our application's structure. It's a lot simpler than you might expect.

Application Architecture

By now, we've established that embedded machine learning applications do the following sequence of things:

1. Obtain an input.
2. Preprocess the input to extract features suitable to feed into a model.
3. Run inference on the processed input.
4. Postprocess the model's output to make sense of it.
5. Use the resulting information to make things happen.

In Chapter 7 we saw this applied to wake-word detection, which uses audio as its input. This time around, our input will be image data. This might sound more complicated, but it's actually much simpler to work with than audio.

Image data is commonly represented as an array of pixel values. We'll be obtaining our image data from embedded camera modules, which all provide data in this format. Our model also expects its input to be an array of pixel values. Because of this, we won't have to do much preprocessing before feeding data into our model.

Given that we don't have to do much preprocessing, our app will be fairly straightforward. It takes a snapshot of data from a camera, feeds it into a model, and determines which output class was detected. It then displays the result in some simple manner.

Before we move on, let's learn a little more about the model we'll be using.

Introducing Our Model

Back in Chapter 7, we learned that convolutional neural networks are neural networks designed to work well with multidimensional tensors, for which information is contained in the relationships between groups of adjacent values. They're particularly well suited to working with image data.

Our person-detection model is a convolutional neural network trained on the Visual Wake Words dataset (*https://oreil.ly/EC6nd*). This dataset consists of 115,000 images, each one labeled with whether or not it contains a person.

The model is 250 KB, which is significantly larger than our speech model. As well as occupying more memory, this additional size means that it will take a lot longer to run a single inference.

The model accepts 96 × 96–pixel grayscale images as input. Each image is provided as a 3D tensor with shape (96, 96, 1), where the final dimension contains an 8-bit value that represents a single pixel. The value specifies the shade of the pixel, ranging from 0 (fully black) to 255 (fully white).

Our camera modules can return images in a variety of resolutions, so we need to ensure they are resized to 96 × 96 pixels. We also need to convert full-color images to grayscale so that they work with the model.

You might think 96 × 96 pixels sounds like a tiny resolution, but it will be more than sufficient to allow us to detect a person in each image. Models that work with images often accept surprisingly small resolutions. Increasing a model's input size gives diminishing returns, and the complexity of the network increases greatly as the size of the input scales. For this reason, even state-of-the-art image classification models commonly work with a maximum of 320 × 320 pixels.

The model outputs two probabilities: one indicating the probability that a person was present in the input, and another indicating the probability that there was nobody there. The probabilities range from 0 to 255.

Our person detection model uses the *MobileNet* architecture, which is a well-known and battle-tested architecture designed for image classification on devices like mobile phones. In Chapter 10, you will learn how this model was adapted to fit on microcontrollers and how you can train your own. For now, let's continue exploring how our application works.

All the Moving Parts

Figure 9-1 shows the structure of our person detection application.

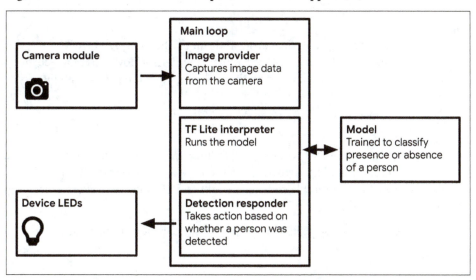

Figure 9-1. The components of our person detection application

As we mentioned previously, this is a lot simpler than the wake-word application, because we can pass image data directly into the model—there's no preprocessing required.

Another aspect that keeps things simple is that we don't average the model's output. Our wake-word model ran multiple times per second, so we had to average its output to get a stable result. Our person detection model is much larger, and it takes a lot longer to run inference. This means that there's no need to average its output.

The code has five main parts:

Main loop

Like the other examples, our application runs in a continuous loop. However, because our model is a lot larger and more complex, it will take longer to run inference. Depending on the device, we can expect one inference every few seconds rather than several inferences per second.

Image provider

This component captures image data from the camera and writes it to the input tensor. The methods for capturing images vary from device to device, so this component can be overridden and customized.

TensorFlow Lite interpreter

The interpreter runs the TensorFlow Lite model, transforming the input image into a set of probabilities.

Model

The model is included as a data array and run by the interpreter. At 250 KB, this model is unreasonably large to commit to the TensorFlow GitHub repository. Because of this, it is downloaded by the Makefile when the project is built. If you want to take a look, you can download it yourself at *tf_lite_micro_person_data_grayscale.zip* (*https://oreil.ly/Ylq9m*).

Detection responder

The detection responder takes the probabilities output by the model and uses the device's output capabilities to display them. We can override it for different device types. In our example code it will light an LED, but you can extend it to do pretty much anything.

To get a sense for how these parts fit together, we'll take a look at their tests.

Walking Through the Tests

This application is nice and simple, since there are only a few tests to walk through. You can find them all in the GitHub repository (*https://oreil.ly/31vB5*):

person_detection_test.cc (https://oreil.ly/r4ny8)
> Shows how to run inference on an array representing a single image

image_provider_test.cc (https://oreil.ly/Js6M3)
> Shows how to use the image provider to capture an image

detection_responder_test.cc (https://oreil.ly/KBVLF)
> Shows how to use the detection responder to output the results of detection

Let's begin by exploring *person_detection_test.cc* to see how inference is run on image data. Because this is the third example we've walked through, this code should feel pretty familiar. You're well on your way to being an embedded ML developer!

The Basic Flow

First up, *person_detection_test.cc*. We begin by pulling in the ops that our model is going to need:

```
namespace tflite {
namespace ops {
namespace micro {
TfLiteRegistration* Register_DEPTHWISE_CONV_2D();
TfLiteRegistration* Register_CONV_2D();
TfLiteRegistration* Register_AVERAGE_POOL_2D();
}  // namespace micro
}  // namespace ops
}  // namespace tflite
```

Next, we define a tensor arena that is appropriately sized for the model. As usual, this number was determined by trial and error:

```
const int tensor_arena_size = 70 * 1024;
uint8_t tensor_arena[tensor_arena_size];
```

We then do the typical setup work, to get the interpreter ready to go, which includes registering the necessary ops using the `MicroMutableOpResolver`:

```
// Set up logging.
tflite::MicroErrorReporter micro_error_reporter;
tflite::ErrorReporter* error_reporter = &micro_error_reporter;

// Map the model into a usable data structure. This doesn't involve any
// copying or parsing, it's a very lightweight operation.
const tflite::Model* model = ::tflite::GetModel(g_person_detect_model_data);
if (model->version() != TFLITE_SCHEMA_VERSION) {
error_reporter->Report(
```

```
    "Model provided is schema version %d not equal "
    "to supported version %d.\n",
    model->version(), TFLITE_SCHEMA_VERSION);
}

// Pull in only the operation implementations we need.
tflite::MicroMutableOpResolver micro_mutable_op_resolver;
micro_mutable_op_resolver.AddBuiltin(
    tflite::BuiltinOperator_DEPTHWISE_CONV_2D,
    tflite::ops::micro::Register_DEPTHWISE_CONV_2D());
micro_mutable_op_resolver.AddBuiltin(tflite::BuiltinOperator_CONV_2D,
                                     tflite::ops::micro::Register_CONV_2D());
micro_mutable_op_resolver.AddBuiltin(
    tflite::BuiltinOperator_AVERAGE_POOL_2D,
    tflite::ops::micro::Register_AVERAGE_POOL_2D());

// Build an interpreter to run the model with.
tflite::MicroInterpreter interpreter(model, micro_mutable_op_resolver,
                                     tensor_arena, tensor_arena_size,
                                     error_reporter);
interpreter.AllocateTensors();
```

Our next step is to inspect the input tensor. We check whether it has the expected number of dimensions and whether its dimensions are sized appropriately:

```
// Get information about the memory area to use for the model's input.
TfLiteTensor* input = interpreter.input(0);

// Make sure the input has the properties we expect.
TF_LITE_MICRO_EXPECT_NE(nullptr, input);
TF_LITE_MICRO_EXPECT_EQ(4, input->dims->size);
TF_LITE_MICRO_EXPECT_EQ(1, input->dims->data[0]);
TF_LITE_MICRO_EXPECT_EQ(kNumRows, input->dims->data[1]);
TF_LITE_MICRO_EXPECT_EQ(kNumCols, input->dims->data[2]);
TF_LITE_MICRO_EXPECT_EQ(kNumChannels, input->dims->data[3]);
TF_LITE_MICRO_EXPECT_EQ(kTfLiteUInt8, input->type);
```

From this, we can see that the input is technically a 5D tensor. The first dimension is just a wrapper containing a single element. The subsequent two dimensions represent the rows and columns of the image's pixels. The final dimension holds the number of color channels used to represent each pixel.

The constants that tell us the expected dimensions, kNumRows, kNumCols, and kNum Channels, are defined in *model_settings.h* (*https://oreil.ly/ae2OI*). They look like this:

```
constexpr int kNumCols = 96;
constexpr int kNumRows = 96;
constexpr int kNumChannels = 1;
```

As you can see, the model is expected to accept a 96 × 96–pixel bitmap. The image will be grayscale, with one color channel for each pixel.

Next in the code, we copy a test image into the input tensor using a straightforward for loop:

```
// Copy an image with a person into the memory area used for the input.
const uint8_t* person_data = g_person_data;
for (int i = 0; i < input->bytes; ++i) {
    input->data.uint8[i] = person_data[i];
}
```

The variable that stores image data, g_person_data, is defined by *person_image_data.h*. To avoid adding more large files to the repository, the data itself is downloaded along with the model, as part of *tf_lite_micro_person_data_grayscale.zip*, when the tests are first run.

After we've populated the input tensor, we run inference. It's just as simple as ever:

```
// Run the model on this input and make sure it succeeds.
TfLiteStatus invoke_status = interpreter.Invoke();
if (invoke_status != kTfLiteOk) {
    error_reporter->Report("Invoke failed\n");
}
TF_LITE_MICRO_EXPECT_EQ(kTfLiteOk, invoke_status);
```

We now check the output tensor to make sure it's the expected size and shape:

```
TfLiteTensor* output = interpreter.output(0);
TF_LITE_MICRO_EXPECT_EQ(4, output->dims->size);
TF_LITE_MICRO_EXPECT_EQ(1, output->dims->data[0]);
TF_LITE_MICRO_EXPECT_EQ(1, output->dims->data[1]);
TF_LITE_MICRO_EXPECT_EQ(1, output->dims->data[2]);
TF_LITE_MICRO_EXPECT_EQ(kCategoryCount, output->dims->data[3]);
TF_LITE_MICRO_EXPECT_EQ(kTfLiteUInt8, output->type);
```

The model's output has four dimensions. The first three are just wrappers around the fourth, which contains one element for each category the model was trained on.

The total number of categories is available as a constant, kCategoryCount, which resides in *model_settings.h* along with some other helpful values:

```
constexpr int kCategoryCount = 3;
constexpr int kPersonIndex = 1;
constexpr int kNotAPersonIndex = 2;
extern const char* kCategoryLabels[kCategoryCount];
```

As kCategoryCount shows, there are three categories in the output. The first happens to be an unused category, which we can ignore. The "person" category comes second, as we can see from its index, stored in the constant kPersonIndex. The "not a person" category comes third, with its index shown by kNotAPersonIndex.

There's also an array of category labels, kCategoryLabels, which is implemented in *model_settings.cc* (*https://oreil.ly/AB0zS*):

```
const char* kCategoryLabels[kCategoryCount] = {
    "unused",
    "person",
    "notperson",
};
```

Extra Dimensions

The output tensor's structure has some redundancy. Why does it have four dimensions when it needs to hold only three values, one for each category probability? And why does it have three categories when we're only attempting to discriminate between "person" and "not a person"?

You'll find that models often have slightly funky input and output shapes, or extra categories that don't seem to do much. Sometimes, this is a characteristic of their architecture; other times it's just an implementation detail. Whatever the reason, we don't need to worry about it. Because the data content of tensors is stored as a flat in-memory array, it doesn't really make much difference whether it is wrapped in unnecessary extra dimensions. We can still access a given element easily via its index.

The next chunk of code logs the "person" and "no person" scores, and asserts that the "person" score is greater—as it should be given that we passed in an image of a person:

```
uint8_t person_score = output->data.uint8[kPersonIndex];
uint8_t no_person_score = output->data.uint8[kNotAPersonIndex];
error_reporter->Report(
    "person data.  person score: %d, no person score: %d\n", person_score,
    no_person_score);
TF_LITE_MICRO_EXPECT_GT(person_score, no_person_score);
```

Since the only data content of the output tensor is the three `uint8` values representing class scores, with the first one being unused, we can access the scores directly by using `output->data.uint8[kPersonIndex]` and `output->data.uint8[kNotAPersonIndex]`. As `uint8` types, they have a minimum value of 0 and a maximum value of 255.

 If the "person" and "no person" scores are similar, it can signify that the model isn't very confident of its prediction. In this case, you might choose to consider the result inconclusive.

Next, we test for an image without a person, held by `g_no_person_data`:

```
const uint8_t* no_person_data = g_no_person_data;
for (int i = 0; i < input->bytes; ++i) {
```

```
  input->data.uint8[i] = no_person_data[i];
}
```

After inference has run, we then assert that the "not a person" score is higher:

```
person_score = output->data.uint8[kPersonIndex];
no_person_score = output->data.uint8[kNotAPersonIndex];
error_reporter->Report(
    "no person data.  person score: %d, no person score: %d\n", person_score,
    no_person_score);
TF_LITE_MICRO_EXPECT_GT(no_person_score, person_score);
```

As you can observe, there's nothing fancy going on here. We may be feeding in images instead of scalars or spectrograms, but the process of inference is similar to what we've seen before.

Running the test is similarly straightforward. Just issue the following command from the root of the TensorFlow repository:

```
make -f tensorflow/lite/micro/tools/make/Makefile \
  test_person_detection_test
```

The first time the test is run, the model and image data will be downloaded. If you want to take a look at the downloaded files, you can find them in *tensorflow/lite/micro/tools/make/downloads/person_model_grayscale*.

Next up, we check out the interface for the image provider.

The Image Provider

The image provider is responsible for grabbing data from the camera and returning it in a format suitable for writing to the model's input tensor. The file *image_provider.h* (*https://oreil.ly/5Vjbe*) defines its interface:

```
TfLiteStatus GetImage(tflite::ErrorReporter* error_reporter, int image_width,
                      int image_height, int channels, uint8_t* image_data);
```

Because its actual implementation is platform-specific, there's a reference implementation in *person_detection/image_provider.cc* (*https://oreil.ly/QoQ3O*) that returns dummy data.

The test in *image_provider_test.cc* (*https://oreil.ly/Nbl9x*) calls this reference implementation to show how it is used. Our first order of business is to create an array to hold the image data. This happens in the following line:

```
uint8_t image_data[kMaxImageSize];
```

The constant kMaxImageSize comes from our old friend, *model_settings.h* (*https://oreil.ly/5naFK*).

After we've set up this array, we can call the GetImage() function to capture an image from the camera:

```
TfLiteStatus get_status =
    GetImage(error_reporter, kNumCols, kNumRows, kNumChannels, image_data);
TF_LITE_MICRO_EXPECT_EQ(kTfLiteOk, get_status);
TF_LITE_MICRO_EXPECT_NE(image_data, nullptr);
```

We call it with an ErrorReporter instance; the number of columns, rows, and channels that we want; and a pointer to our image_data array. The function will write the
image data into this array. We can check the function's return value to determine
whether the capture process was successful; it will be set to kTfLiteError if there is a
problem, or kTfLiteOk otherwise.

Finally, the test walks through the returned data to show that all of the memory locations are readable. Even though the image technically has rows, columns, and channels, in practice the data is flattened into a 1D array:

```
uint32_t total = 0;
for (int i = 0; i < kMaxImageSize; ++i) {
    total += image_data[i];
}
```

To run this test, use the following command:

```
make -f tensorflow/lite/micro/tools/make/Makefile \
  test_image_provider_test
```

We'll examine the device-specific implementations of *image_provider.cc* later in the
chapter; for now, let's take a look at the detection responder's interface.

The Detection Responder

Our final test shows how the detection responder is used. This is the code responsible
for communicating the results of inference. Its interface is defined in *detection_res-
ponder.h* (*https://oreil.ly/cTptj*), and the test is in *detection_responder_test.cc* (*https://
oreil.ly/Igx7a*).

The interface is pretty simple:

```
void RespondToDetection(tflite::ErrorReporter* error_reporter,
                        uint8_t person_score, uint8_t no_person_score);
```

We just call it with the scores for both the "person" and "not a person" categories, and
it will decide what to do from there.

The reference implementation in *detection_responder.cc* (*https://oreil.ly/5Wjjt*) just
logs these values. The test in *detection_responder_test.cc* calls the function a couple of
times:

```
RespondToDetection(error_reporter, 100, 200);
RespondToDetection(error_reporter, 200, 100);
```

To run the test and see the output, use the following command:

```
make -f tensorflow/lite/micro/tools/make/Makefile \
  test_detection_responder_test
```

We've explored all of the tests and the interfaces they exercise. Let's now walk through the program itself.

Detecting People

The application's core functions reside in *main_functions.cc* (*https://oreil.ly/64oHW*). They're short and sweet, and we've seen much of their logic in the tests.

First, we pull in all of the ops that our model needs:

```
namespace tflite {
namespace ops {
namespace micro {
TfLiteRegistration* Register_DEPTHWISE_CONV_2D();
TfLiteRegistration* Register_CONV_2D();
TfLiteRegistration* Register_AVERAGE_POOL_2D();
}  // namespace micro
}  // namespace ops
}  // namespace tflite
```

Next, we declare a bunch of variables to hold the important moving parts:

```
tflite::ErrorReporter* g_error_reporter = nullptr;
const tflite::Model* g_model = nullptr;
tflite::MicroInterpreter* g_interpreter = nullptr;
TfLiteTensor* g_input = nullptr;
```

After that, we allocate some working memory for tensor operations:

```
constexpr int g_tensor_arena_size = 70 * 1024;
static uint8_t tensor_arena[kTensorArenaSize];
```

In the setup() function, which is run before anything else happens, we create an error reporter, load our model, set up an interpreter instance, and grab a reference to the model's input tensor:

```
void setup() {
  // Set up logging.
  static tflite::MicroErrorReporter micro_error_reporter;
  g_error_reporter = &micro_error_reporter;

  // Map the model into a usable data structure. This doesn't involve any
  // copying or parsing, it's a very lightweight operation.
  g_model = tflite::GetModel(g_person_detect_model_data);
  if (g_model->version() != TFLITE_SCHEMA_VERSION) {
    g_error_reporter->Report(
        "Model provided is schema version %d not equal "
        "to supported version %d.",
        g_model->version(), TFLITE_SCHEMA_VERSION);
    return;
```

```
    }

    // Pull in only the operation implementations we need.
    static tflite::MicroMutableOpResolver micro_mutable_op_resolver;
    micro_mutable_op_resolver.AddBuiltin(
        tflite::BuiltinOperator_DEPTHWISE_CONV_2D,
        tflite::ops::micro::Register_DEPTHWISE_CONV_2D());
    micro_mutable_op_resolver.AddBuiltin(tflite::BuiltinOperator_CONV_2D,
                                         tflite::ops::micro::Register_CONV_2D());
    micro_mutable_op_resolver.AddBuiltin(
        tflite::BuiltinOperator_AVERAGE_POOL_2D,
        tflite::ops::micro::Register_AVERAGE_POOL_2D());

    // Build an interpreter to run the model with.
    static tflite::MicroInterpreter static_interpreter(
        model, micro_mutable_op_resolver, tensor_arena, kTensorArenaSize,
        error_reporter);
    interpreter = &static_interpreter;

    // Allocate memory from the tensor_arena for the model's tensors.
    TfLiteStatus allocate_status = interpreter->AllocateTensors();
    if (allocate_status != kTfLiteOk) {
      error_reporter->Report("AllocateTensors() failed");
      return;
    }

    // Get information about the memory area to use for the model's input.
    input = interpreter->input(0);
}
```

The next part of the code is called continually in the program's main loop. It first grabs an image using the image provider, passing a reference to the input tensor so that the image is written directly there:

```
void loop() {
    // Get image from provider.
    if (kTfLiteOk != GetImage(g_error_reporter, kNumCols, kNumRows, kNumChannels,
                              g_input->data.uint8)) {
      g_error_reporter->Report("Image capture failed.");
    }
```

It then runs inference, obtains the output tensor, and reads the "person" and "no person" scores from it. These scores are passed into the detection responder's RespondTo Detection() function:

```
    // Run the model on this input and make sure it succeeds.
    if (kTfLiteOk != g_interpreter->Invoke()) {
      g_error_reporter->Report("Invoke failed.");
    }

    TfLiteTensor* output = g_interpreter->output(0);
```

```
  // Process the inference results.
  uint8_t person_score = output->data.uint8[kPersonIndex];
  uint8_t no_person_score = output->data.uint8[kNotAPersonIndex];
  RespondToDetection(g_error_reporter, person_score, no_person_score);
}
```

After `RespondToDetection()` has finished outputting the results, the `loop()` function will return, ready to be called again by the program's main loop.

The loop itself is defined within the program's `main()` function, which is located in *main.cc* (*https://oreil.ly/_PR3L*). It calls the `setup()` function once and then calls the `loop()` function repeatedly and indefinitely:

```
int main(int argc, char* argv[]) {
  setup();
  while (true) {
    loop();
  }
}
```

And that's the entire program! This example is great because it shows that working with sophisticated machine learning models can be surprisingly simple. The model contains all of the complexity, and we just need to feed it data.

Before we move along, you can run the program locally to give it a try. The reference implementation of the image provider just returns dummy data, so you won't get meaningful recognition results, but you'll at least see the code at work.

First, use this command to build the program:

```
make -f tensorflow/lite/micro/tools/make/Makefile person_detection
```

Once the build completes, you can run the example with the following command:

```
tensorflow/lite/micro/tools/make/gen/osx_x86_64/bin/ \
person_detection
```

You'll see the program's output scroll past until you press Ctrl-C to terminate it:

```
person score:129 no person score 202
person score:129 no person score 202
person score:129 no person score 202
person score:129 no person score 202
person score:129 no person score 202
person score:129 no person score 202
```

In the next section, we walk through the device-specific code that will capture camera images and output the results on each platform. We also show how to deploy and run this code.

Deploying to Microcontrollers

In this section, we deploy our code to two familiar devices:

- Arduino Nano 33 BLE Sense (*https://oreil.ly/6qlMD*)
- SparkFun Edge (*https://oreil.ly/-hoL-*)

There's one big difference this time around: because neither of these devices has a built-in camera, we recommend that you buy a camera module for whichever device you're using. Each device has its own implementation of *image_provider.cc*, which interfaces with the camera module to capture images. There's also device-specific output code in *detection_responder.cc*.

This nice and simple, so it will make an excellent template to start from when you're creating your own vision-based ML applications.

Let's begin by exploring the Arduino implementation.

Arduino

As an Arduino board, the Arduino Nano 33 BLE Sense has access to a massive ecosystem of compatible third-party hardware and libraries. We're using a third-party camera module designed to work with Arduino, along with a couple of Arduino libraries that will interface with our camera module and make sense of the data it outputs.

Which camera module to buy

This example uses the Arducam Mini 2MP Plus (*https://oreil.ly/LAwhb*) camera module. It's easy to connect to the Arduino Nano 33 BLE Sense, and it can be powered by the Arduino board's power supply. It has a large lens and is capable of capturing high-quality 2-megapixel images—though we'll be using its on-board image rescaling feature to obtain a smaller resolution. It's not particularly power-efficient, but its high image quality makes it ideal for building image capture applications, like for recording wildlife.

Capturing images on arduino

We connect the Arducam module to the Arduino board via a number of pins. To obtain image data, we send a command from the Arduino board to the Arducam that instructs it to capture an image. The Arducam will do that, storing the image in its internal data buffer. We then send further commands that allow us to read the image data from the Arducam's internal buffer and store it in the Arduino's memory. To do all of this, we use the official Arducam library.

The Arducam camera module has a 2-megapixel image sensor, with a resolution of 1920 × 1080. Our person detection model has an input size of only 96 × 96, so we don't need all of that data. In fact, the Arduino itself doesn't have enough memory to hold a 2-megapixel image, which would be several megabytes in size.

Fortunately, the Arducam hardware has the ability to resize its output to a much smaller resolution, 160 × 120 pixels. We can easily crop this down to 96 × 96 in our code, by keeping only the central 96 × 96 pixels. However, to complicate matters, the Arducam's resized output is encoded using JPEG (*https://oreil.ly/gwWDh*), a common compression format for images. Our model requires an array of pixels, not a JPEG-encoded image, which means that we need to decode the Arducam's output before we use it. We can do this using an open source library.

Our final task is to convert the Arducam's color image output into grayscale, which is what our person-detection model expects. We'll write the grayscale data into our model's input tensor.

The image provider is implemented in *arduino/image_provider.cc* (*https://oreil.ly/ kGx0-*). We won't explain its every detail, because the code is specific to the Arducam camera module. Instead, let's step through what happens at a high level.

The `GetImage()` function is the image provider's interface with the world. It's called in our application's main loop to obtain a frame of image data. The first time it is called, we need to initialize the camera. This happens with a call to the `InitCamera()` function, as follows:

```
static bool g_is_camera_initialized = false;
if (!g_is_camera_initialized) {
  TfLiteStatus init_status = InitCamera(error_reporter);
  if (init_status != kTfLiteOk) {
    error_reporter->Report("InitCamera failed");
    return init_status;
  }
  g_is_camera_initialized = true;
}
```

The `InitCamera()` function is defined further up in *image_provider.cc*. We won't walk through it here because it's very device-specific, and if you want to use it in your own code you can just copy and paste it. It configures the Arduino's hardware to communicate with the Arducam and then confirms that communication is working. Finally, it instructs the Arducam to output 160 × 120–pixel JPEG images.

The next function called by `GetImage()` is `PerformCapture()`:

```
TfLiteStatus capture_status = PerformCapture(error_reporter);
```

We won't go into the details of this one, either. All it does is send a command to the camera module, instructing it to capture an image and store the image data in its internal buffer. It then waits for confirmation that an image was captured. At this point, there's image data waiting in the Arducam's internal buffer, but there isn't yet any image data on the Arduino itself.

The next function we call is `ReadData()`:

```
TfLiteStatus read_data_status = ReadData(error_reporter);
```

The `ReadData()` function uses more commands to fetch the image data from the Arducam. After the function has run, the global variable `jpeg_buffer` will be filled with the JPEG-encoded image data retrieved from the camera.

When we have the JPEG-encoded image, our next step is to decode it into raw image data. This happens in the `DecodeAndProcessImage()` function:

```
TfLiteStatus decode_status = DecodeAndProcessImage(
    error_reporter, image_width, image_height, image_data);
```

The function uses a library named JPEGDecoder to decode the JPEG data and write it directly into the model's input tensor. In the process, it crops the image, discarding some of the 160 × 120 data so that all that remains are 96 × 96 pixels, roughly at the center of the image. It also reduces the image's 16-bit color representation down to 8-bit grayscale.

After the image has been captured and stored in the input tensor, we're ready to run inference. Next, we show how the model's output is displayed

Responding to detections on Arduino

The Arduino Nano 33 BLE Sense has a built-in RGB LED, which is a single component that contains distinct red, green, and blue LEDs that you can control separately. The detection responder's implementation flashes the blue LED every time inference is run. When a person is detected, it lights the green LED; when a person is not detected, it lights the red LED.

The implementation is in *arduino/detection_responder.cc* (*https://oreil.ly/-WsSN*). Let's take a quick walk through.

The `RespondToDetection()` function accepts two scores, one for the "person" category and the other for "not a person." The first time it is called, it sets up the blue, green, and yellow LEDs for output:

```
void RespondToDetection(tflite::ErrorReporter* error_reporter,
                        uint8_t person_score, uint8_t no_person_score) {
  static bool is_initialized = false;
  if (!is_initialized) {
    pinMode(led_green, OUTPUT);
    pinMode(led_blue, OUTPUT);
    is_initialized = true;
  }
```

Next, to indicate that an inference has just completed, we switch off all the LEDs and then flash the blue LED very briefly:

```
// Note: The RGB LEDs on the Arduino Nano 33 BLE
// Sense are on when the pin is LOW, off when HIGH.

// Switch the person/not person LEDs off
digitalWrite(led_green, HIGH);
digitalWrite(led_red, HIGH);

// Flash the blue LED after every inference.
digitalWrite(led_blue, LOW);
delay(100);
digitalWrite(led_blue, HIGH);
```

You'll notice that unlike with the Arduino's built-in LED, these LEDs are switched on with LOW and off with HIGH. This is just a factor of how the LEDs are connected to the board.

Next, we switch on and off the appropriate LEDs depending on which category score is higher:

```
// Switch on the green LED when a person is detected,
// the red when no person is detected
if (person_score > no_person_score) {
  digitalWrite(led_green, LOW);
  digitalWrite(led_red, HIGH);
} else {
  digitalWrite(led_green, HIGH);
  digitalWrite(led_red, LOW);
}
```

Finally, we use the `error_reporter` instance to output the scores to the serial port:

```
  error_reporter->Report("Person score: %d No person score: %d", person_score,
                         no_person_score);
}
```

And that's it! The core of the function is a basic `if` statement, and you could easily use similar logic to control other types of output. There's something very exciting about such a complex visual input being transformed into a single Boolean output: "person" or "no person."

Running the example

Running this example is a little more complex than our other Arduino examples, because we need to connect the Arducam to the Arduino board. We also need to install and configure the libraries that interface with the Arducam and decode its JPEG output. But don't worry, it's still very easy!

To deploy this example, here's what we'll need:

- An Arduino Nano 33 BLE Sense board
- An Arducam Mini 2MP Plus
- Jumper cables (and optionally a breadboard)
- A micro-USB cable
- The Arduino IDE

Our first task is to connect the Arducam to the Arduino using jumper cables. This isn't an electronics book, so we won't go into the details of using the cables. Instead, Table 9-1 shows how the pins should be connected. The pins are labeled on each device.

Table 9-1. Arducam Mini 2MP Plus to Arduino Nano 33 BLE Sense connections

Arducam pin	Arduino pin
CS	D7 (unlabeled, immediately to the right of D6)
MOSI	D11
MISO	D12
SCK	D13
GND	GND (either pin marked GND is fine)
VCC	3.3 V
SDA	A4
SCL	A5

After you've set up the hardware, you can continue with installing the software.

 There's always a chance that the build process might have changed since this book was written, so check *README.md* (*https://oreil.ly/ CR5Pb*) for the latest instructions.

The projects in this book are available as example code in the TensorFlow Lite Arduino library. If you haven't already installed the library, open the Arduino IDE and select Manage Libraries from the Tools menu. In the window that appears, search for and install the library named *Arduino_TensorFlowLite*. You should be able to use the latest version, but if you run into issues, the version that was tested with this book is 1.14-ALPHA.

You can also install the library from a *.zip* file, which you can either download (*https://oreil.ly/blgB8*) from the TensorFlow Lite team or generate yourself using the TensorFlow Lite for Microcontrollers Makefile. If you'd prefer to do the latter, see Appendix A.

After you've installed the library, the `person_detection` example will show up in the File menu under Examples→Arduino_TensorFlowLite, as shown in Figure 9-2.

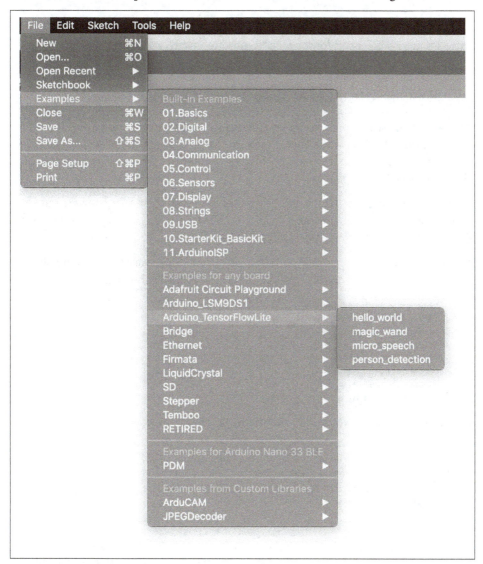

Figure 9-2. The Examples menu

Click "person_detection" to load the example. It will appear as a new window, with a tab for each of the source files. The file in the first tab, *person_detection*, is equivalent to the *main_functions.cc* we walked through earlier.

"Running the Example" on page 101 already explained the structure of the Arduino example, so we won't cover it again here.

In addition to the TensorFlow library, we need to install two other libraries:

- The Arducam library, so our code can interface with the hardware
- The JPEGDecoder library, so we can decode JPEG-encoded images

The Arducam Arduino library is available from GitHub (*https://oreil.ly/93OKK*). To install it, download or clone the repository. Next, copy its *ArduCAM* subdirectory into your *Arduino/libraries* directory. To find the *libraries* directory on your machine, check the Sketchbook location in the Arduino IDE's Preferences window.

After downloading the library, you'll need to edit one of its files to make sure it is configured for the Arducam Mini 2MP Plus. To do this, open *Arduino/libraries/ArduCAM/memorysaver.h*.

You should see a bunch of #define statements listed. Make sure that they are all commented out except for #define OV2640_MINI_2MP_PLUS, as shown here:

```
//Step 1: select the hardware platform, only one at a time
//#define OV2640_MINI_2MP
//#define OV3640_MINI_3MP
//#define OV5642_MINI_5MP
//#define OV5642_MINI_5MP_BIT_ROTATION_FIXED
#define OV2640_MINI_2MP_PLUS
//#define OV5642_MINI_5MP_PLUS
//#define OV5640_MINI_5MP_PLUS
```

After you save the file, you're done configuring the Arducam library.

The example was developed using commit #e216049 of the Arducam library. If you run into problems with the library, you can try downloading this specific commit to make sure you're using the exact same code.

The next step is to install the JPEGDecoder library. You can do this from within the Arduino IDE. In the Tools menu, select the Manage Libraries option and search for JPEGDecoder. You should install version 1.8.0 of the library.

After you've installed the library, you'll need to configure it to disable some optional components that are not compatible with the Arduino Nano 33 BLE Sense. Open *Arduino/libraries/JPEGDecoder/src/User_Config.h* and make sure that both `#define LOAD_SD_LIBRARY` and `#define LOAD_SDFAT_LIBRARY` are commented out, as shown in this excerpt from the file:

```
// Comment out the next #defines if you are not using an SD Card to store
// the JPEGs
// Commenting out the line is NOT essential but will save some FLASH space if
// SD Card access is not needed. Note: use of SdFat is currently untested!

//#define LOAD_SD_LIBRARY // Default SD Card library
//#define LOAD_SDFAT_LIBRARY // Use SdFat library instead, so SD Card SPI can
                            // be bit bashed
```

After you've saved the file, you're done installing libraries. You're now ready to run the person detection application!

To begin, plug in your Arduino device via USB. Make sure the correct device type is selected from the Board drop-down list in the Tools menu, as shown in Figure 9-3.

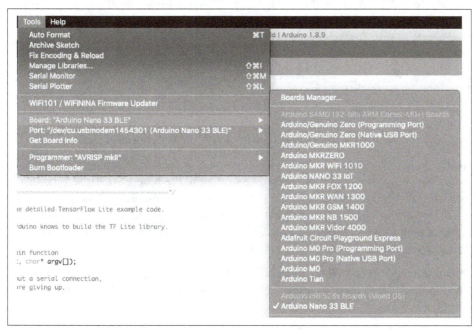

Figure 9-3. The Board drop-down list

If your device's name doesn't appear in the list, you'll need to install its support package. To do this, click Boards Manager. In the window that appears, search for your device and install the latest version of the corresponding support package.

Also in the Tools menu, make sure the device's port is selected in the Port drop-down list, as demonstrated in Figure 9-4.

Figure 9-4. The Port drop-down list

Finally, in the Arduino window, click the upload button (highlighted in white in Figure 9-5) to compile and upload the code to your Arduino device.

Figure 9-5. The upload button

As soon as the upload has successfully completed, the program will run.

To test it, start by pointing the device's camera at something that is definitely not a person, or just covering up the lens. The next time the blue LED flashes, the device will capture a frame from the camera and begin to run inference. Because the vision model we are using for person detection is relatively large, this will take a long time inference—around 19 seconds at the time of writing, though it's possible TensorFlow Lite has become faster since then.

When inference is complete, the result will be translated into another LED being lit. You pointed the camera at something that isn't a person, so the red LED should illuminate.

Now, try pointing the device's camera at yourself! The next time the blue LED flashes, the device will capture another image and begin to run inference. After roughly 19 seconds, the green LED should turn on.

Remember, image data is captured as a snapshot before each inference, whenever the blue LED flashes. Whatever the camera is pointed at during that moment is what will be fed into the model. It doesn't matter where the camera is pointed until the next time an image is captured, when the blue LED will flash again.

If you're getting seemingly incorrect results, make sure you are in an environment with good lighting. You should also make sure that the camera is oriented correctly, with the pins pointing downward, so that the images it captures are the right way up —the model was not trained to recognize upside-down people. In addition, it's good to remember that this is a tiny model, which trades accuracy for small size. It works very well, but it isn't accurate 100% of the time.

You can also see the results of inference via the Arduino Serial Monitor. To do this, from the Tools menu, open the Serial Monitor. You'll see a detailed log showing what is happening while the application runs. It's also interesting to check the "Show time-stamp" box, so you can see how long each part of the process takes:

```
14:17:50.714 -> Starting capture
14:17:50.714 -> Image captured
14:17:50.784 -> Reading 3080 bytes from ArduCAM
14:17:50.887 -> Finished reading
14:17:50.887 -> Decoding JPEG and converting to greyscale
14:17:51.074 -> Image decoded and processed
14:18:09.710 -> Person score: 246 No person score: 66
```

From this log, we can see that it took around 170 ms to capture and read the image data from the camera module, 180 ms to decode the JPEG and convert it to grayscale, and 18.6 seconds to run inference.

Making your own changes

Now that you've deployed the basic application, try playing around and making some changes to the code. Just edit the files in the Arduino IDE and save, and then repeat the previous instructions to deploy your modified code to the device.

Here are a few things you could try:

- Modify the detection responder so that it ignores ambiguous inputs, where there isn't much difference between the "person" and "no person" scores.
- Use the results of person detection to control other components, like additional LEDs or servos.
- Build a smart security camera, by storing or transmitting images—but only those that contain a person.

SparkFun Edge

The SparkFun Edge board is optimized for low power consumption. When paired with a similarly efficient camera module, it's the ideal platform for building vision applications that will be running on battery power. It's easy to plug in a camera module via the board's ribbon cable adapter.

Which camera module to buy

This example uses SparkFun's Himax HM01B0 breakout camera module (*https:// oreil.ly/H24xS*). It's based on a 320 × 320–pixel image sensor that consumes an extremely small amount of power: less than 2 mW when capturing at 30 frames per second (FPS).

Capturing images on SparkFun Edge

To begin capturing images with the Himax HM01B0 camera module, we first must initialize the camera. After this is done, we can read a frame from the camera every time we need a new image. A frame is an array of bytes representing what the camera can currently see.

Working with the camera will involve heavy use of both the Ambiq Apollo3 SDK, which is downloaded as part of the build process, and the HM01B0 driver, which is located in *sparkfun_edge/himax_driver* (*https://oreil.ly/OhBj0*).

The image provider is implemented in *sparkfun_edge/image_provider.cc* (*https:// oreil.ly/ZdU9N*). We won't explain its every detail, because the code is specific to the SparkFun board and the Himax camera module. Instead, let's step through what happens at a high level.

The GetImage() function is the image provider's interface with the world. It's called in our application's main loop to obtain a frame of image data. The first time it is called, we'll need to initialize the camera. This happens with a call to the InitCamera() function, as follows:

```
// Capture single frame.  Frame pointer passed in to reduce memory usage.  This
// allows the input tensor to be used instead of requiring an extra copy.
TfLiteStatus GetImage(tflite::ErrorReporter* error_reporter, int frame_width,
                      int frame_height, int channels, uint8_t* frame) {
  if (!g_is_camera_initialized) {
    TfLiteStatus init_status = InitCamera(error_reporter);
    if (init_status != kTfLiteOk) {
      am_hal_gpio_output_set(AM_BSP_GPIO_LED_RED);
      return init_status;
    }
```

If `InitCamera()` returns anything other than a `kTfLiteOk` status, we switch on the board's red LED (using `am_hal_gpio_output_set(AM_BSP_GPIO_LED_RED)`) to indicate a problem. This is helpful for debugging.

The `InitCamera()` function is defined further up in *image_provider.cc*. We won't walk through it here because it's very device-specific, and if you want to use it in your own code you can just copy and paste it.

It calls a bunch of Apollo3 SDK functions to configure the microcontroller's inputs and outputs so that it can communicate with the camera module. It also enables *interrupts*, which are the mechanism used by the camera to send over new image data. When this is all set up, it uses the camera driver to switch on the camera and configures it to start continually capturing images.

The camera module has an autoexposure feature, which calibrates its exposure setting automatically as frames are captured. To allow it the opportunity to calibrate before we attempt to perform inference, the next part of the `GetImage()` function uses the camera driver's `hm01b0_blocking_read_oneframe_scaled()` function to capture several frames. We don't do anything with the captured data; we are only doing this to give the camera module's autoexposure function some material to work with:

```
// Drop a few frames until auto exposure is calibrated.
for (int i = 0; i < kFramesToInitialize; ++i) {
  hm01b0_blocking_read_oneframe_scaled(frame, frame_width, frame_height,
                                       channels);
}
g_is_camera_initialized = true;
}
```

After setup is out of the way, the rest of the `GetImage()` function is very simple. All we do is call `hm01b0_blocking_read_oneframe_scaled()` to capture an image:

```
hm01b0_blocking_read_oneframe_scaled(frame, frame_width, frame_height,
                                     channels);
```

When `GetImage()` is called during the application's main loop, the `frame` variable is a pointer to our input tensor, so the data is written directly by the camera driver to the area of memory allocated to the input tensor. We also specify the width, height, and number of channels we want.

With this implementation, we're able to capture image data from our camera module. Next, let's look at how we respond to the model's output.

Responding to detections on SparkFun Edge

The detection responder's implementation is very similar to our wake-word example's command responder. It toggles the device's blue LED every time inference is run. When a person is detected, it lights the green LED, and when a person is not detected it lights the yellow LED.

The implementation is in *sparkfun_edge/detection_responder.cc* (*https://oreil.ly/ OeN1M*). Let's take a quick walk through.

The `RespondToDetection()` function accepts two scores, one for the "person" category, and the other for "not a person." The first time it is called, it sets up the blue, green, and yellow LEDs for output:

```
void RespondToDetection(tflite::ErrorReporter* error_reporter,
                        uint8_t person_score, uint8_t no_person_score) {
  static bool is_initialized = false;
  if (!is_initialized) {
    // Setup LED's as outputs.  Leave red LED alone since that's an error
    // indicator for sparkfun_edge in image_provider.
    am_hal_gpio_pinconfig(AM_BSP_GPIO_LED_BLUE, g_AM_HAL_GPIO_OUTPUT_12);
    am_hal_gpio_pinconfig(AM_BSP_GPIO_LED_GREEN, g_AM_HAL_GPIO_OUTPUT_12);
    am_hal_gpio_pinconfig(AM_BSP_GPIO_LED_YELLOW, g_AM_HAL_GPIO_OUTPUT_12);
    is_initialized = true;
  }
```

Because the function is called once per inference, the next snippet of code causes it to toggle the blue LED on and off each time inference is performed:

```
// Toggle the blue LED every time an inference is performed.
static int count = 0;
if (++count & 1) {
    am_hal_gpio_output_set(AM_BSP_GPIO_LED_BLUE);
} else {
    am_hal_gpio_output_clear(AM_BSP_GPIO_LED_BLUE);
}
```

Finally, it turns on the green LED if a person was detected, or the blue LED if not. It also logs the score using the `ErrorReporter` instance:

```
am_hal_gpio_output_clear(AM_BSP_GPIO_LED_YELLOW);
am_hal_gpio_output_clear(AM_BSP_GPIO_LED_GREEN);
if (person_score > no_person_score) {
    am_hal_gpio_output_set(AM_BSP_GPIO_LED_GREEN);
} else {
    am_hal_gpio_output_set(AM_BSP_GPIO_LED_YELLOW);
}

error_reporter->Report("person score:%d no person score %d", person_score,
                       no_person_score);
```

And that's it! The core of the function is a basic `if` statement, and you could easily use similar logic could to control other types of output. There's something very exciting about such a complex visual input being transformed into a single Boolean output: "person" or "no person."

Running the example

Now that we've seen how the SparkFun Edge implementation works, let's get it up and running.

 There's always a chance that the build process might have changed since this book was written, so check *README.md* (*https://oreil.ly/ kaSXN*) for the latest instructions.

To build and deploy our code, we'll need the following:

- A SparkFun Edge board with the Himax HM01B0 breakout (*https://oreil.ly/ jNtyv*) attached
- A USB programmer (we recommend the SparkFun Serial Basic Breakout, which is available in both micro-B USB (*https://oreil.ly/wXo-f*) and USB-C (*https:// oreil.ly/-YvfN*) variants)
- A matching USB cable
- Python 3 and some dependencies

 If you're unsure whether you have the correct version of Python installed, "Running the Example" on page 110 has instructions on how to check.

In a terminal, clone the TensorFlow repository and change into its directory:

```
git clone https://github.com/tensorflow/tensorflow.git
cd tensorflow
```

Next, we're going to build the binary and run some commands that get it ready for downloading to the device. To avoid some typing, you can copy and paste these commands from *README.md* (*https://oreil.ly/kaSXN*).

Build the binary. The following command downloads all of the required dependencies and then compiles a binary for the SparkFun Edge:

```
make -f tensorflow/lite/micro/tools/make/Makefile \
  TARGET=sparkfun_edge person_detection_bin
```

The binary is created as a *.bin* file, in the following location:

```
tensorflow/lite/micro/tools/make/gen/
  sparkfun_edge_cortex-m4/bin/person_detection.bin
```

To check that the file exists, you can use the following command:

```
test -f tensorflow/lite/micro/tools/make/gen \
/sparkfun_edge_cortex-m4/bin/person_detection.bin \
&& echo "Binary was successfully created" || echo "Binary is missing"
```

When you run that command, you should see `Binary was successfully created` printed to the console.

If you see `Binary is missing`, there was a problem with the build process. If so, it's likely that there are some clues to what went wrong in the output of the `make` command.

Sign the binary. The binary must be signed with cryptographic keys to be deployed to the device. Let's now run some commands that will sign the binary so that it can be flashed to the SparkFun Edge. The scripts used here come from the Ambiq SDK, which is downloaded when the Makefile is run.

Enter the following command to set up some dummy cryptographic keys that you can use for development:

```
cp tensorflow/lite/micro/tools/make/downloads/AmbiqSuite-Rel2.0.0 \
  /tools/apollo3_scripts/keys_info0.py \
tensorflow/lite/micro/tools/make/downloads/AmbiqSuite-Rel2.0.0 \
  /tools/apollo3_scripts/keys_info.py
```

Next, run the following command to create a signed binary. Substitute `python3` with python if necessary:

```
python3 tensorflow/lite/micro/tools/make/downloads/ \
  AmbiqSuite-Rel2.0.0/tools/apollo3_scripts/create_cust_image_blob.py \
  --bin tensorflow/lite/micro/tools/make/gen/ \
  sparkfun_edge_cortex-m4/bin/person_detection.bin \
  --load-address 0xC000 \
  --magic-num 0xCB \
  -o main_nonsecure_ota \
  --version 0x0
```

This creates the file *main_nonsecure_ota.bin*. Now run this command to create a final version of the file that you can use to flash your device with the script you will use in the next step:

```
python3 tensorflow/lite/micro/tools/make/downloads/ \
  AmbiqSuite-Rel2.0.0/tools/apollo3_scripts/create_cust_wireupdate_blob.py \
  --load-address 0x20000 \
```

```
--bin main_nonsecure_ota.bin \
-i 6 \
-o main_nonsecure_wire \
--options 0x1
```

You should now have a file called *main_nonsecure_wire.bin* in the directory where you ran the commands. This is the file you'll be flashing to the device.

Flash the binary.   The SparkFun Edge stores the program it is currently running in its 1 megabyte of flash memory. If you want the board to run a new program, you need to send it to the board, which will store it in flash memory, overwriting any program that was previously saved.

As we've mentioned earlier in the book, this process is called *flashing*.

Attach the programmer to the board.   To download new programs to the board, you'll use the SparkFun USB-C Serial Basic serial programmer. This device allows your computer to communicate with the microcontroller via USB.

To attach this device to your board, perform the following steps:

1. On the side of the SparkFun Edge, locate the six-pin header.

2. Plug the SparkFun USB-C Serial Basic into these pins, ensuring that the pins labeled BLK and GRN on each device are lined up correctly, as demonstrated in Figure 9-6.

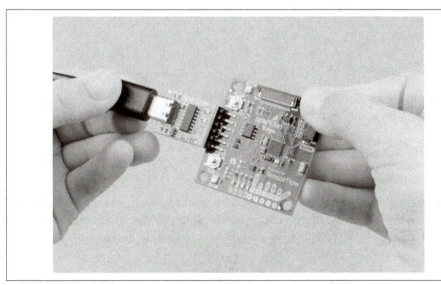

Figure 9-6. Connecting the SparkFun Edge and USB-C Serial Basic (courtesy of SparkFun)

Attach the programmer to your computer. You connect the board to your computer via USB. To program the board, you need to find out the name that your computer gives the device. The best way of doing this is to list all of the computer's devices before and after attaching it and then look to see which device is new.

 Some people have reported issues with their operating system's default drivers for the programmer, so we strongly recommend installing the driver (*https://oreil.ly/yI-NR*) before you continue.

Before attaching the device via USB, run the following command:

```
# macOS:
ls /dev/cu*

# Linux:
ls /dev/tty*
```

This should output a list of attached devices that looks something like the following:

```
/dev/cu.Bluetooth-Incoming-Port
/dev/cu.MALS
/dev/cu.SOC
```

Now, connect the programmer to your computer's USB port and run the following command again:

```
# macOS:
ls /dev/cu*

# Linux:
ls /dev/tty*
```

You should see an extra item in the output, as in the example that follows. Your new item might have a different name. This new item is the name of the device:

```
/dev/cu.Bluetooth-Incoming-Port
/dev/cu.MALS
/dev/cu.SOC
/dev/cu.wchusbserial-1450
```

This name will be used to refer to the device. However, it can change depending on which USB port the programmer is attached to, so if you disconnect the board from the computer and then reattach it, you might have to look up its name again.

Some users have reported two devices appearing in the list. If you see two devices, the correct one to use begins with the letters "wch"; for example, /dev/wchusbserial-14410.

After you've identified the device name, put it in a shell variable for later use:

```
export DEVICENAME=<your device name here>
```

This is a variable that you can use when running commands that require the device name, later in the process.

Run the script to flash your board. To flash the board, you need to put it into a special "bootloader" state that prepares it to receive the new binary. You'll then run a script to send the binary to the board.

First create an environment variable to specify the baud rate, which is the speed at which data will be sent to the device:

```
export BAUD_RATE=921600
```

Now paste the following command into your terminal—but *do not press Enter yet*! The ${DEVICENAME} and ${BAUD_RATE} in the command will be replaced with the values you set in the previous sections. Remember to substitute python3 with python if necessary.

```
python3 tensorflow/lite/micro/tools/make/downloads/ \
    AmbiqSuite-Rel2.0.0/tools/apollo3_scripts/uart_wired_update.py -b \
    ${BAUD_RATE} ${DEVICENAME} -r 1 -f main_nonsecure_wire.bin -i 6
```

Next, you'll reset the board into its bootloader state and flash the board. On the board, locate the buttons marked RST and 14, as shown in Figure 9-7.

Perform the following steps:

1. Ensure that your board is connected to the programmer, and the entire thing is connected to your computer via USB.

2. On the board, press and hold the button marked 14. *Continue holding it.*

3. While still holding the button marked 14, press the button marked RST to reset the board.

4. Press Enter on your computer to run the script. *Continue on holding button 14.*

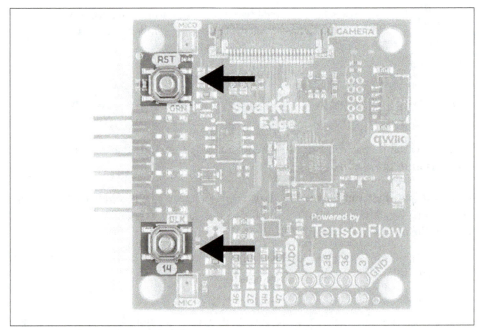

Figure 9-7. The SparkFun Edge's buttons

You should now see something like the following appearing on your screen:

```
Connecting with Corvette over serial port /dev/cu.usbserial-1440...
Sending Hello.
Received response for Hello
Received Status
length =  0x58
version =  0x3
Max Storage =  0x4ffa0
Status =  0x2
State =  0x7
AMInfo =
0x1
0xff2da3ff
0x55fff
0x1
0x49f40003
0xffffffff
[...lots more 0xffffffff...]
Sending OTA Descriptor =  0xfe000
Sending Update Command.
number of updates needed =  1
Sending block of size  0x158b0  from  0x0  to  0x158b0
Sending Data Packet of length  8180
Sending Data Packet of length  8180
[...lots more Sending Data Packet of length  8180...]
```

Keep holding button 14 until you see `Sending Data Packet of length 8180`. You can release the button after seeing this (but it's okay if you keep holding it).

The program will continue to print lines on the terminal. Eventually, you'll see something like the following:

```
[...lots more Sending Data Packet of length  8180...]
Sending Data Packet of length  8180
Sending Data Packet of length  6440
Sending Reset Command.
Done.
```

This indicates a successful flashing.

 If the program output ends with an error, check whether `Sending Reset Command.` was printed. If so, flashing was likely successful despite the error. Otherwise, flashing might have failed. Try running through these steps again (you can skip over setting the environment variables).

Testing the program

Start by pressing the RST button, to make sure the program is running.

When the program is running the blue LED will toggle on and off, once for each inference. Because the vision model we are using for person detection is relatively large, it takes a long time to run inference—around 6 seconds in total.

Start by pointing the device's camera at something that is definitely not a person, or just covering up the lens. The next time the blue LED toggles, the device will capture a frame from the camera and begin to run inference. After 6 seconds or so, the inference result will be translated into another LED being lit. Given that you pointed the camera at something that isn't a person, the orange LED should light up.

Now, try pointing the device's camera at yourself. The next time the blue LED toggles, the device will capture another frame and begin to run inference. This time, the green LED should light up.

Remember, image data is captured as a snapshot before each inference, whenever the blue LED toggles. Whatever the camera is pointed at during that moment is what will be fed into the model. It doesn't matter where the camera is pointed until the next time a frame is captured, when the blue LED will toggle again.

If you're getting seemingly incorrect results, make sure that you are in an environment with good lighting. It's also good to remember that this is a tiny model, which trades accuracy for small size. It works very well, but it isn't accurate 100% all of the time.

What If It Didn't Work?

Here are some possible issues and how to debug them:

Problem: When flashing, the script hangs for a while at `Sending Hello.` and then prints an error.

Solution: You need to hold down the button marked 14 while running the script. Hold down button 14, press the RST button, and then run the script, while holding the button marked 14 the entire time.

Problem: After flashing, none of the LEDs are coming on.

Solution: Try pressing the RST button or disconnecting the board from the programmer and then reconnecting it. If neither of these works, try flashing the board again.

Problem: After flashing, the red LED illuminates.

Solution: The red LED indicates a problem with the camera module. Ensure that the camera module is connected properly and, if so try disconnecting and reconnecting it.

Viewing debug data

The program will log detection results to the serial port. To view them, we can monitor the board's serial port output using a baud rate of 115200. On macOS and Linux, the following command should work:

```
screen ${DEVICENAME} 115200
```

You should initially see output that looks something like the following:

```
Apollo3 Burst Mode is Available

                              Apollo3 operating in Burst Mode (96MHz)
```

As the board captures frames and runs inference, you should see it printing debug information:

```
Person score: 130 No person score: 204
Person score: 220 No person score: 87
```

To stop viewing the debug output with `screen`, press Ctrl-A, immediately followed by the K key, and then press the Y key.

Making your own changes

Now that you've deployed the basic application, try playing around and making some changes. You can find the application's code in the *tensorflow/lite/micro/examples/person_detection* folder. Just edit and save, and then repeat the preceding instructions to deploy your modified code to the device.

Here are a few things you could try:

- Modify the detection responder so that it ignores ambiguous inputs, where there isn't much difference between the "person" and "no person" scores.
- Use the results of person detection to control other components, like additional LEDs or servos.
- Build a smart security camera, by storing or transmitting images—but only those that contain a person.

Wrapping Up

The vision model we've used in this chapter is an amazing thing. It accepts raw and messy input, no preprocessing required, and gives us a beautifully simple output: yes, a person is present, or no, there is no one present. This is the magic of machine learning: it can filter information from noise, leaving us with only the signals we care about. As developers, it's easy to use these signals to build amazing experiences for our users.

When building machine learning applications, it's very common to use pretrained models like this one, which already contain the knowledge required to perform a task. Roughly equivalent to code libraries, models encapsulate specific functionality and are easily shared between projects. You'll often find yourself exploring and evaluating models, looking for the proper fit for your task.

In Chapter 10, we'll examine how the person detection model works. You'll also learn how to train your own vision models to spot different types of objects.

Person Detection: Training a Model

In Chapter 9, we showed how you can deploy a pretrained model for recognizing people in images, but we didn't explain where that model came from. If your product has different requirements, you'll want to be able to train your own version, and this chapter explains how to do that.

Picking a Machine

Training this image model takes a lot more compute power than our previous examples, so if you want your training to complete in a reasonable amount of time, you'll need to use a machine with a high-end graphics processing unit (GPU). Unless you expect to be running a lot of training jobs, we recommend starting off by renting a cloud instance rather than buying a special machine. Unfortunately the free Colaboratory service from Google that we've used in previous chapters for smaller models won't work, and you will need to pay for access to a machine. There are many great providers available, but our instructions will assume you're using Google Cloud Platform because that's the service we're most familiar with. If you are already using Amazon Web Services (AWS) or Microsoft Azure, they also have TensorFlow support and the training instructions should be the same, but you'll need to follow their tutorials for setting up a machine.

Setting Up a Google Cloud Platform Instance

You can rent a virtual machine with TensorFlow and NVIDIA drivers preinstalled from Google Cloud Platform, and with support for a Jupyter Notebook web interface, which can be very convenient. The route to setting this up can be a bit involved, though. As of September 2019, here are the steps you need to take to create a machine:

1. Sign in to *console.cloud.google.com* (*https://oreil.ly/Of6oo*). You'll need to create a Google account if you don't already have one, and you'll have to set up billing to pay for the instance you create. If you don't already have a project, you'll need to create one.

2. In the upper-left corner of the screen, open the hamburger menu (the main menu with three horizontal lines as an icon, as illustrated in Figure 10-1) and scroll down until you find the Artificial Intelligence section.

3. In this section, select AI Platform→Notebooks, as shown in Figure 10-1.

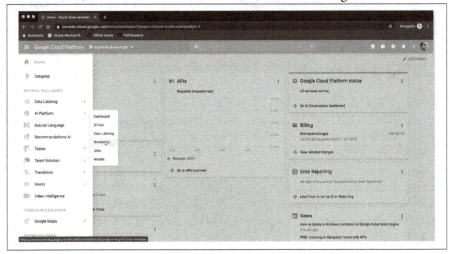

Figure 10-1. The AI Platform menu

4. You might see a prompt asking you to enable the Compute Engine API to proceed, as depicted in Figure 10-2; go ahead and approve it. This can take several minutes to go through.

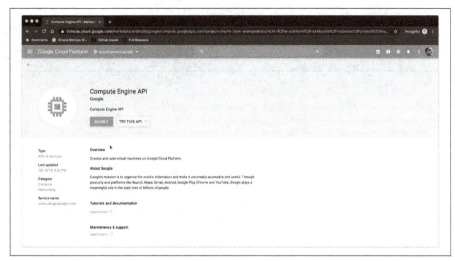

Figure 10-2. The Compute Engine API screen

5. A "Notebook instances" screen will open. In the menu bar at the top, select NEW INSTANCE. On the submenu that opens, choose "Customize instance," as shown in Figure 10-3.

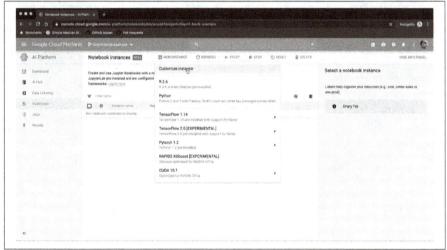

Figure 10-3. The instance creation menu

6. On the "New notebook instance" page, in the "instance name" box, give your machine a name, as illustrated in Figure 10-4, and then scroll down to set up the environment.

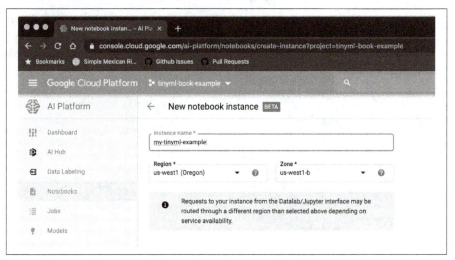

Figure 10-4. The naming interface

7. As of September 2019, the correct TensorFlow version to choose is TensorFlow 1.14. The recommended version will likely have increased to 2.0 or beyond by the time you're reading this, but there might be some incompatibilities, so if it's still possible start by selecting 1.14 or another version in the 1.x branch.

8. In the "Machine configuration" section, choose at least 4 CPUs and 15 GB of RAM, as shown in Figure 10-5.

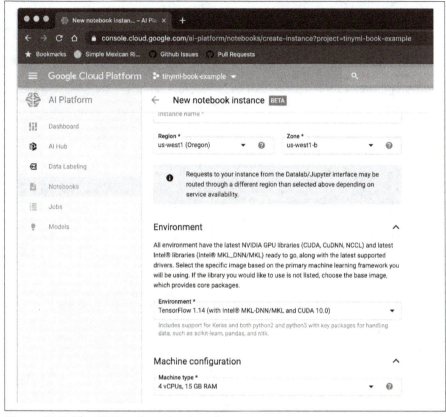

Figure 10-5. The CPU and version interface

9. Picking the right GPU will make the biggest difference in your training speed. It can be tricky because not all zones offer the same kind of hardware. In our case, we're using "us-west1 (Oregon)" as the region and "us-west-1b" as the zone because we know that they currently offer high-end GPUs. You can get the detailed pricing information using Google Cloud Platform's pricing calculator (*https://oreil.ly/t2XO0*), but for this example we're choosing one NVIDIA Tesla V100 GPU, as illustrated in Figure 10-6. This costs $1,300 a month to run but allows us to train the person-detector model in around a day, so the model training cost works out to about $45.

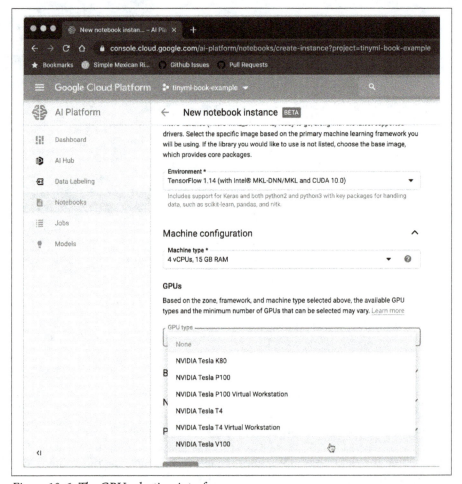

Figure 10-6. The GPU selection interface

These high-end machines are expensive to run, so make sure you stop your instance when you're not actively using it for training. Otherwise, you'll be paying for an idle machine.

10. It makes life easier to have the GPU drivers installed automatically, so make sure you select that option, as demonstrated in Figure 10-7.

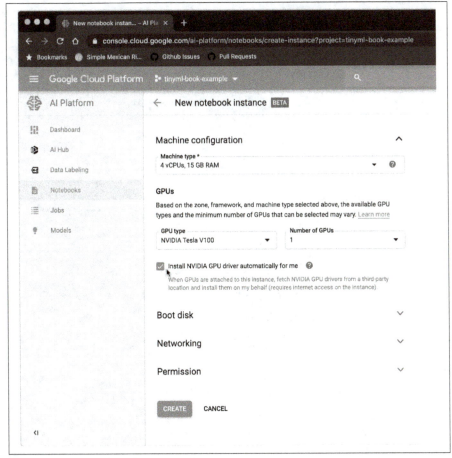

Figure 10-7. The GPU driver interface

11. Because you'll be downloading a dataset to this machine, we recommend making the boot disk a bit larger than the default 100 GB; maybe as big as 500 GB, as shown in Figure 10-8.

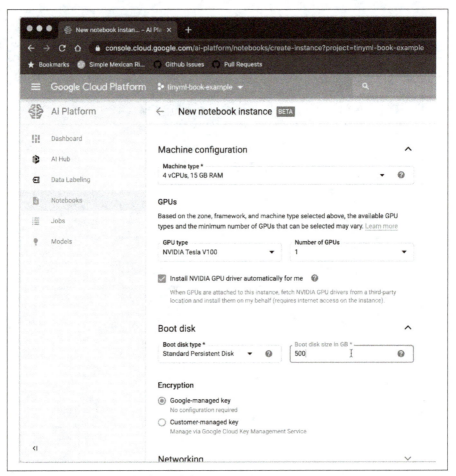

Figure 10-8. Increasing the boot disk size

12. When you've set all those options, at the bottom of the page, click the CREATE button, which should return you to the "Notebook instances" screen. There should be a new instance in the list with the name you gave to your machine. There will be spinners next to it for a few minutes while the instance is being set up. When that's complete click the OPEN JUPYTERLAB link, as depicted in Figure 10-9.

Figure 10-9. The instances screen

13. In the screen that opens, choose to create a Python 3 notebook (see Figure 10-10).

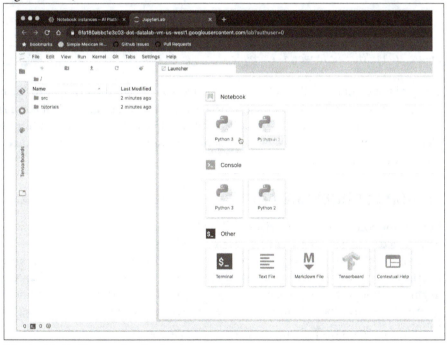

Figure 10-10. The notebook selection screen

This gives you a Jupyter notebook connected to your instance. If you're not familiar with Jupyter, it gives you a nice web interface to a Python interpreter running on a machine, and stores the commands and results in a notebook you can share. To start using it, in the panel on the right, type `print("Hello World!")` and then press Shift+Return. You should see "Hello World!'" printed just below, as shown in Figure 10-11. If so, you've successfully set up your machine instance. We use this notebook as the place in which we enter commands for the rest of this tutorial.

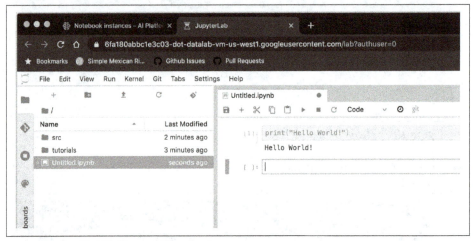

Figure 10-11. The "hello world" example

Many of the commands that follow assume that you're running from a Jupyter notebook, so they begin with a !, which indicates they should be run as shell commands rather than Python statements. If you're running directly from a terminal (for example, after opening a Secure Shell connection to commmunicate with an instance) you can remove the initial !.

Training Framework Choice

Keras is the recommended interface for building models in TensorFlow, but when the person detection model was being created it didn't yet support all the features we needed. For that reason, we show you how to train a model using *tf.slim*, an older interface. It is still widely used but deprecated, so future versions of TensorFlow might not support this approach. We hope to publish Keras instructions online in the future; check tinymlbook.com/persondetector (*https://oreil.ly/sxP6q*) for updates.

The model definitions for Slim are part of the TensorFlow models repository (*https:// oreil.ly/iamdB*), so to get started, you'll need to download it from GitHub:

```
! cd ~
! git clone https://github.com/tensorflow/models.git
```

The following guide assumes that you've done this from your home directory, so the model repository code is at *~/models*, and that all commands are run from the home directory unless otherwise noted. You can place the repository somewhere else, but you'll need to update all references to it.

To use Slim, you need to make sure that Python can find its modules and install one dependency. Here's how to do this in an iPython notebook:

```
! pip install contextlib2
import os
new_python_path = (os.environ.get("PYTHONPATH") or '') + ":models/research/slim"
%env PYTHONPATH=$new_python_path
```

Updating PYTHONPATH through an EXPORT statement like this works only for the current Jupyter session, so if you're using bash directly you should add it to a persistent startup script, running something like this:

```
echo 'export PYTHONPATH=$PYTHONPATH:models/research/slim' >> ~/.bashrc
source ~/.bashrc
```

If you see import errors running the Slim scripts, make sure the PYTHONPATH is set up correctly and that contextlib2 has been installed. You can find more general information on *tf.slim* in the repository's README (*https://oreil.ly/azuvk*).

Building the Dataset

To train our person detection model, we need a large collection of images that are labeled depending on whether they have people in them. The ImageNet 1,000-class dataset that's widely used for training image classifiers doesn't include labels for people, but luckily the COCO dataset (*http://cocodataset.org/#home*) does.

The dataset is designed to be used for training models for localization, so the images aren't labeled with the "person," "not person" categories for which we want to train. Instead, each image comes with a list of bounding boxes for all of the objects it contains. "Person" is one of these object categories, so to get to the classification labels we want, we need to look for images with bounding boxes for people. To make sure that they aren't too tiny to be recognizable we also need to exclude very small bounding boxes. Slim contains a convenient script to both download the data and convert bounding boxes into labels:

```
! python download_and_convert_data.py \
  --dataset_name=visualwakewords \
  --dataset_dir=data/visualwakewords
```

This is a large download, about 40 GB, so it will take a while and you'll need to make sure you have at least 100 GB free on your drive to allow space for unpacking and further processing. Don't be surprised if the process takes around 20 minutes to complete. When it's done, you'll have a set of TFRecords in *data/visualwakewords* holding the labeled image information. This dataset was created by Aakanksha Chowdhery and is known as the Visual Wake Words dataset (*https://oreil.ly/EC6nd*). It's designed to be useful for benchmarking and testing embedded computer vision because it represents a very common task that we need to accomplish with tight resource constraints. We're hoping to see it drive even better models for this and similar tasks.

Training the Model

One of the nice things about using *tf.slim* to handle the training is that the parameters we commonly need to modify are available as command-line arguments, so we can just call the standard *train_image_classifier.py* script to train our model. You can use this command to build the model we use in the example:

```
! python models/research/slim/train_image_classifier.py \
    --train_dir=vww_96_grayscale \
    --dataset_name=visualwakewords \
    --dataset_split_name=train \
    --dataset_dir=data/visualwakewords \
    --model_name=mobilenet_v1_025 \
    --preprocessing_name=mobilenet_v1 \
    --train_image_size=96 \
    --use_grayscale=True \
    --save_summaries_secs=300 \
    --learning_rate=0.045 \
    --label_smoothing=0.1 \
    --learning_rate_decay_factor=0.98 \
    --num_epochs_per_decay=2.5 \
    --moving_average_decay=0.9999 \
    --batch_size=96 \
    --max_number_of_steps=1000000
```

It will take a couple of days on a single-GPU V100 instance to complete all one million steps, but you should be able to get a fairly accurate model after a few hours if you want to experiment early. Following are some additional considerations:

- The checkpoints and summaries will be saved in the folder given in the --train_dir argument. This is where you'll need to look for the results.

- The --dataset_dir parameter should match the one where you saved the TFRecords from the Visual Wake Words build script.

- The architecture we use is defined by the --model_name argument. The mobilenet_v1 prefix instructs the script to use the first version of MobileNet. We did experiment with later versions, but these used more RAM for their intermediate activation buffers, so for now we're sticking with the original. The `025` is the depth multiplier to use, which mostly affects the number of weight parameters; this low setting ensures the model fits within 250 KB of flash memory.

- `--preprocessing_name` controls how input images are modified before they're fed into the model. The `mobilenet_v1` version shrinks the width and height of the images to the size given in `--train_image_size` (in our case 96 pixels because we want to reduce the compute requirements). It also scales the pixel values from integers in the range 0 to 255 to floating-point numbers in the range −1.0 to +1.0 floating-point numbers (though we'll be quantizing those after pass: [training).

- The HM01B0 camera (*https://oreil.ly/RGciN*) we're using on the SparkFun Edge board is monochrome, so to get the best results, we need to train our model on black-and-white images. We pass in the `--use_grayscale` flag to enable that preprocessing.

- The `--learning_rate`, `--label_smoothing`, `--learning_rate_decay_factor`, `--num_epochs_per_decay`, `--moving_average_decay`, and `--batch_size` parameters all control how weights are updated during the the training process. Training deep networks is still a bit of a dark art, so these exact values we found through experimentation for this particular model. You can try tweaking them to speed up training or gain a small boost in accuracy, but we can't give much guidance for how to make those changes, and it's easy to get combinations where the training accuracy never converges.

- `--max_number_of_steps` defines how long the training should continue. There's no good way to establish this threshold in advance; you need to experiment to determine when the accuracy of the model is no longer improving to know when to cut it off. In our case, we default to a million steps because with this particular model we know that's a good point to stop.

After you start the script, you should see output that looks something like this:

```
INFO:tensorflow:global step 4670: loss = 0.7112 (0.251 sec/step)
    I0928 00:16:21.774756 140518023943616 learning.py:507] global step 4670: loss
    = 0.7112 (0.251 sec/step)
INFO:tensorflow:global step 4680: loss = 0.6596 (0.227 sec/step)
    I0928 00:16:24.365901 140518023943616 learning.py:507] global step 4680: loss
    = 0.6596 (0.227 sec/step)
```

Don't worry about the line duplication: this is just a side effect of the way TensorFlow log printing interacts with Python. Each line has two key bits of information about the training process. The global step is a count of how far through the training we are. Because we've set the limit as a million steps, in this case we're nearly 5% complete. Together with the steps-per-second estimate, this is useful because you can use it to estimate a rough duration for the entire training process. In this case, we're completing about 4 steps per second, so a million steps will take about 70 hours, or 3 days. The other crucial piece of information is the loss. This is a measure of how close the partially trained model's predictions are to the correct values, and lower values are better. This will show a lot of variation but should on average decrease during training if the model is learning. Because it's so noisy the amounts will bounce around a lot over short time periods, but if things are working well you should see a noticeable drop if you wait an hour or so and check back. This kind of variation is a lot easier to see in a graph, which is one of the main reasons to try TensorBoard.

TensorBoard

TensorBoard is a web application that lets you view data visualizations from Tensor-Flow training sessions, and it's included by default in most cloud instances. If you're using Google Cloud AI Platform, you can start up a new TensorBoard session by opening the command palette from the left tabs in the notebook interface and then scrolling down to select "Create a new tensorboard." You're then prompted for the location of the summary logs. Enter the path you used for `--train_dir` in the training script—in the previous example, the folder name is *vww_96_grayscale*. One common error to watch out for is adding a slash to the end of the path, which will cause TensorBoard to fail to find the directory.

If you're starting TensorBoard from the command line in a different environment you'll need to pass in this path as the `--logdir` argument to the TensorBoard command-line tool, and point your browser to *http://localhost:6006* (or the address of the machine you're running it on).

After navigating to the TensorBoard address or opening the session through Google Cloud, you should see a page that looks something like Figure 10-12. It might take a little while for the graphs to have anything useful in them given that the script only saves summaries every five minutes. Figure 10-12 shows the results after training for more than a day. The most important graph is called "clone_loss"; it shows the progression of the same loss value that's displayed in the logging output. As you can see in this example it fluctuates a lot, but the overall trend is downward over time. If you don't see this sort of progression after a few hours of training, it's a good sign that your model isn't converging to a good solution, and you might need to debug what's going wrong either with your dataset or the training parameters.

TensorBoard defaults to the SCALARS tab when it opens, but the other section that can be useful during training is IMAGES (Figure 10-13). This shows a random selection of the pictures the model is currently being trained on, including any distortions and other preprocessing. In the figure, you can see that the image has been flipped and that it's been converted to grayscale before being fed to the model. This information isn't as essential as the loss graphs, but it can be useful to ensure that the dataset is what you expect, and it is interesting to see the examples updating as training progresses.

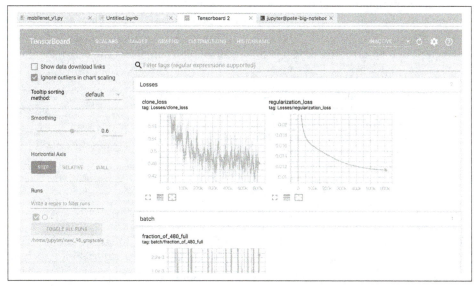

Figure 10-12. Graphs in TensorBoard

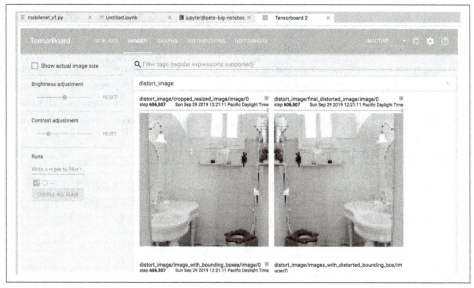

Figure 10-13. Images in TensorBoard

Evaluating the Model

The loss function correlates with how well your model is training, but it isn't a direct, understandable metric. What we really care about is how many people our model detects correctly, but to get it to calculate this we need to run a separate script. You don't need to wait until the model is fully trained, you can check the accuracy of any checkpoints in the --train_dir folder. To do this, run the following command:

```
! python models/research/slim/eval_image_classifier.py \
    --alsologtostderr \
    --checkpoint_path=vww_96_grayscale/model.ckpt-698580 \
    --dataset_dir=data/visualwakewords \
    --dataset_name=visualwakewords \
    --dataset_split_name=val \
    --model_name=mobilenet_v1_025 \
    --preprocessing_name=mobilenet_v1 \
    --use_grayscale=True \
    --train_image_size=96
```

You'll need to make sure that --checkpoint_path is pointing to a valid set of checkpoint data. Checkpoints are stored in three separate files, so the value should be their common prefix. For example, if you have a checkpoint file called *model.ckpt-5179.data-00000-of-00001*, the prefix would be *model.ckpt-5179*. The script should produce output that looks something like this:

```
INFO:tensorflow:Evaluation [406/406]
I0929 22:52:59.936022 140225887045056 evaluation.py:167] Evaluation [406/406]
eval/Accuracy[0.717438412]eval/Recall_5[1]
```

The important number here is the accuracy. It shows the proportion of the images that were classified correctly, which is 72% in this case, after converting to a percentage. If you follow the example script, you should expect a fully trained model to achieve an accuracy of around 84% after one million steps and show a loss of around 0.4.

Exporting the Model to TensorFlow Lite

When the model has trained to an accuracy you're happy with, you'll need to convert the results from the TensorFlow training environment into a form you can run on an embedded device. As we've seen in previous chapters, this can be a complex process, and *tf.slim* adds a few of its own wrinkles, too.

Exporting to a GraphDef Protobuf File

Slim generates the architecture from the model_name every time one of its scripts is run, so for a model to be used outside of Slim, it needs to be saved in a common format. We're going to use the GraphDef protobuf serialization format because that's understood by both Slim and the rest of TensorFlow:

```
! python models/research/slim/export_inference_graph.py \
    --alsologtostderr \
    --dataset_name=visualwakewords \
    --model_name=mobilenet_v1_025 \
    --image_size=96 \
    --use_grayscale=True \
    --output_file=vww_96_grayscale_graph.pb
```

If this succeeds, you should have a new *vww_96_grayscale_graph.pb* file in your home directory. This contains the layout of the operations in the model, but it doesn't yet have any of the weight data.

Freezing the Weights

The process of storing the trained weights together with the operation graph is known as *freezing*. This converts all of the variables in the graph to constants, after loading their values from a checkpoint file. The command that follows uses a checkpoint from the millionth training step, but you can supply any valid checkpoint path. The graph-freezing script is stored in the main TensorFlow repository, so you'll need to download this from GitHub before running this command:

```
! git clone https://github.com/tensorflow/tensorflow
! python tensorflow/tensorflow/python/tools/freeze_graph.py \
    --input_graph=vww_96_grayscale_graph.pb \
    --input_checkpoint=vww_96_grayscale/model.ckpt-1000000 \
    --input_binary=true --output_graph=vww_96_grayscale_frozen.pb \
    --output_node_names=MobilenetV1/Predictions/Reshape_1
```

After this, you should see a file called *vww_96_grayscale_frozen.pb*.

Quantizing and Converting to TensorFlow Lite

Quantization is a tricky and involved process, and it's still very much an active area of research, so taking the float graph that we've trained so far and converting it down to an 8-bit entity takes quite a bit of code. You can find more of an explanation of what quantization is and how it works in Chapter 15, but here we'll show you how to use it with the model we've trained. The majority of the code is preparing example images to feed into the trained network so that the ranges of the activation layers in typical use can be measured. We rely on the TFLiteConverter class to handle the quantization and conversion into the TensorFlow Lite FlatBuffer file that we need for the inference engine:

```
import tensorflow as tf
import io
import PIL
import numpy as np

def representative_dataset_gen():
```

```
record_iterator = tf.python_io.tf_record_iterator
    (path='data/visualwakewords/val.record-00000-of-00010')

count = 0
for string_record in record_iterator:
  example = tf.train.Example()
  example.ParseFromString(string_record)
  image_stream = io.BytesIO
      (example.features.feature['image/encoded'].bytes_list.value[0])
  image = PIL.Image.open(image_stream)
  image = image.resize((96, 96))
  image = image.convert('L')
  array = np.array(image)
  array = np.expand_dims(array, axis=2)
  array = np.expand_dims(array, axis=0)
  array = ((array / 127.5) - 1.0).astype(np.float32)
  yield([array])
  count += 1
  if count > 300:
      break

converter = tf.lite.TFLiteConverter.from_frozen_graph \
    ('vww_96_grayscale_frozen.pb', ['input'],  ['MobilenetV1/Predictions/ \
    Reshape_1'])
converter.inference_input_type = tf.lite.constants.INT8
converter.inference_output_type = tf.lite.constants.INT8
converter.optimizations = [tf.lite.Optimize.DEFAULT]
converter.representative_dataset = representative_dataset_gen

tflite_quant_model = converter.convert()
open("vww_96_grayscale_quantized.tflite", "wb").write(tflite_quant_model)
```

Converting to a C Source File

The converter writes out a file, but most embedded devices don't have a filesystem. To access the serialized data from our program, we must compile it into the executable and store it in flash. The easiest way to do that is to convert the file to a C data array, as we've done in previous chapters:

```
# Install xxd if it is not available
! apt-get -qq install xxd
# Save the file as a C source file
! xxd -i vww_96_grayscale_quantized.tflite > person_detect_model_data.cc
```

You can now replace the existing *person_detect_model_data.cc* file with the version you've trained and will be able to run your own model on embedded devices.

Training for Other Categories

There are more than 60 different object types in the COCO dataset, so an easy way to customize your model would be to choose one of those instead of `person` when you build the training dataset. Here's an example that looks for cars:

```
! python models/research/slim/datasets/build_visualwakewords_data.py \
    --logtostderr \
    --train_image_dir=coco/raw-data/train2014 \
    --val_image_dir=coco/raw-data/val2014 \
    --train_annotations_file=coco/raw-data/annotations/instances_train2014.json \
    --val_annotations_file=coco/raw-data/annotations/instances_val2014.json \
    --output_dir=coco/processed_cars \
    --small_object_area_threshold=0.005 \
    --foreground_class_of_interest='car'
```

You should be able to follow the same steps as you did for the person detector, substituting in the new `coco/processed_cars` path wherever `data/visualwakewords` used to be.

If the kind of object you're interested in isn't present in COCO, you might be able to use transfer learning to help you train on a custom dataset you've gathered, even if it's much smaller. Although we don't have an example of this to share yet, you can check *tinymlbook.com* for updates on this approach.

Understanding the Architecture

MobileNets (*https://oreil.ly/tK57G*) are a family of architectures designed to provide good accuracy for as few weight parameters and arithmetic operations as possible. There are now multiple versions, but in our case we're using the original v1 because it requires the smallest amount of RAM at runtime. The core concept behind the architecture is *depthwise separable convolution*. This is a variant of classic 2D convolutions that works in a much more efficient way, without sacrificing very much accuracy. Regular convolution calculates an output value based on applying a filter of a particular size across all channels of the input. This means that the number of calculations involved in each output is the width of the filter multiplied by the height, multiplied by the number of input channels. Depthwise convolution breaks this large calculation into separate parts. First, each input channel is filtered by one or more rectangular filters to produce intermediate values. These values are then combined using pointwise convolutions. This dramatically reduces the number of calculations needed, and in practice produces similar results to regular convolution.

MobileNet v1 is a stack of 14 of these depthwise separable convolution layers with an average pool and then a fully connected layer followed by a softmax at the end. We have specified a *width multiplier* of 0.25, which has the effect of reducing the number of computations down to around 60 million per inference, by shrinking the number of channels in each activation layer by 75% compared to the standard model. In essence it's very similar to a normal convolutional neural network in operation, with each layer learning patterns in the input. Earlier layers act more like edge recognition filters, spotting low-level structure in the image, and later layers synthesize that information into more abstract patterns that help with the final object classification.

Wrapping Up

Image recognition using machine learning requires large amounts of data and a lot of processing power. In this chapter you learned how to train a model from scratch, given nothing but a dataset, and how to convert that model into a form that is optimized for embedded devices.

This experience should give you a good foundation for tackling the machine vision problems that you need to solve for your product. There's still something a bit magical about computers being able to see and understand the world around them, so we can't wait to see what you come up with!

## CHAPTER 11

Magic Wand: Building an Application

So far, our example applications have worked with data that human beings can easily comprehend. We have entire areas of our brain devoted to understanding speech and vision, so it's not difficult for us to interpret visual or audio data and form an idea of what's going on.

A lot of data, however, is not so easily understood. Machines and their sensors generate huge streams of information that don't map easily onto our human senses. Even when represented visually, it can be difficult for our brains to grasp the trends and patterns within the data.

For example, the two graphs presented in Figure 11-1 and Figure 11-2 show sensor data captured by mobile phones placed in the front pockets of people doing exercise. The sensor in question is an *accelerometer*, which measures acceleration in three dimensions (we'll talk more about these later). The graph in Figure 11-1 shows accelerometer data for a person who is jogging, whereas the graph in Figure 11-2 shows data for the same person walking down stairs.

As you can see, it's tough to distinguish between the two activities, even though the data represents a simple and relatable activity. Imagine trying to distinguish between the operating states of a complex industrial machine, which might have hundreds of sensors measuring all sorts of obscure properties.

It's often possible to write handcrafted algorithms that can make sense of this type of data. For example, an expert in human gait might recognize the telltale signs of walking up stairs, and be able to express this knowledge as a function in code. This type of function is called a *heuristic*, and it's commonly used in all sorts of applications, from industrial automation to medical devices.

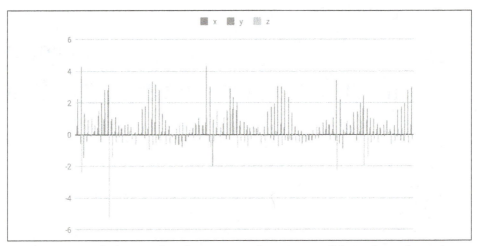

Figure 11-1. Graph showing data for a person who is jogging (MotionSense dataset) (https://oreil.ly/ZUPV5)

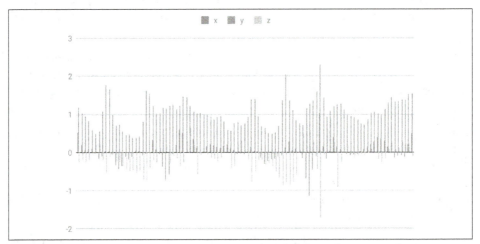

Figure 11-2. Graph showing data for a person who is walking down stairs (MotionSense dataset) (https://oreil.ly/ZUPV5)

To create a heuristic, you need two things. The first is domain knowledge. A heuristic algorithm expresses human knowledge and understanding, so to write one, you need to already understand what the data means. To understand this, imagine a heuristic that determines whether a person has a fever based on their body temperature. Whoever created it must have had knowledge of the temperature changes that indicate a fever.

The second requirement for building a heuristic is programming and mathematical expertise. Although it's fairly easy to determine whether someone's temperature is too high, other problems can be far more complex. Discerning a system's state based on complex patterns in multiple streams of data might require knowledge of some advanced techniques, like statistical analysis or signal processing. For example, imagine creating a heuristic to distinguish between walking and running based on accelerometer data. To build this, you might need to know how to mathematically filter the accelerometer data to get an estimate of step frequency.

Heuristics can be extremely useful, but the fact that they require domain knowledge and programming expertise means that they can be a challenge to build. First, domain knowledge is not always available. For example, a small company might not have the resources to conduct the basic research necessary to know what indicates one state versus another. Similarly, even given domain knowledge, not everyone has the expertise required to design and implement the heuristic algorithm in code.

Machine learning gives us an opportunity to shortcut these requirements. A model trained on labeled data can learn to recognize the signals that indicate one class or another, meaning there's less need for deep domain knowledge. For example, a model can learn the human temperature fluctuations that indicate a fever without ever being told which specific temperatures are important—all it needs is temperature data labelled with "fever" or "nonfever." In addition, the engineering skills required to work with machine learning are arguably easier to acquire than those that might be required to implement a sophisticated heuristic.

Instead of having to design a heuristic algorithm from scratch, a machine learning developer can find a suitable model architecture, collect and label a dataset, and iteratively create a model through training and evaluation. Domain knowledge is still extremely helpful, but it might no longer be a prerequisite to getting something working. And in some cases, the resulting model can actually be more accurate than the best handcoded algorithms.

In fact, a recent paper[1] showed how a simple convolutional neural network is able to detect congestive heart failure in a patient from a single heartbeat *with 100% accuracy*. This is better performance than any previous diagnostic technique. The paper is a fascinating read, even if you don't understand every detail.

By training a deep learning model to understand complex data and embedding it in a microcontroller program, we can create smart sensors that are able to understand the complexities of their environments and tell us, at a high level, what is going on. This has huge implications across dozens of fields. Here are just a few potential applications:

---

1 Mihaela Porumb et al., "A convolutional neural network approach to detect congestive heart failure." *Biomedical Signal Processing and Control* (Jan 2020). *https://oreil.ly/4HBFt*

- Environmental monitoring in remote places with poor connectivity
- Automated industrial processes that adjust to problems in real time
- Robots that react to complex external stimuli
- Disease diagnosis without the need for medical professionals
- Computer interfaces that understand physical movement

In this chapter, we build a project in the final category: a digital "magic wand," which can be waved by its owner to cast a variety of spells. As its input, it takes complex, multidimensional sensor data that would be inscrutable to a human. Its output will be a simple classification that alerts us if one of several classes of movements has recently occurred. We'll look at how deep learning can transform strange numerical data into meaningful information—to magical effect.

What We're Building

Our "magic wand" can be used to cast several types of spells. To do so, the wielder need only wave the wand in one of three gestures, named "wing," "ring," and "slope," as shown in Figure 11-3.

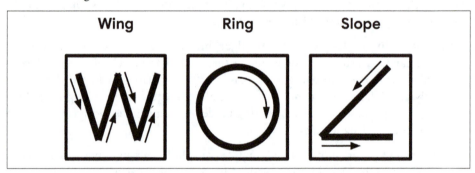

Figure 11-3. The three magic wand gestures

The wand will react to each spell by lighting an LED. In case the magic of electric light is not sufficiently exciting, it will also output information to its serial port, which can be used to control an attached computer.

To understand physical gestures, the magic wand application uses a device's accelerometer to collect information about its motion through space. An accelerometer measures the degree of acceleration that it is currently experiencing. For example, imagine that we've attached an accelerometer to a car that has stopped at a red light and is about to drive away.

When the light turns green, the car starts moving forward, increasing in speed until it reaches the speed limit. During this period, the accelerometer will output a value that indicates the car's rate of acceleration. After the car has reached a steady speed, it is no longer accelerating, so the accelerometer will output zero.

The SparkFun Edge and Arduino Nano 33 BLE Sense boards are both equipped with three-axis accelerometers contained within components that are soldered to each board. These measure acceleration in three directions, which means they can be used to track the motion of the device in 3D space. To construct our magic wand, we'll attach the microcontroller board to the end of a stick so it can be waved in a sorcerous manner. We'll then feed the accelerometer's output into a deep learning model, which will perform classification to tell us whether a known gesture was made.

We provide instructions on deploying this application to the following microcontroller platforms:

- Arduino Nano 33 BLE Sense (*https://oreil.ly/6qlMD*)
- SparkFun Edge (*https://oreil.ly/-hoL-*)

Because the ST Microelectronics STM32F746G Discovery kit (*https://oreil.ly/SSsVJ*) doesn't include an accelerometer (and is too big to attach to the end of a magic wand), we won't be featuring it here.

 TensorFlow Lite regularly adds support for new devices, so if the device you'd like to use isn't listed here, it's worth checking the example's *README.md* (*https://oreil.ly/dkZfA*). You can also check there for updated deployment instructions if you run into trouble.

In the next section, we'll look at the structure of our application and learn more about how its model works.

Application Architecture

Our application will again follow the now-familiar pattern of obtaining input, running inference, processing the output, and using the resulting information to make things happen.

A three-axis accelerometer outputs three values representing the amount of acceleration on the device's x, y, and z-axes. The accelerometer on the SparkFun Edge board can do this 25 times per second (a rate of 25 Hz). Our model takes these values directly as its input, meaning we won't need to do any preprocessing.

After data has been captured and inference has been run, our application will determine whether a valid gesture was detected, print some output to the terminal, and light an LED.

Introducing Our Model

Our gesture-detecting model is a convolutional neural network, weighing in at around 20 KB, that accepts raw accelerometer values as its input. It takes in 128 sets of *x*, *y*, and *z* values at once, which at a rate of 25 Hz adds up to a little more than five seconds' worth of data. Each value is a 32-bit floating-point number that indicates the amount of acceleration in that direction.

The model was trained on four gestures performed by numerous people. It outputs probability scores for four classes: one representing each gesture ("wing," "ring," and "slope"), and one representing no recognized gesture. The probability scores sum to 1, with a score above 0.8 being considered confident.

Because we'll be running multiple inferences per second, we'll need to make sure a single errant inference while a gesture is performed doesn't skew our results. Our mechanism for doing this will be to consider a gesture as being detected only after it has been confirmed by a certain number of inferences. Given that each gesture takes a different amount of time to perform, the number of required inferences is different for each gesture, with the optimal numbers being determined through experimentation. Likewise, inference runs at varying rates on different devices, so these thresholds are also set per device.

In Chapter 12, we'll explore how to train a model on our own gesture data and dig deeper into how the model works. Until then, let's continue walking through our application.

All the Moving Parts

Figure 11-4 shows the structure of our magic wand application.

As you can see, it's almost as simple as our person detection application. Our model accepts raw accelerometer data, meaning we don't need to do any preprocessing.

The code's six main parts follow a similar structure as in our person detection example. Let's walk through them in turn:

Main loop
> Our application runs in a continuous loop. Since its model is small and simple and there's no preprocessing required, we'll be able to run multiple inferences per second.

Accelerometer handler
> This component captures data from the accelerometer and writes it to the model's input tensor. It uses a buffer to hold data.

TF Lite interpreter
> The interpreter runs the TensorFlow Lite model, as in our earlier examples.

Model

The model is included as a data array and run by the interpreter. It's nice and small, weighing in at only 19.5 KB.

Gesture predictor

This component takes the model's output and decides whether a gesture has been detected, based on thresholds for both probability and the number of consecutive positive predictions.

Output handler

The output handler lights LEDs and prints output to the serial port depending on which gesture was recognized.

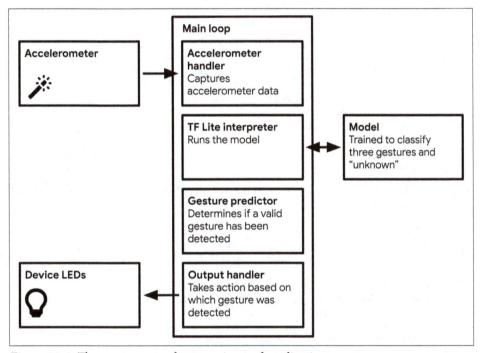

Figure 11-4. The components of our magic wand application

Walking Through the Tests

You can find the application's tests in the GitHub repository (*https://oreil.ly/h4iYb*):

magic_wand_test.cc (https://oreil.ly/X0AJP)

Shows how to run inference on a sample of accelerometer data

accelerometer_handler_test.cc (https://oreil.ly/MwM7g)

Shows how to use the accelerometer handler to obtain fresh data

gesture_predictor_test.cc (https://oreil.ly/cGbim)
Shows how to use the gesture predictor to interpret the results of inference

output_handler_test.cc (https://oreil.ly/MYwUW)
Shows how to use the output handler to show results of inference

Let's begin by walking through *magic_wand_test.cc*, which will show us the end-to-end process of inference with our model.

The Basic Flow

We step through the basic flow in *magic_wand_test.cc*.

First, we list the ops our model will need:

```
namespace tflite {
namespace ops {
namespace micro {
TfLiteRegistration* Register_DEPTHWISE_CONV_2D();
TfLiteRegistration* Register_MAX_POOL_2D();
TfLiteRegistration* Register_CONV_2D();
TfLiteRegistration* Register_FULLY_CONNECTED();
TfLiteRegistration* Register_SOFTMAX();
}  // namespace micro
}  // namespace ops
}  // namespace tflite
```

The test itself begins (as usual) by setting up everything required for inference and grabbing a pointer to the model's input tensor:

```
// Set up logging
tflite::MicroErrorReporter micro_error_reporter;
tflite::ErrorReporter* error_reporter = &micro_error_reporter;

// Map the model into a usable data structure. This doesn't involve any
// copying or parsing, it's a very lightweight operation.
const tflite::Model* model =
    ::tflite::GetModel(g_magic_wand_model_data);
if (model->version() != TFLITE_SCHEMA_VERSION) {
error_reporter->Report(
    "Model provided is schema version %d not equal "
    "to supported version %d.\n",
    model->version(), TFLITE_SCHEMA_VERSION);
}

static tflite::MicroMutableOpResolver micro_mutable_op_resolver;
micro_mutable_op_resolver.AddBuiltin(
    tflite::BuiltinOperator_DEPTHWISE_CONV_2D,
    tflite::ops::micro::Register_DEPTHWISE_CONV_2D());
micro_mutable_op_resolver.AddBuiltin(
    tflite::BuiltinOperator_MAX_POOL_2D,
    tflite::ops::micro::Register_MAX_POOL_2D());
```

```
micro_mutable_op_resolver.AddBuiltin(
    tflite::BuiltinOperator_CONV_2D,
    tflite::ops::micro::Register_CONV_2D());
micro_mutable_op_resolver.AddBuiltin(
    tflite::BuiltinOperator_FULLY_CONNECTED,
    tflite::ops::micro::Register_FULLY_CONNECTED());
micro_mutable_op_resolver.AddBuiltin(tflite::BuiltinOperator_SOFTMAX,
                                     tflite::ops::micro::Register_SOFTMAX());

// Create an area of memory to use for input, output, and intermediate arrays.
// Finding the minimum value for your model may require some trial and error.
const int tensor_arena_size = 60 * 1024;
uint8_t tensor_arena[tensor_arena_size];

// Build an interpreter to run the model with
tflite::MicroInterpreter interpreter(model, micro_mutable_op_resolver, ten
sor_arena,
                                     tensor_arena_size, error_reporter);

// Allocate memory from the tensor_arena for the model's tensors
interpreter.AllocateTensors();

// Obtain a pointer to the model's input tensor
TfLiteTensor* input = interpreter.input(0);
```

We then inspect the input tensor to ensure that it's the expected shape:

```
// Make sure the input has the properties we expect
TF_LITE_MICRO_EXPECT_NE(nullptr, input);
TF_LITE_MICRO_EXPECT_EQ(4, input->dims->size);
// The value of each element gives the length of the corresponding tensor.
TF_LITE_MICRO_EXPECT_EQ(1, input->dims->data[0]);
TF_LITE_MICRO_EXPECT_EQ(128, input->dims->data[1]);
TF_LITE_MICRO_EXPECT_EQ(3, input->dims->data[2]);
TF_LITE_MICRO_EXPECT_EQ(1, input->dims->data[3]);
// The input is a 32 bit floating point value
TF_LITE_MICRO_EXPECT_EQ(kTfLiteFloat32, input->type);
```

Our input's shape is (1, 128, 3, 1). The first dimension is just a wrapper around
the second, which holds 128 three-axis accelerometer readings. Each reading has
three values, one for each axis, and each value is wrapped within a single-element
tensor. The inputs are all 32-bit floating-point values.

After we've confirmed the input shape, we write some data to the input tensor:

```
// Provide an input value
const float* ring_features_data = g_circle_micro_f9643d42_nohash_4_data;
error_reporter->Report("%d", input->bytes);
for (int i = 0; i < (input->bytes / sizeof(float)); ++i) {
    input->data.f[i] = ring_features_data[i];
}
```

The constant g_circle_micro_f9643d42_nohash_4_data is defined in *circle_micro_features_data.cc*; it contains an array of floating-point values representing one person's attempt at performing a circle gesture. In the for loop, we step through this data and write each value into the input. We write only as many float values as the input tensor can hold.

Next, we run inference in the familiar manner:

```
// Run the model on this input and check that it succeeds
TfLiteStatus invoke_status = interpreter.Invoke();
if (invoke_status != kTfLiteOk) {
  error_reporter->Report("Invoke failed\n");
}
TF_LITE_MICRO_EXPECT_EQ(kTfLiteOk, invoke_status);
```

Afterward, we investigate our output tensor to ensure that it's the shape we expect:

```
// Obtain a pointer to the output tensor and make sure it has the
// properties we expect.
TfLiteTensor* output = interpreter.output(0);
TF_LITE_MICRO_EXPECT_EQ(2, output->dims->size);
TF_LITE_MICRO_EXPECT_EQ(1, output->dims->data[0]);
TF_LITE_MICRO_EXPECT_EQ(4, output->dims->data[1]);
TF_LITE_MICRO_EXPECT_EQ(kTfLiteFloat32, output->type);
```

It should have two dimensions: a single-element wrapper, and a set of four values that indicate our four probabilities ("wing," "ring," "slope," and unknown). Each of these will be a 32-bit floating-point number.

We can then test our data to make sure the inference result is what we expect. We passed in data for a circle gesture, so we expect the "ring" score to be the highest:

```
// There are four possible classes in the output, each with a score.
const int kWingIndex = 0;
const int kRingIndex = 1;
const int kSlopeIndex = 2;
const int kNegativeIndex = 3;

// Make sure that the expected "Ring" score is higher than the other
// classes.
float wing_score = output->data.f[kWingIndex];
float ring_score = output->data.f[kRingIndex];
float slope_score = output->data.f[kSlopeIndex];
float negative_score = output->data.f[kNegativeIndex];
TF_LITE_MICRO_EXPECT_GT(ring_score, wing_score);
TF_LITE_MICRO_EXPECT_GT(ring_score, slope_score);
TF_LITE_MICRO_EXPECT_GT(ring_score, negative_score);
```

We then repeat this entire process for the "slope" gesture:

```
// Now test with a different input, from a recording of "Slope".
const float* slope_features_data = g_angle_micro_f2e59fea_nohash_1_data;
for (int i = 0; i < (input->bytes / sizeof(float)); ++i) {
```

```
    input->data.f[i] = slope_features_data[i];
  }

  // Run the model on this "Slope" input.
  invoke_status = interpreter.Invoke();
  if (invoke_status != kTfLiteOk) {
    error_reporter->Report("Invoke failed\n");
  }
  TF_LITE_MICRO_EXPECT_EQ(kTfLiteOk, invoke_status);

  // Make sure that the expected "Slope" score is higher than the other classes.
  wing_score = output->data.f[kWingIndex];
  ring_score = output->data.f[kRingIndex];
  slope_score = output->data.f[kSlopeIndex];
  negative_score = output->data.f[kNegativeIndex];
  TF_LITE_MICRO_EXPECT_GT(slope_score, wing_score);
  TF_LITE_MICRO_EXPECT_GT(slope_score, ring_score);
  TF_LITE_MICRO_EXPECT_GT(slope_score, negative_score);
```

And that's it! We've seen how we can run inference on raw accelerometer data. Like the previous example, the fact that we can avoid preprocessing keeps things nice and simple.

To run this test, use the following command:

```
make -f tensorflow/lite/micro/tools/make/Makefile test_magic_wand_test
```

The Accelerometer Handler

Our next test shows the interface for the accelerometer handler. This component's task is to populate the input tensor with accelerometer data for each inference.

Because both of these things depend on how the device's accelerometer works, a different accelerometer handler implementation is provided for each individual device. We'll walk through these implementations later on, but for now, the tests located in *accelerometer_handler_test.cc* (*https://oreil.ly/MwM7g*) will show us how the handler should be called.

The first test is very simple:

```
TF_LITE_MICRO_TEST(TestSetup) {
  static tflite::MicroErrorReporter micro_error_reporter;
  TfLiteStatus setup_status = SetupAccelerometer(&micro_error_reporter);
  TF_LITE_MICRO_EXPECT_EQ(kTfLiteOk, setup_status);
}
```

The SetupAccelerometer() function performs the one-time setup that needs to happen in order to obtain values from the accelerometer. The test shows how the function should be called (with a pointer to an ErrorReporter) and that it returns a TfLiteStatus indicating that setup was successful.

The next test shows how the accelerometer handler is used to fill the input tensor with data:

```
TF_LITE_MICRO_TEST(TestAccelerometer) {
  float input[384] = {0.0};
  tflite::MicroErrorReporter micro_error_reporter;
  // Test that the function returns false before insufficient data is available
  bool inference_flag =
      ReadAccelerometer(&micro_error_reporter, input, 384, false);
  TF_LITE_MICRO_EXPECT_EQ(inference_flag, false);

  // Test that the function returns true once sufficient data is available to
  // fill the model's input buffer (128 sets of values)
  for (int i = 1; i <= 128; i++) {
    inference_flag =
        ReadAccelerometer(&micro_error_reporter, input, 384, false);
  }
  TF_LITE_MICRO_EXPECT_EQ(inference_flag, true);
}
```

First, we prepare a `float` array named `input` to simulate the model's input tensor. Because there are 128 three-axis readings, it has a total length of 384 readings (128 * 3). We initialize every value in the array to `0.0`.

We then call `ReadAccelerometer()`. We provide an `ErrorReporter` instance, the array to which we want data to be written (`input`), and the total amount of data that we want to obtain (384 bytes). The final argument is a Boolean flag that instructs `ReadAccelerometer()` whether to clear the buffer before reading more data, which needs to be done after a gesture has been successfully recognized.

When called, the `ReadAccelerometer()` function attempts to write 384 bytes of data to the array passed to it. If the accelerometer has only just started collecting data, the full 384 bytes might not yet be available. In this case, the function will do nothing and return a value of `false`. We can use this to avoid running inference if no data is available.

The dummy implementation of the accelerometer handler, located in *accelerometer_handler.cc (https://oreil.ly/MwM7g)*, simulates another reading being available every time it is called. By calling it 127 additional times we ensure it will have accrued enough data to start returning `true`.

To run these tests, use the following command:

```
make -f tensorflow/lite/micro/tools/make/Makefile \
  test_gesture_accelerometer_handler_test
```

The Gesture Predictor

After inference has occurred, our output tensor will be filled with probabilities that indicate to us which gesture, if any, was made. However, because machine learning is not an exact science, there's a chance that any single inference might result in a false positive.

To reduce the impact of false positives, we can stipulate that for a gesture to be recognized, it must have been detected in at least a certain number of consecutive inferences. Given that we run inference multiple times per second, we can quickly determine whether a result is valid. This is the job of the gesture predictor.

It defines a single function, PredictGesture(), which takes the model's output tensor as its input. To determine whether a gesture has been detected, the function does two things:

1. Checks whether the gesture's probability meets a minimum threshold
2. Checks whether the gesture has been consistently detected over a certain number of inferences

The minimum number of inferences required varies per gesture because some take longer to perform than others. It also varies per device, given that faster devices are able to run inference more frequently. The default values, tuned for the SparkFun Edge board, are located in *constants.cc* (*https://oreil.ly/ktGgw*):

```
const int kConsecutiveInferenceThresholds[3] = {15, 12, 10};
```

The values are defined in the same order as the gestures appear in the model's output tensor. Other platforms, such as Arduino, have device-specific versions of this file that contain values tuned to their own performance.

Let's walk through the code in *gesture_predictor.cc* (*https://oreil.ly/f3I6U*) to see how these are used.

First, we define some variables that are used to keep track of the last gesture seen and how many of the same gesture have been recorded in a row:

```
// How many times the most recent gesture has been matched in a row
int continuous_count = 0;
// The result of the last prediction
int last_predict = -1;
```

Next, we define the PredictGesture() function and determine whether any of the gesture categories had a probability of greater than 0.8 in the most recent inference:

```
// Return the result of the last prediction
// 0: wing("W"), 1: ring("O"), 2: slope("angle"), 3: unknown
int PredictGesture(float* output) {
  // Find whichever output has a probability > 0.8 (they sum to 1)
```

```
int this_predict = -1;
for (int i = 0; i < 3; i++) {
  if (output[i] > 0.8) this_predict = i;
}
```

We use `this_predict` to store the index of the gesture that was predicted.

The variable `continuous_count` is used to track how many times the most recently spotted gesture has been predicted in a row. If none of the gesture categories meet the probability threshold of 0.8, we reset any ongoing detection process by setting `continuous_count` to 0, and `last_predict` to 3 (the index of the "unknown" category), indicating that the most recent result was no known gesture:

```
// No gesture was detected above the threshold
if (this_predict == -1) {
  continuous_count = 0;
  last_predict = 3;
  return 3;
}
```

Next, if the most recent prediction aligns with the previous one, we increment `continuous_count`. Otherwise, we reset it to 0. We also store the most recent prediction in `last_predict`:

```
if (last_predict == this_predict) {
  continuous_count += 1;
} else {
  continuous_count = 0;
}
last_predict = this_predict;
```

In the next section of `PredictGesture()`, we use `continuous_count` to check whether the current gesture has met its threshold yet. If it hasn't, we return a 3, indicating an unknown gesture:

```
// If we haven't yet had enough consecutive matches for this gesture,
// report a negative result
if (continuous_count < kConsecutiveInferenceThresholds[this_predict]) {
  return 3;
}
```

If we get past this point, it means that we've confirmed a valid gesture. In this case, we reset all of our variables:

```
// Otherwise, we've seen a positive result, so clear all our variables
// and report it
continuous_count = 0;
last_predict = -1;
return this_predict;
}
```

The function ends by returning the current prediction. This will be passed by our main loop into the output handler, which displays the result to the user.

The gesture predictor's tests are located in *gesture_predictor_test.cc* (*https://oreil.ly/ 5BZzt*). The first test demonstrates a successful prediction:

```
TF_LITE_MICRO_TEST(SuccessfulPrediction) {
  // Use the threshold from the 0th gesture
  int threshold = kConsecutiveInferenceThresholds[0];
  float probabilities[4] = {1.0, 0.0, 0.0, 0.0};
  int prediction;
  // Loop just too few times to trigger a prediction
  for (int i = 0; i <= threshold - 1; i++) {
    prediction = PredictGesture(probabilities);
    TF_LITE_MICRO_EXPECT_EQ(prediction, 3);
  }
  // Call once more, triggering a prediction
  // for category 0
  prediction = PredictGesture(probabilities);
  TF_LITE_MICRO_EXPECT_EQ(prediction, 0);
}
```

The PredictGesture() function is fed a set of probabilities that strongly indicate that the first category should be matched. However, until it has been called with these probabilities threshold number of times, it returns a 3, signifying an "unknown" result. After it has been called threshold number of times, it returns a positive prediction for category 0.

The next test shows what happens if a consecutive run of high probabilities for one category is interrupted by a high probability for a different category:

```
TF_LITE_MICRO_TEST(FailPartWayThere) {
  // Use the threshold from the 0th gesture
  int threshold = kConsecutiveInferenceThresholds[0];
  float probabilities[4] = {1.0, 0.0, 0.0, 0.0};
  int prediction;
  // Loop just too few times to trigger a prediction
  for (int i = 0; i <= threshold - 1; i++) {
    prediction = PredictGesture(probabilities);
    TF_LITE_MICRO_EXPECT_EQ(prediction, 3);
  }
  // Call with a different prediction, triggering a failure
  probabilities[0] = 0.0;
  probabilities[2] = 1.0;
  prediction = PredictGesture(probabilities);
  TF_LITE_MICRO_EXPECT_EQ(prediction, 3);
}
```

In this case, we feed in a set of consecutive high probabilities for category 0, but not a sufficient number to meet the threshold. We then change the probabilities so that category 2 is the highest, which results in a category 3 prediction, signifying an "unknown" gesture.

The final test shows how PredictGesture() ignores probabilities that are below its threshold. In a loop, we feed in exactly the correct number of predictions to meet category 0's threshold. However, although category 0 has the highest probability, its value is 0.7, which is below PredictGesture()'s internal threshold of 0.8. This results in a category 3 "unknown" prediction:

```
TF_LITE_MICRO_TEST(InsufficientProbability) {
  // Use the threshold from the 0th gesture
  int threshold = kConsecutiveInferenceThresholds[0];
  // Below the probability threshold of 0.8
  float probabilities[4] = {0.7, 0.0, 0.0, 0.0};
  int prediction;
  // Loop the exact right number of times
  for (int i = 0; i <= threshold; i++) {
    prediction = PredictGesture(probabilities);
    TF_LITE_MICRO_EXPECT_EQ(prediction, 3);
  }
}
```

To run these tests, use the following command:

```
make -f tensorflow/lite/micro/tools/make/Makefile \
  test_gesture_predictor_test
```

The Output Handler

The output handler is very simple; it just takes the class index returned by Predict Gesture() and displays the results to the user. Its test, in *output_handler_test.cc* (*https://oreil.ly/QWkeL*), shows its interface:

```
TF_LITE_MICRO_TEST(TestCallability) {
  tflite::MicroErrorReporter micro_error_reporter;
  tflite::ErrorReporter* error_reporter = &micro_error_reporter;
  HandleOutput(error_reporter, 0);
  HandleOutput(error_reporter, 1);
  HandleOutput(error_reporter, 2);
  HandleOutput(error_reporter, 3);
}
```

To run this test, use the following command:

```
make -f tensorflow/lite/micro/tools/make/Makefile \
  test_gesture_output_handler_test
```

Detecting Gestures

All of these components come together in *main_functions.cc* (*https://oreil.ly/ggNtD*), which contains the core logic of our program. First it sets up the usual variables, along with some extras:

```
namespace tflite {
namespace ops {
namespace micro {
TfLiteRegistration* Register_DEPTHWISE_CONV_2D();
TfLiteRegistration* Register_MAX_POOL_2D();
TfLiteRegistration* Register_CONV_2D();
TfLiteRegistration* Register_FULLY_CONNECTED();
TfLiteRegistration* Register_SOFTMAX();
}  // namespace micro
}  // namespace ops
}  // namespace tflite

// Globals, used for compatibility with Arduino-style sketches.
namespace {
tflite::ErrorReporter* error_reporter = nullptr;
const tflite::Model* model = nullptr;
tflite::MicroInterpreter* interpreter = nullptr;
TfLiteTensor* model_input = nullptr;
int input_length;

// Create an area of memory to use for input, output, and intermediate arrays.
// The size of this will depend on the model you're using, and may need to be
// determined by experimentation.
constexpr int kTensorArenaSize = 60 * 1024;
uint8_t tensor_arena[kTensorArenaSize];

// Whether we should clear the buffer next time we fetch data
bool should_clear_buffer = false;
}  // namespace
```

The input_length variable stores the length of the model's input tensor, and the should_clear_buffer variable is a flag that indicates whether the accelerometer handler's buffer should be cleared the next time it runs. Clearing the buffer is done after a successful detection result in order to provide a clean slate for subsequent inferences.

Next, the setup() function does all of the usual housekeeping so that we're ready to run inference:

```
void setup() {
  // Set up logging. Google style is to avoid globals or statics because of
  // lifetime uncertainty, but since this has a trivial destructor it's okay.
  static tflite::MicroErrorReporter micro_error_reporter;  //NOLINT
  error_reporter = &micro_error_reporter;

  // Map the model into a usable data structure. This doesn't involve any
```

```
  // copying or parsing, it's a very lightweight operation.
  model = tflite::GetModel(g_magic_wand_model_data);
  if (model->version() != TFLITE_SCHEMA_VERSION) {
    error_reporter->Report(
        "Model provided is schema version %d not equal "
        "to supported version %d.",
        model->version(), TFLITE_SCHEMA_VERSION);
    return;
  }

  // Pull in only the operation implementations we need.
  // This relies on a complete list of all the ops needed by this graph.
  // An easier approach is to just use the AllOpsResolver, but this will
  // incur some penalty in code space for op implementations that are not
  // needed by this graph.
  static tflite::MicroMutableOpResolver micro_mutable_op_resolver; // NOLINT
  micro_mutable_op_resolver.AddBuiltin(
      tflite::BuiltinOperator_DEPTHWISE_CONV_2D,
      tflite::ops::micro::Register_DEPTHWISE_CONV_2D());
  micro_mutable_op_resolver.AddBuiltin(
      tflite::BuiltinOperator_MAX_POOL_2D,
      tflite::ops::micro::Register_MAX_POOL_2D());
  micro_mutable_op_resolver.AddBuiltin(
      tflite::BuiltinOperator_CONV_2D,
      tflite::ops::micro::Register_CONV_2D());
  micro_mutable_op_resolver.AddBuiltin(
      tflite::BuiltinOperator_FULLY_CONNECTED,
      tflite::ops::micro::Register_FULLY_CONNECTED());
  micro_mutable_op_resolver.AddBuiltin(tflite::BuiltinOperator_SOFTMAX,
                                       tflite::ops::micro::Register_SOFTMAX());

  // Build an interpreter to run the model with
  static tflite::MicroInterpreter static_interpreter(model,
                                                     micro_mutable_op_resolver,
                                                     tensor_arena,
                                                     kTensorArenaSize,
                                                     error_reporter);
  interpreter = &static_interpreter;

  // Allocate memory from the tensor_arena for the model's tensors
  interpreter->AllocateTensors();

  // Obtain pointer to the model's input tensor
  model_input = interpreter->input(0);
  if ((model_input->dims->size != 4) || (model_input->dims->data[0] != 1) ||
      (model_input->dims->data[1] != 128) ||
      (model_input->dims->data[2] != kChannelNumber) ||
      (model_input->type != kTfLiteFloat32)) {
    error_reporter->Report("Bad input tensor parameters in model");
    return;
  }
```

```
input_length = model_input->bytes / sizeof(float);

TfLiteStatus setup_status = SetupAccelerometer(error_reporter);
if (setup_status != kTfLiteOk) {
  error_reporter->Report("Set up failed\n");
}
}
```

The more interesting stuff happens in the loop() function, which is still very simple:

```
void loop() {
  // Attempt to read new data from the accelerometer
  bool got_data = ReadAccelerometer(error_reporter, model_input->data.f,
                                     input_length, should_clear_buffer);
  // Don't try to clear the buffer again
  should_clear_buffer = false;
  // If there was no new data, wait until next time
  if (!got_data) return;
  // Run inference, and report any error
  TfLiteStatus invoke_status = interpreter->Invoke();
  if (invoke_status != kTfLiteOk) {
    error_reporter->Report("Invoke failed on index: %d\n", begin_index);
    return;
  }
  // Analyze the results to obtain a prediction
  int gesture_index = PredictGesture(interpreter->output(0)->data.f);
  // Clear the buffer next time we read data
  should_clear_buffer = gesture_index < 3;
  // Produce an output
  HandleOutput(error_reporter, gesture_index);
}
```

First, we attempt to read some values from the accelerometer. After the attempt, we set should_clear_buffer to false to ensure that we stop trying to clear it for the time being.

If obtaining new data was unsuccessful, ReadAccelerometer() will return a false value, and we'll return from the loop() function so that we can try again the next time it is called.

If the value returned by ReadAccelerometer() is true, we'll run inference on our freshly populated input tensor. We pass the result into PredictGesture(), which gives us the index of which gesture was detected. If the index is less than 3, the gesture was valid, so we set the should_clear_buffer flag in order to clear the buffer next time ReadAccelerometer() is called. We then call HandleOutput() to report any results to the user.

Over in *main.cc*, the main() function kicks off our program, runs setup(), and calls the loop() function in a loop:

```
int main(int argc, char* argv[]) {
  setup();
  while (true) {
    loop();
  }
}
```

And that's it! To build the program on your development computer, use the following command:

```
make -f tensorflow/lite/micro/tools/make/Makefile magic_wand
```

Then, to run the program, enter the following:

```
./tensorflow/lite/micro/tools/make/gen/osx_x86_64/bin/magic_wand
```

The program won't produce any output, because there isn't any accelerometer data available, but you can confirm that it builds and runs.

Next, we walk through the code for each platform that captures accelerometer data and produces an output. We also show how to deploy and run the application.

Deploying to Microcontrollers

In this section, we'll deploy our code to two devices:

- Arduino Nano 33 BLE Sense (*https://oreil.ly/6qlMD*)
- SparkFun Edge (*https://oreil.ly/-hoL-*)

Let's begin with the Arduino implementation.

Arduino

The Arduino Nano 33 BLE Sense has a three-axis accelerometer as well as Bluetooth support, and is small and lightweight—ideal for building a magic wand.

Bluetooth

The implementation in this chapter doesn't demonstrate how to use Bluetooth, but Arduino provides a library with example code that you can use create your own implementation. You can find the details in "Making your own changes" on page 326.

There's also a chance that Bluetooth support might have been added to the example since the book was published. Check the latest version in the TensorFlow repository (*https://oreil.ly/1ZC4g*).

Let's walk through the Arduino-specific implementations of some of the application's key files.

Arduino constants

The constant kConsecutiveInferenceThresholds is redefined in the file *arduino/ constants.cc* (*https://oreil.ly/5bBt0*):

```
// The number of expected consecutive inferences for each gesture type.
// Established with the Arduino Nano 33 BLE Sense.
const int kConsecutiveInferenceThresholds[3] = {8, 5, 4};
```

As mentioned earlier in the chapter, this constant stores the number of consecutive positive inferences required for each gesture to be considered detected. The number depends on how many inferences are run per second, which varies per device. Because the default numbers were calibrated for the SparkFun Edge, the Arduino implementation needs its own set of numbers. You can modify these thresholds to make inference more difficult or easier to trigger, but setting them too low will result in false positives.

Capturing accelerometer data on Arduino

The Arduino accelerometer handler is located in *arduino/accelerometer_handler.cc* (*https://oreil.ly/jV_Qm*). It has the task of capturing data from the accelerometer and writing it to the model's input buffer.

The model we are using was trained using data from the SparkFun Edge board. The Edge's accelerometer provides a set of readings at a rate of 25 Hz, or 25 times per second. To work correctly, it needs to be fed data that is captured at the same rate. As it turns out, the accelerometer on the Arduino Nano 33 BLE Sense board returns measurements at a rate of 119 Hz. This means that in addition to capturing data, we need to *downsample* it to suit our model.

Although it sounds very technical, downsampling is actually pretty easy. To reduce the sample rate of a signal, we can just throw away some of the data. We look at how this works in the following code.

First the implementation includes its own header file, along with some others:

```
#include "tensorflow/lite/micro/examples/magic_wand/
  accelerometer_handler.h"

#include <Arduino.h>
#include <Arduino_LSM9DS1.h>

#include "tensorflow/lite/micro/examples/magic_wand/constants.h"
```

The file *Arduino.h* provides access to some basic features of the Arduino platform. The file *Arduino_LSM9DS1.h* is part of the Arduino_LSM9DS1 (*https://oreil.ly/eb3Zs*) library, which we'll be using to communicate with the board's accelerometer.

Next, we set up some variables:

```
// A buffer holding the last 200 sets of 3-channel values
float save_data[600] = {0.0};
// Most recent position in the save_data buffer
int begin_index = 0;
// True if there is not yet enough data to run inference
bool pending_initial_data = true;
// How often we should save a measurement during downsampling
int sample_every_n;
// The number of measurements since we last saved one
int sample_skip_counter = 1;
```

These include a buffer we'll be filling with our data, `save_data`, along with some variables for tracking our current position in the buffer and whether we have enough data to start running inference. The most interesting two variables, `sample_every_n` and `sample_skip_counter`, are used in the downsampling process. We'll look at this more closely in a moment.

Next in the file, the `SetupAccelerometer()` function is called by the program's main loop to get the board ready to capture data:

```
TfLiteStatus SetupAccelerometer(tflite::ErrorReporter* error_reporter) {
  // Wait until we know the serial port is ready
  while (!Serial) {
  }

  // Switch on the IMU
  if (!IMU.begin()) {
    error_reporter->Report("Failed to initialize IMU");
    return kTfLiteError;
  }
```

Because we'll be outputting a message to indicate that everything is ready to go, the first thing it does is make sure that the device's serial port is ready. It then switches on the *inertial measurement unit* (IMU), which is the electronic component that contains the accelerometer. The IMU object comes from the Arduino_LSM9DS1 library.

The next step is to start thinking about downsampling. We first query the IMU library to determine the board's sample rate. When we have that number, we divide it by our target sample rate, which is defined in `kTargetHz` as part of *constants.h* (*https://oreil.ly/rQaSw*):

```
// Determine how many measurements to keep in order to
// meet kTargetHz
float sample_rate = IMU.accelerationSampleRate();
sample_every_n = static_cast<int>(roundf(sample_rate / kTargetHz));
```

Our target rate is 25 Hz, and the board's sample rate is 119 Hz; thus, the result of our division is 4.76. This lets us know how many of the 119 Hz samples we need to keep in order to attain the target sample rate of 25 Hz: 1 sample in every 4.76.

Because keeping a fractional number of samples is difficult, we use the roundf() function to round to the nearest number, 5. To downsample our signal, then, we need to keep one in every five measurements. This will result in an effective sample rate of 23.8 Hz, which is a close enough approximation that our model should work well. We store this value in the sample_every_n variable for use later.

Now that we've established the parameters of our downsampling, we give the user a message to inform them that the application is ready to go and then return from the SetupAccelerometer() function:

```
    error_reporter->Report("Magic starts!");

    return kTfLiteOk;
}
```

Next up, we define ReadAccelerometer(). This function is tasked with capturing new data and writing it to the model's output tensor. It begins with some code that is used to clear its internal buffer after a gesture has been successfully recognized, cleaning the slate for any subsequent gestures:

```
bool ReadAccelerometer(tflite::ErrorReporter* error_reporter, float* input,
                       int length, bool reset_buffer) {
  // Clear the buffer if required, e.g. after a successful prediction
  if (reset_buffer) {
    memset(save_data, 0, 600 * sizeof(float));
    begin_index = 0;
    pending_initial_data = true;
  }
```

Next, we use the IMU library to check for available data in a loop. If there's data available, we read it:

```
  // Keep track of whether we stored any new data
  bool new_data = false;
  // Loop through new samples and add to buffer
  while (IMU.accelerationAvailable()) {
    float x, y, z;
    // Read each sample, removing it from the device's FIFO buffer
    if (!IMU.readAcceleration(x, y, z)) {
      error_reporter->Report("Failed to read data");
      break;
    }
```

The accelerometer on the Arduino Nano 33 BLE Sense board is equipped with something called a *FIFO buffer* (*https://oreil.ly/kFEa0*). This is a special memory buffer, located on the accelerometer itself, which holds the most recent 32 measurements.

Because it's part of the accelerometer hardware, the FIFO buffer continues to accrue measurements even while our application code is running. If it weren't for the FIFO buffer, we might lose a lot of data, meaning we wouldn't have an accurate record of the gestures being made.

When we call `IMU.accelerationAvailable()`, we are querying the accelerometer to see whether new data is available in its FIFO buffer. Using our loop, we continue to read all the data from the buffer until there is none remaining.

Next up, we implement our super-simple downsampling algorithm:

```
// Throw away this sample unless it's the nth
if (sample_skip_counter != sample_every_n) {
  sample_skip_counter += 1;
  continue;
}
```

Our approach is to keep one in every n samples, where n is the number stored in `sample_every_n`. To do this, we maintain a counter, `sample_skip_counter`, which lets us know how many samples have been read since the last one we kept. For every measurement we read, we check whether it is the nth. If it isn't, we `continue` the loop without writing the data anywhere, effectively throwing it away. This simple process leads to our data being downsampled.

If execution gets further than this point, we're planning on keeping the data. To do this, we write it to consecutive positions in our `save_data` buffer:

```
// Write samples to our buffer, converting to milli-Gs
// and flipping y and x order for compatibility with
// model (sensor orientation is different on Arduino
// Nano BLE Sense compared with SparkFun Edge)
save_data[begin_index++] = y * 1000;
save_data[begin_index++] = x * 1000;
save_data[begin_index++] = z * 1000;
```

Our model accepts accelerometer measurements in the order x, y, z. You'll notice here that we're writing the y value to the buffer before the x. This is because our model was trained on data captured on the SparkFun Edge board, whose accelerometer has its axes pointing in different physical directions to the one on the Arduino. This difference means that the SparkFun Edge's x-axis is equivalent to the Arduino's y-axis, and vice versa. By swapping these axes' data in our code, we can make sure our model is being fed data that it can understand.

The final few lines of our loop do some housework, setting some state variables that are used in our loop:

```
// Since we took a sample, reset the skip counter
sample_skip_counter = 1;
// If we reached the end of the circle buffer, reset
if (begin_index >= 600) {
```

```
      begin_index = 0;
    }
    new_data = true;
  }
```

We reset our downsampling counter, make sure we don't run off the end of our sample buffer, and set a flag to indicate that new data has been saved.

After grabbing this new data, we do some more checks. This time, we're making sure that we have sufficient data to perform an inference. If not, or if new data was not captured this time around, we return from the function without doing anything:

```
// Skip this round if data is not ready yet
if (!new_data) {
  return false;
}

// Check if we are ready for prediction or still pending more initial data
if (pending_initial_data && begin_index >= 200) {
  pending_initial_data = false;
}

// Return if we don't have enough data
if (pending_initial_data) {
  return false;
}
```

By returning false when there's no new data, we make sure the calling function knows not to bother running inference.

If we got this far, we've obtained some new data. We copy the appropriate amount of data, including our new samples, to the input tensor:

```
// Copy the requested number of bytes to the provided input tensor
for (int i = 0; i < length; ++i) {
  int ring_array_index = begin_index + i - length;
  if (ring_array_index < 0) {
    ring_array_index += 600;
  }
  input[i] = save_data[ring_array_index];
}

return true;
}
```

And that's it! We've populated the input tensor and are ready to run inference. After inference has been run, the results are passed into the gesture predictor, which determines whether a valid gesture has been spotted. The result is passed into the output handler, which we walk through next.

Responding to gestures on Arduino

The output handler is defined in *arduino/output_handler.cc* (*https://oreil.ly/kdVLW*). It's nice and simple: all it does is log information to the serial port depending on which gesture was detected, and toggle the board's LED each time inference is run.

The first time the function runs, the LED is configured for output:

```
void HandleOutput(tflite::ErrorReporter* error_reporter, int kind) {
  // The first time this method runs, set up our LED
  static bool is_initialized = false;
  if (!is_initialized) {
    pinMode(LED_BUILTIN, OUTPUT);
    is_initialized = true;
  }
```

Next, the LED is toggled on and off with each inference:

```
// Toggle the LED every time an inference is performed
static int count = 0;
++count;
if (count & 1) {
  digitalWrite(LED_BUILTIN, HIGH);
} else {
  digitalWrite(LED_BUILTIN, LOW);
}
```

Finally, we print some beautiful ASCII art depending on which gesture was matched:

```
// Print some ASCII art for each gesture
if (kind == 0) {
  error_reporter->Report(
      "WING:\n\r*         *         *\n\r *         *  *         "
      "*\n\r *    *    *\n\r  *    *    *    *\n\r   *  *         "
      "*  *\n\r     *          *\n\r");
} else if (kind == 1) {
  error_reporter->Report(
      "RING:\n\r          *\n\r       *     *\n\r     *         "
      "*\n\r    *           *\n\r     *         *\n\r       *     "
      "*\n\r          *\n\r");
} else if (kind == 2) {
  error_reporter->Report(
      "SLOPE:\n\r        *\n\r       *\n\r      *\n\r     *     "
      "\n\r    *\n\r   *\n\r  * * * * * * * *\n\r");
}
```

It's difficult to read now, but you'll be rewarded with the output's full glory when you deploy the application to your board.

Running the example

To deploy this example, here's what we'll need:

- An Arduino Nano 33 BLE Sense board
- A micro-USB cable
- The Arduino IDE

There's always a chance that the build process might have changed since this book was written, so check *README.md* (*https://oreil.ly/Zkd3x*) for the latest instructions.

The projects in this book are available as example code in the TensorFlow Lite Arduino library. If you haven't already installed the library, open the Arduino IDE and select Manage Libraries from the Tools menu. In the window that appears, search for and install the library named TensorFlowLite. You should be able to use the latest version, but if you run into issues, the version that was tested with this book is 1.14-ALPHA.

You can also install the library from a *.zip* file, which you can either download (*https://oreil.ly/blgB8*) from the TensorFlow Lite team or generate yourself using the TensorFlow Lite for Microcontrollers Makefile. If you'd prefer to do the latter, see Appendix A.

After you've installed the library, the `magic_wand` example will show up in the File menu under Examples→Arduino_TensorFlowLite, as shown in Figure 11-5.

Click "magic_wand" to load the example. It will appear as a new window, with a tab for each of the source files. The file in the first tab, *magic_wand*, is equivalent to the *main_functions.cc* we walked through earlier.

"Running the Example" on page 101 already explained the structure of the Arduino example, so we won't cover it again here.

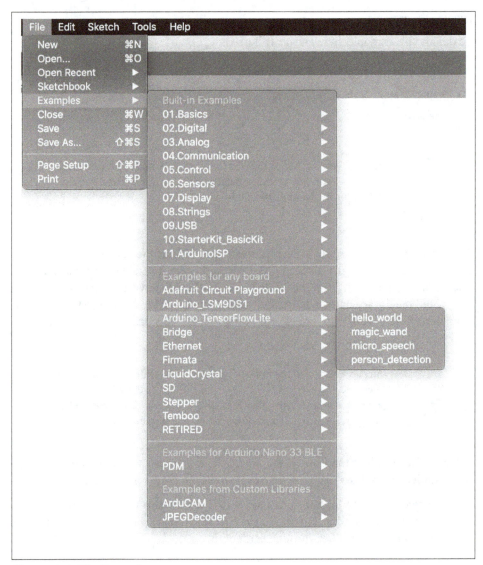

Figure 11-5. The Examples menu

In addition to the TensorFlow library, we also need to install and patch the Arduino_LSM9DS1 library. By default, the library doesn't enable the FIFO buffer that is required by the example, so we have to make some modifications to its code.

In the Arduino IDE, select Tools→Manage Libraries and then search for Arduino_LSM9DS1. To ensure the following instructions work, you must install version 1.0.0 of the driver.

It's possible that the driver might have been fixed by the time you are reading this chapter. You can find the latest deployment instructions in *README.md* (*https://oreil.ly/pk61J*).

The driver will be installed to your *Arduino/libraries* directory, in the subdirectory *Arduino_LSM9DS1*.

Open the *Arduino_LSM9DS1/src/LSM9DS1.cpp* driver source file and then go to the function named `LSM9DS1Class::begin()`. Insert the following lines at the end of the function, immediately before the `return 1` statement:

```
// Enable FIFO (see docs https://www.st.com/resource/en/datasheet/
DM00103319.pdf)
// writeRegister(LSM9DS1_ADDRESS, 0x23, 0x02);
// Set continuous mode
writeRegister(LSM9DS1_ADDRESS, 0x2E, 0xC0);
```

Next, locate the function named `LSM9DS1Class::accelerationAvailable()`. You will see the following lines:

```
if (readRegister(LSM9DS1_ADDRESS, LSM9DS1_STATUS_REG) & 0x01) {
  return 1;
}
```

Comment out those lines and then replace them with the following:

```
// Read FIFO_SRC. If any of the rightmost 8 bits have a value, there is data.
if (readRegister(LSM9DS1_ADDRESS, 0x2F) & 63) {
  return 1;
}
```

Save the file. Patching is now complete!

To run the example, plug in your Arduino device via USB. On the Tools menu, make sure that the correct device type is selected from the Board drop-down list, as shown in Figure 11-6.

If your device's name doesn't appear in the list, you'll need to install its support package. To do this, click Boards Manager and then, in the window that appears, search for your device and install the latest version of the corresponding support package.

Next, make sure the device's port is selected in the Port drop-down, also in the Tools menu, as demonstrated in Figure 11-7.

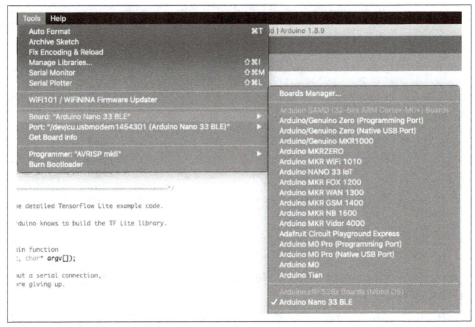

Figure 11-6. The Board drop-down list

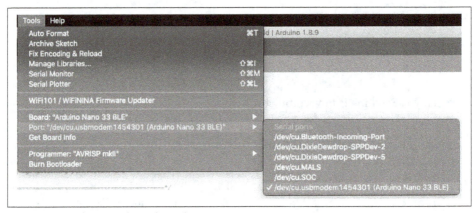

Figure 11-7. The Port drop-down list

Finally, click the upload button in the Arduino window (highlighted in white in Figure 11-8) to compile and upload the code to your Arduino device.

Figure 11-8. The upload button

After the upload has successfully completed, you should see the LED on your Arduino board begin to flash.

To try some gestures, select Serial Monitor in the Tools menu. You should initially see the following output:

```
Magic starts!
```

You can now try to make some gestures. Hold the board up with one hand, with the components facing up and the USB adapter facing toward the left, as shown in Figure 11-9.

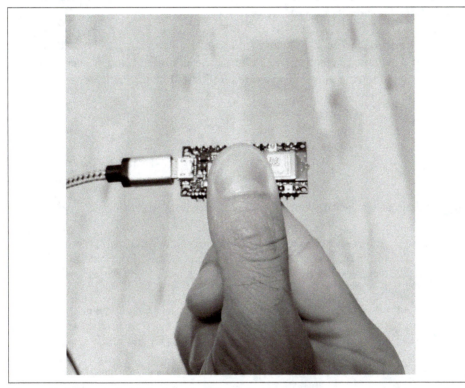

Figure 11-9. How to hold the board while performing gestures

Figure 11-10 presents a diagram showing how to perform each gesture. Because the model was trained on data collected when the board was attached to a wand, you might need a few tries to get them to work.

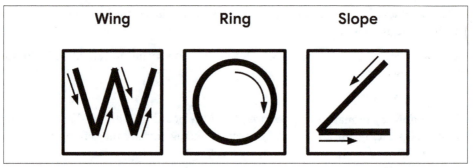

| Wing | Ring | Slope |

Figure 11-10. The three magic wand gestures

The easiest one to start with is "wing." You should move your hand quickly enough that it takes around one second to perform the gesture. If you're successful, you should see the following output, and the red LED should illuminate:

```
WING:
*           *           *
   *        * *         *
     *      *   *       *
       *   *     *    *
         * *       * *
           *         *
```

Congratulations, you've cast your first magic spell using the Arduino!

At this point, you might choose to be creative and attach the board to the tip of a magic wand, at the point furthest from your hand. Any stick, ruler, or other household item with a length of around a foot (30 cm) should work well.

Make sure the device is attached firmly, and in the same orientation, with the components facing up and the USB adapter facing toward the left. And pick a rigid wand, not a flexible one; any wobbling will affect the accelerometer readings.

Next, try the "ring" gesture, by tracing a clockwise circle with your hand (or the tip of your wand). Again, aim to take around a second to perform the gesture. You should see the following appear, as if by magic:

```
RING:
           *
        *     *
      *         *
     *           *
      *         *
       *       *
        *     *
           *
```

For the final gesture, trace the corner of a triangle in the air. It's best described by its ASCII art demonstration, shown here:

```
SLOPE:
        *
       *
      *
     *
    *
   *
  *
 * * * * * * *
```

Like any good magic spells, you might have to practice these a bit before you can perform them perfectly each time. You can see video demonstrations of the gestures in *README.md (https://oreil.ly/O1LqD)*.

What If It Didn't Work?

Here are some possible issues and how to debug them:

Problem: The LED isn't coming on.

Solution: Try pressing the reset button or disconnecting the board from the USB cable and then reconnecting it. If neither of these works, try flashing the board again.

Problem: The LED is stuck on or off.

Solution: It's normal for the LED to stop flashing immediately after an inference, while the program waits for enough new data to be available. If the LED stops flashing for more than a few seconds, the program might have crashed. In that case, press the reset button.

Problem: You can't get the gestures to work.

Solution: First, make sure the LED is blinking, which indicates that inference is happening. If it isn't, press the reset button. Next, make sure you're holding the board in the correct orientation, as shown earlier.

To learn the gestures, start with the "W," which is the easiest to master. The "O" is a little more difficult because the circle needs to be quite smooth. The angle gesture is the trickiest. Try watching the videos in *README.md (https://oreil.ly/GkpP5)* for guidance.

Making your own changes

Now that you deployed the basic application, try playing around and making some changes to the code. Just edit the files in the Arduino IDE and save them, and then repeat the previous instructions to deploy your modified code to the device.

Here are a few things you could try:

- Experiment with the threshold values in *arduino/constants.cc* (*https://oreil.ly/ H49iS*) to make the gestures easier or more difficult to perform (at the cost of more false positives or negatives).
- Write a program on your computer that lets you perform tasks using physical gestures.
- Extend the program to transmit detection results via Bluetooth. There are examples showing how to do this included with the ArduinoBLE library (*https:// oreil.ly/xW4SN*), which you can download via the Arduino IDE.

SparkFun Edge

The SparkFun Edge features a three-axis accelerometer, a battery mount, and Bluetooth support. This makes it perfect for a magic wand because it can operate wirelessly.

Bluetooth

The implementation in this chapter doesn't demonstrate how to use Bluetooth, but there's an example in the Ambiq SDK that shows how you can do it. We provide a link in "Making your own changes" on page 326.

There's also a chance that Bluetooth support might have been added to the example since the book was published. Check the latest version in the TensorFlow repository (*https://oreil.ly/FJB4h*).

Capturing accelerometer data on SparkFun Edge

The code that captures accelerometer data is located in *sparkfun_edge/accelerometer_handler.cc* (*https://oreil.ly/yZi0v*). A lot of it is device-specific, but we'll skip over the implementation details and focus on the important stuff.

The first step involved with capturing accelerometer data is configuring the hardware. The `SetupAccelerometer()` function kicks this off by setting various low-level parameters required by the accelerometer:

```
TfLiteStatus SetupAccelerometer(tflite::ErrorReporter* error_reporter) {
  // Set the clock frequency.
```

```
am_hal_clkgen_control(AM_HAL_CLKGEN_CONTROL_SYSCLK_MAX, 0);

// Set the default cache configuration
am_hal_cachectrl_config(&am_hal_cachectrl_defaults);
am_hal_cachectrl_enable();

// Configure the board for low power operation.
am_bsp_low_power_init();

// Collecting data at 25Hz.
int accInitRes = initAccelerometer();
```

You'll notice a call to a function named `initAccelerometer()`. This is defined in the SparkFun Edge BSP's accelerometer example (*https://oreil.ly/JC0b6*), which is pulled down as a dependency when our project is built. It performs various tasks to switch on and configure the board's accelerometer.

After the accelerometer is running, we enable its FIFO buffer (*https://oreil.ly/kFEa0*). This is a special memory buffer, located on the accelerometer itself, which holds the last 32 datapoints. By enabling it, we're able to continue collecting accelerometer measurements even while our application code is busy running inference. The remainder of the function sets up the buffer and logs errors if anything goes wrong:

```
// Enable the accelerometer's FIFO buffer.
// Note: LIS2DH12 has a FIFO buffer which holds up to 32 data entries. It
// accumulates data while the CPU is busy. Old data will be overwritten if
// it's not fetched in time, so we need to make sure that model inference is
// faster than 1/25Hz * 32 = 1.28s
if (lis2dh12_fifo_set(&dev_ctx, 1)) {
  error_reporter->Report("Failed to enable FIFO buffer.");
}

if (lis2dh12_fifo_mode_set(&dev_ctx, LIS2DH12_BYPASS_MODE)) {
  error_reporter->Report("Failed to clear FIFO buffer.");
  return 0;
}

if (lis2dh12_fifo_mode_set(&dev_ctx, LIS2DH12_DYNAMIC_STREAM_MODE)) {
  error_reporter->Report("Failed to set streaming mode.");
  return 0;
}

error_reporter->Report("Magic starts!");

return kTfLiteOk;
}
```

When we're done with initialization, we can call the `ReadAccelerometer()` function to get the latest data. This will happen between every inference.

First, if the reset_buffer argument is true, ReadAccelerometer() performs a reset of its data buffer. This is done after a valid gesture has been detected in order to provide a clean slate for further gestures. As part of this process, we use am_util_delay_ms() to make our code wait for 10 ms. Without this delay, the code often hangs when reading new data (as of this writing, the cause was unclear, but the TensorFlow open source project welcomes pull requests if you determine a better fix):

```
bool ReadAccelerometer(tflite::ErrorReporter* error_reporter, float* input,
                       int length, bool reset_buffer) {
  // Clear the buffer if required, e.g. after a successful prediction
  if (reset_buffer) {
    memset(save_data, 0, 600 * sizeof(float));
    begin_index = 0;
    pending_initial_data = true;
    // Wait 10ms after a reset to avoid hang
    am_util_delay_ms(10);
  }
```

After resetting the main buffer, ReadAccelerometer() checks whether there is any new data available in the accelerometer's FIFO buffer. If there's nothing available yet, we just return from the function:

```
  // Check FIFO buffer for new samples
  lis2dh12_fifo_src_reg_t status;
  if (lis2dh12_fifo_status_get(&dev_ctx, &status)) {
    error_reporter->Report("Failed to get FIFO status.");
    return false;
  }

  int samples = status.fss;
  if (status.ovrn_fifo) {
    samples++;
  }

  // Skip this round if data is not ready yet
  if (samples == 0) {
    return false;
  }
```

Our application's main loop will continue calling, meaning as soon as there's data available, we can move past this point.

The next part of the function loops through the new data and stores it in another, larger buffer. First we set up a special struct of type axis3bit16_t, designed to hold accelerometer data. We then call lis2dh12_acceleration_raw_get() to fill it with the next available measurement. This function will return zero if it fails, at which point we display an error:

```
  // Load data from FIFO buffer
  axis3bit16_t data_raw_acceleration;
  for (int i = 0; i < samples; i++) {
```

```
// Zero out the struct that holds raw accelerometer data
memset(data_raw_acceleration.u8bit, 0x00, 3 * sizeof(int16_t));
// If the return value is non-zero, sensor data was successfully read
if (lis2dh12_acceleration_raw_get(&dev_ctx, data_raw_acceleration.u8bit)) {
  error_reporter->Report("Failed to get raw data.");
```

If the measurement was obtained successfully, we convert it into milli-Gs, the unit of measurement expected by the model, and then write it into save_data[], which is an array we're using as a buffer to store values that we'll use for inference. The values for each axis of the accelerometer are stored consecutively:

```
} else {
  // Convert each raw 16-bit value into floating point values representing
  // milli-Gs, a unit of acceleration, and store in the current position of
  // our buffer
  save_data[begin_index++] =
      lis2dh12_from_fs2_hr_to_mg(data_raw_acceleration.i16bit[0]);
  save_data[begin_index++] =
      lis2dh12_from_fs2_hr_to_mg(data_raw_acceleration.i16bit[1]);
  save_data[begin_index++] =
      lis2dh12_from_fs2_hr_to_mg(data_raw_acceleration.i16bit[2]);
  // Start from beginning, imitating loop array.
  if (begin_index >= 600) begin_index = 0;
  }
}
```

Our save_data[] array can store 200 sets of three-axis values, so we set our begin_index counter back to 0 when it reaches 600.

We've now incorporated all of the new data into our save_data[] buffer. Next, we check whether we have enough data to make a prediction. When testing the model, it was discovered that around a third of our total buffer size is the bare minimum amount of data that results in a reliable prediction; therefore, if we have at least this much data, we set the pending_initial_data flag to false (it defaults to true):

```
// Check if we are ready for prediction or still pending more initial data
if (pending_initial_data && begin_index >= 200) {
  pending_initial_data = false;
}
```

Next, if there is still insufficient data to run an inference, we return false:

```
// Return if we don't have enough data
if (pending_initial_data) {
  return false;
}
```

If we got this far, there's sufficient data in the buffer to run an inference. The final part of the function copies the requested data from the buffer into the input argument, which is a pointer to the model's input tensor:

```
// Copy the requested number of bytes to the provided input tensor
for (int i = 0; i < length; ++i) {
  int ring_array_index = begin_index + i - length;
  if (ring_array_index < 0) {
    ring_array_index += 600;
  }
  input[i] = save_data[ring_array_index];
}
return true;
```

The variable `length` is an argument passed into `ReadAccelerometer()` that determines how much data should be copied. Because our model takes 128 three-axis readings as its input, the code in *main_functions.cc* calls `ReadAccelerometer()` with a `length` of 384 (128 * 3).

At this point, our input tensor is filled with fresh accelerometer data. Inference will be run, the results will be interpreted by the gesture predictor, and the result will be passed to the output handler to display to the user.

Responding to gestures on SparkFun Edge

The output handler, located in *sparkfun_edge/output_handler.cc* (*https://oreil.ly/ix1o1*), is very simple. The first time it runs, we configure the LEDs for output:

```
void HandleOutput(tflite::ErrorReporter* error_reporter, int kind) {
  // The first time this method runs, set up our LEDs correctly
  static bool is_initialized = false;
  if (!is_initialized) {
    am_hal_gpio_pinconfig(AM_BSP_GPIO_LED_RED, g_AM_HAL_GPIO_OUTPUT_12);
    am_hal_gpio_pinconfig(AM_BSP_GPIO_LED_BLUE, g_AM_HAL_GPIO_OUTPUT_12);
    am_hal_gpio_pinconfig(AM_BSP_GPIO_LED_GREEN, g_AM_HAL_GPIO_OUTPUT_12);
    am_hal_gpio_pinconfig(AM_BSP_GPIO_LED_YELLOW, g_AM_HAL_GPIO_OUTPUT_12);
    is_initialized = true;
  }
```

Next, we toggle the yellow LED with each inference:

```
// Toggle the yellow LED every time an inference is performed
static int count = 0;
++count;
if (count & 1) {
  am_hal_gpio_output_set(AM_BSP_GPIO_LED_YELLOW);
} else {
  am_hal_gpio_output_clear(AM_BSP_GPIO_LED_YELLOW);
}
```

After that, we check which gesture was detected. For each individual gesture, we light an LED, clear all the others, and output some beautiful ASCII art via the serial port. Here's the code that handles the "wing" gesture:

```
// Set the LED color and print a symbol (red: wing, blue: ring, green: slope)
if (kind == 0) {
```

```
error_reporter->Report(
    "WING:\n\r*            *            *\n\r *       * *       "
    "*\n\r  *      *    *    *\n\r  *    *    *    *\n\r   * *       * *       "
    "* *\n\r     *            *\n\r");
am_hal_gpio_output_set(AM_BSP_GPIO_LED_RED);
am_hal_gpio_output_clear(AM_BSP_GPIO_LED_BLUE);
am_hal_gpio_output_clear(AM_BSP_GPIO_LED_GREEN);
```

On a serial port monitor, the output will look like this:

```
WING:
*            *            *
 *          * *          *
  *        *   *        *
   *      *     *      *
    * *         * *
     *           *
```

A different serial output and LED are used for each gesture.

Running the example

We've now seen how the SparkFun Edge code works. Next, let's get it running on our hardware.

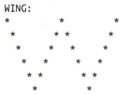

> There's always a chance that the build process might have changed since this book was written, so check *README.md* (*https://oreil.ly/ Ts6MT*) for the latest instructions.

To build and deploy our code, we'll need the following:

- A SparkFun Edge board with the Himax HM01B0 breakout (*https://oreil.ly/ f23oa*) attached
- A USB programmer (we recommend the SparkFun Serial Basic Breakout, which is available in micro-B USB (*https://oreil.ly/KKfyI*) and USB-C (*https://oreil.ly/ ztUrB*) variants)
- A matching USB cable
- Python 3 and some dependencies

> If you're unsure whether you have the correct version of Python installed, "Running the Example" on page 110 has instructions on how to check.

Open a terminal window, clone the TensorFlow repository, and then change into its directory:

```
git clone https://github.com/tensorflow/tensorflow.git
cd tensorflow
```

Next, we're going to build the binary and run some commands that get it ready for downloading to the device. To avoid some typing, you can copy and paste these commands from *README.md* (*https://oreil.ly/MQmWw*).

Build the binary. The following command downloads all the required dependencies and then compiles a binary for the SparkFun Edge:

```
make -f tensorflow/lite/micro/tools/make/Makefile \
  TARGET=sparkfun_edge magic_wand_bin
```

The binary will be created as a *.bin* file, in the following location:

```
tensorflow/lite/micro/tools/make/gen/
  sparkfun_edge_cortex-m4/bin/magic_wand.bin
```

To check that the file exists, you can use the following command:

```
test -f tensorflow/lite/micro/tools/make/gen/sparkfun_edge_ \
  cortex-m4/bin/magic_wand.bin &&  echo "Binary was successfully created" || \
  echo "Binary is missing"
```

If you run that command, you should see `Binary was successfully created` printed to the console.

If you see `Binary is missing`, there was a problem with the build process. If so, it's likely that there are some clues to what went wrong in the output of the `make` command.

Sign the binary. The binary must be signed with cryptographic keys to be deployed to the device. Let's run some commands that will sign the binary so that it can be flashed to the SparkFun Edge. The scripts used here come from the Ambiq SDK, which is downloaded when the Makefile is run.

Enter the following command to set up some dummy cryptographic keys you can use for development:

```
cp tensorflow/lite/micro/tools/make/downloads/AmbiqSuite-Rel2.0.0/ \
  tools/apollo3_scripts/keys_info0.py
  tensorflow/lite/micro/tools/make/downloads/AmbiqSuite-Rel2.0.0/ \
  tools/apollo3_scripts/keys_info.py
```

Next, run the following command to create a signed binary. Substitute `python3` with `python` if necessary:

```
python3 tensorflow/lite/micro/tools/make/downloads/ \
  AmbiqSuite-Rel2.0.0/tools/apollo3_scripts/create_cust_image_blob.py \
```

```
--bin tensorflow/lite/micro/tools/make/gen/ \
sparkfun_edge_cortex-m4/bin/micro_vision.bin \
--load-address 0xC000 \
--magic-num 0xCB \
-o main_nonsecure_ota \
--version 0x0
```

This creates the file *main_nonsecure_ota.bin*. Now, run this command to create a final version of the file that you can use to flash your device with the script you will use in the next step:

```
python3 tensorflow/lite/micro/tools/make/downloads/ \
AmbiqSuite-Rel2.0.0/tools/apollo3_scripts/create_cust_wireupdate_blob.py \
--load-address 0x20000 \
--bin main_nonsecure_ota.bin \
-i 6 \
-o main_nonsecure_wire \
--options 0x1
```

You should now have a file called *main_nonsecure_wire.bin* in the directory where you ran the commands. This is the file you'll be flashing to the device.

Flash the binary. The SparkFun Edge stores the program it is currently running in its 1 megabyte of flash memory. If you want the board to run a new program, you need to send it to the board, which will store it in flash memory, overwriting any program that was previously saved. This process is called flashing.

Attach the programmer to the board. To download new programs to the board, you'll use the SparkFun USB-C Serial Basic serial programmer. This device allows your computer to communicate with the microcontroller via USB.

To attach this device to your board, perform the following steps:

1. On the side of the SparkFun Edge, locate the six-pin header.
2. Plug the SparkFun USB-C Serial Basic into these pins, ensuring that the pins labeled BLK and GRN on each device are lined up correctly.

You can see the correct arrangement in Figure 11-11.

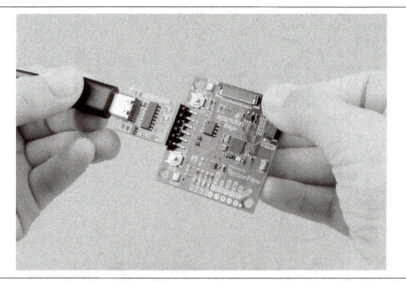

Figure 11-11. Connecting the SparkFun Edge and USB-C Serial Basic (image courtesy of SparkFun)

Attach the programmer to your computer. Next, connect the board to your computer via USB. To program the board, you need to determine the name that your computer gives the device. The best way of doing this is to list all the computer's devices before and after attaching it and then look to see which device is new.

 Some people have reported issues with their operating system's default drivers for the programmer, so we strongly recommend installing the driver (*https://oreil.ly/vLavS*) before you continue.

Before attaching the device via USB, run the following command:

```
# macOS:
ls /dev/cu*

# Linux:
ls /dev/tty*
```

This should output a list of attached devices that looks something like the following:

```
/dev/cu.Bluetooth-Incoming-Port
/dev/cu.MALS
/dev/cu.SOC
```

Now, connect the programmer to your computer's USB port and run the command again:

```
# macOS:
ls /dev/cu*

# Linux:
ls /dev/tty*
```

You should see an extra item in the output, as in the example that follows. Your new item might have a different name. This new item is the name of the device:

```
/dev/cu.Bluetooth-Incoming-Port
/dev/cu.MALS
/dev/cu.SOC
/dev/cu.wchusbserial-1450
```

This name will be used to refer to the device. However, it can change depending on which USB port the programmer is attached to, so if you disconnect the board from your computer and then reattach it you might need to look up its name again.

 Some users have reported two devices appearing in the list. If you see two devices, the correct one to use begins with the letters "wch"; for example, "/dev/wchusbserial-14410."

After you've identified the device name, put it in a shell variable for later use:

```
export DEVICENAME=<your device name here>
```

This is a variable that you can use when running commands that require the device name, later in the process.

Run the script to flash your board. To flash the board, you need to put it into a special "bootloader" state that prepares it to receive the new binary. You can then run a script to send the binary to the board.

First create an environment variable to specify the baud rate, which is the speed at which data will be sent to the device:

```
export BAUD_RATE=921600
```

Now paste the command that follows into your terminal—but *do not press Enter yet!*. The ${DEVICENAME} and ${BAUD_RATE} in the command will be replaced with the values you set in the previous sections. Remember to substitute python3 with python if necessary:

```
python3 tensorflow/lite/micro/tools/make/downloads/ \
    AmbiqSuite-Rel2.0.0/tools/apollo3_scripts/uart_wired_update.py -b \
    ${BAUD_RATE} ${DEVICENAME} -r 1 -f main_nonsecure_wire.bin -i 6
```

Next you'll reset the board into its bootloader state and flash the board.

On the board, locate the buttons marked RST and 14, as shown in Figure 11-12.

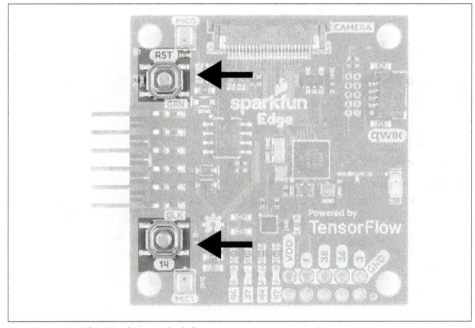

Figure 11-12. The SparkFun Edge's buttons

Perform the following steps:

1. Ensure that your board is connected to the programmer, and the entire thing is connected to your computer via USB.

2. On the board, press and hold the button marked 14. *Continue holding it.*

3. While still holding the button marked 14, press the button marked RST to reset the board.

4. Press Enter on your computer to run the script. *Continue holding button 14.*

You should now see something like the following appearing on your screen:

```
Connecting with Corvette over serial port /dev/cu.usbserial-1440...
Sending Hello.
Received response for Hello
Received Status
length =  0x58
version =  0x3
Max Storage =  0x4ffa0
Status =  0x2
State =  0x7
```

```
AMInfo =
0x1
0xff2da3ff
0x55fff
0x1
0x49f40003
0xffffffff
[...lots more 0xffffffff...]
Sending OTA Descriptor = 0xfe000
Sending Update Command.
number of updates needed = 1
Sending block of size  0x158b0  from  0x0  to  0x158b0
Sending Data Packet of length  8180
Sending Data Packet of length  8180
[...lots more Sending Data Packet of length  8180...]
```

Keep holding button 14 until you see `Sending Data Packet of length 8180`. You can release the button after seeing this (but it's okay if you keep holding it).

The program will continue to print lines on the terminal. Eventually, you'll see something like the following:

```
[...lots more Sending Data Packet of length  8180...]
Sending Data Packet of length  8180
Sending Data Packet of length  6440
Sending Reset Command.
Done.
```

This indicates a successful flashing.

 If the program output ends with an error, check whether `Sending Reset Command.` was printed. If so, flashing was likely successful despite the error. Otherwise, flashing might have failed. Try running through these steps again (you can skip over setting the environment variables).

Testing the Program

Start by pressing the RST button to make sure the program is running. When the program is running, the yellow LED will toggle on and off, once for each inference.

Next, use the following command to start printing the serial output of the device:

```
screen ${DEVICENAME} 115200
```

You should initially see the following output:

```
Magic starts!
```

You can now try to make some gestures. Hold the board up with one hand, with the components facing up and the USB adapter facing toward the left, as shown in Figure 11-13.

Figure 11-13. How to hold the board while performing gestures

Figure 11-14 presents a diagram showing how to perform each gesture. Because the model was trained on data collected when the board was attached to a wand, you might need a few tries to get them to work.

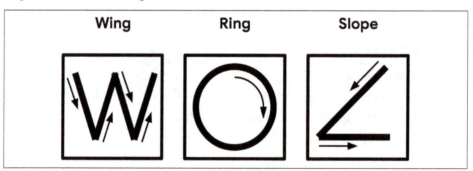

Figure 11-14. The three magic wand gestures

The easiest one to start with is "wing." You should move your hand quickly enough that it takes around one second to perform the gesture. If you're successful, the red LED should illuminate, and you should see the following output:

```
WING:
*           *           *
  *        *  *         *
    *      *    *      *
      *  *        *  *
        * *        * *
          *          *
```

Congratulations, you've cast your first magic spell using the SparkFun Edge!

At this point, you might choose to be creative and attach the board to the tip of a magic wand, at the point furthest from your hand. Any stick, ruler, or other household item with a length of around a foot (30 cm) should work well.

Make sure the device is attached firmly, and in the same orientation, with the components facing up and the USB adapter facing toward the left. And pick a rigid wand, not a flexible one because any wobbling will affect the accelerometer readings.

Next try the "ring" gesture, by tracing a clockwise circle with your hand (or the tip of your wand). Again, aim to take around a second to perform the gesture. You should see the following appear, as if by magic:

```
RING:
          *
       *     *
     *         *
   *             *
   *             *
     *         *
       *     *
          *
```

For the final gesture, trace the corner of a triangle in the air. It's best described by its ASCII art demonstration, shown here:

```
SLOPE:
          *
         *
        *
       *
      *
     *
    *
   * * * * * * *
```

Like any good magic spells, you might have to practice these a bit before you can perform them perfectly each time. You can see video demonstrations of the gestures in *README.md* (*https://oreil.ly/ilGJY*).

What If It Didn't Work?

Here are some possible issues and how to debug them:

Problem: When flashing, the script hangs for a while at `Sending Hello.` and then prints an error.

Solution: You need to hold down the button marked 14 while running the script. Hold down button 14, press the RST button, and then run the script, while holding the button marked 14 the whole time.

Problem: After flashing, none of the LEDs are coming on.

Solution: Try pressing the RST button or disconnecting the board from the programmer and then reconnecting it. If neither of these works, try flashing the board again.

Problem: The LEDs are stuck on or off.

Solution: It's normal for the LEDs to stop flashing immediately after an inference, while the program waits for enough new data to be available. If the LED stops flashing for more than a few seconds, the program might have crashed. In that case, press the RST button.

Problem: You can't get the gestures to work.

Solution: First, make sure the yellow LED is blinking, which indicates that inference is happening. If it isn't, press the RST button. Next, make sure you're holding the board in the correct orientation, as shown earlier.

To learn the gestures, start with the "W," which is the easiest to master. The "O" is a little more difficult because the circle needs to be quite smooth. The angle gesture is the trickiest. For guidance, try watching the videos in *README.md* (*https://oreil.ly/k-kU3*).

Making your own changes

Now that you've deployed the basic application, try playing around and making some changes. You can find the application's code in the *tensorflow/lite/micro/examples/magic_wand* folder. Just edit and save, and then repeat the previous instructions to deploy your modified code to the device.

Here are a few things you could try:

- Experiment with the threshold values in *constants.cc* (*https://oreil.ly/s5bdg*) to make the gestures easier or more difficult to perform (at the cost of more false positives or negatives).

- Write a program on your computer that lets you perform tasks using physical gestures.

- Extend the program to transmit detection results via Bluetooth. There's an example of how to do this in the Ambiq SDK (*https://oreil.ly/Bci3a*), in *AmbiqSuite-Rel2.0.0/boards/apollo3_evb/examples/uart_ble_bridge*. When the magic wand application is built, the SDK is downloaded to *tensorflow/tensorflow/lite/micro/tools/make/downloads/AmbiqSuite-Rel2.0.0*.

Wrapping Up

In this chapter, you saw a fun example of how obscure sensor data can be interpreted by an embedded machine learning application into a much more useful form. By seeing the patterns in noise, embedded machine learning models allow devices to understand the world around them and alert us to events, even when the raw data might be difficult for a human to digest.

In Chapter 12, we explore how our magic wand model works and learn how to collect data and train our own magic spells.

Magic Wand: Training a Model

In Chapter 11, we used a 20 KB pretrained model to interpret raw accelerometer data, using it to identify which of a set of gestures was performed. In this chapter, we show you how this model was trained, and then we talk about how it actually works.

Our wake-word and person detection models both required large amounts of data to train. This is mostly due to the complexity of the problems they were trying to solve. There are a huge number of different ways in which a person can say "yes" or "no"—think of all the variations of accent, intonation, and pitch that make someone's voice unique. Similarly, a person can appear in image in an infinite variety of ways; you might see their face, their whole body, or a single hand, and they could be standing in any possible pose.

So that it can accurately classify such a diversity of valid inputs, a model needs to be trained on an equally diverse set of training data. This is why our datasets for wake-word and person detection training were so large, and why training takes so long.

Our magic wand gesture recognition problem is a lot simpler. In this case, rather than trying to classify a huge range of natural voices or human appearances and poses, we're attempting to understand the differences between three specific and deliberately selected gestures. Although there'll be some variation in the way different people per-form each gesture, we're hoping that our users will strive to perform the gestures as correctly and uniformly as possible.

This means that there'll be a lot less variation in our expected valid inputs, which makes it a lot easier to train an accurate model without needing vast amounts of data. In fact, the dataset we'll be using to train the model contains only around 150 exam-ples for each gesture and is only 1.5 MB in size. It's exciting to think about how a use-ful model can be trained on such a small dataset, because obtaining sufficient data is often the most difficult part of a machine learning project.

In the first part of this chapter, you'll learn how to train the original model used in the magic wand application. In the second part, we'll talk about how this model actually works. And finally, you'll see how you can capture your own data and train a new model that recognizes different gestures.

Training a Model

To train our model, we use training scripts located in the TensorFlow repository. You can find them in *magic_wand/train* (*https://oreil.ly/LhZGT*).

The scripts perform the following tasks:

- Prepare raw data for training.
- Generate synthetic data.[1]
- Split the data for training, validation, and testing.
- Perform data augmentation.
- Define the model architecture.
- Run the training process.
- Convert the model into the TensorFlow Lite format.

To make life easy, the scripts are accompanied by a Jupyter notebook which demonstrates how to use them. You can run the notebook in Colaboratory (Colab) on a GPU runtime. With our tiny dataset, training will take only a few minutes.

To begin, let's walk through the training process in Colab.

Training in Colab

Open the Jupyter notebook at *magic_wand/train/train_magic_wand_model.ipynb* (*https://oreil.ly/2BLtj*) and click the "Run in Google Colab" button, as shown in Figure 8-1.

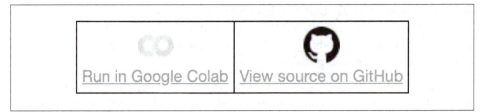

Figure 12-1. The "Run in Google Colab" button

---

1 This is a new term, which we'll talk about later.

As of this writing, there's a bug in GitHub that results in intermittent error messages when displaying Jupyter notebooks. If you see the message "Sorry, something went wrong. Reload?" when trying to access the notebook, follow the instructions in "Building Our Model" on page 34.

This notebook walks through the process of training the model. It includes the following steps:

- Installing dependencies
- Downloading and preparing the data
- Loading TensorBoard to visualize the training process
- Training the model
- Generating a C source file

Enable GPU Training

Training this model should be very quick, but it will be even faster if we use a GPU runtime. To enable this option, go to Colab's Runtime menu and choose "Change runtime type," as illustrated in Figure 12-2.

This opens the "Notebook settings" dialog box shown in Figure 12-3.

From the "Hardware accelerator" drop-down list, select GPU, as depicted in Figure 12-4, and then click SAVE.

You're now ready to run the notebook.

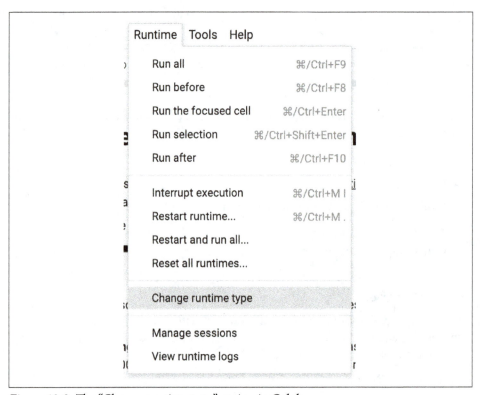

Figure 12-2. The "Change runtime type" option in Colab

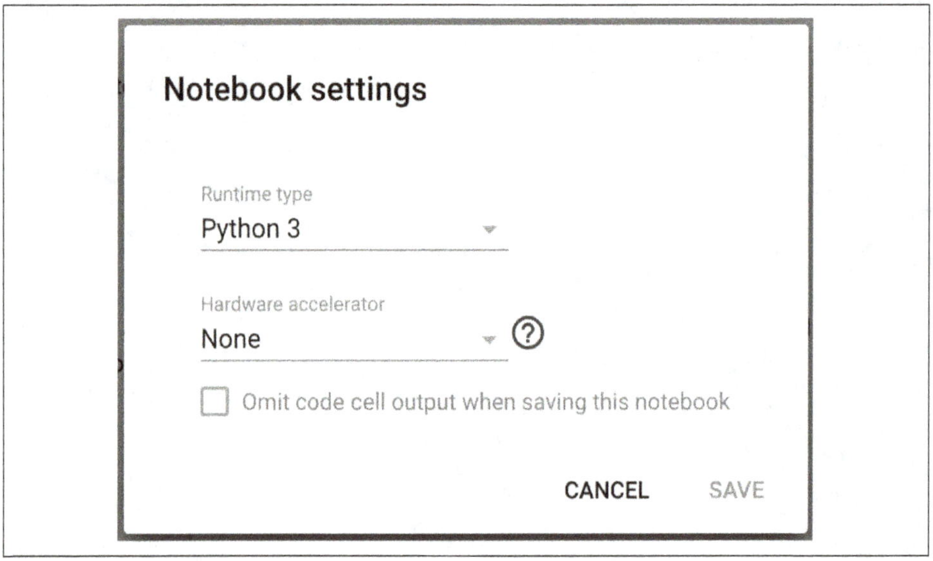

Notebook settings

Runtime type
Python 3

Hardware accelerator
None

☐ Omit code cell output when saving this notebook

CANCEL   SAVE

Figure 12-3. The "Notebook settings" dialog box

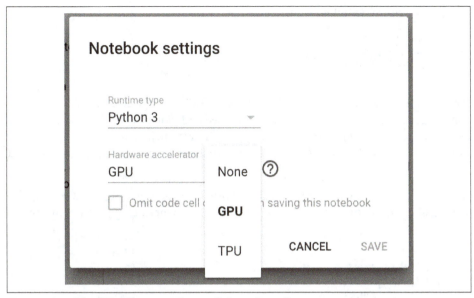

Figure 12-4. The "Hardware accelerator" drop-down list

Install dependencies

The first step is to install the required dependencies. In the "Install dependencies" section, run the cells to install the correct versions of TensorFlow and grab a copy of the training scripts.

Prepare the data

Next, in the "Prepare the data" section, run the cells to download the dataset and split it into training, validation, and test sets.

The first cell downloads and extracts the dataset into the training scripts' directory. The dataset consists of four directories, one for each gesture ("wing," "ring," and "slope") plus a "negative" directory for data that represents no distinct gesture. Each directory contains files that represent raw data resulting from the capture process for the gesture being performed:

```
data/
├── slope
│   ├── output_slope_dengyl.txt
│   ├── output_slope_hyw.txt
│   └── ...
├── ring
│   ├── output_ring_dengyl.txt
│   ├── output_ring_hyw.txt
│   └── ...
├── negative
```

```
|       ├── output_negative_1.txt
|       └── ...
└── wing
        ├── output_wing_dengyl.txt
        ├── output_wing_hyw.txt
        └── ...
```

There are 10 files for each gesture, which we'll walk through later on. Each file contains a gesture being demonstrated by a named individual, with the last part of the filename corresponding to their user ID. For example, the file *output_slope_dengyl.txt* contains data for the "slope" gesture being demonstrated by a user whose ID is dengyl.

There are approximately 15 individual performances of a given gesture in each file, one accelerometer reading per row, with each performance being prefixed by the row -,-,-:

```
    -,-,-
-766.0,132.0,709.0
-751.0,249.0,659.0
-714.0,314.0,630.0
-709.0,244.0,623.0
-707.0,230.0,659.0
```

Each performance consists of a log of up to a few seconds' worth of data, with 25 rows per second. The gesture itself occurs at some point within that window, with the device being held still for the remainder of the time.

Due to the way the measurements were captured, the files also contain some garbage characters. Our first training script, *data_prepare.py* (*https://oreil.ly/SCZe9*), which is run in our second training cell, will clean up this dirty data:

```
# Prepare the data
!python data_prepare.py
```

This script is designed to read the raw data files from their folders, ignore any garbage characters, and write them in a sanitized form to another location within the training scripts' directory (*data/complete_data*). Cleaning up messy data sources is a common task when training machine learning models given that it's very common for errors, corruption, and other issues to creep into large datasets.

In addition to cleaning the data, the script generates some *synthetic data*. This is a term for data that is generated algorithmically, rather than being captured from the real world. In this case, the generate_negative_data() function in *data_prepare.py* creates synthetic data that is equivalent to movement of the accelerometer that doesn't correspond to any particular gesture. This data is used to train our "unknown" category.

Because creating synthetic data is much faster than capturing real-world data, it's useful to help augment our training process. However, real-world variation is unpredictable, so it's not often possible to create an entire dataset from synthetic data. In our case, it's helpful for making our "unknown" category more robust, but it wouldn't be helpful for classifying the known gestures.

The next script to run in the second cell is *data_split_person.py* (*https://oreil.ly/ 1U0FW*):

```
# Split the data by person
!python data_split_person.py
```

This script splits the data into training, validation, and test sets. Because our data is labeled with the person who created it, we're able to use one set of people's data for training, another set for validation, and a final set for test. The data is split as follows:

```
train_names = [
    "hyw", "shiyun", "tangsy", "dengyl", "jiangyh", "xunkai", "negative3",
    "negative4", "negative5", "negative6"
]
valid_names = ["lsj", "pengxl", "negative2", "negative7"]
test_names = ["liucx", "zhangxy", "negative1", "negative8"]
```

We use six people's data for training, two for validation, and two for testing. In addition, we mix in our negative data, which isn't associated with a particular user. Our total data is split between the three sets at a ratio of roughly 60%/20%/20%, which is pretty standard for machine learning.

In splitting by person, we're trying to ensure that our model will be able to generalize to new data. Because the model will be validated and tested on data from individuals who were not included in the training dataset, the model will need to be robust against individual variations in how each person performs each gesture.

It's also possible to split the data randomly, instead of by person. In this case, the training, validation, and testing datasets would each contain some samples of each gesture from every single individual. The resulting model will have been trained on data from every single person rather than just six, so it will have had more exposure to people's varying gesturing styles.

However, because the validation and training sets also contain data from every individual, we'd have no way of testing whether the model is able to generalize to new gesturing styles that it has not seen before. A model developed in this way might report higher accuracy during validation and testing, but it would not be guaranteed to work as well with new data.

Make sure you've run both cells in the "Prepare the data" section before continuing.

Load TensorBoard

After the data has been prepared, we can run the next cell to load TensorBoard, which will help us monitor the training process:

```
# Load TensorBoard
%load_ext tensorboard
%tensorboard --logdir logs/scalars
```

Training logs will be written to the *logs/scalars* subdirectory of the training scripts' directory, so we pass this in to TensorBoard.

Begin training

After TensorBoard has loaded, it's time to begin training. Run the following cell:

```
!python train.py --model CNN --person true
```

The script *train.py* (*https://oreil.ly/S3w0X*) sets up the model architecture, loads the data using *data_load.py* (*https://oreil.ly/aCZgu*), and begins the training process.

As the data is loaded, *load_data.py* also performs data augmentation using code defined in *data_augmentation.py* (*https://oreil.ly/zL6wm*). The function augment_data() takes data representing a gesture and creates a number of new versions of it, each modified slightly from the original. The modifications include shifting and warping the datapoints in time, adding random noise, and increasing the amount of acceleration. This augmented data is used alongside the original data to train the model, helping make the most of our small dataset.

As training ramps up, you'll see some output appearing below the cell you just ran. There's a lot there, so let's pick out the most noteworthy parts. First, Keras generates a nice table that shows the architecture of our model:

Layer (type)	Output Shape	Param #
conv2d (Conv2D)	(None, 128, 3, 8)	104
max_pooling2d (MaxPooling2D)	(None, 42, 1, 8)	0

```
dropout (Dropout)              (None, 42, 1, 8)          0

conv2d_1 (Conv2D)              (None, 42, 1, 16)         528

max_pooling2d_1 (MaxPooling2   (None, 14, 1, 16)         0

dropout_1 (Dropout)            (None, 14, 1, 16)         0

flatten (Flatten)              (None, 224)               0

dense (Dense)                  (None, 16)                3600

dropout_2 (Dropout)            (None, 16)                0

dense_1 (Dense)                (None, 4)                 68
==================================================================
```

It tells us all the layers that are used, along with their shapes and their numbers of parameters—which is another term for weights and biases. You can see that our model uses Conv2D layers, as it's a convolutional model. Not shown in this table is the fact that our model's input shape is (None, 128, 3). We'll look more closely at the model's architecture later.

The output will also show us an estimate of the model's size:

```
Model size: 16.796875 KB
```

This represents the amount of memory that will be taken up by the model's trainable parameters. It doesn't include the extra space required to store the model's execution graph, so our actual model file will be slightly larger, but it gives us an idea of the correct order of magnitude. This will definitely qualify as a tiny model!

You'll eventually see the training process itself begin:

```
1000/1000 [==============================] - 12s 12ms/step - loss: 7.6510 -
accuracy: 0.5207 - val_loss: 4.5836 - val_accuracy: 0.7206
```

At this point, you can take a look at TensorBoard to see the training process moving along.

Evaluate the results

When training is complete, we can look at the cell's output for some useful information. First, we can see that the validation accuracy in our final epoch looks very promising at 0.9743, and the loss is nice and low, too:

```
Epoch 50/50
1000/1000 [==============================] - 7s 7ms/step - loss: 0.0568 -

accuracy: 0.9835 - val_loss: 0.1185 - val_accuracy: 0.9743
```

This is great, especially as we're using a per-person data split, meaning our validation data is from a completely different set of individuals. However, we can't just rely on our validation accuracy to evaluate our model. Because the model's hyperparameters and architecture were hand-tuned on the validation dataset, we might have overfit it.

To get a better understanding of our model's final performance, we can evaluate it against our test dataset by calling Keras's `model.evaluate()` function. The next line of output shows the results of this:

```
6/6 [==============================] - 0s 6ms/step - loss: 0.2888 - accuracy:
0.9323
```

Although not as amazing as the validation numbers, the model shows a good-enough accuracy of 0.9323, with a loss that is still low. The model will predict the correct class 93% of the time, which should be fine for our purposes.

The next few lines show the *confusion matrix* for the results, calculated by the `tf.math.confusion_matrix()` (*https://oreil.ly/xlIKj*) function:

```
tf.Tensor(
[[ 75   3   0   4]
 [  0  69   0  15]
 [  0   0  85   3]
 [  0   0   1 129]], shape=(4, 4), dtype=int32)
```

A confusion matrix is a helpful tool for evaluating the performance of classification models. It shows how well the predicted class of each input in the test dataset agrees with its actual value.

Each column of the confusion matrix corresponds to a predicted label, in order ("wing," "ring," "slope," then "unknown"). Each row, from the top down, corresponds to the actual label. From our confusion matrix, we can see that the vast majority of predictions agree with the actual labels. We can also see the specific places where confusion is occurring: most significantly, a fair number of inputs were misclassified as "unknown," especially those belonging to the "ring" category.

The confusion matrix gives us an idea of where our model's weak points are. In this case, it informs us that it might be beneficial to obtain more training data for the "ring" gesture in order to help the model better learn the differences between "ring" and "unknown."

The final thing that *train.py* does is convert the model to TensorFlow Lite format, in both floating-point and quantized variations. The following output reveals the sizes of each variant:

```
Basic model is 19544 bytes
Quantized model is 8824 bytes
Difference is 10720 bytes
```

Our 20 KB model shrinks down to 8.8 KB after quantization. This is a *very* tiny model, and a great result.

Create a C array

The next cell, in the "Create a C source file" section, transforms this into a C source file. Run this cell to see the output:

```
# Install xxd if it is not available
!apt-get -qq install xxd
# Save the file as a C source file
!xxd -i model_quantized.tflite > /content/model_quantized.cc
# Print the source file
!cat /content/model_quantized.cc
```

We can copy and paste the contents of this file into our project so that we can use the newly trained model in our application. Later, you'll learn how to collect new data and teach the application to understand new gestures. For now, let's keep moving.

Other Ways to Run the Scripts

If you'd prefer not to use Colab, or you're making changes to the model training scripts and would like to test them out locally, you can easily run the scripts from your own development machine. You can find the instructions in *README.md* (*https://oreil.ly/6-KPf*).

Next up, we walk through how the model itself works.

How the Model Works

So far, we've established that our model is a convolutional neural network (CNN) and that it transforms a sequence of 128 three-axis accelerometer readings, representing around five seconds of time, into an array of four probabilities: one for each gesture, and one for "unknown."

CNNs are used when the relationships between adjacent values contain important information. In the first part of our explanation, we'll take a look at our data and learn why a CNN is well suited to making sense of it.

Visualizing the Input

In our time-series accelerometer data, adjacent accelerometer readings give us clues about the device's motion. For example, if acceleration on one axis changes rapidly from zero to positive, then back to zero, the device might have begun motion in that direction. Figure 12-5 shows a hypothetical example of this.

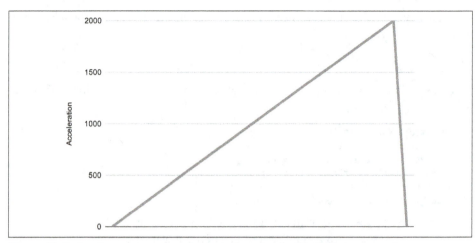

Figure 12-5. Accelerometer values for a single axis of a device being moved

Any given gesture is composed of a series of motions, one after the other. For example, consider our "wing" gesture, shown in Figure 12-6.

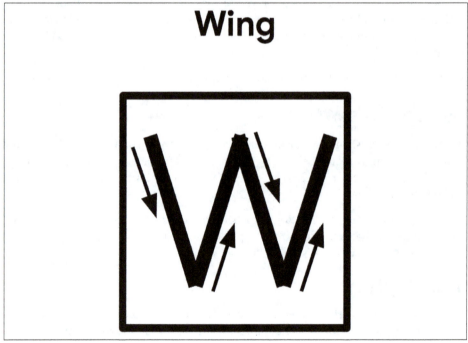

Figure 12-6. The "wing" gesture

The device is first moved down and to the right, then up and to the right, then down and to the right, then up and to the right again. Figure 12-7 shows a sample of real data captured during the "wing" gesture, measured in milli-Gs.

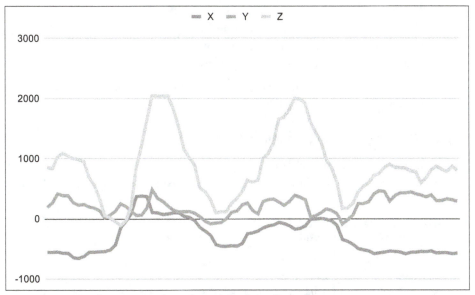

Figure 12-7. Accelerometer values during the "wing" gesture

By looking at this graph and breaking it down into its component parts, we can understand which gesture is being made. From the z-axis acceleration, it's very clear that the device is being moved up and down in the way we would expect given the "wing" gesture's shape. More subtly, we can see how the acceleration on the x-axis correlates with the z-axis changes in a way that indicates the device's motion across the width of the gesture. Meanwhile, we can observe that the y-axis remains mostly stable.

Similarly, a CNN with multiple layers is able to learn how to discern each gesture through its telltale component parts. For example, a network might learn to distinguish an up-and-down motion, and that two of them, when combined with the appropriate z- and y-axis movements, indicates a "wing" gesture.

To do this, a CNN learns a series of *filters*, arranged in layers. Each filter learns to spot a particular type of feature in the data. When it notices this feature, it passes this high-level information to the next layer of the network. For example, one filter in the first layer of the network might learn to spot something simple, like a period of upward acceleration. When it identifies such a structure, it passes this information to the next layer of the network.

Subsequent layers of filters learn how the outputs of earlier, simpler filters are composed together to form larger structures. For example, a series of four alternating upward and downward accelerations might fit together to represent the "W" shape in our "wing" gesture.

In this process, the noisy input data is progressively transformed into a high-level, symbolic representation. Subsequent layers of our network can analyze this symbolic representation to guess which gesture was performed.

In the next section, we walk through the actual model architecture and see how it maps onto this process.

Understanding the Model Architecture

The architecture of our model is defined in *train.py* (*https://oreil.ly/vxT1v*), in the build_cnn() function. This function uses the Keras API to define a model, layer by layer:

```
model = tf.keras.Sequential([
    tf.keras.layers.Conv2D( # input_shape=(batch, 128, 3)
        8, (4, 3),
        padding="same",
        activation="relu",
        input_shape=(seq_length, 3, 1)),  # output_shape=(batch, 128, 3, 8)
    tf.keras.layers.MaxPool2D((3, 3)),  # (batch, 42, 1, 8)
    tf.keras.layers.Dropout(0.1),  # (batch, 42, 1, 8)
    tf.keras.layers.Conv2D(16, (4, 1), padding="same",
                        activation="relu"),  # (batch, 42, 1, 16)
    tf.keras.layers.MaxPool2D((3, 1), padding="same"),  # (batch, 14, 1, 16)
    tf.keras.layers.Dropout(0.1),  # (batch, 14, 1, 16)
    tf.keras.layers.Flatten(),  # (batch, 224)
    tf.keras.layers.Dense(16, activation="relu"),  # (batch, 16)
    tf.keras.layers.Dropout(0.1),  # (batch, 16)
    tf.keras.layers.Dense(4, activation="softmax")  # (batch, 4)
])
```

This is a sequential model, meaning the output of each layer is passed directly into the next one. Let's walk through the layers one by one and explore what's going on. The first layer is a Conv2D:

```
tf.keras.layers.Conv2D(
    8, (4, 3),
    padding="same",
    activation="relu",
    input_shape=(seq_length, 3, 1)),  # output_shape=(batch, 128, 3, 8)
```

This is a convolutional layer; it directly receives our network's input, which is a sequence of raw accelerometer data. The input's shape is provided in the input_shape argument. It's set to (seq_length, 3, 1), where seq_length is the total number of accelerometer measurements that are passed in (128 by default). Each measurement is composed of three values, representing the x-, y-, and z-axes. The input is visualized in Figure 12-8.

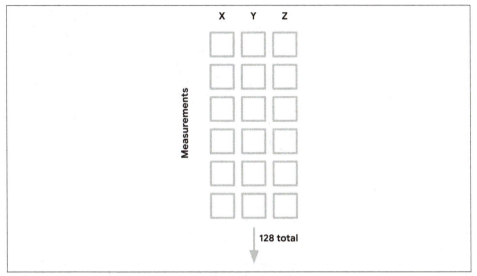

Figure 12-8. The model's input

The job of our convolutional layer is to take this raw data and extract some basic features that can be interpreted by subsequent layers. The arguments to the Conv2D() function determine how many features will be extracted. The arguments are described in the tf.keras.layers.Conv2D() documentation (*https://oreil.ly/hqXJF*).

The first argument determines how many filters the layer will have. During training, each filter learns to identify a particular feature in the raw data—for example, one filter might learn to identify the telltale signs of an upward motion. For each filter, the layer outputs a *feature map* that shows where the feature it has learned occurs within the input.

The layer defined in our code has eight filters, meaning that it will learn to recognize and output eight different types of high-level features from the input data. You can see this reflected in the output shape, (batch_size, 128, 3, 8), which has eight *feature channels* in its final dimension, one for each feature. The value in each channel indicates the degree to which a feature was present in that location of the input.

As we learned in Chapter 8, convolutional layers slide a window across the data and decide whether a given feature is present in that window. The second argument to

Conv2D() is where we provide the dimensions of this window. In our case, it's (4, 3). This means that the features for which our filters are hunting span four consecutive accelerometer measurements and all three axes. Because the window spans four measurements, each filter analyzes a small snapshot of time, meaning it can generate features that represent a change in acceleration over time. You can see how this works in Figure 12-9.

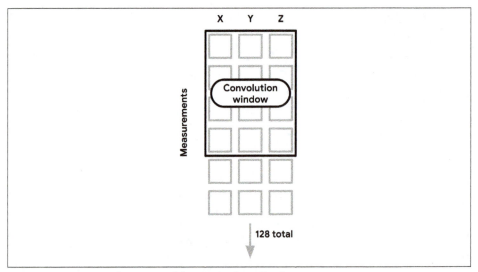

Figure 12-9. A convolution window overlaid on the data

The padding argument determines how the window will be moved across the data. When padding is set to "same", the layer's output will have the same length (128) and width (3) as the input. Because every movement of the filter window results in a single output value, the "same" argument means the window must be moved three times across the data, and 128 times down it.

Because the window has a width of 3, this means it must start by overhanging the left-hand side of the data. The empty spaces, where the filter window doesn't cover an actual value, are *padded* with zeros. To move a total of 128 times down the length of the data, the filter must also overhang the top of the data. You can see how this works in Figures 12-10 and 12-11.

As soon as the convolution window has moved across all the data, using each filter to create eight different feature maps, the output will be passed to our next layer, Max Pool2D:

```
tf.keras.layers.MaxPool2D((3, 3)),  # (batch, 42, 1, 8)
```

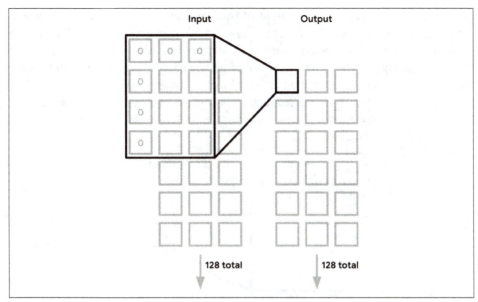

Figure 12-10. The convolution window in its first position, necessitating padding on the top and left sides

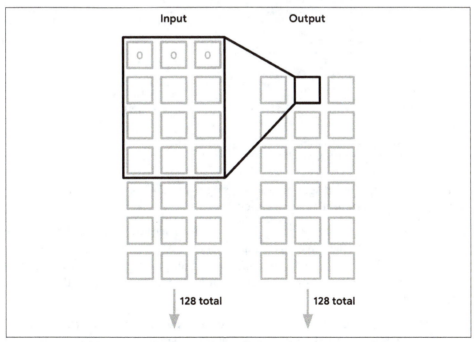

Figure 12-11. The same convolution window having moved to its second position, requiring padding only on the top

This `MaxPool2D` layer takes the output of the previous layer, a `(128, 3, 8)` tensor, and shrinks it down to a `(42, 1, 8)` tensor—a third of its original size. It does this by looking at a window of input data and then selecting the largest value in the window and propagating only that value to the output. The process is then repeated with the next window of data. The argument provided to the `MaxPool2D()` (*https://oreil.ly/ HZo0q*) function, `(3, 3)`, specifies that a 3 × 3 window should be used. By default, the window is always moved so that it contains entirely new data. Figure 12-12 shows how this process works.

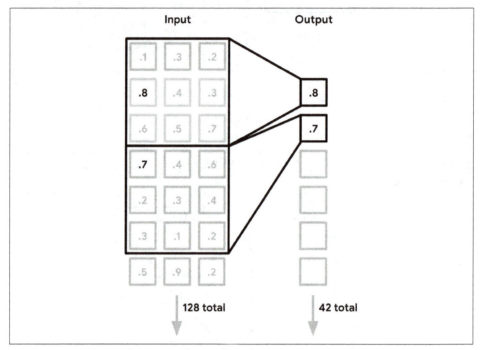

Figure 12-12. Max pooling at work

Note that although the diagram shows a single value for each element, our data actually has eight feature channels per element.

But why do we need to shrink our input like this? When used for classification, the goal of a CNN is to transform a big, complex input tensor into a small, simple output. The `MaxPool2D` layer helps make this happen. It boils down the output of our first convolutional layer into a concentrated, high-level representation of the relevant information that it contains.

By concentrating the information, we begin to strip out things that aren't relevant to the task of identifying which gesture was contained within the input. Only the most significant features, which were maximally represented in the first convolutional layer's output, are preserved. It's interesting to note that even though our original input had three accelerometer axes for each measurement, a combination of Conv2D and MaxPool2D has now merged these together into a single value.

After we've shrunk our data down, it goes through a Dropout layer (*https://oreil.ly/ JuQtU*):

```
tf.keras.layers.Dropout(0.1),  # (batch, 42, 1, 8)
```

The Dropout layer randomly sets some of a tensor's values to zero during training. In this case, by calling Dropout(0.1), we set 10% of the values to zero, entirely obliterating that data. This might seem like a strange thing to do, so let's explain.

Dropout is a regularization technique. As mentioned earlier in the book, *regularization* is the process of improving machine learning models so that they are less likely to overfit their training data. Dropout is a simple but effective way to limit overfitting. By randomly removing some data between one layer and the next, we force the neural network to learn how to cope with unexpected noise and variation. Adding dropout between layers is a common and effective practice.

The dropout layer is only active during training. During inference, it has no effect; all of the data is allowed through.

After the Dropout layer, we again feed the data through a MaxPool2D layer and a Dropout layer:

```
tf.keras.layers.Conv2D(16, (4, 1), padding="same",
                       activation="relu"),  # (batch, 42, 1, 16)
```

This layer has 16 filters and a window size of (4, 1). These numbers are part of the model's hyperparameters, and they were chosen in an iterative process while the model was being developed. Designing an effective architecture is a process of trial and error, and these magic numbers are what was arrived at after a lot of experimentation. It's unlikely that you'll ever select the exact right values the first time around.

Like the first convolutional layer, this one also learns to spot patterns in adjacent values that contain meaningful information. Its output is an even higher-level representation of the content of a given input. The features it recognizes are compositions of the features identified by our first convolutional layer.

After this convolutional layer, we do another MaxPool2D and Dropout:

```
tf.keras.layers.MaxPool2D((3, 1), padding="same"),  # (batch, 14, 1, 16)
tf.keras.layers.Dropout(0.1),  # (batch, 14, 1, 16)
```

This continues the process of distilling the original input down to a smaller, more manageable representation. The output, with a shape of (14, 1, 16), is a multidimensional tensor that symbolically represents only the most significant structures contained within the input data.

If we wanted to, we could continue with the process of convolution and pooling. The number of layers in a CNN is just another hyperparameter that we can tune during model development. However, during the development of this model, we found that two convolutional layers was sufficient.

Up until this point, we've been running our data through convolutional layers, which care only about the relationships between adjacent values—we haven't really been considering the bigger picture. However, because we now have high-level representations of the major features contained within our input, we can "zoom out" and study them in aggregate. To do so, we flatten our data and feed it into a `Dense` layer (also known as a *fully connected layer*):

```
tf.keras.layers.Flatten(),  # (batch, 224)
tf.keras.layers.Dense(16, activation="relu"),  # (batch, 16)
```

The `Flatten` layer (*https://oreil.ly/TUIZc*) is used to transform a multidimensional tensor into one with a single dimension. In this case, our `(14, 1, 16)` tensor is squished down into a single dimension with shape `(224)`.

It's then fed into a `Dense` layer (*https://oreil.ly/FbpDB*) with 16 neurons. This is one of the most basic tools in the deep learning toolbox: a layer where every input is connected to every neuron. By considering all of our data, all at once, this layer can learn the meanings of various combinations of inputs. The output of this `Dense` layer will be a set of 16 values representing the content of the original input in a highly compressed form.

Our final task is to shrink these 16 values down into 4 classes. To do this, we first add some more dropout and then a final `Dense` layer:

```
tf.keras.layers.Dropout(0.1),  # (batch, 16)
tf.keras.layers.Dense(4, activation="softmax")  # (batch, 4)
```

This layer has four neurons; one representing each class of gesture. Each of them is connected to all 16 of the outputs from the previous layer. During training, each neuron will learn the combination of previous-layer activations that correspond to the gesture it represents.

The layer is configured with a `"softmax"` activation function, which results in the layer's output being a set of probabilities that sum to 1. This output is what we see in the model's output tensor.

This type of model architecture—a combination of convolutional and fully connected layers—is very useful in classifying time-series sensor data like the measurements we obtain from our accelerometer. The model learns to identify the high-level features that represent the "fingerprint" of a particular class of input. It's small, runs fast, and doesn't take long to train. This architecture will be a valuable tool in your belt as an embedded machine learning engineer.

Training with Your Own Data

In this section, we'll show you how to train your own, custom model that recognizes new gestures. We'll walk through how to capture accelerometer data, modify the training scripts to incorporate it, train a new model, and integrate it into the embedded application.

Capturing Data

To obtain training data, we can use a simple program to log accelerometer data to the serial port while gestures are being performed.

SparkFun Edge

The fastest way to get started is by modifying one of the examples in the SparkFun Edge Board Support Package (BSP) (*https://oreil.ly/z4eHX*). First, follow SparkFun's "Using SparkFun Edge Board with Ambiq Apollo3 SDK" (*https://oreil.ly/QqKPa*) guide to set up the Ambiq SDK and SparkFun Edge BSP.

After you've downloaded the SDK and BSP, you'll need to tweak the example code so it does what we want.

First, open the file *AmbiqSuite-Rel2.2.0/boards/SparkFun_Edge_BSP/examples/example1_edge_test/src/tf_adc/tf_adc.c* in your text editor of choice. Find the call to `am_hal_adc_samples_read()`, on line 61 of the file:

```
if (AM_HAL_STATUS_SUCCESS != am_hal_adc_samples_read(g_ADCHandle,
                                                     NULL,
                                                     &ui32NumSamples,
                                                     &Sample))
```

Change its second parameter to `true` so that the entire function call looks like this:

```
if (AM_HAL_STATUS_SUCCESS != am_hal_adc_samples_read(g_ADCHandle,
                                                     true,
                                                     &ui32NumSamples,
                                                     &Sample))
```

Next, you'll need to modify the file *AmbiqSuite-Rel2.2.0/boards/SparkFun_Edge_BSP/examples/example1_edge_test/src/main.c*. Find the `while` loop on line 51:

```
/*
 * Read samples in polling mode (no int)
 */
while(1)
{
    // Use Button 14 to break the loop and shut down
    uint32_t pin14Val = 1;
    am_hal_gpio_state_read( AM_BSP_GPIO_14, AM_HAL_GPIO_INPUT_READ, &pin14Val);
```

Change the code to add the following extra line:

```
/*
 * Read samples in polling mode (no int)
 */
while(1)
{
    am_util_stdio_printf("-,-,-\r\n");
    // Use Button 14 to break the loop and shut down
    uint32_t pin14Val = 1;
    am_hal_gpio_state_read( AM_BSP_GPIO_14, AM_HAL_GPIO_INPUT_READ, &pin14Val);
```

Now find this line a little further along in the while loop:

```
am_util_stdio_printf("Acc [mg] %04.2f x, %04.2f y, %04.2f z,
                      Temp [deg C] %04.2f, MIC0 [counts / 2^14] %d\r\n",
        acceleration_mg[0], acceleration_mg[1], acceleration_mg[2],
        temperature_degC, (audioSample) );
```

Delete the original line and replace it with the following:

```
am_util_stdio_printf("%04.2f,%04.2f,%04.2f\r\n", acceleration_mg[0],
                      acceleration_mg[1], acceleration_mg[2]);
```

The program will now output data in the format expected by the training scripts.

Next, follow the instructions in SparkFun's guide (*https://oreil.ly/BPJMG*) to build the example1_edge_test example application and flash it to the device.

Logging data

After you've built and flashed the example code, follow these instructions to capture some data.

First, open a new terminal window. Then run the following command to begin logging all of the terminal's output to a file named *output.txt*:

```
script output.txt
```

Next, in the same window, use screen to connect to the device:

```
screen ${DEVICENAME} 115200
```

Measurements from the accelerometer will be shown on the screen and saved to *output.txt* in the same comma-delimited format expected by the training scripts.

You should aim to capture multiple performances of the same gesture in a single file. To start capturing a single performance of a gesture, press the button marked RST. The characters -,-,- will be written to the serial port; this output is used by the training scripts to identify the start of a gesture performance. After you've performed the gesture, press the button marked 14 to stop logging data.

When you've logged the same gesture a number of times, exit `screen` by pressing Ctrl- A, immediately followed by the K key, and then the Y key. After you've exited `screen`, enter the following command to stop logging data to *output.txt*:

```
exit
```

You now have a file, *output.txt*, which contains data for one person performing a single gesture. To train an entirely new model, you should aim to collect a similar amount of data as in the original dataset, which contains around 15 performances of each gesture by 10 people.

If you don't care about your model working for people other than yourself, you can probably get away with capturing only your own performances. That said, the more variation in performances you can collect, the better.

For compatibility with the training scripts, you should rename your captured data files in the following format:

```
output_<gesture_name>_<person_name>.txt
```

For example, data for a hypothetical "triangle" gesture made by "Daniel" would have the following name:

```
output_triangle_Daniel.txt
```

The training scripts will expect the data to be organized in directories for each gesture name; for example:

```
data/
├── triangle
│   ├── output_triangle_Daniel.txt
│   └── ...
├── square
│   ├── output_square_Daniel.txt
│   └── ...
└── star
    ├── output_star_Daniel.txt
    └── ...
```

You'll also need to provide data for the "unknown" category, in a directory named *negative*. In this case, you can just reuse the data files from the original dataset.

Note that because the model architecture is designed to output probabilities for four classes (three gestures plus "unknown"), you should provide three gestures of your own. If you want to train on more or fewer gestures, you'll need to change the training scripts and adjust the model architecture.

Modifying the Training Scripts

To train a model with your new gestures, you need to make some changes to the training scripts.

First, replace all of the gesture names within the following files:

- *data_load.py* (*https://oreil.ly/1Tplr*)
- *data_prepare.py* (*https://oreil.ly/O7eym*)
- *data_split.py* (*https://oreil.ly/w8ORq*)

Next, replace all of the person names within the following files:

- *data_prepare.py* (*https://oreil.ly/3swnY*)
- *data_split_person.py* (*https://oreil.ly/xhVh7*)

Note that if you have a different number of person names (the original dataset has 10) and you want to split the data by person during training, you'll need to decide on a new split. If you have data from only a few people, it won't be possible to split by person during training, so don't worry about *data_split_person.py*.

Training

To train a new model, copy your data files directories into the training scripts' directory and follow the process we walked through earlier in this chapter.

If you have data from only a few people, you should split the data randomly rather than per person. To do this, run *data_split.py* instead of *data_split_person.py* when preparing for training.

Because you're training on new gestures, it's worth playing with the model's hyperparameters to obtain the best accuracy. For example, you can see whether you get better results by training for more or fewer epochs, or with a different arrangement of layers or number of neurons, or with different convolutional hyperparameters. You can use TensorBoard to monitor your progress.

Once you have a model with acceptable accuracy, you'll need to make a few changes to the project to make sure it works.

Using the New Model

First, you'll need to copy the new model's data, as formatted by xxd -i, into *magic_wand_model_data.cc*. Make sure you also update the value of g_magic_wand_model_data_len to match the number output by xxd.

Next, in the array `should_continuous_count`, you'll need to update the values in *accelerometer_handler.cc* that specify the number of continuous predictions required for each gesture. The value corresponds to how long the gesture takes to perform. Given that the original "wing" gesture requires a continuous count of 15, estimate how long your new gestures will take relative to that, and update the values in the array. You can tune these values iteratively until you get the most reliable performance.

Finally, update the code in *output_handler.cc* to print the correct names for your new gestures. When this is done, you can build your code and flash your device.

Wrapping Up

In this chapter, we've taken our deepest dive yet into the architecture of a typical embedded machine learning model. This type of convolutional model is a powerful tool for classifying time-series data, and you'll come across it often.

By now, you hopefully have an understanding of what embedded machine learning applications look like, and how their application code works together with models to understand the world around them. As you build your own projects, you'll begin to put together a toolbox of familiar models that you can use to solve different problems.

Learning Machine Learning

This book is intended to provide a gentle introduction to the possibilities of embedded machine learning, but it's not a complete reference on machine learning itself. If you'd like to dig deeper into building your own models, there are some amazing and highly accessible resources that are suitable for students of all backgrounds and will give you a running start.

Here are some of our favorites, which will build on what you've learned here:

- François Chollet's *Deep Learning with Python* (*https://oreil.ly/PFF3r*) (Manning)
- Aurélien Géron's *Hands-on Machine Learning with Scikit-Learn, Keras, and TensorFlow*, 2nd Edition (*https://oreil.ly/M5KrN*) (O'Reilly)
- Deeplearning.ai's Deep Learning Specialization (*https://oreil.ly/xKQMP*) and TensorFlow in Practice (*https://oreil.ly/4q7HY*) courses
- Udacity's Intro to TensorFlow for Deep Learning (*https://oreil.ly/YJlYd*) course

What's Next

The remaining chapters of this book take a deeper dive into the tools and workflows of embedded machine learning. You'll learn how to think about designing your own TinyML applications, how to optimize models and application code to run well on low-powered devices, how to port existing machine learning models to embedded devices, and how to debug embedded machine learning code. We'll also address some high-level concerns, like deployment, privacy, and security.

But first, let's learn a bit more about TensorFlow Lite, the framework that powers all of the examples in this book.

## CHAPTER 13

TensorFlow Lite for Microcontrollers

In this chapter we look at the software framework we've been using for all of the examples in the book: TensorFlow Lite for Microcontrollers. We go into a lot of detail, but you don't need to understand everything we cover to use it in an application. If you're not interested in what's happening under the hood, feel free to skip this chapter; you can always return to it when you have questions. If you do want to better understand the tool you're using to run machine learning, we cover the history and inner workings of the library here.

What Is TensorFlow Lite for Microcontrollers?

The first question you might ask is what the framework actually does. To understand that, it helps to break the (rather long) name down a bit and explain the components.

TensorFlow

You may well have heard of TensorFlow itself if you've looked into machine learning. TensorFlow (*https://tensorflow.org*) is Google's open source machine learning library, with the motto "An Open Source Machine Learning Framework for Everyone." It was developed internally at Google and first released to the public in 2015. Since then a large external community has grown up around the software, with more contributors outside Google than inside. It's aimed at Linux, Windows, and macOS desktop and server platforms and offers a lot of tools, examples, and optimizations around training and deploying models in the cloud. It's the main machine learning library used within Google to power its products, and the core code itself is the same across the internal and published versions.

There are also a large number of examples and tutorials available from Google and other sources. These can show you how to train and use models for everything from speech recognition to data center power management or video analysis.

The biggest need when TensorFlow was launched was the ability to train models and run them in desktop environments. This influenced a lot of the design decisions, such as trading the size of the executable for lower latency and more functionality—on a cloud server where even RAM is measured in gigabytes and there are terabytes of storage space, having a binary that's a couple of hundred megabytes in size is not a problem. Another example is that its main interface language at launch was Python, a scripting language widely used on servers.

These engineering trade-offs weren't as appropriate for other platforms, though. On Android and iPhone devices, adding even a few megabytes to the size of an app can decrease the number of downloads and customer satisfaction dramatically. You can build TensorFlow for these phone platforms, but by default it adds 20 MB to the application size, and even with some work never shrinks below 2 MB.

TensorFlow Lite

To meet these lower size requirements for mobile platforms, in 2017 Google started a companion project to mainline TensorFlow called TensorFlow Lite. This library is aimed at running neural network models efficiently and easily on mobile devices. To reduce the size and complexity of the framework, it drops features that are less common on these platforms. For example, it doesn't support training, just running inference on models that were previously trained on a cloud platform. It also doesn't support the full range of data types (such as `double`) available in mainline Tensor-Flow. Additionally, some less-used operations aren't present, like `tf.depth_to_space`. You can find the latest compatibility information on the TensorFlow website (*https://oreil.ly/otEIp*).

In return for these trade-offs, TensorFlow Lite can fit within just a few hundred kilobytes, making it much easier to fit into a size-constrained application. It also has highly optimized libraries for Arm Cortex-A-series CPUs, along with support for Android's Neural Network API for accelerators, and GPUs through OpenGL. Another key advantage is that it has good support for 8-bit quantization of networks. Because a model might have millions of parameters, the 75% size reduction from 32-bit floats to 8-bit integers alone makes it worthwhile, but there are also specialized code paths that allow inference to run much faster on the smaller data type.

TensorFlow Lite for Microcontrollers

TensorFlow Lite has been widely adopted by mobile developers, but its engineering trade-offs didn't meet the requirements of all platforms. The team noticed that there were a lot of Google and external products that could benefit from machine learning being build on embedded platforms, on which the existing TensorFlow Lite library wouldn't fit. Again, the biggest constraint was binary size. For these environments even a few hundred kilobytes was too large; they needed something that would fit within 20 KB or less. A lot of the dependencies that mobile developers take for granted, like the C Standard Library, weren't present either, so no code that relied on these libraries could be used. A lot of the requirements were very similar, though. Inference was the primary use case, quantized networks were important for performance, and having a code base that was simple enough for developers to explore and modify was a priority.

With those needs in mind, in 2018 a team at Google (including the authors of this book) started experimenting with a specialized version of TensorFlow Lite aimed just at these embedded platforms. The goal was to reuse as much of the code, tooling, and documentation from the mobile project as possible, while satisfying the tough requirements of embedded environments. To make sure Google was building something practical, the team focused on the real-world use case of recognizing a spoken "wake word," similar to the "Hey Google" or "Alexa" examples from commercial voice interfaces. Aiming at an end-to-end example of how to tackle this problem, Google worked to ensure the system we designed was usable for production systems.

Requirements

The Google team knew that running in embedded environments imposed a lot of constraints on how the code could be written, so it identified some key requirements for the library:

No operating system dependencies
A machine learning model is fundamentally a mathematical black box where numbers are fed in, and numbers are returned as the results. Access to the rest of the system shouldn't be necessary to perform these operations, so it's possible to write a machine learning framework without calls to the underlying operating system. Some of the targeted platforms don't have an OS at all, and avoiding any references to files or devices in the basic code made it possible to port to those chips.

No standard C or C++ library dependencies at linker time
This is a bit subtler than the OS requirement, but the team was aiming to deploy on devices that might have only a few tens of kilobytes of memory to store a program, so the binary size was very important. Even apparently simple functions like `sprintf()` can easily take up 20 KB by themselves, so the team aimed to avoid anything that had to be pulled in from the library archives that hold the implementations of the C and C++ standard libraries. This was tricky because there's no well-defined boundary between header-only dependencies (like *stdint.h*, which holds the sizes of data types) and linker-time parts of the standard

libraries (such as many string functions or `sprintf()`). In practice the team had to use some common sense to understand that, generally, compile-time constants and macros were fine, but anything more complex should be avoided. The one exception to this linker avoidance is the standard C `math` library, which is relied on for things like trigonometric functions that do need to be linked in.

No floating-point hardware expected

Many embedded platforms don't have support for floating-point arithmetic in hardware, so the code had to avoid any performance-critical uses of floats. This meant focusing on models with 8-bit integer parameters, and using 8-bit arithmetic within operations (though for compatibility the framework also supports float ops if they're needed).

No dynamic memory allocation

A lot of applications using microcontrollers need to run continuously for months or years. If the main loop of a program is allocating and deallocating memory using `malloc()`/new and `free()`/delete, it's very difficult to guarantee that the heap won't eventually end up in a fragmented state, causing an allocation failure and a crash. There's also very little memory available on most embedded systems, so upfront planning of this limited resource is more important than on other platforms, and without an OS there might not even be a heap and allocation routines. This means that embedded applications often avoid using dynamic memory allocation entirely. Because the library was designed to be used by those applications, it needed do the same. In practice the framework asks the calling application to pass in a small, fixed-size arena that the framework can use for temporary allocations (like activation buffers) at initialization time. If the arena is too small, the library will return an error immediately and the client will need to recompile with a larger arena. Otherwise, the calls to perform inference happen with no further memory allocations, so they can be made repeatedly with no risk of heap fragmentation or memory errors.

The team also decided against some other constraints that are common in the embedded community because they would make sharing code and maintaining compatibility with mobile TensorFlow Lite too difficult. Therefore:

It requires C++11

It's common to write embedded programs in C, and some platforms don't have toolchains that support C++ at all, or support older versions than the 2011 revision of the standard. TensorFlow Lite is mostly written in C++, with some plain C APIs, which makes calling it from other languages easier. It doesn't rely on advanced features like complex templates; its style is in the spirit of a "better C" with classes to help modularize the code. Rewriting the framework in C would have taken a lot of work and been a step backward for users on mobile platforms, and when we surveyed the most popular platforms we found, they all had C++11 support already, so the team decided to trade support for older devices against making it easier to share code across all flavors of TensorFlow Lite.

It expects 32-bit processors

There are a massive number of different hardware platforms available in the embedded world, but the trend in recent years has been toward 32-bit processors, rather than the 16-bit or 8-bit chips that used to be common. After surveying the ecosystem, Google decided to focus its development on the newer 32-bit devices because that kept assumptions like the C int data type being 32 bits the same across mobile and embedded versions of the framework. We have had reports of successful ports to some 16-bit platforms, but these rely on modern toolchains that compensate for the limitations, and are not our main priority.

Why Is the Model Interpreted?

One question that comes up a lot is why we chose to interpret models at runtime rather than doing code generation from a model ahead of time. Explaining that decision involves teasing apart some of the benefits and problems of the different approaches involved.

Code generation involves converting a model directly into C or C++ code, with all of the parameters stored as data arrays in the code and the architecture expressed as a series of function calls that pass activations from one layer to the next. This code is often output into a single large source file with a handful of entry points. That file can then be included in an IDE or toolchain directly, and compiled like any other code. Here are a few of the key advantages of code generation:

Ease of building

Users told us the number one benefit was how easy it makes integrating into build systems. If all you have is a few C or C++ files, with no external library dependencies, you can easily drag and drop them into almost any IDE and get a project built with few chances for things to go wrong.

Modifiability

When you have a small amount of code in a single implementation file, it's much simpler to step through and change the code if you need to, at least compared to a large library for which you first need to establish what implementations are even being used.

Inline data

The data for the model itself can be stored as part of the implementation source code, so no additional files are required. It can also be stored directly as an in-memory data structure, so no loading or parsing step is required.

Code size

> If you know what model and platform you're building for ahead of time, you can avoid including code that will never be called, so the size of the program segment can be kept minimal.

Interpreting a model is a different approach, and relies on loading a data structure that defines the model. The executed code is static; only the model data changes, and the information in the model controls which operations are executed and where parameters are drawn from. This is more like running a script in an interpreted language like Python, whereas you can see code generation as being closer to traditional compiled languages like C. Here are some of the drawbacks of code generation, compared to interpreting a model data structure:

Upgradability

> What happens if you've locally modified the generated code but you want to upgrade to a newer version of the overall framework to get new functionality or optimizations? You'll either need to manually cherry-pick changes into your local files or regenerate them entirely and try to patch back in your local changes.

Multiple models

> It's difficult to support more than one model at a time through code generation without a lot of source duplication.

Replacing models

> Each model is expressed as a mixture of source code and data arrays within the program, so it's difficult to change the model without recompiling the entire program.

What the team realized was that it's possible to get a lot of the benefits of code generation, without incurring the drawbacks, using what we term *project generation*.

Project Generation

In TensorFlow Lite, project generation is a process that creates a copy of just the source files you need to build a particular model, without making any changes to them, and also optionally sets up any IDE-specific project files so that they can be built easily. It retains most of the benefits of code generation, but it has some key advantages:

Upgradability

> All of the source files are just copies of originals from the main TensorFlow Lite code base, and they appear in the same location in the folder hierarchy, so if you make local modifications they can easily be ported back to the original source, and library upgrades can be merged simply using standard merge tools.

Multiple and replacement models
> The underlying code is an interpreter, so you can have more than one model or swap out a data file easily without recompiling.

Inline data
> The model parameters themselves can still be compiled into the program as a C data array if needed, and the use of the FlatBuffers serialization format means that this representation can be used directly in memory with no unpacking or parsing required.

External dependencies
> All of the header and source files required to build the project are copied into the folder alongside the regular TensorFlow code, so no dependencies need to be downloaded or installed separately.

The biggest advantage that doesn't come automatically is code size, because the interpreter structure makes it more difficult to spot code paths that will never be called. This is addressed separately in TensorFlow Lite by manually using the OpResolver mechanism to register only the kernel implementations that you expect to use in your application.

Build Systems

TensorFlow Lite was originally developed in a Linux environment, so a lot of our tooling is based around traditional Unix tools like shell scripts, Make, and Python. We know that's not a common combination for embedded developers, though, so we aim to support other platforms and compilation toolchains as first-class citizens.

The way we do that is through the aforementioned project generation. If you grab the TensorFlow source code from GitHub, you can build for a lot of platforms using a standard Makefile approach on Linux. For example, this command line should compile and test an x86 version of the library:

```
make -f tensorflow/lite/micro/tools/make/Makefile test
```

You can build a specific target, like the speech wake-word example for the SparkFun Edge platform, with a command like this:

```
make -f tensorflow/lite/micro/tools/make/Makefile \
  TARGET="sparkfun_edge" micro_speech_bin
```

What if you're running on a Windows machine or want to use an IDE like Keil, Mbed, Arduino, or another specialized build system? That's where the project generation comes in. You can generate a folder that's ready to use with the Mbed IDE by running the following command line from Linux:

```
make -f tensorflow/lite/micro/tools/make/Makefile \
  TARGET="disco_f746ng" generate_micro_speech_mbed_project
```

You should now see a set of source files in *tensorflow/lite/micro/tools/make/gen/disco_f746ng_x86_64/prj/micro_speech/mbed/*, along with all the dependencies and project files you need to build within the Mbed environment. The same approach works for Keil and Arduino, and there's a generic version that just outputs the folder hierarchy of source files without project metainformation (though it does include a Visual Studio Code file that defines a couple of build rules).

You might be wondering how this Linux command-line approach helps people on other platforms. We automatically run this project-generation process as part of our nightly continuous integration workflow and whenever we do a major release. Whenever it's run, it automatically puts the resulting files up on a public web server. This means that users on all platforms should be able to find a version for their preferred IDE, and download the project as a self-contained folder instead of through GitHub.

Specializing Code

One of the benefits of code generation is that it's easy to rewrite part of the library to work well on a particular platform, or even just optimize a function for a particular set of parameters that you know are common in your use case. We didn't want to lose this ease of modification, but we also wanted to make it as easy as possible for more generally useful changes to be merged back into the main framework's source code. We had the additional constraint that some build environments don't make it easy to pass in custom #define macros during compilation, so we couldn't rely on switching to different implementations at compile time using macro guards.

To solve this problem we've broken the library into small modules, each of which has a single C++ file implementing a default version of its functionality, along with a C++ header that defines the interface that other code can call to use the module. We then adopted a convention that if you want to write a specialized version of a module, you save your new version out as a C++ implementation file with the same name as the original but in a subfolder of the directory that the original is in. This subfolder should have the name of the platform or feature you're specializing for (see Figure 13-1), and will be automatically used by the Makefile or generated projects instead of the original implementation when you're building for that platform or feature. This probably sounds pretty complicated, so let's walk through a couple of concrete examples.

The speech wake-word sample code needs to grab audio data from a microphone, but unfortunately there's no cross-platform way to capture audio. Because we need to at least compile across a wide range of devices, we wrote a default implementation that just returns a buffer full of zero values, without using a microphone. Here's what the interface to that module looks like, from *audio_provider.h* (*https://oreil.ly/J5N0N*):

```
TfLiteStatus GetAudioSamples(tflite::ErrorReporter* error_reporter,
                             int start_ms, int duration_ms,
                             int* audio_samples_size, int16_t** audio_samples);
int32_t LatestAudioTimestamp();
```

Figure 13-1. Screenshot of a specialized audio provider file

The first function outputs a buffer filled with audio data for a given time period, returning an error if something goes wrong. The second function returns when the most recent audio data was captured, so the client can ask for the correct range of time, and know when new data has arrived.

Because the default implementation can't rely on a microphone being present, the implementations of the two functions in *audio_provider.cc* (*https://oreil.ly/8V1Ll*) are very simple:

```
namespace {
int16_t g_dummy_audio_data[kMaxAudioSampleSize];
int32_t g_latest_audio_timestamp = 0;
} // namespace

TfLiteStatus GetAudioSamples(tflite::ErrorReporter* error_reporter,
                             int start_ms, int duration_ms,
                             int* audio_samples_size, int16_t** audio_samples) {
  for (int i = 0; i < kMaxAudioSampleSize; ++i) {
    g_dummy_audio_data[i] = 0;
  }
  *audio_samples_size = kMaxAudioSampleSize;
  *audio_samples = g_dummy_audio_data;
  return kTfLiteOk;
}

int32_t LatestAudioTimestamp() {
  g_latest_audio_timestamp += 100;
  return g_latest_audio_timestamp;
}
```

The timestamp is incremented automatically every time the function is called, so that clients will behave as if new data were coming in, but the same array of zeros is returned every time by the capture routine. The benefit of this is that it allows you to prototype and experiment with the sample code even before you have a microphone working on a system. kMaxAudioSampleSize is defined in the model header and is the largest number of samples that the function will ever be asked for.

On a real device the code needs to be a lot more complex, so we need a new implementation. Earlier, we compiled this example for the STM32F746NG Discovery kit board, which has microphones built in and uses a separate Mbed library to access them. The code is in *disco_f746ng/audio_provider.cc* (*https://oreil.ly/KrdSO*). It's not included inline here because it's too big, but if you look at that file, you'll see it implements the same two public functions as the default *audio_provider.cc*: GetAudioSam ples() and LatestAudioTimestamp(). The definitions of the functions are a lot more complex, but their behavior from a client's perspective is the same. The complexity is hidden, and the calling code can remain the same despite the change in platform— and now, instead of receiving an array of zeros every time, captured audio will show up in the returned buffer.

If you look at the full path of this specialized implementation, *tensorflow/lite/micro/ examples/micro_speech/disco_f746ng/audio_provider.cc*, you'll see it's almost identical to that of the default implementation at *tensorflow/lite/micro/examples/micro_speech/ audio_provider.cc*, but it's inside a *disco_f746ng* subfolder at the same level as the original *.cc* file. If you look back at the command line for building the STM32F746NG Mbed project, you'll see we passed in TARGET=disco_f746ng to specify what platform we want. The build system always looks for *.cc* files in subfolders with the target name for possible specialized implementations, so in this case *disco_f746ng/ audio_provider.cc* is used instead of the default *audio_provider.cc* version in the parent folder. When the source files are being assembled for the Mbed project copy, that parent-level *.cc* file is ignored, and the one in the subfolder is copied over; thus, the specialized version is used by the resulting project.

Capturing audio is done differently on almost every platform, so we have a lot of different specialized implementations of this module. There's even a macOS version, *osx/audio_provider.cc* (*https://oreil.ly/ZaMtF*), which is useful if you're debugging locally on a Mac laptop.

This mechanism isn't just used for portability, though; it's also flexible enough to use for optimizations. We actually use this approach in the speech wake-word example to help speed up the depthwise convolution operation. If you look in *tensorflow/lite/ micro/kernels* (*https://oreil.ly/0yHNd*) you'll see implementations of all the operations that TensorFlow Lite for Microcontrollers supports. These default implementations are written to be short, be easy to understand, and run on any platform, but meeting those goals means that they often miss opportunities to run as fast as they could. Optimization usually involves making the algorithms more complicated and more difficult to understand, so these reference implementations are expected to be comparatively slow. The idea is that we want to enable developers to get code running in the simplest possible way first and ensure that they're getting correct results, and then be able to incrementally change the code to improve performance. This means that every small change can be tested to make sure it doesn't break correctness, making debugging much easier.

The model used in the speech wake-word example relies heavily on the depthwise convolution operation, which has an unoptimized implementation at *tensorflow/lite/micro/kernels/depthwise_conv.cc* (*https://oreil.ly/a16dw*). The core algorithm is implemented in *tensorflow/lite/kernels/internal/reference/depthwiseconv_uint8.h* (*https://oreil.ly/2gQ-e*), and it's written as a straightforward set of nested loops. Here's the code itself:

```
for (int b = 0; b < batches; ++b) {
  for (int out_y = 0; out_y < output_height; ++out_y) {
    for (int out_x = 0; out_x < output_width; ++out_x) {
      for (int ic = 0; ic < input_depth; ++ic) {
        for (int m = 0; m < depth_multiplier; m++) {
          const int oc = m + ic * depth_multiplier;
          const int in_x_origin = (out_x * stride_width) - pad_width;
          const int in_y_origin = (out_y * stride_height) - pad_height;
          int32 acc = 0;
          for (int filter_y = 0; filter_y < filter_height; ++filter_y) {
            for (int filter_x = 0; filter_x < filter_width; ++filter_x) {
              const int in_x =
                  in_x_origin + dilation_width_factor * filter_x;
              const int in_y =
                  in_y_origin + dilation_height_factor * filter_y;
              // If the location is outside the bounds of the input image,
              // use zero as a default value.
              if ((in_x >= 0) && (in_x < input_width) && (in_y >= 0) &&
                  (in_y < input_height)) {
                int32 input_val =
                    input_data[Offset(input_shape, b, in_y, in_x, ic)];
                int32 filter_val = filter_data[Offset(
                    filter_shape, 0, filter_y, filter_x, oc)];
                acc += (filter_val + filter_offset) *
                       (input_val + input_offset);
              }
            }
          }
          if (bias_data) {
            acc += bias_data[oc];
          }
          acc = DepthwiseConvRound<output_rounding>(acc, output_multiplier,
                                                    output_shift);
          acc += output_offset;
          acc = std::max(acc, output_activation_min);
          acc = std::min(acc, output_activation_max);
          output_data[Offset(output_shape, b, out_y, out_x, oc)] =
              static_cast<uint8>(acc);
```

```
                }
              }
            }
          }
        }
```

You might be able to see lots of opportunities to speed this up just from a quick look, like precalculating all the array indices that we figure out every time in the inner loop. Those changes would add to the complexity of the code, so for this reference implementation we've avoided them. The speech wake-word example needs to run multiple times a second on a microcontroller, though, and it turns out that this naive implementation is the main speed bottleneck preventing that on the SparkFun Edge Cortex-M4 processor. To make the example run at a usable speed, we needed to add some optimizations.

To provide an optimized implementation, we created a new subfolder called *portable_optimized* inside *tensorflow/lite/micro/kernels*, and added a new C++ source file called *depthwise_conv.cc* (*https://oreil.ly/BYRho*). This is much more complex than the reference implementation, and takes advantage of particular features of the speech model to enable specialized optimizations. For example, the convolution windows are multiples of 8 wide, so we can load the values as two 32-bit words from memory, rather than as 8 individual bytes.

You'll notice that we've named the subfolder *portable_optimized*, rather than something platform-specific as we did for the previous example. This is because none of the changes we've made are tied to a particular chip or library; they're generic optimizations that are expected to help across a wide variety of processors, such as precalculating array indices or loading multiple byte values as larger words. We then specify that this implementation should be used inside the make project files, by adding portable_optimized to the ALL_TAGS list (*https://oreil.ly/XSWFk*). Because this tag is present, and there's an implementation of *depthwise_conv.cc* inside the subfolder with the same name, the optimized implementation is linked in rather than the default reference version.

Hopefully these examples show how you can use the subfolder mechanism to extend and optimize the library code while keeping the core implementations small and easy to understand.

Makefiles

On the topic of being easy to understand, Makefiles aren't. The Make build system (*https://oreil.ly/8Ft1J*) is now more than 40 years old and has a lot of features that can be confusing, such as its use of tabs as meaningful syntax or the indirect specification of build targets through declarative rules. We chose to use Make over alternatives such as Bazel or Cmake because it was flexible enough to implement complex behaviors like project generation, and we hope that most users of TensorFlow Lite for

Microcontrollers will use those generated projects in more modern IDEs rather than interacting with Makefiles directly.

If you're making changes to the core library, you might need to understand more about what's going on under the hood in the Makefiles, though, so this section covers some of the conventions and helper functions that you'll need to be familiar with to make modifications.

 If you're using a bash terminal on Linux or macOS, you should be able to see all of the available targets (names of things you can build) by typing the normal `make -f tensorflow/lite/micro/tools/make/Makefile` command and then pressing the Tab key. This autocomplete feature can be very useful when finding or debugging targets.

If you're just adding a specialized version of a module or operation, you shouldn't need to update the Makefile at all. There's a custom function called `specialize()` (*https://oreil.ly/teIF6*) that automatically takes the `ALL_TAGS` list of strings (populated with the platform name, along with any custom tags) and a list of source files, and returns the list with the correct specialized versions substituted for the originals. This does also give you the flexibility to manually specify tags on the command line if you want to. For example, this:

```
make -f tensorflow/lite/micro/tools/make/Makefile \
    TARGET="bluepill" TAGS="portable_optimized foo" test
```

would produce an `ALL_TAGS` list that looked like "bluepill portable_optimized foo," and for every source file the subfolders would be searched in order to find any specialized versions to substitute.

You also don't need to alter the Makefile if you're just adding new C++ files to standard folders, because most of these are automatically picked up by wildcard rules, like the definition of `MICROLITE_CC_BASE_SRCS` (*https://oreil.ly/QAtDk*).

The Makefile relies on defining lists of source and header files to build at the root level and then modifying them depending on which platform and tags are specified. These modifications happen in sub-Makefiles included from the parent build project. For example, all of the *.inc* files in the *tensorflow/lite/micro/tools/make/targets* (*https://oreil.ly/79zOB*) folder are automatically included. If you look in one of these, like the *apollo3evb_makefile.inc* (*https://oreil.ly/gKKXO*) used for Ambiq and SparkFun Edge platforms, you can see that it checks whether the chips it's targeting have been specified for this build; if they have, it defines a lot of flags and modifies the source lists. Here's an abbreviated version including some of the most interesting bits:

```
ifeq ($(TARGET),$(filter $(TARGET),apollo3evb sparkfun_edge))
    export PATH := $(MAKEFILE_DIR)/downloads/gcc_embedded/bin/:$(PATH)
```

```
TARGET_ARCH := cortex-m4
TARGET_TOOLCHAIN_PREFIX := arm-none-eabi-
...
$(eval $(call add_third_party_download,$(GCC_EMBEDDED_URL), \
    $(GCC_EMBEDDED_MD5),gcc_embedded,))
$(eval $(call add_third_party_download,$(CMSIS_URL),$(CMSIS_MD5),cmsis,))
...
PLATFORM_FLAGS = \
  -DPART_apollo3 \
  -DAM_PACKAGE_BGA \
  -DAM_PART_APOLLO3 \
  -DGEMMLOWP_ALLOW_SLOW_SCALAR_FALLBACK \
...
LDFLAGS += \
  -mthumb -mcpu=cortex-m4 -mfpu=fpv4-sp-d16 -mfloat-abi=hard \
  -nostartfiles -static \
  -Wl,--gc-sections -Wl,--entry,Reset_Handler \
...
MICROLITE_LIBS := \
  $(BOARD_BSP_PATH)/gcc/bin/libam_bsp.a \
  $(APOLLO3_SDK)/mcu/apollo3/hal/gcc/bin/libam_hal.a \
  $(GCC_ARM)/lib/gcc/arm-none-eabi/7.3.1/thumb/v7e-m/fpv4-sp/hard/crtbegin.o \
  -lm
INCLUDES += \
  -isystem$(MAKEFILE_DIR)/downloads/cmsis/CMSIS/Core/Include/ \
  -isystem$(MAKEFILE_DIR)/downloads/cmsis/CMSIS/DSP/Include/ \
  -I$(MAKEFILE_DIR)/downloads/CMSIS_ext/ \
...
MICROLITE_CC_SRCS += \
  $(APOLLO3_SDK)/boards/apollo3_evb/examples/hello_world/gcc_patched/ \
      startup_gcc.c \
  $(APOLLO3_SDK)/utils/am_util_delay.c \
  $(APOLLO3_SDK)/utils/am_util_faultisr.c \
  $(APOLLO3_SDK)/utils/am_util_id.c \
  $(APOLLO3_SDK)/utils/am_util_stdio.c
```

This is where all of the customizations for a particular platform happen. In this snippet, we're indicating to the build system where to find the compiler that we want to use, and what architecture to specify. We're specifying some extra external libraries to download, like the GCC toolchain and Arm's CMSIS library. We're setting up compilation flags for the build, and arguments to pass to the linker, including extra library archives to link in and include paths to look in for headers. We're also adding some extra C files we need to build successfully on Ambiq platforms.

A similar kind of sub-Makefile inclusion is used for building the examples. The speech wake-word sample code has its own Makefile at *micro_speech/Makefile.inc* (*https://oreil.ly/XjuJP*), and it defines its own lists of source code files to compile, along with extra external dependencies to download.

You can generate standalone projects for different IDEs by using the generate_micro lite_projects() (*https://oreil.ly/iv94T*) function. This takes a list of source files and flags and then copies the required files to a new folder, together with any additional project files that are needed by the build system. For some IDEs this is very simple, but the Arduino, for example, requires all *.cc* files to be renamed to *.cpp* and some include paths to be altered in the source files as they are copied.

External libraries such as the C++ toolchain for embedded Arm processors are automatically downloaded as part of the Makefile build process. This happens because of the add_third_party_download (*https://oreil.ly/E9tS-*) rule that's invoked for every needed library, passing in a URL to pull from and an MD5 sum to check the archive against to ensure that it's correct. These are expected to be ZIP, GZIP, BZ2, or TAR files, and the appropriate unpacker will be called depending on the file extension. If headers or source files from any of these are needed by build targets, they should be explicitly included in the file lists in the Makefile so that they can be copied over to any generated projects, so each project's source tree is self-contained. This is easy to forget with headers because setting up include paths is enough to get the Makefile compilation working without explicitly mentioning each included file, but the generated projects will then fail to build. You should also ensure that any license files are included in your file lists, so that the copies of the external libraries retain the proper attribution.

Writing Tests

TensorFlow aims to have unit tests for all of its code, and we've already covered some of these tests in detail in Chapter 5. The tests are usually arranged as *_test.cc* files in the same folder as the module that's being tested, and with the same prefix as the original source file. For example, the implementation of the depthwise convolution operation is tested by *tensorflow/lite/micro/kernels/depthwise_conv_test.cc* (*https://oreil.ly/eIiRO*). If you're adding a new source file, you must add an accompanying unit test that exercises it if you want to submit your modifications back into the main tree. This is because we need to support a lot of different platforms and models and many people are building complex systems on top of our code, so it's important that our core components can be checked for correctness.

If you add a file in a direct subfolder of *tensorflow/tensorflow/lite/experimental/micro*, you should be able to name it *<something>_test.cc* and it will be picked up automatically. If you're testing a module inside an example, you'll need to add an explicit call to the microlite_test Makefile helper function, like this (*https://oreil.ly/wkYgu*):

```
# Tests the feature provider module using the mock audio provider.
$(eval $(call microlite_test,feature_provider_mock_test,\
$(FEATURE_PROVIDER_MOCK_TEST_SRCS),$(FEATURE_PROVIDER_MOCK_TEST_HDRS)))
```

The tests themselves need to be run on microcontrollers, so they must stick to the same constraints around dynamic memory allocation, avoiding OS and external library dependencies that the framework aims to satisfy. Unfortunately, this means that popular unit test systems like Google Test (*https://oreil.ly/GZWdj*) aren't acceptable. Instead, we've written our own very minimal test framework, defined and implemented in the *micro_test.h* (*https://oreil.ly/GcIbP*) header.

To use it, create a *.cc* file that includes the header. Start with a TF_LITE_MICRO_TESTS_BEGIN statement on a new line, and then define a series of test functions, each with a TF_LITE_MICRO_TEST() macro. Inside each test, you call macros like TF_LITE_MICRO_EXPECT_EQ() to assert the expected results that you want to see from the functions being tested. At the end of all the test functions you'll need TF_LITE_MICRO_TESTS_END. Here's a basic example:

```
#include "tensorflow/lite/micro/testing/micro_test.h"

TF_LITE_MICRO_TESTS_BEGIN

TF_LITE_MICRO_TEST(SomeTest) {
  TF_LITE_LOG_EXPECT_EQ(true, true);
}

TF_LITE_MICRO_TESTS_END
```

If you compile this for your platform, you'll get a normal binary that you should be able to run. Executing it will output logging information like this to stderr (or whatever equivalent is available and written to by ErrorReporter on your platform):

```
-------------------------------------------------------------------
Testing SomeTest
1/1 tests passed
~~~ALL TESTS PASSED~~~
-------------------------------------------------------------------
```

This is designed to be human-readable, so you can just run tests manually, but the string ~~~ALL TESTS PASSED~~~ should appear only if all of the tests do actually pass. This makes it possible to integrate with automated test systems by scanning the output logs and looking for that magic value. This is how we're able to run tests on microcontrollers. As long as there's some debug logging connection back, the host can flash the binary and then monitor the output log to ensure the expected string appears to indicate whether the tests succeeded.

Supporting a New Hardware Platform

One of the main goals of the TensorFlow Lite for Microcontrollers project is to make it easy to run machine learning models across many different devices, operating systems, and architectures. The core code is designed to be as portable as possible, and the build system is written to make bringing up new environments straightforward. In this section, we present a step-by-step guide to getting TensorFlow Lite for Microcontrollers running on a new platform.

Printing to a Log

The only platform dependency that TensorFlow Lite absolutely requires is the ability to print strings to a log that can be inspected externally, typically from a desktop host machine. This is so that we can see whether tests have been run successfully and generally debug what's happening inside the programs we're running. Because this is a difficult requirement, the first thing you will need to do on your platform is determine what kind of logging facilities are available and then write a small program to print something out to exercise them.

On Linux and most other desktop operating systems, this would be the canonical "hello world" example that begins many C training curriculums. It would typically look something like this:

```
#include <stdio.h>

int main(int argc, char** argv) {
  fprintf(stderr, "Hello World!\n");
}
```

If you compile and build this on Linux, macOS, or Windows and then run the executable from the command line, you should see "Hello World!" printed to the terminal. It might also work on a microcontroller if it's running an advanced OS, but at the very least you'll need to figure out where the text itself appears given that embedded systems don't have displays or terminals themselves. Typically you'll need to connect to a desktop machine over USB or another debugging connection to see any logs, even if fprintf() is supported when compiling.

There are a few tricky parts about this code from a microcontroller perspective. One of them is that the *stdio.h* library requires functions to be linked in, and some of them are quite large, which can increase the binary size beyond the resources available on a small device. The library also assumes that there are all the normal C standard library facilities available, like dynamic memory allocation and string functions. And there's no natural definition for where stderr should go on an embedded system, so the API is unclear.

Instead, most platforms define their own debug logging interfaces. How these are called often depends on what kind of connection is being used between the host and microcontroller, as well as the hardware architecture and the OS (if any) being run on the embedded system. For example, Arm Cortex-M microcontrollers support *semihosting* (*https://oreil.ly/LmC4k*), which is a standard for communicating between the host and target systems during the development process. If you're using a connection like OpenOCD (*https://oreil.ly/lSn0n*) from your host machine, calling the SYS_WRITE0 (*https://oreil.ly/6IyrK*) system call from the microcontroller will cause the zero-terminated string argument in register 1 to be shown on the OpenOCD terminal. In this case, the code for an equivalent "hello world" program would look like this:

```
void DebugLog(const char* s) {
  asm("mov r0, #0x04\n"  // SYS_WRITE0
      "mov r1, %[str]\n"
      "bkpt #0xAB\n"
      :
      : [ str ] "r"(s)
      : "r0", "r1");
}

int main(int argc, char** argv) {
  DebugLog("Hello World!\n");
}
```

The need for assembly here shows how platform-specific this solution is, but it does avoid the need to bring in any external libraries at all (even the standard C library).

Exactly how to do this will vary widely across different platforms, but one common approach is to use a serial UART connection to the host. Here's how you do that on Mbed:

```
#include <mbed.h>

// On mbed platforms, we set up a serial port and write to it for debug logging.
void DebugLog(const char* s) {
  static Serial pc(USBTX, USBRX);
  pc.printf("%s", s);
}

int main(int argc, char** argv) {
  DebugLog("Hello World!\n");
}
```

And here's a slightly more complex example for Arduino:

```
#include "Arduino.h"

// The Arduino DUE uses a different object for the default serial port shown in
// the monitor than most other models, so make sure we pick the right one. See
// https://github.com/arduino/Arduino/issues/3088#issuecomment-406655244
#if defined(__SAM3X8E__)
#define DEBUG_SERIAL_OBJECT (SerialUSB)
#else
#define DEBUG_SERIAL_OBJECT (Serial)
#endif

// On Arduino platforms, we set up a serial port and write to it for debug
```

```
// logging.
void DebugLog(const char* s) {
  static bool is_initialized = false;
  if (!is_initialized) {
    DEBUG_SERIAL_OBJECT.begin(9600);
    // Wait for serial port to connect. Only needed for some models apparently?
    while (!DEBUG_SERIAL_OBJECT) {
    }
    is_initialized = true;
  }
  DEBUG_SERIAL_OBJECT.println(s);
}

int main(int argc, char** argv) {
  DebugLog("Hello World!\n");
}
```

Both of these examples create a serial object, and then expect that the user will hook up a serial connection to the microcontroller over USB to their host machine.

The key first step in the porting effort is to create a minimal example for your platform, running in the IDE you want to use, that gets a string printed to the host console somehow. If you can get this working, the code you use will become the basis of a specialized function that you'll add to the TensorFlow Lite code.

Implementing DebugLog()

If you look in *tensorflow/lite/micro/debug_log.cc* (*https://oreil.ly/Lka3T*), you'll see that there's an implementation of the DebugLog() function that looks very similar to the first "hello world" example we showed, using *stdio.h* and fprintf() to output a string to the console. If your platform supports the standard C library fully and you don't mind the extra binary size, you can just use this default implementation and ignore the rest of this section. It's more likely that you'll need to use a different approach, though, unfortunately.

As a first step, we'll use the test that already exists for the DebugLog() function. To begin, run this command line:

```
make -f tensorflow/lite/micro/tools/make/Makefile \
  generate_micro_error_reporter_test_make_project
```

When you look inside *tensorflow/lite/micro/tools/make/gen/linux_x86_64/prj/ micro_error_reporter_test/make/* (replacing *linux* with *osx* or *windows* if you're on a different host platform) you should see some folders like *tensorflow* and *third_party*. These folders contain C++ source code, and if you drag them into your IDE or build system and compile all the files, you should end up with an executable that tests out the error reporting functionality we need to create. It's likely that your first attempt to build this code will fail, because it's still using the default DebugLog() implementation in *debug_log.cc* (*https://oreil.ly/fDkLh*), which relies on *stdio.h* and the C standard

library. To work around that problem, change *debug_log.cc* to remove the #include
<cstdio> statement and replace the DebugLog() implementation with one that does
nothing:

```
#include "tensorflow/lite/micro/debug_log.h"

extern "C" void DebugLog(const char* s) {
  // Do nothing for now.
}
```

With that changed, try to get the set of source files successfully compiling. After
you've done that, take the resulting binary and load it onto your embedded system. If
you can, check that the program runs without crashing, even though you won't be
able to see any output yet.

When the program seems to build and run correctly, see whether you can get the
debug logging working. Take the code that you used for the "hello world" program in
the previous section and put it into the DebugLog() implementation inside
debug_log.cc.

The actual test code itself exists in *tensorflow/lite/micro/micro_error_reporter_test.cc*
(*https://oreil.ly/0jD00*), and it looks like this:

```
int main(int argc, char** argv) {
  tflite::MicroErrorReporter micro_error_reporter;
  tflite::ErrorReporter* error_reporter = &micro_error_reporter;
  error_reporter->Report("Number: %d", 42);
  error_reporter->Report("Badly-formed format string %");
  error_reporter->Report("Another % badly-formed %% format string");
  error_reporter->Report("~~~%s~~~", "ALL TESTS PASSED");
}
```

It's not calling DebugLog() directly—it goes through the ErrorReporter interface that
handles things like variable numbers of arguments first—but it does rely on the code
you've just written as its underlying implementation. You should see something like
this in your debug console if everything's working correctly:

```
Number: 42
Badly-formed format string
Another  badly-formed  format string
~~~ALL TESTS PASSED~~~
```

After you have that working, you'll want to put your implementation of DebugLog()
back into the main source tree. To do this, you'll use the subfolder specialization technique that we discussed earlier. You'll need to decide on a short name (with no capital
letters, spaces, or other special characters) to use to identify your platform. For example, we use *arduino*, *sparkfun_edge*, and *linux* for some of the platforms we already
support. For the purposes of this tutorial, we'll use *my_mcu*. Start by creating a new
subfolder in *tensorflow/lite/micro/* called *my_mcu* in the copy of the source code you

checked out from GitHub (not the one you just generated or downloaded). Copy the *debug_log.cc* file with your implementation into that *my_mcu* folder, and add it to source tracking using Git. Copy your generated project files to a backup location and then run the following commands:

```
make -f tensorflow/lite/micro/tools/make/Makefile TARGET=my_mcu clean
make -f tensorflow/lite/micro/tools/make/Makefile \
  TARGET=my_mcu generate_micro_error_reporter_test_make_project
```

If you now look in *tensorflow/lite/micro/tools/make/gen/my_mcu_x86_64/prj/ micro_error_reporter_test/make/tensorflow/lite/micro/* you should see that the default *debug_log.cc* is no longer present, but your implementation is in the *my_mcu* sub-folder. If you drag this set of source files back into your IDE or build system, you should now see a program that successfully builds, runs, and outputs to the debug console.

Running All the Targets

If that works, congratulations: you've now enabled all of the TensorFlow test and executable targets! Implementing debug logging is the only required platform-specific change you need to make; everything else in the code base should be written in a portable enough way that it will build and run on any C++11-supporting toolchain, with no need for standard library linking beyond the math library. To create all of the targets so that you can try them in your IDE, you can run the following command from the terminal:

```
make -f tensorflow/lite/micro/tools/make/Makefile generate_projects \
  TARGET=my_mcu
```

This creates a large number of folders in similar locations to the generated error reporter test, each exercising different parts of the library. If you want to get the speech wake-word example running on your platform, you can look at *tensorflow/ lite/micro/tools/make/gen/my_mcu_x86_64/prj/micro_speech/make/*.

Now that you have DebugLog() implemented, it should run on your platform, but it won't do anything useful because the default *audio_provider.cc* implementation is always returning arrays full of zeros. To get it working properly, you'll need to create a specialized *audio_provider.cc* module that returns captured sound, using the sub-folder specialization approach described earlier. If you don't care about a working demonstration, you can still look at things like the inference latency of neural networks on your platform using the same sample code, or some of the other tests.

As well as hardware support for sensors and output devices like LEDs, you may well want to implement versions of the neural network operators that run faster by taking advantage of special features of your platform. We welcome this kind of specialized optimization and hope that the subfolder specialization technique will be a good way to integrate them back into the main source tree if they prove to be useful.

Integrating with the Makefile Build

So far we've talked only about using your own IDE, given that it's often simpler and more familiar to many embedded programmers than using our Make system. If you want to be able to have your code tested by our continuous integration builds, or have it available outside of a particular IDE, you might want to integrate your changes more fully with our Makefiles. One of the essentials for this is finding a publicly downloadable toolchain for your platform, along with public downloads for any SDKs or other dependencies, so that a shell script can automatically grab everything it needs to build without having to worry about website logins or registrations. For example, we download the macOS and Linux versions of the GCC Embedded toolchain from Arm, with the URLs in *tensorflow/lite/micro/tools/make/ third_party_downloads.inc (https://oreil.ly/WBrIy)*.

You'll then need to determine the correct command-line flags to pass into the compiler and linker, along with any extra source files you need that aren't found using subfolder specialization, and encode that information into a sub-Makefile in *tensorflow/lite/micro/tools/make/targets (https://oreil.ly/zusVM)*. If you want extra credit, you can then figure out how to emulate your microcontroller on an x86 server using a tool like Renode (*https://renode.io/*) so that we can run the tests during our continuous integration, not just confirm the build. You can see an example of the script we run to test the "Bluepill" binaries using Renode at *tensorflow/lite/micro/testing/ test_bluepill_binary.sh (https://oreil.ly/A80CN)*.

If you have all of the build settings configured correctly, you'll be able to run something like this to generate a flashable binary (setting the target as appropriate for your platform):

```
make -f tensorflow/lite/micro/tools/make/Makefile \
  TARGET=bluepill micro_error_reporter_test_bin
```

If you have the script and environment for running tests working correctly, you can do this to run all the tests for the platform:

```
make -f tensorflow/lite/micro/tools/make/Makefile TARGET=bluepill test
```

Supporting a New IDE or Build System

TensorFlow Lite for Microcontrollers can create standalone projects for Arduino, Mbed, and Keil toolchains, but we know that a lot of other development environments are used by embedded engineers. If you need to run the framework in a new environment, the first thing we recommend is seeing whether the "raw" set of files that are generated when you generate a Make project can be imported into your IDE. This kind of project archive contains only the source files needed for a particular target, including any third-party dependencies, so in many cases you can just point your toolchain at the root folder and ask it to include everything.

When you have only a few files, it can seem odd to keep them in the nested subfolders (like *tensorflow/lite/micro/examples/ micro_speech*) of the original source tree when you export them to a generated project. Wouldn't it make more sense to flatten out the directory hierarchy?

The reason we chose to keep the deeply nested folders is to make merging back into the main source tree as straightforward as possible, even if it is a little less convenient when working with the generated project files. If the paths always match between the original code checked out of GitHub and the copies in each project, keeping track of changes and updates is a lot easier.

This approach won't work for all IDEs, unfortunately. For example, Arduino libraries require all C++ source code files to have the suffix *.cpp* rather than TensorFlow's default of *.cc,* and they're also unable to specify include paths, so we need to change the paths in the code when we copy over the original files to the Arduino destination. To support these more complex transformations we have some rules and scripts in the Makefile build, with the root function `generate_microlite_projects()` (*https:// oreil.ly/YYoHm*) calling into specialized versions for each IDE, which then rely on more rules (*https://oreil.ly/KHo7G*), Python scripts (*https://oreil.ly/BKLhn*), and template files (*https://oreil.ly/tDFhh*) to create the final output. If you need to do something similar for your own IDE, you'll need to add similar functionality using the Makefile, which won't be straightforward to implement because the build system is quite complex to work with.

Integrating Code Changes Between Projects and Repositories

One of the biggest disadvantages of a code generation system is that you end up with multiple copies of the source scattered in different locations, which makes dealing with code updates very tricky. To minimize the cost of merging changes, we've adopted some conventions and recommended procedures that should help. The most common use case is that you've made some modifications to files within the local copy of your project, and you'd like to update to a newer version of the TensorFlow Lite framework to get extra features or bug fixes. Here's how we suggest handling that process:

1. Either download a prebuilt archive of the project file for your IDE and target or generate one manually from the Makefile using the version of the framework you're interested in.

2. Unpack this new set of files into a folder and make sure that the folder structures match between the new folder and the folder containing the project files that

you've been modifying. For example, both should have *tensorflow* subfolders at the top level.

3. Run a merge tool between the two folders. Which tool you use will depend on your OS, but Meld (*https://meldmerge.org/*) is a good choice that works on Linux, Windows, and macOS. The complexity of the merge process will depend on how many files you've changed locally, but it's expected most of the differences will be updates on the framework side, so you should usually be able to choose the equivalent of "accept theirs."

If you have changed only one or two files locally, it might be easier to just copy the modified code from the old version and manually merge it into the new exported project.

You could also get more advanced by checking your modified code into Git, importing the latest project files as a new branch, and then using Git's built-in merging facilities to handle integration. We're still not advanced enough Git masters (*https://oreil.ly/sIe1F*) to offer advice on this approach, so we haven't used it ourselves.

The big difference between this process and doing the same with more traditional code-generation approaches is that the code is still separated into many logical files whose paths remain constant over time. Typical code generation will concatenate all of the source into a single file, which makes merging or tracking changes very difficult because trivial changes to the order or layout make historical comparisons impossible.

Sometimes you might want to port changes in the other direction, merging from project files to the main source tree. This main source tree doesn't need to be the official repository on GitHub (*https://oreil.ly/o8Ytb*); it could be a local fork that you maintain and don't distribute. We love to get pull requests to the main repository with fixes or upgrades, but we know that's not always possible with proprietary embedded development, so we're also happy to help keep forks healthy. The key thing to watch is that you try to keep a single "source of truth" for your development files. Especially if you have multiple developers, it's easy to have incompatible changes being made in different local copies of the source files inside project archives, which makes updating and debugging a nightmare. Whether it's only internal or shared publicly, we highly recommend having a source-control system that has a single copy of each file, rather than checking in multiple versions.

To handle migrating changes back to the source of truth repository, you'll need to keep track of which files you've modified. If you don't have that information handy, you can always go back to the project files you originally downloaded or generated and run a diff to see what has changed. As soon as you know what files are modified or new, just copy them into the Git (or other source-control system) repository at the same paths they occur at in the project files.

The only exceptions to this approach are files that are part of third-party libraries, given that these don't exist in the TensorFlow repository. Getting changes to those files submitted is beyond the scope of this book—the process will depend on the rules of each individual repository—but as a last resort, if you have changes that aren't being accepted, you can often fork the project on GitHub and point your platform's build system to that new URL rather than the original. Assuming that you're changing just TensorFlow source files, you should now have a locally modified repository that contains your changes. To verify that the modifications have been successfully integrated, you'll need to run `generate_projects()` using Make and then ensure that the project for your IDE and target has your updates applied as you'd expect. When that's complete, and you've run tests to ensure nothing else has been broken, you can submit your changes to your fork of TensorFlow. As soon as that's done, the final stage is to submit a pull request if you'd like to see your changes made public.

Contributing Back to Open Source

There are already more contributors to TensorFlow outside of Google than inside, and the microcontroller work has a larger reliance on collaboration than most other areas. We're very keen to get help from the community, and one of the most important ways of helping is through pull requests (though there are plenty of other ways, like Stack Overflow (*https://oreil.ly/7btPw*)) or creating your own example projects). GitHub has great documentation (*https://oreil.ly/8rDKL*) covering the basics of pull requests, but there are some details that are helpful to know when working with TensorFlow:

- We have a code review process run by project maintainers inside and outside Google. This is managed through GitHub's code review system, so you should expect to see a discussion about your submission there.

- Changes that are more than just a bug fix or optimization usually need a design document first. There's a group called SIG Micro (*https://oreil.ly/JKiwD*) that's run by external contributors to help define our priorities and roadmap, so that's a good forum to talk about new designs. The document can be just a page or two for a smaller change; it's helpful to understand the context and motivation behind a pull request.

- Maintaining a public fork can be a great way of getting feedback on experimental changes before they're submitted to the main branch because you can make changes with any cumbersome processes to slow you down.

- There are automated tests that run against all pull requests, both publicly and with some additional Google internal tools that check the integration against our own projects that depend on this. The results of these tests can sometimes be difficult to interpret, unfortunately, and even worse, they're occasionally "flakey," with tests failing for reasons unrelated to your changes. We're constantly trying to improve this process because we know it's a bad experience, but please do ping the maintainers in the conversation thread if you're having trouble understanding test failures.

- We aim for 100% test coverage, so if a change isn't exercised by an existing test, we'll ask you for a new one. These tests can be quite simple; we just want to make sure there's some coverage of everything we do.

- For readability's sake, we use the Google style guide for C and C++ code formatting consistently across the entire TensorFlow code base, so we request any new or modified code be in this style. You can use `clang-format` (*https://oreil.ly/ KkRKL*) with the `google` style argument to automatically format your code.

Thanks in advance for any contributions you can make to TensorFlow, and for your patience with the work involved in getting changes submitted. It's not always easy, but you'll be making a difference to many developers around the world!

Supporting New Hardware Accelerators

One of the goals of TensorFlow Lite for Microcontrollers is to be a reference software platform to help hardware developers make faster progress with their designs. What we've observed is that a lot of the work around getting a new chip doing something useful with machine learning is in tasks like writing exporters from the training environment, especially with regard to tricky details like quantization and implementing the "long tail" of operations that are needed for typical machine learning models. These tasks take so little time that they aren't good candidates for hardware optimization.

To address these problems, we hope that the first step that hardware developers will take is getting the unoptimized reference code for TensorFlow Lite for Microcontrollers running on their platform and producing the correct results. This will demonstrate that everything but the hardware optimization is working, so that can be the focus of the remaining work. One challenge might be if the chip is an accelerator that doesn't support general-purpose C++ compilation, because it only has specialized functionality rather than a traditional CPU. For embedded use cases, we've found that it's almost always necessary to have some general-purpose computation available, even if it's slow (like a small microcontroller), because many users' graphs have operations that can't be compactly expressed except as arbitrary C++ implementations. We've also made the design decision that the TensorFlow Lite for Microcontrollers interpreter won't support asynchronous execution of subgraphs, because that would complicate the code considerably and also seems uncommon in the embedded domain (unlike the mobile world, where Android's Neural Network API is popular).

This means that the kinds of architectures TensorFlow Lite for Microcontrollers supports look more like synchronous coprocessors that run in lockstep with a traditional processor, with the accelerator speeding up compute-intensive functions that would otherwise take a long time but deferring the smaller ops with more flexible requirements to a CPU. The result in practice is that we recommend starting off by replacing individual operator implementations at the kernel level with calls to any specialized hardware. This does mean that the results and inputs are expected to be in normal memory addressable by the CPU (because you don't have any guarantees about what processor subsequent ops will run on), and you will either need to wait for the accelerator to complete before continuing or use platform-specific code to switch to threads outside of the Micro framework. These restrictions should at least enable some quick prototyping, though, and hopefully offer the ability to make incremental changes while always being able to test the correctness of each small modification.

Understanding the File Format

The format TensorFlow Lite uses to store its models has many virtues, but unfortunately simplicity is not one of them. Don't be put off by the complexity, though; it's actually fairly straightforward to work with after you understand some of the fundamentals.

As we touched on in Chapter 3, neural network models are graphs of operations with inputs and outputs. Some of the inputs to an operation might be large arrays of learned values, known as weights, and others will come from the results of earlier operations, or input value arrays fed in by the application layer. These inputs might be image pixels, audio sample data, or accelerometer time-series data. At the end of running a single pass of the model, the final operations will leave arrays of values in their outputs, typically representing things like classification predictions for different categories.

Models are usually trained on desktop machines, so we need a way of transferring them to other devices like phones or microcontrollers. In the TensorFlow world, we do this using a converter that can take a trained model from Python and export it as a TensorFlow Lite file. This exporting stage can be fraught with problems, because it's easy to create a model in TensorFlow that relies on features of the desktop environment (like being able to execute Python code snippets or use advanced operations) that are not supported on simpler platforms. It's also necessary to convert all the values that are variable in training (such as weights) into constants, remove operations that are needed only for gradient backpropagation, and perform optimizations like fusing neighboring ops or folding costly operations like batch normalization into less expensive forms. What makes this even trickier is that there are more than 800 operations in mainline TensorFlow, and more are being added all the time. This means that it's fairly straightforward to write your own converter for a small set of models, but handling the broader range of networks that users can create in TensorFlow reliably is much more difficult. Just keeping up to date with new operations is a full-time job.

The TensorFlow Lite file that you get out of the conversion process doesn't suffer from most of these issues. We try to produce a simpler and more stable representation of a trained model with clear inputs and outputs, variables that are *frozen* into weights, and common graph optimizations like fusing already applied. This means that even if you're not intending to use TensorFlow Lite for Microcontrollers, we recommend using the TensorFlow Lite file format as the way you access TensorFlow models for inference instead of writing your own converter from the Python layer.

FlatBuffers

We use FlatBuffers (*https://oreil.ly/jfoBx*) as our serialization library. It was designed for applications for which performance is critical, so it's a good fit for embedded systems. One of the nice features is that its runtime in-memory representation is exactly the same as its serialized form, so models can be embedded directly into flash memory and accessed immediately, with no need for any parsing or copying. This does mean that the generated code classes to read properties can be a bit difficult to follow because there are a couple of layers of indirection, but the important data (such as weights) is stored directly as little-endian blobs that can be accessed like raw C arrays. There's also very little wasted space, so you aren't paying a size penalty by using FlatBuffers.

FlatBuffers work using a *schema* that defines the data structures we want to serialize, together with a compiler that turns that schema into native C++ (or C, Python, Java, etc.) code for reading and writing the information. For TensorFlow Lite, the schema is in *tensorflow/lite/schema/schema.fbs* (*https://oreil.ly/JoDE9*), and we cache the generated C++ accessor code at *tensorflow/lite/schema/schema_generated.h* (*https://oreil.ly/LjxOp*). We could generate the C++ code every time we do a fresh build rather than storing it in source control, but this would require every platform we build on to include the `flatc` compiler as well as the rest of the toolchain, and we decided to trade the convenience of automatic generation for ease of porting.

If you want to understand the format at the byte level, we recommend looking at the internals page (*https://oreil.ly/EBg3-*) of the FlatBuffers C++ project or the equivalent for the C library (*https://oreil.ly/xXkZg*). We're hopeful that most needs will be met through the various high-level language interfaces, though, and you won't need to work at that granularity. To introduce you to the concepts behind the format, we're going to walk through the schema and the code in `MicroInterpreter` that reads a model; hopefully, having some concrete examples will help it all make sense.

Ironically, to get started we need to scroll to the very end of the schema (*https://oreil.ly/aHYM-*). Here we see a line declaring that the `root_type` is `Model`:

```
root_type Model;
```

FlatBuffers need a single container object that acts as the root for the tree of other data structures held within the file. This statement tells us that the root of this format is going to be a Model. To find out what that means, we scroll up a few more lines to the definition of Model:

```
table Model {
```

This tells us that Model is what FlatBuffers calls a table. You can think of this like a Dict in Python or a struct in C or C++ (though it's more flexible than that). It defines what properties an object can have, along with their names and types. There's also a less-flexible type in FlatBuffers called struct that's more memory-efficient for arrays of objects, but we don't currently use this in TensorFlow Lite.

You can see how this is used in practice by looking at the micro_speech example's main() function (*https://oreil.ly/StkFf*):

```
// Map the model into a usable data structure. This doesn't involve any
// copying or parsing, it's a very lightweight operation.
const tflite::Model* model =
    ::tflite::GetModel(g_tiny_conv_micro_features_model_data);
```

The g_tiny_conv_micro_features_model_data variable is a pointer to an area of memory containing a serialized TensorFlow Lite model, and the call to ::tflite::GetModel() is effectively just a cast to get a C++ object backed up by that underlying memory. It doesn't require any memory allocation or walking of data structures, so it's a very quick and efficient call. To understand how we can use it, look at the next operation we perform on the data structure:

```
if (model->version() != TFLITE_SCHEMA_VERSION) {
  error_reporter->Report(
      "Model provided is schema version %d not equal "
      "to supported version %d.\n",
      model->version(), TFLITE_SCHEMA_VERSION);
  return 1;
}
```

If you look at the start of the Model definition in the schema (*https://oreil.ly/vPpDw*), you can see the definition of the version property this code is referring to:

```
// Version of the schema.
version:uint;
```

This informs us that the version property is a 32-bit unsigned integer, so the C++ code generated for model->version() returns that type of value. Here we're just doing error checking to make sure the version is one that we can understand, but the same kind of accessor function is generated for all the properties that are defined in the schema.

To understand the more complex parts of the file format, it's worth following the flow of the `MicroInterpreter` class as it loads a model and prepares to execute it. The constructor is passed a pointer to a model in memory, such as the previous example's `g_tiny_conv_micro_features_model_data`. The first property it accesses is buffers (*https://oreil.ly/nQjwY*):

```
const flatbuffers::Vector<flatbuffers::Offset<Buffer>>* buffers =
    model->buffers();
```

You might see the `Vector` name in the type definition, and be worried we're trying to use objects similar to Standard Template Library (STL) types inside an embedded environment without dynamic memory management, which would be a bad idea. Happily, though, the FlatBuffers `Vector` class is just a read-only wrapper around the underlying memory, so just like with the root `Model` object, there's no parsing or memory allocation required to create it.

To understand more about what this `buffers` array represents, it's worth taking a look at the schema definition (*https://oreil.ly/QOTlY*):

```
// Table of raw data buffers (used for constant tensors). Referenced by tensors
// by index. The generous alignment accommodates mmap-friendly data structures.
table Buffer {
  data:[ubyte] (force_align: 16);
}
```

Each buffer is defined as a raw array of unsigned 8-bit values, with the first value 16-byte-aligned in memory. This is the container type used for all of the arrays of weights (and any other constant values) held in the graph. The type and shape of the tensors are held separately; this array just holds the raw bytes that back up the data inside the arrays. Operations refer to these constant buffers by index inside this top-level vector.

The next property we access is a list of subgraphs (*https://oreil.ly/9Fa9V*):

```
auto* subgraphs = model->subgraphs();
if (subgraphs->size() != 1) {
  error_reporter->Report("Only 1 subgraph is currently supported.\n");
  initialization_status_ = kTfLiteError;
  return;
}
subgraph_ = (*subgraphs)[0];
```

A subgraph is a set of operators, the connections between them, and the buffers, inputs, and outputs that they use. There are some advanced models that might require multiple subgraphs in the future—for example, to support control flow—but all of the networks we want to support on microcontrollers at the moment have a single subgraph, so we can simplify our subsequent code by making sure the current model meets that requirement. To get more of an idea of what's in a subgraph, we can look back at the schema (*https://oreil.ly/Z9mLn*):

```
// The root type, defining a subgraph, which typically represents an entire
// model.
table SubGraph {
  // A list of all tensors used in this subgraph.
  tensors:[Tensor];

  // Indices of the tensors that are inputs into this subgraph. Note this is
  // the list of non-static tensors that feed into the subgraph for inference.
  inputs:[int];

  // Indices of the tensors that are outputs out of this subgraph. Note this is
  // the list of output tensors that are considered the product of the
  // subgraph's inference.
  outputs:[int];

  // All operators, in execution order.
  operators:[Operator];

  // Name of this subgraph (used for debugging).
  name:string;
}
```

The first property every subgraph has is a list of tensors, and the MicroInterpreter code accesses it like this (*https://oreil.ly/EsO7M*):

```
tensors_ = subgraph_->tensors();
```

As we mentioned earlier, the Buffer objects just hold raw values for weights, without any metadata about their types or shapes. Tensors are the place where this extra information is stored for constant buffers. They also hold the same information for temporary arrays like inputs, outputs, or activation layers. You can see this metadata in their definition near the top of the schema file (*https://oreil.ly/mH0IL*):

```
table Tensor {
  // The tensor shape. The meaning of each entry is operator-specific but
  // builtin ops use: [batch size, height, width, number of channels] (That's
  // Tensorflow's NHWC).
  shape:[int];
  type:TensorType;
  // An index that refers to the buffers table at the root of the model. Or,
  // if there is no data buffer associated (i.e. intermediate results), then
  // this is 0 (which refers to an always existent empty buffer).
  //
  // The data_buffer itself is an opaque container, with the assumption that the
  // target device is little-endian. In addition, all builtin operators assume
  // the memory is ordered such that if `shape` is [4, 3, 2], then index
  // [i, j, k] maps to data_buffer[i*3*2 + j*2 + k].
  buffer:uint;
  name:string;  // For debugging and importing back into tensorflow.
  quantization:QuantizationParameters;  // Optional.
```

```
        is_variable:bool = false;
    }
```

The shape is a simple list of integers that indicates the tensor's dimensions, whereas type is an enum mapping to the possible data types that are supported in TensorFlow Lite. The buffer property indicates which Buffer in the root-level list has the actual values backing up this tensor if it's a constant read from a file, or is zero if the values are calculated dynamically (for example, for an activation layer). The name is there only to give a human-readable label for the tensor, which can help with debugging, and the quantization property defines how to map low-precision values into real numbers. Finally, the is_variable member exists to support future training and other advanced applications, but it doesn't need to be used on microcontroller units (MCUs).

Going back to the MicroInterpreter code, the second major property we pull from the subgraph is a list of operators (*https://oreil.ly/6Yl8d*):

```
operators_ = subgraph_->operators();
```

This list holds the graph structure of the model. To understand how this is encoded, we can go back to the schema definition of Operator (*https://oreil.ly/xTs7j*):

```
// An operator takes tensors as inputs and outputs. The type of operation being
// performed is determined by an index into the list of valid OperatorCodes,
// while the specifics of each operations is configured using builtin_options
// or custom_options.
table Operator {
    // Index into the operator_codes array. Using an integer here avoids
    // complicate map lookups.
    opcode_index:uint;

    // Optional input and output tensors are indicated by -1.
    inputs:[int];
    outputs:[int];

    builtin_options:BuiltinOptions;
    custom_options:[ubyte];
    custom_options_format:CustomOptionsFormat;

    // A list of booleans indicating the input tensors which are being mutated by
    // this operator.(e.g. used by RNN and LSTM).
    // For example, if the "inputs" array refers to 5 tensors and the second and
    // fifth are mutable variables, then this list will contain
    // [false, true, false, false, true].
    //
    // If the list is empty, no variable is mutated in this operator.
    // The list either has the same length as `inputs`, or is empty.
    mutating_variable_inputs:[bool];
}
```

The `opcode_index` member is an index into the root-level `operator_codes` vector inside `Model`. Because a particular kind of operator, like `Conv2D`, might show up many times in one graph, and some ops require a string to define them, it saves serialization size to keep all of the op definitions in one top-level array and refer to them indirectly from subgraphs.

The `inputs` and `outputs` arrays define the connections between an operator and its neighbors in the graph. These are lists of integers that refer to the tensor array in the parent subgraph, and may refer to constant buffers read from the model, inputs fed into the network by the application, the results of running other operations, or output destination buffers that will be read by the application after calculations have finished.

One important thing to know about this list of operators held in the subgraph is that they are always in topological order, so that if you execute them from the beginning of the array to the end, all of the inputs for a given operation that rely on previous operations will have been calculated by the time that operation is reached. This makes writing interpreters much simpler, because the execution loop doesn't need to do any graph operations beforehand and can just execute the operations in the order they're listed. It does mean that running the same subgraph in different orders (for example, to use back-propagation with training) is not straightforward, but TensorFlow Lite's focus is on inference so this is a worthwhile trade-off.

Operators also usually require parameters, like the shape and stride for the filters for a `Conv2D` kernel. The representation of these is unfortunately pretty complex. For historical reasons, TensorFlow Lite supports two different families of operations. Built-in operations came first, and are the most common ops that are used in mobile applications. You can see a list in the schema (*https://oreil.ly/HjdHn*). As of November 2019 there are only 122, but TensorFlow supports more than 800 operations—so what can we do about the remainder? Custom operations are defined by a string name instead of a fixed enum like built-ins, so they can be added more easily without touching the schema.

For built-in ops, the parameter structures are listed in the schema. Here's an example for `Conv2D`:

```
table Conv2DOptions {
  padding:Padding;
  stride_w:int;
  stride_h:int;
  fused_activation_function:ActivationFunctionType;
  dilation_w_factor:int = 1;
  dilation_h_factor:int = 1;
}
```

Hopefully most of the members listed look somewhat familiar, and they are accessed in the same way as other FlatBuffers objects: through the `builtin_options` union of each `Operator` object, with the appropriate type picked based on the operator code (though the code to do so is based on a monster `switch` statement) (*https://oreil.ly/ SkzaA*).

If the operator code turns out to indicate a custom operator, we don't know the structure of the parameter list ahead of time, so we can't generate a code object. Instead, the argument information is packed into a FlexBuffer (*https://oreil.ly/qPwo9*). This is a format that the FlatBuffer library offers for encoding arbitrary data when you don't know the structure in advance, which means the code implementing the operator needs to access the resulting data specifying what the type is, and with messier syntax than a built-in's. Here's an example from some object detection code (*https://oreil.ly/ xQoTR*):

```
const flexbuffers::Map& m = flexbuffers::GetRoot(buffer_t, length).AsMap();
op_data->max_detections = m["max_detections"].AsInt32();
```

The buffer pointer being referenced in this example ultimately comes from the `custom_options` member of the `Operator` table, showing how you can access parameter data from this property.

The final member of `Operator` is `mutating_variable_inputs`. This is an experimental feature to help manage Long Short-Term Memory (LSTM) and other ops that might want to treat their inputs as variables, and shouldn't be relevant for most MCU applications.

Those are the key parts of the TensorFlow Lite serialization format. There are a few other members we haven't covered (like `metadata_buffer` in `Model`), but these are for nonessential features that are optional and so can usually be ignored. Hopefully this overview will be enough to get you started on reading, writing, and debugging your own model files.

Porting TensorFlow Lite Mobile Ops to Micro

There are more than one hundred "built-in" operations in the mainline TensorFlow Lite version targeting mobile devices. TensorFlow Lite for Microcontrollers reuses most of the code, but because the default implementations of these ops bring in dependencies like pthreads, dynamic memory allocation, or other features unavailable on embedded systems, the op implementations (also known as kernels) require some work to make them available on Micro.

Eventually, we hope to unify the two branches of op implementations, but that effort requires some design and API changes across the framework, so it won't be happening in the short term. Most ops should already have Micro implementations, but if you discover one that's available on mobile TensorFlow Lite but not through the embedded version, this section walks you through the conversion process. After you've identified the operation you're going to port, there are several stages.

Separate the Reference Code

All of the ops listed should already have reference code, but the functions are likely to be in *reference_ops.h* (*https://oreil.ly/QmW4H*). This is a monolithic header file that's almost 5,000 lines long. Because it covers so many operations, it pulls in a lot of dependencies that are not available on embedded platforms. To begin the porting process, you first need to extract the reference functions that are required for the operation you're working on into a separate header file. You can see examples of these smaller headers in *https://oreil.ly/vH-6[_conv.h]* and *pooling.h* (*https://oreil.ly/pwP_0*). The reference functions themselves should have names that match the operation they implement, and there will typically be multiple implementations for different data types, sometimes using templates.

As soon as the file is separated from the larger header, you'll need to include it from *reference_ops.h* so that all the existing users of that header still see the functions you've moved (though our Micro code will include only the separated headers individually). You can see how we do this for conv2d here (*https://oreil.ly/jtXLU*). You'll also need to add the header to the kernels/internal/BUILD:reference_base and kernels/internal/BUILD:legacy_reference_base build rules. After you've made those changes, you should be able to run the test suite and see all of the existing mobile tests passing:

```
bazel test tensorflow/lite/kernels:all
```

This is a good point to create an initial pull request for review. You haven't ported anything to the micro branch yet, but you've prepared the existing code for the change, so it's worth trying to get this work reviewed and submitted while you work on the following steps.

Create a Micro Copy of the Operator

Each micro operator implementation is a modified copy of a mobile version held in *tensorflow/lite/kernels/*. For example, the micro *conv.cc* is based on the mobile *conv.cc*. There are a few big differences. First, dynamic memory allocation is trickier in embedded environments, so the creation of the OpData structure that caches calculated values for the calculations used during inference is moved into a separate function so that it can be called during Invoke() rather than returned from Prepare(). This involves a little more work for each Invoke() call, but the reduction in memory overhead usually makes sense for microcontrollers.

Second, most of the parameter-checking code in Prepare() is usually removed. It might be better to enclose this in #if defined(DEBUG) rather than removing it entirely, but the removal keeps the code size to a minimum. All references to external frameworks (Eigen, gemmlowp, cpu_backend_support) should be removed from the includes and the code. In the `Eval()` function, everything but the path that calls the function in the `reference_ops::` namespace should be removed.

The resulting modified operator implementation should be saved in a file with the same name as the mobile version (usually the lowercase version of the operator name) in the *tensorflow/lite/micro/kernels/* folder.

Port the Test to the Micro Framework

We can't run the full Google Test framework on embedded platforms, so we need to use the Micro Test library instead. This should look familiar to users of GTest, but it avoids any constructs that require dynamic memory allocation or C++ global initialization. There's more documentation elsewhere in this book.

You'll want to run the same tests that you run on mobile in the embedded environment, so you'll need to use the version in *tensorflow/lite/kernels/<your op name>_test.cc* as a starting point. For example, look at *tensorflow/lite/kernels/conv_test.cc* (*https://oreil.ly/76KXK*) and the ported version *tensorflow/lite/micro/kernels/conv_test.cc* (*https://oreil.ly/r1wKh*). Here are the big differences:

- The mobile code relies on C++ STL classes like `std::map` and `std::vector`, which require dynamic memory allocation.
- The mobile code also uses helper classes and passes in data objects in a way that involves allocations.
- The micro version allocates all of its data on the stack, using `std::initializer_list` to pass down objects that look a lot like `std::vectors`, but do not require dynamic memory allocation.
- Calls to run a test are expressed as function calls rather than object allocations because this helps reuse a lot of code without hitting allocation issues.
- Most standard error checking macros are available, but with the `TF_LITE_MICRO_` suffix. For example, `EXPECT_EQ` becomes `TF_LITE_MICRO_EXPECT_EQ`.

The tests all have to live in one file, and be surrounded by a single `TF_LITE_MICRO_TESTS_BEGIN`/`TF_LITE_MICRO_TESTS_END` pair. Under the hood this actually creates a `main()` function so that the tests can be run as a standalone binary.

We also try to ensure that the tests rely on only the kernel code and API, not bringing in other classes like the interpreter. The tests should call into the kernel implementations directly, using the C API returned from `GetRegistration()`. This is because we want to ensure that the kernels can be used completely standalone, without needing the rest of the framework, so the testing code should avoid those dependencies, too.

Build a Bazel Test

Now that you have created the operator implementation and test files, you'll want to check whether they work. You'll need to use the Bazel open source build system to do this. Add a `tflite_micro_cc_test` rule to the *BUILD* file (*https://oreil.ly/CbwMI*) and then try building and running this command line (replacing `conv` with your operator name):

```
bazel test ttensorflow/lite/micro/kernels:conv_test --test_output=streamed
```

No doubt there will be compilation errors and test failures, so expect to spend some time iterating on fixing those.

Add Your Op to AllOpsResolver

Applications can choose to pull in only certain operator implementations for binary size reasons, but there's an op resolver that pulls in all available operators, to make getting started easy. You should add a call to register your operator implementation in the constructor of *all_ops_resolver.cc* (*https://oreil.ly/0Nq06*), and make sure the implementation and header files are included in the *BUILD* rules, too.

Build a Makefile Test

So far, everything you've been doing has been within the `micro` branch of TensorFlow Lite, but you've been building and testing on x86. This is the easiest way to develop, and the initial task is to create portable, unoptimized implementations of all the ops, so we recommend doing as much as you can in this domain. At this point, though, you should have a completely working and tested operator implementation running on desktop Linux, so it's time to begin compiling and testing on embedded devices.

The standard build system for Google open source projects is Bazel, but unfortunately it's not easy to implement cross-compilation and support for embedded toolchains using it, so we've had to turn to the venerable Make for deployment. The Makefile itself is very complicated internally, but hopefully your new operator should be automatically picked up based on the name and location of its implementation file and test. The only manual step should be adding the reference header you created to the `MICROLITE_CC_HDRS` file list.

To test your operator in this environment, `cd` to the folder, and run this command (with your own operator name instead of `conv`):

```
make -f tensorflow/lite/micro/tools/make/Makefile test_conv_test
```

Hopefully this will compile and the test will pass. If not, run through the normal debugging procedures to work out what's going wrong.

This is still running natively on your local Intel x86 desktop machine, though it's using the same build machinery as the embedded targets. You can try compiling and flashing your code onto a real microcontroller like the SparkFun Edge now (just passing in `TARGET=sparkfun_edge` on the Makefile line should be enough), but to make life easier we also have software emulation of a Cortex-M3 device available. You should be able to run your test through this by executing the following command:

```
make -f tensorflow/lite/micro/tools/make/Makefile TARGET=bluepill test_conv_test
```

This can be a little flakey because sometimes the emulator takes too long to execute and the process times out, but hopefully giving it a second try will fix it. If you've gotten this far, we encourage you to contribute your changes back to the open source build if you can. The full process of open-sourcing your code can be a bit involved, but the TensorFlow Community guide (*https://oreil.ly/YcbFB*) is a good place to start.

Wrapping Up

After finishing this chapter, you might be feeling like you've been trying to drink from a fire hose. We've given you a lot of information about how TensorFlow Lite for Microcontrollers works. Don't worry if you don't understand it all, or even most of it—we just wanted to give you enough background so that if you do need to delve under the hood, you know where to begin looking. The code is all open source and is the ultimate guide to how the framework operates, but we hope this commentary will help you navigate its structure and understand why some of its design decisions were made.

After seeing how to run some prebuilt examples and taking a deep dive into how the library works, you're probably wondering how you can apply what you've learned to your own applications. The remainder of the book concentrates on the skills you need to be able to deploy custom machine learning in your own products, covering optimization, debugging, and porting models, along with privacy and security.

## CHAPTER 14

Designing Your Own TinyML Applications

So far, we've explored existing reference applications for important areas like audio, image, and gesture recognition. If your problem is similar to one of the examples, you should be able to adapt the training and deployment process—but what if it isn't obvious how to modify one of our examples to fit? In this and the following chapters, we cover the process of building an embedded machine learning solution for a problem for which you don't have an easy starting point. Your experience with the examples will serve as a good foundation for creating your own systems, but you also need to learn more about designing, training, and deploying new models. Because the constraints of our platforms are so tight, we also spend a lot of time discussing how you can make the right optimizations to fit within your storage and computational budgets without missing your accuracy targets. You'll undoubtedly spend a lot of your time trying to understand why things aren't working, so we cover a variety of debugging techniques. Finally, we explore how you can build in safeguards for your users' privacy and security.

The Design Process

Training models can take days or weeks, and bringing up a new embedded hardware platform can also be very time-consuming—so one of the biggest risks to any embedded machine learning project is running out of time before you have something working. The most effective way to reduce this risk is by answering as many of the outstanding questions as early in the process as possible, through planning, research, and experimentation. Each change to your training data or architecture can easily involve a week of coding and retraining, and deployment hardware changes have a ripple effect throughout your software stack, involving a lot of rewriting of previously working code. Anything you can do at the outset to reduce the number of changes required later in the development process can save you the time you would have spent making those changes. This chapter focuses on some of the techniques we recommend for answering important questions before you start coding the final application.

Do You Need a Microcontroller, or Would a Larger Device Work?

The first question you really need to answer is whether you need the advantages of an embedded system or can relax your requirements for battery life, cost, and size, at least for an initial prototype. Programming on a system with a complete modern OS like Linux is a lot easier (and faster) than developing in the embedded world. You can get complete desktop-level systems like a Raspberry Pi for under $25, along with a lot of peripherals like cameras and other sensors. If you need to run compute-heavy neural networks, NVIDIA's Jetson series of boards start at $99 and bring a strong software stack in a small form factor. The biggest downsides to these devices are that they will burn several watts, giving them battery-powered lifetimes on the order of hours or days at most, depending on the physical size of the energy storage. As long as latency isn't a hard constraint, you can even fire up as many powerful cloud servers as you need to handle the neural network workload, leaving the client device to handle the interface and network communications.

We're strong believers in the power of being able to deploy anywhere, but if you're trying to determine whether an idea will work at all, we highly recommend trying to prototype using a device that is easy and quick to experiment with. Developing embedded systems is a massive pain in the behind, so the more you can tease out the real requirements of your application before you dive in, the more chance you have of being successful.

Picking a practical example, imagine that you want to build a device to help monitor the health of sheep. The final product will need to be able to run for weeks or months in an environment without good connectivity, so it must be an embedded system. When you're getting underway, however, you don't want to use such a tricky-to-program device, because you won't yet know crucial details like what models you want to run, which sensors are required, or what actions you need to take based on the data you gather, and you won't yet have any training data. To bootstrap your work, you'll probably want to find a friendly farmer with a small flock of sheep that graze somewhere accessible. You could put together a Raspberry Pi platform that you remove from each monitored sheep every night yourself to recharge, and set up an outdoor WiFi network that covers the range of the grazing field so that the devices can easily communicate with a network. Obviously you can't expect real customers to go to this sort of trouble, but you'll be able to answer a lot of questions about what you need to build with this setup, and experimenting with new models, sensors, and form factors will be much faster than in an embedded version.

Microcontrollers are useful because they scale up in a way no other hardware can. They are cheap, small, and able to run on almost no energy, but these advantages only kick in when you actually need to scale. If you can, put off dealing with scaling until you absolutely must so that you can be confident that you're scaling the right thing.

Understanding What's Possible

It's difficult to know what problems deep learning is able to solve. One rule of thumb we've found very useful is that neural network models are great at the kind of tasks that people can solve "in the blink of an eye." We intuitively seem able to recognize objects, sounds, words, and friends in a comparative instant, and these are the same kinds of tasks that neural networks can perform. Similarly, DeepMind's Go-solving algorithm relies on a convolutional neural network that's able to look at a board and return an estimate of how strong a position each player is in. The longer-term planning parts of that system are then built up using those foundational components.

This is a useful distinction because it draws a line between different kinds of "intelligence." Neural networks are not automatically capable of planning or higher-level tasks like theorem solving. They're much better at taking in large amounts of noisy and confusing data, and spotting patterns robustly. For example, a neural network might not be a good solution for guiding a sheepdog in how to herd a flock through a gate, but it could well be the best approach for taking in a variety of sensor data like body temperature, pulse, and accelerometer readings to predict whether a sheep is feeling unwell. The sorts of judgments that we're able to perform almost unconsciously are more likely to be covered by deep learning than problems that require explicit thinking this doesn't mean that those more abstract problems can't be helped by neural networks, just that they're usually only a component of a larger system that uses their "instinctual" predictions as inputs.

Follow in Someone Else's Footsteps

In the research world, "reviewing the literature" is the rather grand name for reading research papers and other publications related to a problem you're interested in. Even if you're not a researcher this can be a useful process when dealing with deep learning because there are a lot of useful accounts of attempts to apply neural network models to all sorts of challenges, and you'll save a lot of time if you can get some hints on how to get started from the work of others. Understanding research papers can be challenging, but the most useful things to glean are what kinds of models people use for problems similar to yours and whether there are any existing datasets you can use, given that gathering data is one of the most difficult parts of the machine learning process.

For example, if you were interested in predictive maintenance on mechanical bearings, you might search for "deep learning predictive maintenance bearings" on arxiv.org (*https://oreil.ly/xljQN*), which is the most popular online host for machine learning research papers. The top result as of this writing is a survey paper from 2019, "Machine Learning and Deep Learning Algorithms for Bearing Fault Diagnostics: A Comprehensive Review" (*https://oreil.ly/-dqy7*) by Shen Zhang et al. From this, you'll learn that there's a standard public dataset of labeled bearing sensor data called the Case Western Reserve University bearing dataset (*https://oreil.ly/q2_79*). Having an existing dataset is extremely helpful because it will assist you in experimenting with approaches even before you have gathered readings from your own setup. There's also a good overview of the different kinds of model architectures that have been used on the problem, along with discussions of their benefits, costs, and the overall results they achieve.

Find Some Similar Models to Train

After you have some ideas about model architectures and training data to use, it's worth spending some time in a training environment experimenting to see what results you can achieve with no resource constraints. This book focuses on TensorFlow, so we'd recommend that you find an example TensorFlow tutorial or script (depending on your level of experience), get it running as is, and then begin to adapt it to your problem. If you can, look at the training examples in this book for inspiration because they also include all of the steps needed to deploy to an embedded platform.

A good way to think about what models might work is looking at the characteristics of your sensor data and trying to match them to something similar in the tutorials. For example, if you have single-channel vibration data from a wheel bearing, that's going to be a comparatively high-frequency time series, which has a lot in common with audio data from a microphone. As a starting point, you could try converting all of your bearing data into *.wav* format and then feed it into the speech training process (*https://oreil.ly/dG9gQ*) instead of the standard Speech Commands dataset, with the appropriate labels. You'd probably then want to customize the process a lot more, but hopefully you'd at least get a model that was somewhat predictive and be able to use that as a baseline for further experiments. A similar process could apply to adapting the gesture tutorial to any accelerometer-based classification problem, or retraining the person detector for different machine vision applications. If there isn't an obvious example to start with in this book, searching for tutorials that show how to build the model architecture you're interested in using Keras is a good way to get started.

Feature Generation

One topic that many pure machine learning tutorials don't cover well is *feature generation*. Features are the values we feed into our neural networks, the arrays of numbers we pass in as inputs. Typically, for modern machine vision, these are just the RGB pixel arrays directly from image data in memory, but this isn't true for many other sensor types. For example, the speech recognition example takes in 16 KHz pulse-coded modulation data (samples of the current volume captured at 16,000 times per second), but transforms that information into spectrograms (single-channel 2D arrays holding the magnitude of a range of frequencies over time in each row), which are then fed into the neural network model. There's a general desire to get rid of this kind of preprocessing because it requires a lot of experimentation and engineering work to implement, but for many problems it's still necessary to achieve the best results, especially within resource constraints. Unfortunately the best feature generation approaches for particular problems are often not well documented, so you might need to find domain experts to ask advice from if you can't find a good example to follow.

Look at the Data

Most of the focus of machine learning research is on designing new architectures; there's not much coverage of training datasets. This is because in the academic world you're usually given a pregenerated training dataset that is fixed, and you're competing on how well your model can score on it compared to others. Outside of research we usually don't have an existing dataset for our problem, and what we care about is the experience we deliver to the end user, not the score on a fixed dataset, so our priorities become very different.

One of the authors has written a blog post (*https://oreil.ly/ghEbc*) that covers this in more detail, but the summary is that you should expect to spend much more time gathering, exploring, labeling, and improving your data than you do on your model architecture. The return on the time you invest will be much higher.

There are some common techniques that we've found to be very useful when working with data. One that sounds extremely obvious but that we still often forget is: look at your data! If you have images, download them into folders arranged by label on your local machine and browse through them. If you're working with audio files, do the same and listen to a selection of them. You'll quickly discover all sorts of oddities and mistakes that you didn't expect, from Jaguar cars labeled as jaguar cats to recordings in which the audio is too faint or has been cropped and cuts off part of a word. Even if you just have numerical data, looking through the numbers in a comma-separated values (CSV) text file can be extremely helpful. In the past we've spotted problems like many of the values reaching the saturation limits of sensors and maxing out, or even wrapping around, or the sensitivity being too low so that most of the data is crammed into too small a numerical range. You can get much more advanced in your data analysis, and you'll find tools like TensorBoard extremely helpful for clustering and other visualizations of what's happening in your dataset.

Another problem to watch out for is an unbalanced training set. If you are classifying into categories, the frequency at which different classes occur in your training inputs will affect the eventual prediction probabilities. One trap that's easy to fall into is thinking that the results from your network represent true probabilities—for example, a 0.5 score for "yes" meaning that the network is predicting there's a 50% chance the spoken word was "yes." In fact the relationship is a lot more complex, given that the ratio of each class in the training data will control the output values, but the prior probability of each class in the application's real input distribution is needed to understand the real probability. As another example, imagine training a bird image classifier on 10 different species. If you then deployed that in the Antarctic, you'd be very suspicious of a result that indicated you'd seen a parrot; if you were looking at video from the Amazon, a penguin would be equally surprising. It can be challenging to bake this kind of domain knowledge into the training process because you typically want roughly equal numbers of samples for each class so the network "pays attention" equally to each. Instead, there's typically a calibration process that occurs after the model inference has been run, to weight the results based on prior knowledge. In the Antarctic example, you might have a very high threshold before you report a parrot, but a much lower one for penguins.

Wizard of Oz-ing

One of our favorite machine learning design techniques doesn't involve much technology at all. The most difficult problem in engineering is determining what the requirements are, and it's very easy to spend a lot of time and resources on something that doesn't actually work well in practice for a problem, especially because the process of developing a machine learning model takes a long time. To flush out the requirements, we highly recommend the Wizard of Oz approach (*https://oreil.ly/Omr6N*). In this scenario, you create a mock-up of the system you eventually want to build, but instead of having software do the decision making, you have a person as "the man behind the curtain." This lets you test your assumptions before you go through a time-consuming development cycle to make sure you have the specifications well tested before you bake them into your design.

How does this work in practice? Imagine that you're designing a sensor that will detect when people are present in a meeting room, and if there's no one in the room, it will dim the lights. Instead of building and deploying a wireless microcontroller running a person detection model, with the Wizard of Oz approach you'd create a prototype that just fed live video to a person sitting in a nearby room with a switch that controlled the lights and instructions to dim them when nobody was visible. You'd quickly discover usability issues, like if the camera doesn't cover the entire room and so the lights keep getting turned off when somebody's still present, or if there's an unacceptable delay in turning them on when someone enters the room. You can apply this approach to almost any problem, and it will give you precious validation of the assumptions you're making about your product, without you spending time and energy on a machine learning model based on the wrong foundations. Even better, you can set up this process so that you generate labeled data for your training set from it, given that you'll have the input data along with the decisions that your Wizard made based on those inputs.

Get It Working on the Desktop First

The Wizard of Oz approach is one way to get a prototype running as quickly as possible, but even after you've moved on to model training you should be thinking about how to experiment and iterate as quickly as you can. Exporting a model and getting that model running fast enough on an embedded platform can take a long time, so a great shortcut is to stream data from a sensor in the environment to a nearby desktop or cloud machine for processing. This will probably use too much energy to be a deployable solution in production, but as long as you can ensure the latency doesn't affect the overall experience, it's a great way to get feedback on how well your machine learning solution works in the context of the whole product design.

Another big benefit is that you can record a stream of sensor data once, and then use it over and over again for informal evaluations of your model. This is especially useful if there are particularly high-impact errors that a model has made in the past that might not be properly captured in the normal metrics. If your photo classifier labels a baby as a dog, you might want to especially avoid this even if you're overall 95% accurate because it would be so upsetting for the user.

There are a lot of choices for how to run the model on the desktop. The easiest way to begin is by collecting example data using a platform like the Raspberry Pi that has good sensor support, and doing a bulk copy to your desktop machine (or a cloud instance if you prefer). You can then use standard TensorFlow in Python to train and evaluate potential models in an offline way, with no interactivity. When you have a model that seems promising you can take incremental steps, such as converting your TensorFlow model to TensorFlow Lite, but continue evaluating it against batch data on your PC. After that's working, you could try putting your desktop TensorFlow Lite application behind a simple web API and calling it from a device that has the form factor you're aiming at to understand how it works in a real environment.

## CHAPTER 15

Optimizing Latency

Embedded systems don't have much computing power, which means that the intensive calculations needed for neural networks can take longer than on most other platforms. Because embedded systems usually operate on streams of sensor data in real time, running too slowly can cause a lot of problems. Suppose that you're trying to observe something that might occur only briefly (like a bird being visible in a camera's field of view). If your processing time is too long you might sample the sensor too slowly and miss one of these occurrences. Sometimes the quality of a prediction is improved by repeated observations of overlapping windows of sensor data, in the way the wake-word detection example runs a one-second window on audio data for wake-word spotting, but moves the window forward only a hundred milliseconds or less each time, averaging the results. In these cases, reducing latency lets us improve the overall accuracy. Speeding up the model execution might also allow the device to run at a lower CPU frequency, or go to sleep in between inferences, which can reduce the overall energy usage.

Because latency is such an important area for optimization, this chapter focuses on some of the different techniques you can use to reduce the time it takes to run your model.

First Make Sure It Matters

It's possible that your neural network code is such a small part of your overall system latency that speeding it up wouldn't make a big difference to your product's performance. The simplest way to determine whether this is the case is by commenting out the call to `tflite::MicroInterpreter::Invoke()` (*https://oreil.ly/1dLTn*) in your application code. This is the function that contains all of the inference calculations, and it will block until the network has been run, so by removing it you can observe what difference it makes to the overall latency. In an ideal world you'll be able to calculate this change with a timer log statement or profiler, but as described shortly even just blinking an LED and eye balling the frequency difference might be enough to give you a rough idea of what the speed increase is. If the difference between running the network inference and not is small, there's not much to gain from optimizing the deep learning part of the code, and you should focus on other parts of your application first.

Hardware Changes

If you do need to speed up your neural network code, the first question to ask is whether you are able to use a more powerful hardware device. This won't be possible for many embedded products, because the decision on which hardware platform to use is often made very early on or has been set externally, but because it's the easiest factor to change from a software perspective, it's worth explicitly considering. If you do have a choice, the biggest constraints are usually energy, speed, and cost. If you can, trade off energy or cost for speed by switching the chip you're using. You might even get lucky in your research and discover a newer platform that gives you more speed without losing either of the other main factors!

 When neural networks are trained, it's typical to send a large number of training examples at once, in every training step. This allows a lot of calculation optimizations that are not possible when only one sample is submitted at once. For example, a hundred images and labels might be sent as part of a single training call. This collection of training data is called a *batch*.

With embedded systems we're usually dealing with one group of sensor readings at a time, in real time, so we don't want to wait to gather a larger batch before we trigger inference. This "single batch" focus means we can't benefit from some optimizations that make sense on the training side, so the hardware architectures that are helpful for the cloud don't always translate over to our use cases.

Model Improvements

After switching hardware platforms, the easiest place to have a big impact on neural network latency is at the architecture level. If you can create a new model that is accurate enough but involves fewer calculations, you can speed up inference without making any code changes at all. It's usually possible to trade reduced accuracy for increased speed, so if you're able to start with as accurate a model as you can get at the beginning, you'll have a lot more scope for these trade-offs. This means that spending time on improving and expanding your training data can be very helpful throughout the development process, even with apparently unrelated tasks like latency optimization.

When optimizing procedural code, it's typically a better use of your budget to spend time changing the high-level algorithms your code is based on rather than rewriting inner loops in assembly. The focus on model architectures is based on the same idea; it's better to eliminate work entirely if you can rather than improving the speed at which you do it. What is different in our case is that it's actually a lot easier to swap out machine learning models than it is to switch algorithms in traditional code because each model is just a functional black box that takes in input data and returns numerical results. After you have a good set of data gathered, it should be comparatively easy to replace one model with another in the training scripts. You can even experiment with removing individual layers from a model that you're using and observe the effect. Neural networks tend to degrade extremely gracefully, so you should feel free to try lots of different destructive changes and observe their effect on accuracy and latency.

Estimating Model Latency

Most neural network models spend the majority of their time running large matrix multiplications or very close equivalents. This is because every input value must be scaled by a different weight for each output value, so the work involved is approximately the number of input values times the number of output values for each layer in the network. This is often approximated by talking about the number of floating-point operations (or FLOPs) that a network requires for a single inference run. Usually a multiply-add operation (which is often a single instruction at the machine code level) counts as two FLOPs, and even if you're performing 8-bit or lower quantized calculations you might sometimes see them referred to as FLOPs, even though floating-point numbers are no longer involved. The number of FLOPs required for a network can be calculated by hand, layer by layer. For example, a fully connected layer requires a number of FLOPs equal to the size of the input vector, multiplied by the size of the output vector. Thus, if you know those dimensions, you can figure out the work involved. You can also usually find FLOP estimates in papers that discuss and compare model architectures, like MobileNet (*https://arxiv.org/abs/1905.02244*).

FLOPs are useful as a rough metric for how much time a network will take to execute because, all else being equal, a model that involves fewer calculations will run faster and in proportion to the difference in FLOPs. For example, you could reasonably expect a model that requires 100 million FLOPs to run twice as fast as a 200-million-FLOP version. This isn't entirely true in practice, because there are other factors like how well optimized the software is for particular layers that will affect the latency, but it's a good starting point for evaluating different network architectures. It's also useful to help establish what's realistic to expect for your hardware platform. If you're able to run a 1-million-FLOP model in 100 ms on your chip, you'll be able to make an educated guess that a different model requiring 10 million FLOPs will take about a second to calculate.

How to Speed Up Your Model

Model architecture design is still an active research field, so it's not easy to write a good guide for beginners at this point. The best starting point is to find some existing models that have been designed with efficiency in mind and then iteratively experiment with changes. Many models have particular parameters that we can alter to affect the amount of computation required, such as MobileNet's depthwise channel factor, or the input size expected. In other cases, you might look at the FLOPs required for each layer and try to remove particularly slow ones or substitute them with faster alternatives (such as depthwise convolution instead of plain convolution). If you can, it's also worth looking at the actual latency of each layer when running on-device, instead of estimating it through FLOPs. This will require some of the profiling techniques discussed in the sections that follow for code optimizations, though.

 Designing model architectures is difficult and time-consuming, but there have recently been some advances in automating the process, such as MnasNet (*https://arxiv.org/abs/1807.11626*), using approaches like genetic algorithms to improve network designs. These are still not at the point of entirely replacing humans (they often require seeding with known good architectures as starting points, and manual rules about what search space to use, for example), but it's likely we'll see rapid progress in this area.

There are already services like AutoML (*https://cloud.google.com/automl/*) that allow users to avoid many of the gritty details of training, and hopefully this trend will continue, so you'll be able to pick the best possible model for your data and efficiency trade-offs.

Quantization

Running a neural network requires hundreds of thousands or even millions of calculations for every prediction. Most programs that perform such complex calculations are very sensitive to numerical precision; otherwise, errors build up and give a result that's too inaccurate to use. Deep learning models are different—they are able to cope with large losses in numerical precision during intermediate calculations and still produce end results that are accurate overall. This property seems to be a by-product of their training process, in which the inputs are large and full of noise, so the models learn to be robust to insignificant variations and focus on the important patterns that matter.

What this means in practice is that operating with 32-bit floating-point representations is almost always more precise than is required for inference. Training is a bit more demanding because it requires many small changes to the weights to learn, but even there, 16-bit representations are widely used. Most inference applications can produce results that are indistinguishable from the floating-point equivalent, using just 8 bits to store weights and activation values. This is good news for embedded applications given that many of our platforms have strong support for the kind of 8-bit multiply-and-accumulate instructions that these models rely on, because those same instructions are common in signal-processing algorithms.

It isn't straightforward to convert a model from floating point to 8-bit, though. To perform calculations efficiently, the 8-bit values require a linear conversion to real numbers. This is easy for weights because we know the range for each layer from the trained values, so we can derive the correct scaling factor to perform the conversion. It's trickier for activations, though, because it's not obvious from inspecting the model parameters and architecture what the range of each layer's outputs actually is. If we pick a range that's too small, some outputs will be clipped to the minimum or maximum, but if it's too large, the precision of the outputs will be smaller than it could be, and we'll risk losing accuracy in the overall results.

Quantization is still an active research topic and there are a lot of different options, so the TensorFlow team has tried a variety of approaches over the past few years. You can see a discussion of some of these experiments in "Quantizing Deep Convolutional Networks for Efficient Inference: A Whitepaper" by Raghuraman Krishnamoorthi (*https://arxiv.org/pdf/1806.08342.pdf*), and the quantization specification (*https://oreil.ly/toF_E*) covers the recommended approach we now use based on our experience.

We've centralized the quantization process so that it happens during the process of converting a model from the TensorFlow training environment into a TensorFlow Lite graph. We used to recommend a quantization-aware training scheme, but this was difficult to use and we found we could produce equivalent results at export time, using some additional techniques. The easiest type of quantization to use is what's known as post-training weight quantization (*https://oreil.ly/Tz9D_*). This is when the weights are quantized down to 8 bits but the activation layers remain in floating point. This is useful because it shrinks the model file size by 75% and offers some speed benefits. It is the easiest approach to run because it doesn't require any knowledge of the activation layer's ranges, but it does still require fast floating-point hardware that isn't present on many embedded platforms.

Post-training integer quantization (*https://oreil.ly/LDw-y*) means that a model can be executed without any floating-point calculations, which makes it the preferred approach for the use cases we cover in this book. The most challenging part about using it is that you need to provide some example inputs during the model export process, so the ranges of the activation layer outputs can be observed by running some typical images, audio, or other data through the graph. As we discussed earlier, without estimates of these ranges, it's not possible to quantize these layers accurately. In the past, we've used other methods, like recording the ranges during training or capturing them during every inference at runtime, but these had disadvantages like making training much more complicated or imposing a latency penalty, so this is the least-worst approach.

If you look back at our instructions for exporting the person detector model in Chapter 10, you'll see that we provide a `representative_dataset` function to the `converter` object. This is a Python function that produces the inputs that the activation range estimation process needs, and for the person detector model we load some example images from the training dataset. This is something you'll need to figure out for every model you train though, because the expected inputs will change for each application. It can also be tough to discern how the inputs are scaled and transformed as part of the preprocessing, so creating the function can involve some trial and error. We're hoping to make this process easier in the future.

Running fully quantized models has big latency benefits on almost all platforms, but if you're supporting a new device it's likely that you'll need to optimize the most computationally intensive operations to take advantage of specialized instructions offered by your hardware. A good place to begin if you're working on a convolutional network is the `Conv2D` operation (*https://oreil.ly/NrjSo*) and the kernel (*https://oreil.ly/V27Q-*). You'll notice that there are `uint8` and `int8` versions of many kernels; the `uint8` versions are remnants of an older approach to quantization that is no longer used, and all models should now be exported using the `int8` path.

Product Design

You might not think of your product design as a way to optimize latency, but it's actually one of the best places to invest your time. The key is to figure out whether you can loosen the requirements on your network, either for speed or accuracy. For example, you might want to track hand gestures using a camera at many frames per second, but if you have a body pose detection model that takes a second to run, you might be able to use a much faster optical tracking algorithm to follow the identified points at a higher rate, updating it with the more accurate but less frequent neural network results when they're available. As another example, you could have a microcontroller delegate advanced speech recognition to a cloud API accessed over a network while keeping wake-word detection running on the local device. At a broader level, you might be able to relax the accuracy requirements of your network by incorporating uncertainty into the user interface. The wake words chosen for speech recognition systems tend to be short phrases that contain sequences of syllables that are unlikely to show up in regular speech. If you have a hand gesture system, maybe you can require every sequence to end with a thumbs-up to confirm the commands were intentional?

The goal is to provide the best overall user experience you can, so anything you can do in the rest of the system to be more forgiving of mistakes gives you more room to trade off accuracy for speed or other properties you need to improve.

Code Optimizations

We've positioned this topic pretty late in the chapter because there are other approaches to optimizing latency that you should try first, but traditional code optimization is an important way to achieve acceptable performance. In particular, the TensorFlow Lite for Microcontrollers code has been written to run well across a large number of models and systems with as small a binary footprint as possible, so there might well be optimizations that apply only to your particular model or platform that you can benefit from adding yourself. This is one of the reasons we encourage you to delay code optimization as long as possible, though—many of these kinds of changes will not be applicable if you change your hardware platform or the model architecture you're using, so having those things nailed down first is essential.

Performance Profiling

The foundation of any code optimization effort is knowing how long different parts of your program take to run. This can be surprisingly difficult to figure out in the embedded world because you might not even have a simple timer available by default, and even if you do, recording and returning the information you need can be demanding. Here's a variety of approaches we've used, ranging from the easiest to implement to the trickiest.

Blinky

Almost all embedded development boards have at least one LED that you can control from your program. If you're measuring times that are more than about half a second, you can try turning on that LED at the start of the code section that you want to measure and then disabling it afterward. You'll probably be able to roughly estimate the time taken using an external stopwatch and manually counting how many blinks you see in 10 seconds. You can also have two dev boards side by side with different versions of the code, and estimate which one is faster by the comparative frequency of the flashes.

Shotgun profiling

After you have a rough idea of how long a normal run of your application is taking, the simplest way to estimate how long a particular piece of code is taking is to comment it out and see how much faster the overall execution takes. This has been called *shotgun profiling* by analogy with shotgun debugging, in which you remove large chunks of code in order to locate crashes when little other information is available. It can be surprisingly effective for neural network debugging because there are typically no data-dependent branches in the model execution code, so turning any one operation into a no-op by commenting out its internal implementation shouldn't affect the speed of other parts of the model.

Debug logging

In most cases you should have the ability to output a line of text back to a host computer from your embedded development board, so this might seem an ideal way to detect when a piece of code is executing. Unfortunately, the act of communicating with the development machine can itself be very time-consuming. Serial Wire Debug output (*https://oreil.ly/SdsWk*) on an Arm Cortex-M chip can take up to 500 ms, with a lot of variability in the latency, which makes it useless for a simplistic approach to log profiling. Debug logging based on UART connections is usually a lot less expensive, but it's still not ideal.

Logic analyzer

In a similar manner to toggling LEDs but with a lot more precision, you can have your code turn GPIO pins on and off and then use an external logic analyzer (we've used the Saleae Logic Pro 16 (*https://oreil.ly/pig8l*) in the past) to visualize and measure the duration. This requires a bit of wiring, and the equipment itself can be expensive, but it gives a very flexible way to investigate your program's latency without requiring any software support beyond the control of one or more GPIO pins.

Timer

If you have a timer that can give you a consistent current time with enough precision, you can record the time at the start and end of the code section you're interested in and output the duration to logs afterward, where any communication latency won't affect the result. We've considered requiring a platform-agnostic timer interface in TensorFlow Lite for Microcontrollers for exactly this reason, but we decided this would add too much of a burden for people porting to different platforms, given that setting up timers can be complicated. Unfortunately this means that you'll need to explore how to implement this functionality yourself for the chip you're running on. There's also the disadvantage that you need to add the timer calls around any code that you want to investigate, so it does require work and planning to identify the critical sections, and you'll need to keep recompiling and flashing as you explore where the time is going.

Profiler

If you're lucky, you'll be working with a toolchain and platform that support some kind of external profiling tool. These applications will typically use debug information from your program to match statistics on execution that they gather from running your program on-device. They will then be able to visualize which functions are taking the most time, or even which lines of code. This is the fastest way to understand where the speed bottlenecks are in your code because you'll be able to rapidly explore and zoom into the functions that matter.

Optimizing Operations

After you've ensured that you're using as simple a model as you can and you've identified which parts of your code are taking the most time, you should then look at what you can do to speed them up. Most of the execution time for neural networks should be spent inside operation implementations, given that they can involve hundreds of thousands or millions of calculations for each layer, so it's likely that you've found one or more of these to be the bottleneck.

Look for Implementations That Are Already Optimized

The default implementations of all operations in TensorFlow Lite for Microcontrollers are written to be small, understandable, and portable, not fast, so it's expected that you should be able to beat them fairly easily with an approach that uses more lines of code or memory. We do have a set of these faster implementations in the *kernels/portable_optimized directory* (*https://oreil.ly/fmY8R*), using the subfolder specialization approach described in Chapter 13. These implementations shouldn't have any platform dependencies, but they can use more memory than the reference versions. Because they're using subfolder specialization, you can just pass in the TAGS="portable_optimized" argument to generate a project that uses these rather than the defaults.

If you're using a device that has platform-specific implementations—for example through a library like CMSIS-NN—and they aren't automatically being picked when you specify your target, you can choose to use these nonportable versions by passing in the appropriate tag. You'll need to explore your platform's documentation and the TensorFlow Lite for Microcontrollers source tree to find what that is, though.

Write Your Own Optimized Implementation

If you've not been able to find an optimized implementation of the operations that are taking the most time or the available implementations aren't fast enough, you might want to write your own. The good news is that you should be able to narrow the scope to make that work easier. You'll only be calling the operations with a few different input and output sizes and parameters, so you need to focus only on making those paths faster rather than the general case. For example, we found that the depthwise convolution reference code was taking up most of the time for the first version of the speech wake-word example on the SparkFun Edge board, and it was overall running too slowly to be usable. When we looked at what the code was doing, we saw that the width of the convolution filters was always eight, which made it possible to write some optimized code that exploited that pattern (*https://oreil.ly/Kbx22*). We could load four input values and four weights held in bytes at a time by using 32-bit integers to fetch them in parallel.

To start the optimization process, create a new directory inside the *kernels* root using the subfolder specialization approach described earlier. Copy the reference kernel implementation into that subfolder as a starting point for your code. To make sure things are building correctly, run the unit test associated with that op and make sure it still passes; if you're passing in the correct tags, it should use the new implementation:

```
make -f tensorflow/lite/micro/tools/make/Makefile test_depthwise_conv_\
    test TAGS="portable_optimized"
```

We then recommend adding a new test to the unit test code for your op—one that doesn't check the correctness but just reports the time taken to execute the operation. Having a benchmark like this will help you to verify that your changes are improving performance in the way you expect. You should have a benchmark for each scenario for which you see a speed bottleneck in your profiling, with the same sizes and other parameters that the op has at that point in your model (though the weights and inputs can be random values, because in most cases the numbers won't affect the execution latency). The benchmark code itself will need to rely on one of the profiling methods discussed earlier in the chapter, ideally using a high-precision timer to measure duration, but if not at least toggling an LED or logic output. If the granularity of your measurement process is too large, you might need to execute the operation multiple times in a loop and then divide by the number of iterations to capture the real time taken. After you have your benchmark written, make a note of the latency before you've made any changes and ensure that it roughly matches what you saw from profiling your application.

With a representative benchmark available, you should now be able to quickly iterate on potential optimizations. A good first step is finding the innermost loop of the initial implementation. This is the section of code that will be run most frequently, so making improvements to it will have a bigger impact than for other parts of the algorithm. You should hopefully be able to identify this by looking through the code and literally finding the most deeply nested for-loop (or equivalent), but it's worth verifying that you have the appropriate section by commenting it out and running the benchmark again. If the latency drops dramatically (hopefully by 50% or more), you've found the right area to focus on. As an example, take this code from the reference implementation of depthwise convolution (*https://oreil.ly/8S4kS*):

```
for (int b = 0; b < batches; ++b) {
  for (int out_y = 0; out_y < output_height; ++out_y) {
    for (int out_x = 0; out_x < output_width; ++out_x) {
      for (int ic = 0; ic < input_depth; ++ic) {
```

```
for (int m = 0; m < depth_multiplier; m++) {
  const int oc = m + ic * depth_multiplier;
  const int in_x_origin = (out_x * stride_width) - pad_width;
  const int in_y_origin = (out_y * stride_height) - pad_height;
  int32 acc = 0;
  for (int filter_y = 0; filter_y < filter_height; ++filter_y) {
    for (int filter_x = 0; filter_x < filter_width; ++filter_x) {
      const int in_x =
          in_x_origin + dilation_width_factor * filter_x;
      const int in_y =
          in_y_origin + dilation_height_factor * filter_y;
      // If the location is outside the bounds of the input image,
      // use zero as a default value.
      if ((in_x >= 0) && (in_x < input_width) && (in_y >= 0) &&
          (in_y < input_height)) {
        int32 input_val =
            input_data[Offset(input_shape, b, in_y, in_x, ic)];
        int32 filter_val = filter_data[Offset(
            filter_shape, 0, filter_y, filter_x, oc)];
        acc += (filter_val + filter_offset) *
               (input_val + input_offset);
      }
    }
  }
  if (bias_data) {
    acc += bias_data[oc];
  }
  acc = DepthwiseConvRound<output_rounding>(acc, output_multiplier,
                                            output_shift);
  acc += output_offset;
  acc = std::max(acc, output_activation_min);
  acc = std::min(acc, output_activation_max);
  output_data[Offset(output_shape, b, out_y, out_x, oc)] =
      static_cast<uint8>(acc);
}
      }
    }
  }
}
```

Just from examining the indentation, it's possible to identify the correct inner loop as this section:

```
const int in_x =
    in_x_origin + dilation_width_factor * filter_x;
const int in_y =
    in_y_origin + dilation_height_factor * filter_y;
// If the location is outside the bounds of the input image,
// use zero as a default value.
if ((in_x >= 0) && (in_x < input_width) && (in_y >= 0) &&
    (in_y < input_height)) {
  int32 input_val =
      input_data[Offset(input_shape, b, in_y, in_x, ic)];
```

```
        int32 filter_val = filter_data[Offset(
            filter_shape, 0, filter_y, filter_x, oc)];
        acc += (filter_val + filter_offset) *
            (input_val + input_offset);
    }
```

This code is being executed many more times than the other lines in the function by virtue of its position in the middle of all the loops, and commenting it out will confirm it's taking the majority of the time. If you're lucky enough to have line-by-line profiling information, this can help you find the exact section, too.

Now that you've found a high-impact area, the goal is to move as much work as you can outside of it to less critical sections. For example, there's an if statement in the middle, which means a conditional check must be executed on every inner loop iteration, but it's possible to hoist that work outside of this part of the code so that the check is executed much less frequently in an outer loop. You might also notice that some conditions or calculations aren't needed for your particular model and benchmark. In the speech wake-word model, the dilation factors are always 1, so the multiplications involving them can be skipped, saving more work. We recommend that you guard these kind of parameter-specific optimizations with a check at the top level, though, and fall back to a plain reference implementation if the arguments aren't what the optimization requires. This allows speedups for known models, but ensures that if you have ops that don't meet these criteria, they at least work correctly. To make sure that you don't accidentally break correctness it's worth running the unit tests for the op frequently, too, as you're making changes.

It's beyond the scope of this book to cover all the ways that you can optimize numerical processing code, but you can look at the kernels in the *portable_optimized* (*https://oreil.ly/tQkJm*) folder to see some of the techniques that can be useful.

Taking Advantage of Hardware Features

So far we've been talking only about portable optimizations that aren't platform-specific. This is because restructuring your code to avoid work entirely is usually the easiest way to make a big impact. It also simplifies and narrows the focus of more specialized optimizations. You might find yourself on a platform like a Cortex-M device with SIMD instructions (*https://oreil.ly/MBxf5*), which are often a big help for the kinds of repetitive calculations that take up most of the time for neural network inference. You'll be tempted to jump straight into using intrinsics or even assembly to rewrite your inner loop, but resist! At least check the documentation of the vendor-supplied libraries to see whether there's something suitable already written to implement a larger part of the algorithm, because that will hopefully be highly optimized already (though it might miss optimizations you can apply knowing your op parameters). If you can, try calling an existing function to calculate something common like fast Fourier transform, rather than writing your own version.

If you have worked through these stages, it's time to experiment with the assembly level of your platform. Our recommended approach is to begin by replacing individual lines of code with their mechanical equivalents in assembly, one line at a time so that you can verify correctness as you go without initially worrying about a speedup. After you have the necessary code converted, you can experiment with fusing operations and other techniques to reduce the latency. One advantage of working with embedded systems is that they tend to be simpler in behavior than more complex processors without deep instruction pipelines or caches, so it's a lot more feasible to understand potential performance on paper and establish potential assembly-level optimizations without too much risk of unexpected side effects.

Accelerators and Coprocessors

As machine learning workloads become more important in the embedded world, we're seeing more systems emerge that offer specialized hardware to speed them up or reduce the power they need. There isn't a clear programming model or standard API for them yet, however, so it's not always clear how to integrate them with a software framework. With TensorFlow Lite for Microcontrollers, we want to support direct integration with hardware that works in a synchronous way with the main processor, but asynchronous components are beyond the scope of the current project.

What we mean by synchronous is that the acceleration hardware is tightly coupled to the main CPU, sharing a memory space, and that an operator implementation can invoke the accelerator very quickly and will block until the result is returned. It's potentially possible that a threading layer above TensorFlow Lite could assign work to another thread or process during this blocking, but that's unlikely to be feasible on most current embedded platforms. From a programmer's perspective, this kind of accelerator looks more like the kind of floating-point coprocessor that existed on early x86 systems than the alternative model, which is more like a GPU. The reason we're focused on these kinds of synchronous accelerators is that they seem to make the most sense for the low-energy systems that we're targeting, and avoiding asynchronous coordination keeps the runtime much simpler.

Coprocessor-like accelerators need to be very close to the CPU in the system architecture to be able to respond with such low latency. The contrasting model is that used by modern GPUs, in which there's a completely separate system with its own control logic on the other end of a bus. Programming these kinds of processors involves the CPU queuing up a large list of commands that will take a comparatively long time to execute and sending them over as soon as a batch is ready, but immediately continuing with other work and not waiting for the accelerator to complete. In this model any latency in communication between the CPU and accelerator is insignificant, because sending the commands is done infrequently and there's no blocking on the result. Accelerators can benefit from this approach because seeing a lot of commands at once gives lots of opportunities to rearrange and optimize the work involved in a way that's difficult when tasks are much more fine-grained and need to be executed in order. It's perfect for graphics rendering because the result never needs to return to the CPU at all; the rendered display buffer is simply shown to the user. It's been adapted to deep learning training by sending large batches of training samples to ensure that there's a lot of work to be done at once and keeping as much as possible on the card, avoiding copies back to the CPU. As embedded systems become more complex and take on larger workloads, we might revisit the requirements for the framework and support this flow with something like the delegate interface in mobile TensorFlow Lite, but that's outside of our scope for this version of the library.

Contributing Back to Open Source

We're always keen to see contributions to TensorFlow Lite, and after you've put effort into optimizing some framework code, you might be interested in sharing it back to the mainline. A good place to begin is by joining the SIG Micro (*https://oreil.ly/wrtz-*) mailing list and sending a quick email summarizing the work you've done, together with a pointer to a fork of the TensorFlow repository with your proposed changes. It helps if you include the benchmark you're using and some inline documentation discussing where the optimization will be helpful. The community should be able to offer feedback; they'll be looking for something that's possible to build on top of, that is generally useful, and that can be maintained and tested. We can't wait to see what you come up with, and thanks for considering open-sourcing your improvements!

Wrapping Up

In this chapter, we covered the most important things you need to know to speed up the execution of your model. The fastest code is code that you don't run at all, so the key thing to remember is to shrink what you're doing at the model and algorithm level before you begin optimizing individual functions. You'll probably need to tackle latency issues before you can get your application working on a real device and test that it works the way you intend it to. After that, the next priority is likely to be ensuring that your device has the lifetime it needs to be useful—and that's where the next chapter, on optimizing energy use, will be useful.

## CHAPTER 16

Optimizing Energy Usage

The most important advantage that embedded devices have over desktop or mobile systems is that they consume very little energy. A server CPU might consume tens or hundreds of watts, requiring a cooling system and main power supply to run. Even a phone can consume several watts and require daily charging. Microcontrollers can run at less than a milliwatt, more than a thousand times less than a phone's CPU, and so run on a coin battery or energy harvesting for weeks, months, or years.

If you're developing a TinyML product, it's likely that the most challenging constraint you'll have to deal with is battery life. Requiring human intervention to change or recharge batteries is often not feasible, so the useful lifetime of your device (how long it will continue working) will be defined by how much energy it uses, and how much it can store. The battery capacity is typically limited by the physical size of your product (for example, a peel-and-stick sensor is unlikely to be able to accommodate anything more than a coin battery), and even if you're able to use energy harvesting, there are sharp limits on how much power that can supply. This means that the main area you can control to influence the lifetime of your device is how much energy your system uses. In this chapter we talk about how you can investigate what your power usage is and how to improve it.

Developing Intuition

Most desktop engineers have a rough feel for how long different kinds of operations take, and they know that a network request is likely to be slower than reading some data from RAM, and that it will usually be faster to access a file from a solid-state drive (SSD) than a spinning-disk drive. It's much less common to have to think about how much energy different functionality needs, but in order to build a mental model and plan for power efficiency, you'll need to have some rules of thumb for what magnitude of energy your operations require.

We switch back and forth in this chapter between measures of energy and power measurements. Power is energy over time, so for example a CPU that uses one joule (J) of energy every second would be using one watt of power. Since what we care most about is the lifetime of our device, it's often most helpful to focus on average power usage as a metric, because that's directly proportional to the length of time a device can run on a fixed amount of energy stored in a battery. This means that we can easily predict that a system that uses an average of 1 mW of power will last twice as long as one that uses 2 mW. We will sometimes still refer to energy usage for one-off operations that aren't sustained for long periods of time.

Typical Component Power Usage

If you want a deep dive into how much energy system components use, *Smartphone Energy Consumption* by Sasu Tarkoma et al. (Cambridge University Press) (*https://oreil.ly/Z3_TQ*) is a great book to start with. Here are some numbers we've derived from their calculations:

- An Arm Cortex-A9 CPU can use between 500 and 2,000 mW.
- A display might use 400 mW.
- Active cell radio might use 800 mW.
- Bluetooth might use 100 mW.

Going beyond smartphones, here are the best measurements we've observed for embedded components:

- A microphone sensor might use 300 microwatts (μW).
- Bluetooth Low Energy might use 40 mW.
- A 320 × 320-pixel monochrome image sensor (like the Himax HM01B0) could use 1 mW at 30 FPS.
- An Ambiq Cortex-M4F microcontroller might use 1 mW at 48 MHz clock rate.
- An accelerometer might use 1 mW.

These numbers will vary a lot depending on the exact components you use, but they're useful to remember so that you at least know the rough proportions of different operations. One top-level summary is that radio uses a lot more power than other functionality you might need in an embedded product. Additionally, it seems like sensor and processor energy requirements are dropping much faster than communications power, so it's likely that the gap will increase even more in the future.

Once you have an idea of what the active components in your system are likely to use, you'll need to think about how much energy you can store or harvest to power them. Here are some rough figures (thanks to James Meyers (*https://oreil.ly/DLf4t*) for the energy harvesting estimates):

- A CR2032 coin battery might hold 2,500 J. This means that if your system is using one mW of power on average, you could hope to get roughly a month of use.
- An AA battery might have 15,000 J, giving a six-month lifetime for a 1 mW system.
- Harvesting temperature differences from an industrial machine could yield 1 to 10 mW per square centimeter.
- Power from indoor light could give 10 μW per square centimeter.
- Outdoor light might enable you to harvest 10 mW for each square centimeter.

As you can see, only industrial temperature differentials or outdoor lighting is currently practical for self-powering devices, but as the energy requirements of processors and sensors drop, we hope using other methods will start to be possible. You can follow commercial suppliers like Matrix (*https://www.matrixindustries.com/en/energy-harvesting*) or e-peas (*https://e-peas.com*) to see some of the latest energy harvesting devices.

Hopefully these ballpark numbers will help you sketch out what kind of system might be practical for your combination of lifetime, cost, and size requirements. They should be enough for at least an initial feasibility check, and if you can internalize them as intuitions, you'll be able to quickly think through a lot of different potential trade-offs.

Hardware Choice

When you have a rough idea of what kinds of components you might use in your product, you'll need to look at real parts you can purchase. If you're looking for something that's well documented and accessible to hobbyists, it's good to start by browsing sites like SparkFun's (*https://www.sparkfun.com*), Arduino's (*https://www.arduino.cc*), or AdaFruit's (*https://www.adafruit.com*). These offer components that come with tutorials, drivers, and advice on connecting to other parts. They are also the best place to start prototyping, because you might well be able to get a complete system with everything you need already populated. The biggest downsides are that you will have a more limited selection, the integrated systems might not be optimized for overall power usage, and you will be paying a premium for the extra resources.

For more choice and lower prices, but without the valuable support, you can try electronics suppliers like Digi-Key (*https://www.digikey.com*), Mouser Electronics (*https://www.mouser.com*), or even Alibaba (*https://oreil.ly/Td-0l*). What all of these sites have in common is that they should supply datasheets for all of their products. These contain a wealth of detail about each part: everything from how to supply clock signals to mechanical data on the size of the chip and its pins. The first thing you'll probably want to understand, though, is the power usage, and this can be surprisingly difficult to find. As an example, look at the datasheet for an STMicroelectronics Cortex-M0 MCU (*https://oreil.ly/fOuLf*). There are almost a hundred pages, and it's not obvious from glancing at the table of contents how to find the power usage. One trick we've found helpful is to search for "milliamps" or "ma" (with the spaces) within these documents, because they're often the units that are used to express power usage. In this datasheet that search leads to a table on page 47, shown in Figure 16-1, which provides values for current consumption.

Table 25. Typical and maximum current consumption from V$_{DD}$ supply at V$_{DD}$ = 3.6 V[1]

Symbol	Parameter	Conditions	f$_{HCLK}$	All peripherals enabled		Unit
				Typ	Max @ T$_A$[2] 85 °C	
I$_{DD}$	Supply current in Run mode, code executing from Flash	HSI or HSE clock, PLL on	48 MHz	22.0	22.8	mA
			48 MHz	26.8	30.2	
			24 MHz	12.2	13.2	
			24 MHz	14.1	16.2	
		HSI or HSE clock, PLL off	8 MHz	4.4	5.2	
			8 MHz	4.9	5.6	
I$_{DD}$	Supply current in Run mode, code executing from RAM	HSI or HSE clock, PLL on	48 MHz	22.2	23.2	mA
			48 MHz	26.1	29.3	
			24 MHz	11.2	12.2	
			24 MHz	13.3	15.7	
		HSI or HSE clock, PLL off	8 MHz	4.0	4.5	
			8 MHz	4.6	5.2	
I$_{DD}$	Supply current in Sleep mode, code executing from Flash or RAM	HSI or HSE clock, PLL on	48 MHz	14	15.3	mA
			48 MHz	17.0	19.0	
			24 MHz	7.3	7.8	
			24 MHz	8.7	10.1	
		HSI or HSE clock, PLL off	8 MHz	2.6	2.9	
			8 MHz	3.0	3.5	

1. The gray shading is used to distinguish the values for STM32F030xC devices.
2. Data based on characterization results, not tested in production unless otherwise specified.

Figure 16-1. Current consumption table from STMicroelectronics

This still can be tough to interpret, but what we're generally interested in is how many watts (or milliwatts) this chip might use. To get that, we need to multiply the amps shown by the voltage, which is listed as 3.6 volts here (we've highlighted this at the top of the table). If we do that, we can see that the typical power used ranges from nearly a 100 mW down to only 10 when it's in sleep mode. This gives us an idea that the MCU is comparatively power-hungry, though its price at 55 cents might compensate for that, depending on your trade-offs. You should be able to perform similar kinds of detective work for the datasheets of all the components you're interested in using, and assemble a picture of the likely overall power usage based on the sum of all these parts.

Measuring Real Power Usage

Once you have a set of components, you'll need to assemble them into a complete system. That process is beyond the scope of this book, but we do recommend that you try to get something completed as early as possible in the process so that you can try out the product in the real world and learn more about its requirements. Even if you aren't using quite the components you want to or don't have all the software ready, getting early feedback is invaluable.

Another benefit of having a complete system is that you can test the actual power usage. Datasheets and estimates are helpful for planning, but there's always something that doesn't fit into a simple model, and integration testing will often show much higher power consumption than you expect.

There are a lot of tools that you can use to measure the power consumption of a system, and knowing how to use a multimeter (a device for measuring various electrical properties) can be very helpful, but the most reliable method is to place a battery with a known capacity in the device and then see how long it lasts. This is what you actually care about, after all, and although you might be aiming for a lifetime of months or years, most likely your first attempts will run for only hours or days. The advantage of this experimental approach is that it captures all the effects you care about, including things like failures when the voltage drops too low, which probably won't show up in simple modeling calculations. It is also so simple that even a software engineer can manage it!

Estimating Power Usage for a Model

The simplest way to estimate how much power a model will use on a particular device is to measure the latency for running one inference, and then multiply the average power usage of the system for that time period to get the energy usage. At the start of a project you're not likely to have hard figures for the latency and power usage, but you can come up with ballpark figures. If you know how many arithmetic operations a model requires, and roughly how many operations per second a processor can perform, you can roughly estimate the time that model will take to execute. Datasheets will usually give you numbers for the power usage of a device at a particular frequency and voltage, though beware that they probably won't include common parts of the whole system like memory or peripherals. It's worth taking these early estimates with a big pinch of salt and using them as an upper bound on what you might achieve, but at least you can get some idea of the feasibility of your approach.

As an example, if you have a model that takes 60 million operations to execute, like the person detector, and you have a chip like an Arm Cortex-M4 running at 48 MHz, and you believe it can perform two 8-bit multiply/adds per cycle using its DSP extensions, you might guess that the maximum latency would be 30,000,000/48,000,000 = 625 ms. If your chip uses 2 mW, that would work out to 1.25 mJ per inference.

Improving Power Usage

Now that you know the approximate lifetime of your system, you'll probably be looking at ways to improve it. You might be able to find hardware modifications that help, including turning off modules that you don't need or replacing components, but those are beyond what this book will cover. Luckily, there are some common techniques that don't require electrical engineering knowledge but can help a lot. Because these approaches are software-focused, they do assume that the microcontroller itself is taking the bulk of the power. If sensors or other components in your device are power hogs, you will need to do a hardware investigation.

Duty Cycling

Almost all embedded processors have the ability to put themselves into a sleep mode in which they don't perform any computation and use very little power, but are able to wake up either after an interval or when a signal comes in from outside. This means that one of the simplest ways of reducing power is to insert sleeps between inference calls, so that the processor spends more time in a low-power mode. This is commonly known as *duty cycling* in the embedded world. You might worry that this excludes continuous sensor data gathering, but many modern microcontrollers have direct memory access (DMA) capabilities that are able to sample analog-to-digital converters (ADCs) continuously and store the results in memory without any involvement from the main processor.

In a similar way, you might be able to reduce the frequency at which the processor executes instructions so that in effect it runs more slowly, dramatically reducing the power it uses. The datasheet example shown earlier demonstrates how the energy required drops as the clock frequency decreases.

What duty cycling and frequency reduction offer is the ability to trade computation for power usage. What this means in practice is that if you can reduce the latency of your software, you can trade that for a lower power budget. Even if you are able to run within your allotted time, look at ways to optimize latency if you want a reduction in power usage.

Cascading Design

One of the big advantages of machine learning over traditional procedural programming is that it makes it easy to scale up or down the amount of compute and storage resources required, and the accuracy will usually degrade gracefully. It's more difficult to achieve this with manually coded algorithms, since there aren't usually obvious parameters that you can tweak to affect these properties. What this means is that you can create what's known as a *cascade of models*. Sensor data can be fed into a very small model with minimal compute requirements, and even though it's not particularly accurate, it can be tuned so that it has a high likelihood of triggering when a particular condition is present (even if it also produces a lot of false positives). If the result indicates that something interesting has just happened, the same inputs can be fed into a more complex model to produce a more accurate result. This process can potentially be repeated for several more stages.

The reason this is useful is that the inaccurate but tiny model can fit into a very power-efficient embedded device, and running it continuously won't drain much energy. When a potential event is spotted, a more powerful system can be woken up and a larger model run, and so on down the cascade. Because the more powerful systems are operating for only a small fraction of the time, their power usage doesn't break the budget. This is how always-on voice interfaces work on phones. A DSP is constantly monitoring the microphone, with a model listening for "Alexa," "Siri," "Hey Google," or a similar wake word. The main CPU can be left in a sleep mode, but when the DSP thinks it might have heard the right phrase, it will signal to wake it up. The CPU can then run a much larger and more accurate model to confirm whether it really was the right phrase, and perhaps send the following speech to an even more powerful processor in the cloud if it was.

This means that an embedded product might be able to achieve its goals even if it can't host a model that's accurate enough to be actionable by itself. If you are able to train a network that's able to spot most true positives, and the false positives occur at a low enough frequency, you might be able offload the remaining work to the cloud. Radio is very power-hungry, but if you're able to limit its use to rare occasions and for short periods, it might fit in your energy budget.

Wrapping Up

For many of us (your authors included), optimizing for energy consumption is an unfamiliar process. Luckily, a lot of the skills we covered for latency optimization also apply here, just with different metrics to monitor. It's generally a good idea to focus on latency optimizations before energy, because you'll often need to validate that your product works using a version that gives the short-term user experience you want, even if its lifetime isn't long enough to be useful in the real world. In the same way, it often makes sense to tackle the subject of Chapter 17, space optimization, after latency and energy. In practice you're likely to iterate back and forth between all the different trade-offs to meet your constraints, but size is often easiest to work on after the other aspects are fairly stable.

Optimizing Model and Binary Size

Whatever platform you choose, it's likely that flash storage and RAM will be very limited. Most embedded systems have less than 1 MB of read-only storage in flash, and many have only tens of kilobytes. The same is true for memory: there's seldom more than 512 KB of static RAM (SRAM) available, and on low-end devices that figure could be in the low single digits. The good news is that TensorFlow Lite for Microcontrollers is designed to work with as little as 20 KB of flash and 4 KB of SRAM, but you will need to design your application carefully and make engineering trade-offs to keep the footprint low. This chapter covers some of the approaches that you can use to monitor and control your memory and storage requirements.

Understanding Your System's Limits

Most embedded systems have an architecture in which programs and other read-only data are stored in flash memory, which is written to only when new executables are uploaded. There's usually also modifiable memory available, often using SRAM technology. This is the same technology used for caches on larger CPUs, and it gives fast access for low power consumption, but it's limited in size. More advanced microcontrollers can offer a second tier of modifiable memory, using a more power-hungry but scalable technology like dynamic RAM (DRAM).

You'll need to understand what potential platforms offer and what the trade-offs are. For example, a chip that has a lot of secondary DRAM might be attractive for its flexibility, but if enabling that extra memory blows past your power budget, it might not be worth it. If you're operating in the 1 mW-and-below power range that this book focuses on it's usually not possible to use anything beyond SRAM, because larger memory approaches will consume too much energy. That means that the two key metrics you'll need to consider are how much flash read-only storage is available and how much SRAM is available. These numbers should be listed in the description of any chip you're looking at. Hopefully you won't even need to dig as deeply as the datasheet "Hardware Choice" on page 417.

Estimating Memory Usage

When you have an idea of what your hardware options are, you need to develop an understanding of what resources your software will need and what trade offs you can make to control those requirements.

Flash Usage

You can usually determine exactly how much room you'll need in flash by compiling a complete executable, and then looking at the size of the resulting image. This can be confusing, because the first artifact that the linker produces is often an annotated version of the executable with debug symbols and section information, in a format like ELF (which we discuss in more detail in "Measuring Code Size" on page 429. The file you want to look at is the actual one that's flashed to the device, often produced by a tool like objcopy. The simplest equation for gauging the amount of flash memory you need is the sum of the following factors:

Operating system size
> If you're using any kind of real-time operating system (RTOS), you'll need space in your executable to hold its code. This will usually be configurable depending on which features you're using, and the simplest way to estimate the footprint is to build a sample "hello world" program with the features you need enabled. If you look at the image file size, this will give you a baseline for how large the OS program code is. Typical modules that can take up a lot of program space include USB, WiFi, Bluetooth, and cellular radio stacks, so ensure that these are enabled if you intend to use them.

TensorFlow Lite for Microcontrollers code size
> The ML framework needs space for the program logic to load and execute a neural network model, including the operator implementations that run the core arithmetic. Later in this chapter we discuss how to configure the framework to reduce the size for particular applications, but to get started just compile one of the standard unit tests (like the micro_speech test (*https://oreil.ly/7cafy*)) that includes the framework and look at the resulting image size for an estimate.

Model data size
> If you don't yet have a model trained, you can get a good estimate of the amount of flash storage space it will need by counting its weights. For example, a fully connected layer will have a number of weights equal to the size of its input vector multiplied by the size of its output vector. For convolutional layers, it's a bit more complex; you'll need to multiply the width and height of the filter box by the

number of input channels, and multiply this by the number of filters. You also need to add on storage space for any bias vectors associated with each layer. This can quickly become complex to calculate, so it can be easier just to create a candidate model in TensorFlow and then export it to a TensorFlow Lite file. This file will be directly mapped into flash, so its size will give you an exact figure for how much space it will take up. You can also look at the number of weights listed by Keras's `model.summary()` method (*https://keras.io/models/about-keras-models*).

 We introduced quantization in Chapter 4 and discussed it further in Chapter 15, but it's worth a quick refresher in the context of model size. During training, weights are usually stored as floating-point values, taking up 4-bytes each in memory. Because space is such a constraint for mobile and embedded devices, TensorFlow Lite supports compressing those values down to a single byte in a process called *quantization*. It works by keeping track of the minimum and maximum values stored in a float array, and then converting all the values linearly to the closest of 256 values equally spaced within that range. These codes are each stored in a byte, and arithmetic operations can be performed on them with a minimal loss of accuracy.

Application code size

You'll need code to access sensor data, preprocess it to prepare it for the neural network, and respond to the results. You might also need some other kinds of user interface and business logic outside of the machine learning module. This can be difficult to estimate, but you should at least try to understand whether you'll need any external libraries (for example, for fast Fourier transforms) and calculate what their code space requirements will be.

RAM Usage

Determining the amount of modifiable memory you'll need can be more of a challenge than understanding the storage requirements, because the amount of RAM used varies over the life of your program. In a similar way to the process of estimating flash requirements, you'll need to look at the different layers of your software to estimate the overall usage requirements:

Operating system size

Most RTOSs (like FreeRTOS) (*https://www.freertos.org/FAQMem.html*) document how much RAM their different configuration options need, and you should be able to use this information to plan the required size. You will need to watch for modules that might require buffers—especially communication stacks like TCP/IP, WiFi, or Bluetooth. These will need to be added to any core OS requirements.

TensorFlow Lite for Microcontrollers RAM size

The ML framework doesn't have large memory needs for its core runtime and shouldn't require more than a few kilobytes of space in SRAM for its data structures. These are allocated as part of the classes used for the interpreter, so whether your application code creates these as global or local objects will determine whether they're on the stack or in general memory. We generally recommend creating them as global or `static` objects, because the lack of space will usually cause an error at linker time, whereas stack-allocated locals can cause a runtime crash that's more difficult to understand.

Model memory size

When a neural network is executed, the results of one layer are fed into subsequent operations and so must be kept around for some time. The lifetimes of these activation layers vary depending on their position in the graph, and the memory size needed for each is controlled by the shape of the array that a layer writes out. These variations mean that it's necessary to calculate a plan over time to fit all these temporary buffers into as small an area of memory as possible. Currently this is done when the model is first loaded by the interpreter, so if the arena is not big enough, you'll see an error on the console. If you see the difference between the available memory and what's required in the error message and increase the arena by that amount, you should be able to run past that error.

Application memory size

Like the program size, memory usage for your application logic can be difficult to calculate before it's written. You can make some guesses about larger users of memory, though, such as buffers that you'll need for storing incoming sample data, or areas of memory that libraries will need for preprocessing.

Ballpark Figures for Model Accuracy and Size on Different Problems

It's helpful to understand what the current state of the art is for different kinds of problems in order to help you plan for what you might be able to achieve for your application. Machine learning isn't magic, and having a sense of its limitations will help you make smart trade-offs as you're building your product. Chapter 14, which examines the design process, is a good place to begin developing your intuition, but you'll also need to think about how accuracy degrades as models are forced into tight resource constraints. To help with that, here are a few examples of architectures designed for embedded systems. If one of them is close to what you need to do, it might help you to envision what you could achieve at the end of your model creation process. Obviously your actual results will depend a lot on your specific product and environment, so use these as guidelines for planning and don't rely on being able to achieve exactly the same performance.

Speech Wake-Word Model

The small (18 KB) model using 400,000 arithmetic operations that we covered earlier as a code sample is able to achieve 85% top-one accuracy (see "Establish a Metric" on page 441) when distinguishing between four classes of sound: silence, unknown words, "yes," and "no." This is the training evaluation metric, which means it's the result of presenting one-second clips and asking the model to do a one-shot classification of its input. In practice, you'd usually use the model on streaming audio, repeatedly predicting a result based on a one-second window that's incrementally moving forward in time, so the actual accuracy in practical applications is lower than that figure might suggest. You should generally think about an audio model this size as a first-stage gatekeeper in a larger cascade of processing, so that its errors can be tolerated and dealt with by more complex models.

As a rule of thumb, you might need a model with 300 to 400 KB of weights and low-tens-of-millions of arithmetic operations to be able to detect a wake word with acceptable enough accuracy to use in a voice interface. Unfortunately you'll also need a commercial-quality dataset to train on, given that there still aren't enough open repositories of labeled speech data available, but hopefully that restriction will ease over time.

Accelerometer Predictive Maintenance Model

There are a wide range of different predictive maintenance problems, but one of the simpler cases is detecting a bearing failure in a motor. This often appears as distinctive shaking that can be spotted as patterns in accelerometer data. A reasonable model to spot these patterns might require only a few thousand weights, making it less than 10 KB in size, and a few hundred thousand arithmetic operations. You could expect better than 95% accuracy at classifying these events with such a model, and you can imagine scaling up the complexity of your model from there to handle more difficult problems (such as detecting failures on a machine with many moving parts or that's traveling itself). Of course, the number of parameters and operations would scale up, as well.

Person Presence Detection

Computer vision hasn't been a common task on embedded platforms, so we're still figuring out what applications make sense. One common request we've heard is the ability to detect when a person is nearby, to wake up a user interface or do other more power-hungry processing that it's not possible to leave running all the time. We've tried to formally capture the requirements of this problem in the Visual Wake Word Challenge (*https://oreil.ly/E8GoU*), and the results show that you can expect roughly 90% accuracy with binary classification of a small (96 × 96–pixel) monochrome image if you use a 250 KB model and around 60 million arithmetic operations. This is the baseline from using a scaled-down MobileNet v2 architecture (as described earlier in the book), so we hope to see the accuracy improve as more researchers tackle this specialized set of requirements, but it gives you a rough estimate of how well you might be able to do on visual problems within a microcontroller's memory footprint. You might wonder how such a small model would do on the popular ImageNet–1,000 category problem—it's hard to say exactly because the final fully connected layer for a thousand classes quickly takes up a hundred or more kilobytes (the number of parameters is the embedding input multiplied by the class count), but for a total size of around 500 KB, you could expect somewhere around 50% top-one accuracy.

Model Choice

In terms of optimizing model and binary size, we highly recommend starting with an existing model. As we discuss in Chapter 14, the most fruitful area to invest in is data gathering and improvement rather than tweaking architectures, and starting with a known model will let you focus on data improvements as early as possible. Machine learning software on embedded platforms is also still in its early stages, so using an existing model increases the chances that its ops are supported and well-optimized on the devices you care about. We're hoping that the code samples accompanying this book will be good starting points for a lot of different applications—we chose them to cover as many different kinds of sensor input as we could—but if they don't fit your use cases you might be able to search for some alternatives online. If you can't find a size-optimized architecture that's suitable, you can look into building your own from scratch in the training environment of TensorFlow, but as Chapters Chapter 13 and Chapter 19 discuss, it can be an involved process to successfully port that onto a microcontroller.

Reducing the Size of Your Executable

Your model is likely to be one of the biggest consumers of read-only memory in a microcontroller application, but you also must think about how much space your compiled code takes. This constraint on code size is the reason that we can't just use an unmodified version of TensorFlow Lite when targeting embedded platforms: it would take up many hundreds of kilobytes of flash memory. TensorFlow Lite for Microcontrollers can compile down to as little as 20 KB, but this can require you to make some changes to exclude the parts of the code that you don't need for your application.

Measuring Code Size

Before you begin optimizing the size of your code, you need to know how big it is. This can be a little tricky on embedded platforms because the output of the building process is often a file that includes debugging and other information that's not transferred onto the embedded device and so shouldn't count toward the total size limit. On Arm and other modern toolchains this is often known as an Executable and Linking Format (ELF) file, whether or not it has an *.elf* suffix. If you're on a Linux or macOS development machine, you can run the `file` command to investigate the output of your toolchain; it will show you whether a file is an ELF.

The better file to look at is what's often known as the *bin*: the binary snapshot of the code that's actually uploaded to the flash storage of an embedded device. This will usually be exactly the size of the read-only flash memory that will be used, so you can use it to understand what the usage actually is. You can find out its size by using a command line like `ls -l` or `dir` on the host, or even inspecting it in a GUI file viewer. Not all toolchains automatically show you this *bin* file, and it might not have any suffix, but it's the file that you download and drag onto your device through USB on Mbed, and with the gcc toolchain you produce it by running something like `arm-none-eabi-objcopy app.elf app.bin -O binary`. It's not helpful to look at the *.o* intermediates, or even the *.a* libraries that the build process produces, because they contain a lot of metadata that doesn't make it into the final code footprint, and a lot of the code might be pruned as unused.

Because we expect you to compile your model into your executable as a C data array (since you can't rely on a filesystem being present to load it from), the binary size you see for any program including the model will contain the model data. To understand how much space your actual code is taking, you'll need to subtract this model size from the binary file length. The model size should usually be defined in the file that contains the C data array (like at the end of *tiny_conv_micro_features_model_data.cc* (*https://oreil.ly/Vknl2*)), so you can subtract that from the binary file size to understand the real code footprint.

How Much Space Is Tensorflow Lite for Microcontrollers Taking?

When you know your entire application's code footprint size, you might want to investigate how much space is being taken up by TensorFlow Lite. The simplest way to test this is by commenting out all your calls to the framework (including the creation of objects like `OpResolvers` and interpreters) and seeing how much smaller the binary becomes. You should expect at least a 20 to 30 KB decrease, so if you don't see anything like that, you should double-check that you've caught all the references. This should work because the linker will strip out any code that you're never calling, removing it from the footprint. This can be extended to other modules of your code, too—as long as you ensure there are no references—to help create a better understanding of where the space is going.

OpResolver

TensorFlow Lite supports over a hundred operations, but it's unlikely that you'll need all of them within a single model. The individual implementations of each operation might take up only a few kilobytes, but the total quickly adds up with so many available. Luckily, there is a built-in mechanism to remove the code footprint of operations you don't need.

When TensorFlow Lite loads a model, it searches for implementations of each included op using the `OpResolver` interface (*https://oreil.ly/dfwOP*). This is a class you pass into the interpreter to load a model, and it contains the logic to find the function pointers to an op's implementation given the op definition. The reason this exists is so that you can control which implementations are actually linked in. For most of the sample code, you'll see that we're creating and passing in an instance of the `AllOpsResolver` class (*https://oreil.ly/tbzg6*). As we discussed in Chapter 5, this implements the `OpResolver` interface, and as the name implies, it has an entry for every operation that's supported in TensorFlow Lite for Microcontrollers. This is convenient for getting started, because it means that you can load any supported model without worrying about what operations it contains.

When you get to the point of worrying about code size, however, you'll want to revisit this class. Instead of passing in an instance of `AllOpsResolver` in your application's main loop, copy the *all_ops_resolver.cc* and *.h* files into your application and rename them to *my_app_resolver.cc* and *.h*, with the class renamed to `MyAppResolver`. Inside the constructor of your class, remove all the `AddBuiltin()` calls that apply to ops that you don't use within your model. Unfortunately we do not know of an easy automatic way to create the list of operations a model uses, but the Netron (*https://oreil.ly/MKqF9*) model viewer is a nice tool that can help with the process.

Make sure that you replace the `AllOpsResolver` instance you were passing into your interpreter with `MyAppResolver`. Now, as soon as you compile your app, you should see the size noticeably shrink. The reason behind this change is that most linkers automatically try to remove code that can't be called (or *dead code*). By removing the references that were in `AllOpsResolver`, you allow the linker to determine that it can exclude all the op implementations that are no longer listed.

If you use only a few ops, you don't need to wrap registration in a new class, like we do with the large `AllOpsResolver`. Instead, you can create an instance of the `MicroMutableOpResolver` class and directly add the op registrations you need. `MicroMutableOpResolver` implements the `OpResolver` interface, but has additional methods that let you add ops to the list (which is why it's named `Mutable`). This is the class that's used to implement `AllOpsResolver`, and it's a good base for any of your own resolver classes, too, but it can be simpler to call it directly. We use this approach in some of the examples, and you can see how it works in this snippet from the `micro_speech` example (*https://oreil.ly/gdZts*):

```
static tflite::MicroMutableOpResolver micro_mutable_op_resolver;
micro_mutable_op_resolver.AddBuiltin(
    tflite::BuiltinOperator_DEPTHWISE_CONV_2D,
    tflite::ops::micro::Register_DEPTHWISE_CONV_2D());
micro_mutable_op_resolver.AddBuiltin(
    tflite::BuiltinOperator_FULLY_CONNECTED,
    tflite::ops::micro::Register_FULLY_CONNECTED());
micro_mutable_op_resolver.AddBuiltin(tflite::BuiltinOperator_SOFTMAX,
                                    tflite::ops::micro::Register_SOFTMAX());
```

You might notice that we're declaring the resolver object as `static`. This is because the interpreter can call into it at any time, so its lifetime needs to be at least as long as the object we created for the interpreter.

Understanding the Size of Individual Functions

If you're using the GCC toolchain, you can use tools like `nm` to get information on the size of functions and objects in object (*.o*) intermediate files. Here's an example of building a binary and then inspecting the size of items in the compiled *audio_provider.cc* object file:

```
nm -S tensorflow/lite/micro/tools/make/gen/ \
  sparkfun_edge_cortex-m4/obj/tensorflow/lite/micro/ \
  examples/micro_speech/sparkfun_edge/audio_provider.o
```

You should see results that look something like this:

```
00000140 t $d
00000258 t $d
00000088 t $d
00000008 t $d
00000000 b $d
00000000 b $d
00000000 b $d
00000000 b $d
00000000 b $d
00000000 b $d
00000000 b $d
00000000 b $d
00000000 b $d
00000000 b $d
00000000 b $d
00000000 r $d
00000000 r $d
00000000 t $t
```

```
00000000 t $t
00000000 t $t
00000000 t $t
00000001 00000178 T am_adc_isr
         U am_hal_adc_configure
         U am_hal_adc_configure_dma
         U am_hal_adc_configure_slot
         U am_hal_adc_enable
         U am_hal_adc_initialize
         U am_hal_adc_interrupt_clear
         U am_hal_adc_interrupt_enable
         U am_hal_adc_interrupt_status
         U am_hal_adc_power_control
         U am_hal_adc_sw_trigger
         U am_hal_burst_mode_enable
         U am_hal_burst_mode_initialize
         U am_hal_cachectrl_config
         U am_hal_cachectrl_defaults
         U am_hal_cachectrl_enable
         U am_hal_clkgen_control
         U am_hal_ctimer_adc_trigger_enable
         U am_hal_ctimer_config_single
         U am_hal_ctimer_int_enable
         U am_hal_ctimer_period_set
         U am_hal_ctimer_start
         U am_hal_gpio_pinconfig
         U am_hal_interrupt_master_enable
         U g_AM_HAL_GPIO_OUTPUT_12
00000001 0000009c T _Z15GetAudioSamplesPN6tflite13ErrorReporterEiiPiPPs
00000001 000002c4 T _Z18InitAudioRecordingPN6tflite13ErrorReporterE
00000001 0000000c T _Z20LatestAudioTimestampv
00000000 00000001 b _ZN12_GLOBAL__N_115g_adc_dma_errorE
00000000 00000400 b _ZN12_GLOBAL__N_121g_audio_output_bufferE
00000000 00007d00 b _ZN12_GLOBAL__N_122g_audio_capture_bufferE
00000000 00000001 b _ZN12_GLOBAL__N_122g_is_audio_initializedE
00000000 00002000 b _ZN12_GLOBAL__N_122g_ui32ADCSampleBuffer0E
00000000 00002000 b _ZN12_GLOBAL__N_122g_ui32ADCSampleBuffer1E
00000000 00000004 b _ZN12_GLOBAL__N_123g_dma_destination_indexE
00000000 00000004 b _ZN12_GLOBAL__N_124g_adc_dma_error_reporterE
00000000 00000004 b _ZN12_GLOBAL__N_124g_latest_audio_timestampE
00000000 00000008 b _ZN12_GLOBAL__N_124g_total_samples_capturedE
00000000 00000004 b _ZN12_GLOBAL__N_128g_audio_capture_buffer_startE
00000000 00000004 b _ZN12_GLOBAL__N_1L12g_adc_handleE
         U _ZN6tflite13ErrorReporter6ReportEPKcz
```

Many of these symbols are internal details or irrelevant, but the last few are recognizable as functions we define in *audio_provider.cc*, with their names mangled to match C++ linker conventions. The second column shows what their size is in hexadecimal. You can see here that the InitAudioRecording() function is 0x2c4 or 708 bytes, which could be quite significant on a small microcontroller, so if space were tight it would be worth investigating where the size inside the function is coming from.

The best way we've found to do this is to disassemble the functions with the source code intermingled. Luckily, the `objdump` tool lets us do this by using the `-S` flag—but unlike with `nm`, you can't use the standard version that's installed on your Linux or macOS desktop. Instead, you need to use one that came with your toolchain. This will usually be downloaded automatically if you're using the TensorFlow Lite for Micro-controllers Makefile to build. It will exist somewhere like *tensorflow/lite/micro/tools/ make/downloads/gcc_embedded/bin*. Here's a command to run to see more about the functions inside *audio_provider.cc*:

```
tensorflow/lite/micro/tools/make/downloads/gcc_embedded/bin/ \
  arm-none-eabi-objdump -S tensorflow/lite/micro/tools/make/gen/ \
  sparkfun_edge_cortex-m4/obj/tensorflow/lite/micro/examples/ \
  micro_speech/sparkfun_edge/audio_provider.o
```

We won't show all of the output, because it's so long; instead, we present an abridged version showing only the function we were curious about:

```
...
Disassembly of section .text._Z18InitAudioRecordingPN6tflite13ErrorReporterE:

00000000 <_Z18InitAudioRecordingPN6tflite13ErrorReporterE>:

TfLiteStatus InitAudioRecording(tflite::ErrorReporter* error_reporter) {
   0:   b570        push {r4, r5, r6, lr}
   // Set the clock frequency.
   if (AM_HAL_STATUS_SUCCESS !=
       am_hal_clkgen_control(AM_HAL_CLKGEN_CONTROL_SYSCLK_MAX, 0)) {
   2:   2100        movs r1, #0
TfLiteStatus InitAudioRecording(tflite::ErrorReporter* error_reporter) {
   4:   b088        sub  sp, #32
   6:   4604        mov  r4, r0
       am_hal_clkgen_control(AM_HAL_CLKGEN_CONTROL_SYSCLK_MAX, 0)) {
   8:   4608        mov  r0, r1
   a:   f7ff fffe   bl   0 <am_hal_clkgen_control>
   if (AM_HAL_STATUS_SUCCESS !=
   e:   2800        cmp  r0, #0
  10:   f040 80e1   bne.w       1d6 <_Z18InitAudioRecordingPN6tflite13ErrorRe-
porterE+0x1d6>
     return kTfLiteError;
   }

   // Set the default cache configuration and enable it.
   if (AM_HAL_STATUS_SUCCESS !=
       am_hal_cachectrl_config(&am_hal_cachectrl_defaults)) {
  14:   4890        ldr  r0, [pc, #576]  ; (244 <am_hal_cachectrl_config+0x244>)
  16:   f7ff fffe   bl   0 <am_hal_cachectrl_config>
   if (AM_HAL_STATUS_SUCCESS !=
  1a:   2800        cmp  r0, #0
  1c:   f040 80d4   bne.w       1c8 <_Z18InitAudioRecordingPN6tflite13ErrorRe-
porterE+0x1c8>
     error_reporter->Report("Error - configuring the system cache failed.");
```

```
        return kTfLiteError;
    }
    if (AM_HAL_STATUS_SUCCESS != am_hal_cachectrl_enable()) {
    20:    f7ff fffe    bl      0 <am_hal_cachectrl_enable>
    24:    2800         cmp    r0, #0
    26:    f040 80dd    bne.w              1e4 <_Z18InitAudioRecordingPN6tflite13Error\
       ReporterE+0x1e4>
    ...
```

You don't need to understand what the assembly is doing, but hopefully you can see where the space is going by seeing how the function size (the number on the far left of the disassembled lines; for example, hexadecimal *10* at the end of InitAudioRecording()) increases for each of the C++ source lines. What is revealed if you look at the entire function is that all of the hardware initialization code has been inlined within the InitAudioRecording() implementation, which explains why it's so large.

Framework Constants

There are a few places in the library code where we use hardcoded sizes for arrays to avoid dynamic memory allocation. If RAM space becomes very tight, it's worth experimenting to see whether you can reduce them for your application (or, for very complex use cases, you might even need to increase them). One of these arrays is TFLITE_REGISTRATIONS_MAX (*https://oreil.ly/hYTLi*), which controls how many different operations can be registered. The default is 128, which is probably far too many for most applications—especially given that it creates an array of 128 TfLiteRegistra tion structs, which are at least 32 bytes each, requiring 4 KB of RAM. You can also look at lesser offenders like kStackDataAllocatorSize (*https://oreil.ly/wIsPm*) in MicroInterpreter, or try shrinking the size of the arena you pass into the constructor of your interpreter.

Truly Tiny Models

A lot of the advice in this chapter is related to embedded systems that can afford to use 20 KB of code footprint on framework code to run machine learning, and aren't trying to scrape by with less than 10 KB of RAM. If you have a device with extremely tight resource constraints—for example, just a couple of kilobytes of RAM or flash—you aren't going to be able to use the same approach. For those environments, you will need to write custom code and hand-tune everything extremely carefully to reduce the size.

We hope that TensorFlow Lite for Microcontrollers can still be useful in these situations, though. We recommend that you still train a model in TensorFlow, even if it's tiny, and then use the export workflow to create a TensorFlow Lite model file from it. This can be a good starting point for extracting the weights, and you can use the existing framework code to verify the results of your custom version. The reference implementations of the ops you're using should be good starting points for your own op code, too; they should be portable, understandable, and memory efficient, even if they're not optimal for latency.

Wrapping Up

In this chapter, we looked at some of the best techniques to shrink the amount of storage you need for your embedded machine learning project. This is likely to be one of the toughest constraints you'll need to overcome, but when you have an application that's small enough, fast enough, and doesn't use too much energy, you've got a clear path to shipping your product. What remains is rooting out all of the inevitable gremlins that will cause your device to behave in unexpected ways. Debugging can be a frustrating process (we've heard it described as a murder mystery where you're the detective, the victim, and the murderer), but it's an essential skill to learn to get products out the door. Chapter 18 covers the basic techniques that can help you understand what's happening in a machine learning system.

Debugging

You're bound to run into some confusing errors as you integrate machine learning into your product, embedded or otherwise, and probably sooner rather than later. In this chapter, we discuss some approaches to understanding what's happening when things go wrong.

Accuracy Loss Between Training and Deployment

There are a lot of ways for problems to creep in when you take a machine learning model out of an authoring environment like TensorFlow and deploy it into an application. Even after you're able to get a model building and running without reporting any errors, you might still not be getting the results you expect in terms of accuracy. This can be very frustrating because the neural network inference step can seem like a black box, with no visibility into what's happening internally or what's causing any problems.

Preprocessing Differences

An area that doesn't get very much attention in machine learning research is how training samples are converted into a form that a neural network can operate on. If you're trying to do object classification on images, those images must be converted into tensors, which are multidimensional arrays of numbers. You might think that would be straightforward, because images are already stored as 2D arrays, usually with three channels for red, green, and blue values. Even in this case, though, you do still need to make some changes. Classification models expect their inputs to be a particular width and height, for example 224 pixels wide by 224 high, and a camera or other input source is unlikely to produce them in the correct size. This means you'll need to rescale your captured data to match. Something similar has to be done for the training process, because the dataset will probably be a set of arbitrarily sized images on disk.

A subtle problem that often creeps in is that the rescaling method used for a deployment doesn't match the one that was used to train the model. For example, early versions of Inception (*https://oreil.ly/rGKnL*) used bilinear scaling to shrink images, which was confusing to people with a background in image processing because downscaling that way degrades the visual quality of an image and is generally to be avoided. As a result, many developers using these models for inference in their applications instead used the more *correct* approach of area sampling—but it turns out that this actually decreases the accuracy of the results! The intuition is that the trained models had learned to look for the artifacts that bilinear downscaling produces, and their absence caused the top-one error rate to increase by a few percent.

The image preprocessing doesn't stop at the rescaling step, either. There's also the question of how to convert image values typically encoded from 0 to 255 into the floating-point numbers used during training. For several reasons, these are usually linearly scaled into a smaller range: either –1.0 to 1.0 or 0.0 to 1.0. You'll need to do the same value scaling in your application if you're feeding in floating-point values. If you're feeding 8-bit values directly, you won't need to do this at runtime—the original 8-bit values can be used untransformed—but you do still need to pass them into the toco export tool through the `--mean_values` and `--std_values` flags. For a range of –1.0 to 1.0, you'd use `--mean_values=128 --std_values=128`.

Confusingly, it's often not obvious what the correct scale for input image values should be from the model code, since this is a detail that's often buried in the implementation of the APIs used. The Slim framework that a lot of published Google models use defaults to –1.0 to 1.0, so that's a good range to try, but you might end up having to debug through the training Python implementation to figure it out in other cases, if it's not documented.

Even worse, you can end up getting *mostly* correct results even if you get the resizing or value scaling a bit wrong, but you'll degrade the accuracy. This means that your application can appear to work upon a casual inspection, but end up with an overall experience that's less impressive than it should be. And the challenges around image preprocessing are actually a lot simpler than in other areas, like audio or accelerometer data, for which there might be a complex pipeline of feature generation to convert raw data into an array of numbers for the neural network. If you look at the preprocessing code for the `micro_speech` example (*https://oreil.ly/tedw1*), you'll see that we had to implement many stages of signal processing to get from the audio samples to a spectrogram that could be fed into the model, and any difference between this code and the version used in training would degrade the accuracy of the results.

Debugging Preprocessing

Given that these input data transformations are so prone to errors, you might not easily be able to even spot that you have a problem—and if you do, it might be tough to figure out the cause. What are you supposed to do? We've found that there are a few approaches that can help.

It's always best to have some version of your code that you can run on a desktop machine if at all possible, even if the peripherals are stubbed out. You'll have much better debugging tools in a Linux, macOS, or Windows environment, and it's easy to transfer test data between your training tools and the application. For the sample code in TensorFlow Lite for Microcontrollers, we've broken the different parts of our applications into modules and enabled Makefile building for Linux and macOS targets, so we can run the inference and preprocessing stages separately.

The most important tool for debugging preprocessing problems is comparing results between the training environment and what you're seeing in your application. The most difficult part of doing this is extracting the correct values for the nodes you care about during training and controlling what the inputs are. It's beyond the scope of this book to cover how to do this in detail, but you'll need to identify the names of the ops that correspond to the core neural network stages (after file decoding, preprocessing, and the first op that takes in the results of the preprocessing). The first op that takes in the results of the preprocessing corresponds to the `--input_arrays` argument to toco. If you can identify these ops, insert a `tf.print` (*https://oreil.ly/ JYT_m*) op with `summarize` set to `-1` after each of them in Python. You'll then be able to see printouts of the contents of the tensors at each stage in the debug console if you run a training loop.

You should then be able to take these tensor contents and convert them into C data arrays that you can compile into your program. There are some examples of this in the `micro_speech` code, like a one-second audio sample of someone saying "yes" (*https://oreil.ly/qFoMn*), and the expected results of preprocessing that input (*https:// oreil.ly/uKYWo*). After you have these reference values, you should be able to feed them as inputs into the modules holding each stage of your pipeline (preprocessing, neural network inference) and make sure the outputs match what you expect. You can do this with throwaway code if you're short on time, but it's worth the extra investment to turn them into unit tests (*https://oreil.ly/t2E03*) that ensure your preprocessing and model inference continue to be verified as the code changes over time.

On-Device Evaluation

At the end of training, neural networks are evaluated using a test set of inputs, and the predictions are compared to the expected results to characterize the overall accuracy of the model. This happens as a normal part of the training process, but it's rare to do the same evaluation on the code that has been deployed on a device. Often the biggest barrier is just transferring the thousands of input samples that make up a typical test dataset onto an embedded system with limited resources. This is a shame, though; making sure that the on-device accuracy matches what was seen at the end of training is the only way to be sure that the model has been correctly deployed, because there are so many ways to introduce subtle errors that are difficult to spot otherwise. We didn't manage to implement a full test set evaluation for the micro_speech demo, but there is at least an end-to-end test (*https://oreil.ly/4372z*) that makes sure we get the correct labels for two different inputs.

Numerical Differences

A neural network is a chain of complex mathematical operations performed on large arrays of numbers. The original training is usually done in floating point, but we try to convert down to a lower-precision integer representation for embedded applications. The operations themselves can be implemented in many different ways, depending on the platform and optimization trade-offs. All these factors mean that you can't expect bit-wise identical results from a network on different devices, even if it's given the same input. This means you must determine what differences you can tolerate, and, if those differences become too large, how to track down where they come from.

Are the Differences a Problem?

We sometimes joke that the only metric that really matters is the app store rating. Our goal should be to produce products that people are happy with, so all other metrics are just proxies for user satisfaction. Since there are always going to be numerical differences from the training environment, the first challenge is to understand whether they hurt the product experience. This can be obvious if the values you're getting out of your network are nonsensical, but if they only differ by a few percentage points from what's expected, it's worth trying out the resulting network as part of a full application with a realistic use case. It might be that the accuracy loss isn't a problem, or that there are other issues that are more important and should be prioritized.

Establish a Metric

When you are sure that you have a real problem, it helps to quantify it. It can be tempting to pick a numerical measure, like the percentage difference in the output score vector from the expected result. This might not reflect the user experience very well, though. For example, if you're doing image classification and all of the scores are 5% below what you'd expect, but the relative ordering of the results remains the same, the end result might be perfectly fine for many applications.

Instead, we recommend designing a metric that does reflect what the product needs. In the image classification case, you might pick what's called a *top-one* score across a set of test images, because this will show how often the model picks the correct label. The top-one metric is how often the model picks the ground truth label as its highest-scoring prediction (*top-five* is similar, but covers how often the ground truth label is in the five highest-scoring predictions). You can then use the top-one metric to keep track of your progress and, importantly, get an idea of when the changes you've made are good enough.

You should also be careful to assemble a standard set of inputs that reflect what's actually fed into the neural network processing, because as we discussed earlier, there are lots of ways that preprocessing can introduce errors.

Compare Against a Baseline

TensorFlow Lite for Microcontrollers was designed to have reference implementations for all of its functionality, and one of the reasons we did this was so that it's possible to compare their results against optimized code to debug potential differences. Once you have some standard inputs, you should try running them through a desktop build of the framework, with no optimizations enabled so that the reference operator implementations are called. If you want a starting point for this kind of standalone test, take a look at *micro_speech_test.cc* (*https://oreil.ly/x5QYp*). If you run your results through the metric you've established, you should see a score that you expect. If not, there might have been some error during the conversion process or something else might have gone wrong earlier in your workflow, so you'll need to debug back into training to understand what the problem is.

If you do see good results using the reference code, you should then try building and running the same test on your target platform with all optimizations enabled. It might not be as simple as this, of course, since often embedded devices don't have the memory to hold all the input data, and outputting the results can be tricky if all you have is a debug logging connection. It's worth persevering, though, even if you must break your test up into multiple runs. When you have the results, run them through your metric to understand what the deficit actually is.

Swap Out Implementations

Many platforms will enable optimizations by default, given that the reference implementations may take so long to run on an embedded device that they're practically unusable. There are lots of ways to disable these optimizations, but we find the simplest is often just to find all the kernel implementations that are currently being used, usually in subfolders of *tensorflow/lite/micro/kernels* (*https://oreil.ly/k3lln*), and overwrite them with the reference versions that are in that parent directory (making sure you have backups of the files you're replacing). As a first step, replace all of the optimized implementations and rerun the on-device tests, to ensure that you do see the better score that you'd expect.

After you've done this wholesale replacement, try just overwriting half of the optimized kernels and see how that affects the metric. In most cases you'll be able to use a binary search approach to determine which optimized kernel implementation is causing the biggest drop in the score. Once you have narrowed it down to a particular optimized kernel, you should then be able to create a minimal reproducible case by capturing the input values for one of the *bad* runs and the expected output values for those inputs from the reference implementation. The easiest way to do this is by debug logging from within the kernel implementation during one of the test runs.

Now that you have a reproducible case, you should be able to create a unit test out of it. You can look at one of the standard kernel tests (*https://oreil.ly/0rnPW*) to get started, and either create a new standalone test or add it to the existing file for that kernel. That then gives you a tool that you can use to communicate the issue to the team responsible for the optimized implementation, because you'll be able to show that there's a difference in the results from their code and the reference version, and that it affects your application. That same test can then also be added to the main code base if you contribute it back, and ensure that no other optimized implementations cause the same problem. It's also a great tool for debugging an implementation yourself, because you can experiment with the code in isolation and iterate quickly.

Mysterious Crashes and Hangs

One of the most difficult situations to fix on an embedded system is when your program doesn't run, but there's no obvious logging output or error to explain what went wrong. The easiest way to understand the problem is to attach a debugger (like GDB) and either look at a stack trace if it's hung or step through your code to see where execution goes wrong. It's not always easy to set up a debugger, though, or the source of the problem may still not be clear after using one, so there are some other techniques you can try.

Desktop Debugging

Full operating systems like Linux, macOS, and Windows all have extensive debugging tools and error reporting mechanisms, so if at all possible try to keep your program portable to one of those platforms, even if you have to stub out some of the hardware-specific functionality with dummy implementations. This is how TensorFlow Lite for Microcontrollers is designed, and it means that we can first try to reproduce anything that's going wrong on our Linux machines. If the same error occurs in this environment, it's usually much easier and faster to track down using standard tooling, and without having to flash devices, speeding up iterations. Even if it would be too difficult to maintain your full application as a desktop build, at least see whether you can create unit and integration tests for your modules that do compile on a desktop. Then you can try giving them similar inputs to those in the situation you're seeing a problem with and discover whether this also causes a similar error.

Log Tracing

The only platform-specific functionality that TensorFlow Lite for Microcontrollers requires is an implementation of DebugLog(). We have this requirement because it's such an essential tool for understanding what's going on during development, even though it's not something you need for production deployments. In an ideal world, any crashes or program errors should trigger log output—for example, our bare-metal support for STM32 devices has a fault handler (*https://oreil.ly/dsHG8*) that does this—but that's not always feasible.

You should always be able to inject log statements into the code yourself, though. These don't need to be meaningful, just statements of what location in the code has been reached. You can even define an automatic trace macro, like this:

```
#define TRACE DebugLog(__FILE__ ":" __LINE__)
```

Then use it in your code like this:

```
int main(int argc, char**argv) {
  TRACE;
  InitSomething();
  TRACE;
  while (true) {
    TRACE;
    DoSomething();
    TRACE;
  }
}
```

You should see output in your debug console showing how far the code managed to go. It's usually best to start with the highest level of your code and then see where the logging stops. That will give you an idea of the rough area where the crash or hang is happening, and then you can add more TRACE statements to narrow down exactly where the problem is occurring.

Shotgun Debugging

Sometimes tracing doesn't give you enough information about what's going wrong, or the problem might occur only in an environment in which you don't have access to logs, like production. In those cases, we recommend what's sometimes called "shotgun debugging." This is similar to the "shotgun profiling" we covered in Chapter 15, and it's as simple as commenting out parts of your code and seeing whether the error still occurs. If you start at the top level of your application and work your way down, you can usually do the equivalent of a binary search to isolate which lines of code are causing the issue. For example, you might start with something like this in your main loop:

```
int main(int argc, char**argv) {
  InitSomething();
  while (true) {
    // DoSomething();
  }
}
```

If this runs successfully with DoSomething() commented out, you know that the problem is happening within that function. You can then uncomment it and recursively do the same within its body to focus in on the misbehaving code.

Memory Corruption

The most painful errors are caused by values in memory being accidentally overwritten. Embedded systems don't have the same hardware to protect against this that desktop or mobile CPUs do, so these can be particularly challenging to debug. Even tracing or commenting out code can produce confusing results, because the overwriting can occur long before the code that uses the corrupted values runs, so crashes can be a long way from their cause. They might even depend on sensor input or hardware timings, making issues intermittent and maddeningly hard to reproduce.

The number one cause of this in our experience is overrunning the program stack. This is where local variables are stored, and TensorFlow Lite for Microcontrollers uses these extensively for comparatively large objects; thus, it requires more space than is typical for many other embedded applications. The exact size you'll need is not easy to ascertain, unfortunately. Often the biggest contributor is the memory arena you need to pass into SimpleTensorAllocator, which in the examples (*https://oreil.ly/Pb9Pa*) is allocated as a local array:

```
// Create an area of memory to use for input, output, and intermediate arrays.
// The size of this will depend on the model you're using, and may need to be
// determined by experimentation.
const int tensor_arena_size = 10 * 1024;
uint8_t tensor_arena[tensor_arena_size];
tflite::SimpleTensorAllocator tensor_allocator(tensor_arena,
                                               tensor_arena_size);
```

If you are using the same approach, you'll need to make sure the stack size is approximately the size of that arena, plus several kilobytes for miscellaneous variables used by the runtime. If your arena is held elsewhere (maybe as a global variable), you should need only a few kilobytes of stack. The exact amount of memory required depends on your architecture, the compiler, and the model you're running, so unfortunately it's not easy to give an exact value ahead of time. If you are seeing mysterious crashes, it's worth increasing this value as much as you can to see whether that helps, though.

If you're still seeing problems, you should start by trying to establish what variable or area of memory is being overwritten. Hopefully this should be possible using the logging or code elimination approaches described earlier, narrowing down the issue to the read of a value that seems to have been corrupted. Once you know what variable or array entry is being clobbered, you can then write a variation on the TRACE macro that outputs the value of that memory location along with the file and line it's been called from. You might need to do special tricks like storing the memory address in a global variable so that it's accessible from deeper stack frames if it's a local. Then, just like you would for tracking down a normal crash, you can TRACE out the contents of that location as you run through the program and attempt to identify which code is responsible for overwriting it.

Wrapping Up

Coming up with a solution when things work in a training environment but fail on a real device can be a long and frustrating process. In this chapter, we've given you a set of tools to try when you do find yourself stuck and spinning your wheels. Unfortunately there aren't many shortcuts in debugging, but by methodically working through the problem using these approaches, we do have confidence that you can track down any embedded machine learning problems.

Once you've gotten one model working in a product, you'll probably start to wonder about how you can adapt it or even create an entirely new model to tackle different issues. Chapter 19 discusses how you can transfer your own model from the Tensor-Flow training environment into the TensorFlow Lite inference engine.

Porting Models from TensorFlow to TensorFlow Lite

If you've made it this far, you'll understand that we're in favor of reusing existing models for new tasks whenever you can. Training an entirely new model from scratch can take a lot of time and experimentation, and even experts often can't predict the best approach ahead of time without trying a lot of different prototypes. This means that a full guide to creating new architectures is beyond the scope of this book, and we recommend looking in Chapter 21 for further reading on the topic. There are some aspects (like working with a restricted set of operations or preprocessing demands) that are unique to resource-constrained, on-device machine learning, though, so this chapter offers advice on those.

Understand What Ops Are Needed

This book is focused on models created in TensorFlow because the authors work on the team at Google, but even within a single framework there are a lot of different ways of creating models. If you look at the speech commands training script (*https:// oreil.ly/ZTYu7*), you'll see that it's building a model using core TensorFlow ops directly as building blocks, and manually running a training loop. This is quite an old-fashioned way of working these days (the script was originally written in 2017), and modern examples with TensorFlow 2.0 are likely to use Keras as a high-level API that takes care of a lot of the details.

The downside to this is that the underlying operations that a model uses are no longer obvious from inspecting the code. Instead, they will be created as part of layers which represent larger chunks of the graph in a single call. This is a problem because knowing what TensorFlow operations are being used by a model is very important for understanding whether the model will run in TensorFlow Lite, and what the resource requirements will be. Luckily you can access the underlying low-level operations even from Keras, as long as you can retrieve the underlying `Session` object using `tf.keras.backend.get_session()` (*https://oreil.ly/4zurk*). If you're coding directly in TensorFlow, it's likely that you already have the session in a variable, so the following code should still work:

```
for op in sess.graph.get_operations():
    print(op.type)
```

If you've assigned your session to the `sess` variable, this will print out the types of all the ops in your model. You can also access other properties, like `name`, to get more information. Understanding what TensorFlow operations are present will help a lot in the conversion process to TensorFlow Lite; otherwise, any errors you see will be much more difficult to understand.

Look at Existing Op Coverage in Tensorflow Lite

TensorFlow Lite supports only a subset of TensorFlow's operations, and with some restrictions. You can see the latest list in the ops compatibility guide (*https://oreil.ly/Pix9U*). This means that if you're planning a new model, you should ensure at the outset that you aren't relying on features or ops that aren't supported. In particular, LSTMs, GRUs, and other recurrent neural networks are not yet usable. There's also currently a gap between what's available in the full mobile version of TensorFlow Lite and the microcontroller branch. The simplest way to understand what operations are supported by TensorFlow Lite for Microcontrollers at the moment is to look at *all_ops_resolver.cc* (*https://oreil.ly/HNpmM*), because ops are constantly being added.

It can become a bit confusing comparing the ops that show up in your TensorFlow training session and those supported by TensorFlow Lite, because there are several transformation steps that take place during the export process. These turn weights that were stored as variables into constants, for example, and might quantize float operations into their integer equivalents as an optimization. There are also ops that exist only as part of the training loop, like those involved in backpropagation, and these are stripped out entirely. The best way to figure out what issues you might encounter is to try exporting a prospective model as soon as you've created it, before it's trained, so that you can adjust its structure before you've spent a lot of time on the training process.

Move Preprocessing and Postprocessing into Application Code

It's common for deep learning models to have three stages. There's often a preprocessing step, which might be as simple as loading images and labels from disk and decoding the JPEGs, or as complex as the speech example which transforms audio data into spectrograms. There's then a core neural network that takes in arrays of values and outputs results in a similar form. Finally, you need to make sense of these values in a postprocessing step. For many classification problems this is as simple as matching scores in a vector to the corresponding labels, but if you look at a model like MobileSSD (*https://oreil.ly/QT_dS*), the network output is a soup of overlapping bounding boxes that need to go through a complex process called "non-max suppression" to be useful as results.

The core neural network model is usually the most computationally intensive, and is often composed of a comparatively small number of operations like convolutions and activations. The pre- and postprocessing stages frequently require a lot more operations, including control flow, even though their computational load is a lot lower. This means that it often makes more sense to implement the non-core steps as regular code in the application, rather than baking them into the TensorFlow Lite model. For example, the neural network portion of a machine vision model will take in an image of a particular size, like 224 pixels high by 224 pixels wide. In the training environment, we'll use a `DecodeJpeg` op followed by a `ResizeImages` operation to convert the result into the correct size. When we're running on a device, however, we're almost certainly grabbing input images from a fixed-size source with no decompression required, so writing custom code to create the neural network input makes a lot more sense than relying on a general-purpose operation from our library. We'll probably also be dealing with asynchronous capture and might be able to get some benefits from threading the work involved. In the case of speech commands, we do a lot of work to cache intermediate results from the FFT so that we can reuse as many calculations as possible as we're running on streaming input.

Not every model has a significant postprocessing stage in the training environment, but when we're running on a device, it's very common to want to take advantage of coherency over time to improve the results shown to the user. Even though the model is just a classifier, the wake-word detection code runs multiple times a second and uses averaging (*https://oreil.ly/E68Q4*) to increase the accuracy of the results. This sort of code is also best implemented at the application level, given that expressing it as TensorFlow Lite operations is difficult and doesn't offer many benefits. It is possible, as you can see in *detection_postprocess.cc* (*https://oreil.ly/IMlsT*), but it involves a lot of work wiring through from the underlying TensorFlow graph during the export process because the way it's typically expressed as small ops in the TensorFlow is not an efficient way to implement it on-device.

This all means that you should try to exclude non-core parts of the graph, which will require some work determining what parts are which. We find Netron (*https://oreil.ly/qoQNY*) to be a good tool for exploring TensorFlow Lite graphs to understand what ops are present, and get a sense for whether they're part of the core of the neural network or just processing steps. Once you understand what is happening internally, you should be able to isolate the core network, export just those ops, and implement the rest as application code.

Implement Required Ops if Necessary

If you do find that there are TensorFlow operations that you absolutely need that are not supported by TensorFlow Lite, it is possible to save them as *custom* operations inside the TensorFlow Lite file format, and then implement them yourself within the framework. The full process is beyond the scope of this book, but here are the key steps:

- Run `toco` with `allow_custom_ops` enabled, so that unsupported operations are stored as custom ops in the serialized model file.
- Write a kernel implementing the operation and register it using `AddCustom()` in the op resolver you're using in your application.
- Unpack the parameters that are stored in a FlexBuffer format when your `Init()` method is called.

Optimize Ops

Even if you're using supported operations in your new model, you might be using them in a way that hasn't yet been optimized. The TensorFlow Lite team's priorities are driven by particular use cases, so if you are running a new model, you might run into code paths that haven't been optimized yet. We covered this in Chapter 15, but just as we recommend you check export compatibility as soon as possible—even before you've trained a model—it's worth ensuring that you get the performance you need before you plan your development schedule, because you might need to budget some time to work on operation latency.

Wrapping Up

Training a novel neural network to complete a task successfully is already challenging, but figuring out how to build a network that will produce good results and run efficiently on embedded hardware is even tougher! This chapter discussed some of the challenges you'll face, and provided suggestions on approaches to overcome them, but it's a large and growing area of study, so we recommend taking a look at some of the resources in Chapter 21 to see whether there are new sources of inspiration for your model architecture. In particular, this is an area where following the latest research papers on arXiv can be very useful.

After overcoming all these challenges, you should have a small, fast, power-efficient product that's ready to be deployed in the real world. It's worth thinking about what potentially harmful impacts it could have on your users before you release it, though, so Chapter 20 covers questions around privacy and security.

Privacy, Security, and Deployment

After working through the previous chapters in this book, you should hopefully be able to build an embedded application that relies on machine learning. You'll still need to navigate a lot of challenges, though, to turn your project into a product that can be successfully deployed into the world. Two key challenges are protecting the privacy and the security of your users. This chapter covers some of the approaches we've found useful for overcoming those challenges.

Privacy

Machine learning on-device relies on sensor inputs. Some of these sensors, like microphones and cameras, raise obvious privacy concerns (*https://oreil.ly/CEcsR*), but even others, like accelerometers, can be abused; for example, to identify individuals from their gait when wearing your product. We all have a responsibility as engineers to safeguard our users from damage that our products can cause, so it's vital to think about privacy at all stages of the design. There are also legal implications to handling sensitive user data that are beyond the scope of our coverage but about which you should consult your lawyers. If you're part of a large organization, you might have privacy specialists and processes that can help you with specialist knowledge. Even if you don't have access to those resources, you should spend some time running your own privacy review at the outset of the project, and periodically revisit it until you launch. There isn't widespread agreement on what a "privacy review" actually is, but we discuss some best practices, most of which revolve around building a strong Privacy Design Document (PDD).

The Privacy Design Document

The field of privacy engineering (*https://oreil.ly/MEwUE*) is still very new, and it can be difficult to find documentation on how to work through the privacy implications of a product. The way that many large companies handle the process of ensuring privacy in their applications is to create a Privacy Design Document. This is a single place where you can cover the important privacy aspects of your product. Your document should include information about all the topics raised in the subsections that follow.

Data collection

The first section of the PDD should cover what data you'll be gathering, how it will be gathered, and why. You should be as specific as possible and use plain English—for example, "collecting temperature and humidity" rather than "obtaining environmental atmospheric information." While working on this section, you also have the opportunity to think about what you're actually gathering, and ensure that it's the minimum you need for your product. If you're only listening for loud noises to wake up a more complex device, do you really need to sample audio at 16 KHz using a microphone, or can you use a cruder sensor that ensures you won't be able to record speech even if there's a security breach? A simple system diagram can be useful in this section, showing how the information flows between the different components in your product (including any cloud APIs). The overall goal of this section is to provide a good overview of what you'll be collecting to a nontechnical audience, whether it's your lawyers, executives, or board members. One way to think about it is how it would look on the front page of a newspaper, in a story written by an unsympathetic journalist. Make sure you've done everything you can to minimize your users' exposure to malicious actions by others. In concrete terms, think through scenarios like "What could an abusive ex-partner do using this technology?" and try to be as imaginative as possible to ensure there's as much protection built in as you can offer.

Data usage

What is done with any data after you've collected it? For example, many startups are tempted to leverage user data to train their machine learning models, but this is an extremely fraught process from a privacy perspective, because it requires storage and processing of potentially very sensitive information for long periods of time for only indirect user benefits. We strongly suggest treating training data acquisition as an entirely separate program, using paid providers with clear consent rather than collecting data as a side effect of product usage.

One of the benefits of on-device machine learning is that you have the ability to process sensitive data locally and share only aggregated results. For example, you might have a pedestrian-counting device that captures images every second, but the only data that's transmitted is a count of people and vehicles seen. If you can, try to engineer your hardware to ensure that these guarantees can't be broken. If you're using only 224 × 224–pixel images as inputs to a classification algorithm, use a camera sensor that's also low-resolution so that it's physically impossible to recognize faces or license plates. If you plan on transmitting only a few values as a summary (like the pedestrian counts), support only a wireless technology with low bit rates to avoid being able to transmit the source video even if your device is hacked. We're hoping that in the future, special-purpose hardware (*https://oreil.ly/6E2Ya*) will help enforce these guarantees, but even now there's still a lot you can do at the system design level to avoid overengineering and make abuse more difficult.

Data sharing and storage

Who has access to the data you've gathered? What systems are in place to ensure that only those people can see it? How long is it kept, either on-device or in the cloud? If it is kept for any length of time, what are the policies on deleting it? You might think that storing information stripped of obvious user IDs like email addresses or names is safe, but identity can be derived from many sources, like IP addresses, recognizable voices, or even gaits, so you should assume that any sensor data you gather is personally identifiable information (PII). The best policy is to treat this kind of PII like radioactive waste. Avoid gathering it if you possibly can, keep it well guarded while you do need it, and dispose of it as quickly as possible after you're done.

When you think about who has access, don't forget that all your permission systems can be overridden by government pressure, which can cause your users serious harm in repressive countries. That's another reason to limit what is transmitted and stored to the bare minimum possible, to avoid that responsibility and limit your users' exposure.

Consent

Do the people using your product understand what information it's gathering, and have they agreed to how you'll use it? There's a narrow legal question here that you might think can be answered by a click-through end-user license agreement, but we'd encourage you to think about this more broadly as a marketing challenge. Presumably you are convinced that the product benefits are worth the trade-off of gathering more data, so how can you communicate that to prospective customers clearly so that they make an informed choice? If you're having trouble coming up with that message, that's a sign you should rethink your design to reduce the privacy implications or increase the benefits of your product.

Using a PDD

You should treat the PDD as a living document, updated constantly as your product evolves. It's clearly useful for communicating product details to your lawyers and other business stakeholders, but it can also be useful in a lot of other contexts. For instance, you should collaborate with your marketing team to ensure that its messaging is informed by what you're doing, and with any providers of third-party services (like advertising) to ensure they're complying with what you're promising. All of the engineers on the team should have access to it and be able to add comments, given that there might well be some hidden privacy implications that are visible only at the implementation level. For example, you might be using a geocoding cloud API that leaks the IP address of your device, or there might be a WiFi chip on your microcontroller that you're not using but that could theoretically be enabled to transmit sensitive data.

Security

Ensuring total security of an embedded device is very hard. An attacker can easily gain physical possession of a system, and then use all sorts of intrusive techniques to extract information. Your first line of defense is ensuring that as little sensitive information as possible is retained on your embedded system, which is why the PDD is so important. If you are relying on secure communications with a cloud service, you should think about investigating secure cryptoprocessors (*https://oreil.ly/lGLzA*) to ensure that any keys are held safely. These chips can also be used for secure booting, to make sure only the program you've flashed will run on the device.

As with privacy, you should try to craft your hardware design to limit the opportunities for any attackers. If you don't need WiFi or Bluetooth, build a device that doesn't have those capabilities. Don't offer debug interfaces like SWD (*https://oreil.ly/X1I7x*) on shipping products, and look into disabling code readout on Arm platforms (*https://oreil.ly/ag5Vc*). Even though these measures aren't perfect (*https://oreil.ly/R3YG-*), they will raise the cost of an attack.

You should also try to rely on established libraries and services for security and encryption. Rolling your own cryptography is a very bad idea, because it's very easy to make mistakes that are difficult to spot but destroy the security of your system. The full challenge of embedded system security is beyond the scope of this book, but you should think about creating a security design document, similar to the one we recommend for privacy. You should cover what you think likely attacks are, their impacts, and how you'll defend against them.

Protecting Models

We often hear from engineers who are concerned about protecting their machine learning models from unscrupulous competitors, because they require a lot of work to create but are shipped on-device and are usually in an easy-to-understand format. The bad news is that there is no absolute protection against copying. In this sense, models are like any other software: they can be stolen and examined just like regular machine code. Like with software, though, the problem is not as bad as it might seem at first. Just as disassembling a procedural program doesn't reveal the true source code, examining a quantized model doesn't offer any access to the training algorithm or data, so attackers won't be able to effectively modify the model for any other use. It should also be pretty easy to spot a direct copy of a model if it's shipped on a competitor's device and prove legally that the competitor stole your intellectual property, just as you can with any other software.

It can still be worthwhile to make it harder for casual attackers to access your model. A simple technique is to store your serialized model in flash after XOR-ing it with a private key and then copy it into RAM and unencrypt it before use. That will prevent a simple dump of flash from revealing your model, but an attacker with access to RAM at runtime will still be able to access it. You might think that switching away from a TensorFlow Lite FlatBuffer to a proprietary format would help, but because the weight parameters themselves are large arrays of numerical values and it's obvious from stepping through a debugger what operations are called in which order, we've found the value of this kind of obfuscation very limited.

One fun approach to use for spotting misappropriation of models is deliberately building in subtle flaws as part of the training process, and then looking out for them when checking suspected infringements. As an example, you could train a wake-word detection model to not only listen out for "Hello," but also secretly "Ahoy, sailor!" It's extremely unlikely that an independently trained model would show a response for that same phrase, so if there is one, it's a strong signal that the model was copied, even if you can't access the internal workings of a device. This technique is based on the old idea of including a fictitious entry in reference works such as maps, directories, and dictionaries to help spot copyright infringements; it has come to be known as *mountweazeling* after the practice of placing a fictitious mountain (*https://oreil.ly/OpY2G*), "Mountweazel," on maps to help identify copies.

Deployment

With modern microcontrollers it's very tempting to enable over-the-air updates so you have the ability to revise the code that's running on your device at any time, even long after shipping. This opens up such a wide attack surface for security and privacy violations that we urge you to consider whether it is truly essential for your product. It's difficult to ensure that only you have the ability to upload new code without a well-designed secure booting system and other protections, and if you make a mistake, you've handed complete control of your device to malicious actors. As a default, we recommend that you don't allow any kind of code updating after a device has been manufactured. This might sound draconian, given that it prevents updates that fix security holes, for example, but in almost all cases removing the possibility of attackers' code being run on the system will help security much more than it hurts. It also simplifies the network architecture, because there's no longer a need for any protocol to "listen" for updates; the device might effectively be able to operate in a transmit-only mode, which also greatly reduces the attack surface.

This does mean that there's much more of a burden on you to get the code right before a device is released, especially with regard to the model accuracy. We talked earlier about approaches like unit tests and verifying overall model accuracy against a dedicated test set, but they won't catch all problems. When you're preparing for a release, we highly recommend using a dog-fooding approach in which you try the devices in real-world environments, but under the supervision of organization insiders. These experiments are a lot more likely to reveal unexpected behaviors than engineering tests, because tests are limited by the imagination of their creators, and the real world is much more surprising than any of us can predict ahead of time. The good news is that after you have encountered undesirable behaviors, you can then turn them into test cases that can be tackled as part of your normal development process. In fact, developing this kind of institutional memory of the deep requirements of your product, codified into tests, can be one of your biggest competitive advantages, in so much as the only way to acquire it is by painful trial and error.

Moving from a Development Board to a Product

The full process of turning an application running on a development board into a shipping product is beyond the scope of this book, but there are some things worth thinking about during the development process. You should research the bulk prices of the microcontroller you're considering using—for example, on sites like Digi-Key (*https://digikey.com*)—to make sure that the system you're targeting will fit your budget in the end. It should be fairly straightforward to move your code to a production device assuming that it's the same chip you were using during development, so from a programming perspective, the main imperative is to ensure that your development board matches your production target. Debugging any issues that arise will become a lot harder after your code is deployed in a final form factor, especially if you've taken the steps described earlier to secure your platform, so it's worth delaying that step as long as you can.

Wrapping Up

Safeguarding our users' privacy and security is one of our most important responsibilities as engineers, but it's not always clear how to decide on the best approaches. In this chapter, we covered the basic process of thinking about and designing in protections, and some more advanced security considerations. With that, we've completed the foundations of building and deploying an embedded machine learning application, but we know that there's far more to this area than we could cover in a single book. To finish off, the final chapter discusses resources that you can use to continue learning more.

## CHAPTER 21

Learning More

We hope that this book helps you to solve problems that matter, using inexpensive, low-power devices. This is a new and rapidly growing field, so what we've included here is just a snapshot. If you want to stay up to date, here are some resources we recommend.

The TinyML Foundation

The TinyML Summit (*https://www.tinymlsummit.org*) is an annual conference that brings together embedded hardware, software, and machine learning practitioners to discuss collaborations across these disciplines. There are also monthly meetups in the Bay Area (*https://oreil.ly/ZtZu_*) and Austin, TX (*https://oreil.ly/cH9d-*), with more locations expected in the future. You can check the TinyML Foundation website (*https://www.tinymlsummit.org*) for videos, slides, and other materials from the events, even if you can't make it in person.

SIG Micro

This book focuses on TensorFlow Lite for Microcontrollers, and if you're interested in contributing to the framework there's a Special Interest Group (SIG) that enables external developers to collaborate on improvements. SIG Micro (*https://oreil.ly/owmCE*) has public monthly video meetings (*https://oreil.ly/1AdpF*), a mailing list (*https://oreil.ly/qFhbv*), and a Gitter chat room (*https://oreil.ly/btt1p*). If you have an idea or a request for a new feature in the library, this is a good place to discuss it. You'll see all the developers working on the project, both inside and outside Google, sharing roadmaps and plans for upcoming work. The usual process for any changes is to start by sharing a design document, which can be just a single page for simple changes, covering why the change is needed and what it will do. We usually publish this as an RFC ("request for comment") to allow stakeholders to contribute their feedback, and then follow it up with a pull request containing the actual code changes once the approach is agreed.

The TensorFlow Website

The main TensorFlow website has a home page for our work on microcontrollers (*https://oreil.ly/Utc2E*), and you can check there for the latest examples and documentation. In particular, we'll be continuing our migration to TensorFlow 2.0 in our training sample code, so it's worth taking a look if you're having compatibility problems.

Other Frameworks

We've focused on the TensorFlow ecosystem given that this is the library we know best, but there's a lot of interesting work happening on other frameworks, too. We're big fans of Neil Tan's pioneering work on uTensor (*https://oreil.ly/IfTva*), which has a lot of interesting experiments with code generation from TensorFlow models. Microsoft's Embedded Learning Library (*https://oreil.ly/Q-r3d*) supports a large variety of different machine learning algorithms beyond deep neural networks, and is aimed at Arduino and micro:bit platforms.

Twitter

Have you built an embedded machine learning project that you'd like to tell the world about? We'd love to see what problems you're solving, and one great way of reaching us is by sharing a link on Twitter using the *#tinyml* hashtag. We're both on Twitter ourselves as @petewarden (*https://oreil.ly/S60rg*) and @dansitu (*https://oreil.ly/xswxw*), and we'll be posting updates on this book at @tinymlbook (*https://oreil.ly/4NaMB*).

Friends of TinyML

There are a lot of interesting companies working in this space, from early-stage start-ups to large corporations. If you're building a product, you'll want to explore what they have to offer, so here's an alphabetical list of some of the organizations we've worked with:

- Adafruit (*https://www.adafruit.com*)
- Ambiq Micro (*https://ambiqmicro.com*)
- Arduino (*https://www.arduino.cc*)
- Arm (*https://www.arm.com*)

- Cadence/Tensilica (*https://ip.cadence.com/knowledgecenter/know-ten*)
- CEVA/DSP Group (*https://www.ceva-dsp.com*)
- Edge Impulse (*https://www.edgeimpulse.com*)
- Eta Compute (*https://etacompute.com*)
- Everactive (*https://everactive.com*)
- GreenWaves Technologies (*https://greenwaves-technologies.com*)
- Himax (*https://www.himax.com.tw*)
- MATRIX Industries (*https://www.matrixindustries.com*)
- Nordic Semiconductor (*https://www.nordicsemi.com*)
- PixArt (*https://www.pixart.com*)
- Qualcomm (*https://www.qualcomm.com*)
- SparkFun (*https://www.sparkfun.com*)
- STMicroelectronics (*https://www.st.com/content/st_com/en.html*)
- Syntiant (*https://www.syntiant.com*)
- Xnor.ai (*https://www.xnor.ai*)

Wrapping Up

Thanks for joining us on this exploration of machine learning on embedded devices. We hope that we've inspired you to work on your own projects, and we can't wait to see what you build, and how you can drive this exciting new field forward!

Using and Generating an Arduino Library Zip

The Arduino IDE requires source files to be packaged in a certain way. The Tensor-Flow Lite for Microcontrollers Makefile knows how to do this for you, and can generate a *.zip* file containing all the source, which you can import into the Arduino IDE as a library. This will allow you to build and deploy your application.

Instructions on generating this file appear later in this section. However, the easiest way to get started is to use a prebuilt *.zip* file (*https://oreil.ly/blgB8*) that is generated nightly by the TensorFlow team.

After you've downloaded that file, you need to import it. In the Arduino IDE's Sketch menu, select Include Library→Add .ZIP Library, as shown in Figure A-1.

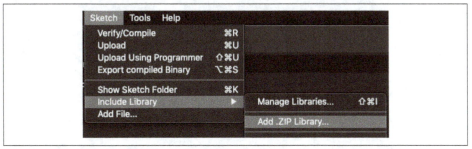

Figure A-1. The "Add .ZIP library..." menu option

In the file browser that appears, locate the *.zip* file and click Choose to import it.

You might instead want to generate the library yourself—for example, if you made changes to the code in the TensorFlow Git repository that you'd like to test out in the Arduino environment.

If you need to generate the file yourself, open a terminal window, clone the Tensor-Flow repository, and change into its directory:

```
git clone https://github.com/tensorflow/tensorflow.git
cd tensorflow
```

Now run the following script to generate the *.zip* file:

```
tensorflow/lite/micro/tools/ci_build/test_arduino.sh
```

The file will be created at the following location:

```
tensorflow/lite/micro/tools/make/gen/arduino_x86_64/ \
  prj/micro_speech/tensorflow_lite.zip
```

You can then import this *.zip* file into the Arduino IDE using the steps documented earlier. If you've previously installed the library, you'll need to remove the original version first. You can do this by deleting the *tensorflow_lite* directory from the Arduino IDE's *libraries* directory, which you can find under "Sketchbook location" in the IDE's Preferences window.

Capturing Audio on Arduino

The following text walks through the audio capture code from the wake-word application in Chapter 7. Since it's not directly related to machine learning, it's provided as an appendix.

The Arduino Nano 33 BLE Sense has an on-board microphone. To receive audio data from the microphone, we can register a callback function that is called when there is a chunk of new audio data ready.

Each time this happens, we'll write the chunk of new data to a *buffer* that stores a reserve of data. Because audio data takes up a lot of memory, the buffer has room for only a set amount of data. This data is overwritten when the buffer becomes full.

Whenever our program is ready to run inference, it can read the last second's worth of data from this buffer. As long as new data keeps coming in faster than we need to access it, there'll always be enough new data in the buffer to preprocess and feed into our model.

Each cycle of preprocessing and inference is complex, and it takes some time to complete. Because of this, we'll only be able to run inference a few times per second on an Arduino. This means that it will be easy for our buffer to stay full.

As we saw in Chapter 7, *audio_provider.h* implements these two functions:

- GetAudioSamples(), which provides a pointer to a chunk of raw audio data
- LatestAudioTimestamp(), which returns the timestamp of the most recently captured audio

The code that implements these for Arduino is located in *arduino/audio_provider.cc* (*https://oreil.ly/Bfh4v*).

In the first part, we pull in some dependencies. The *PDM.h* library defines the API that we'll use to get data from the microphone. The file *micro_model_settings.h* contains constants related to our model's data requirements that will help us provide audio in the correct format:

```
#include "tensorflow/lite/micro/examples/micro_speech/
  audio_provider.h"

#include "PDM.h"
#include "tensorflow/lite/micro/examples/micro_speech/
  micro_features/micro_model_settings.h"
```

The next chunk of code is where we set up some important variables:

```
namespace {
bool g_is_audio_initialized = false;
// An internal buffer able to fit 16x our sample size
constexpr int kAudioCaptureBufferSize = DEFAULT_PDM_BUFFER_SIZE * 16;
int16_t g_audio_capture_buffer[kAudioCaptureBufferSize];
// A buffer that holds our output
int16_t g_audio_output_buffer[kMaxAudioSampleSize];
// Mark as volatile so we can check in a while loop to see if
// any samples have arrived yet.
volatile int32_t g_latest_audio_timestamp = 0;
} // namespace
```

The Boolean `g_is_audio_initialized` is what we'll use to track whether the microphone has started capturing audio. Our audio capture buffer is defined by `g_audio_capture_buffer` and is sized to be 16 times the size of `DEFAULT_PDM_BUFFER_SIZE`, which is a constant defined in *PDM.h* that represents the amount of audio we receive from the microphone each time the callback is called. Having a nice big buffer means that we're unlikely to run out of data if the program slows down for some reason.

In addition to the audio capture buffer, we also keep a buffer of output audio, `g_audio_output_buffer`, that we'll return a pointer to when `GetAudioSamples()` is called. It's the length of `kMaxAudioSampleSize`, which is a constant from *micro_model_settings.h* that defines the number of 16-bit audio samples our preprocessing code can handle at once.

Finally, we use `g_latest_audio_timestamp` to keep track of the time represented by our most recent audio sample. This won't match up with the time on your wristwatch; it's just the number of milliseconds relative to when audio capture began. The variable is declared as `volatile`, which means the processor shouldn't attempt to cache its value. We'll see why later on.

After setting up these variables, we define the callback function that will be called every time there's new audio data available. Here it is in its entirety:

```
void CaptureSamples() {
  // This is how many bytes of new data we have each time this is called
  const int number_of_samples = DEFAULT_PDM_BUFFER_SIZE;
  // Calculate what timestamp the last audio sample represents
  const int32_t time_in_ms =
      g_latest_audio_timestamp +
      (number_of_samples / (kAudioSampleFrequency / 1000));
  // Determine the index, in the history of all samples, of the last sample
  const int32_t start_sample_offset =
      g_latest_audio_timestamp * (kAudioSampleFrequency / 1000);
  // Determine the index of this sample in our ring buffer
  const int capture_index = start_sample_offset % kAudioCaptureBufferSize;
  // Read the data to the correct place in our buffer
  PDM.read(g_audio_capture_buffer + capture_index, DEFAULT_PDM_BUFFER_SIZE);
  // This is how we let the outside world know that new audio data has arrived.
  g_latest_audio_timestamp = time_in_ms;
}
```

This function is a bit complicated, so we'll walk through it in chunks. Its goal is to determine the correct index in the audio capture buffer to write this new data to.

First, we figure out how much new data we'll receive each time the callback is called. We use that to determine a number in milliseconds that represents the time of the most recent audio sample in the buffer:

```
// This is how many bytes of new data we have each time this is called
const int number_of_samples = DEFAULT_PDM_BUFFER_SIZE;
// Calculate what timestamp the last audio sample represents
const int32_t time_in_ms =
    g_latest_audio_timestamp +
    (number_of_samples / (kAudioSampleFrequency / 1000));
```

The number of audio samples per second is kAudioSampleFrequency (this constant is defined in *micro_model_settings.h*). We divide this by 1,000 to get the number of samples per millisecond.

Next, we divide the number of samples per callback (number_of_samples) by the samples per millisecond to obtain the number of milliseconds' worth of data we obtain each callback:

```
(number_of_samples / (kAudioSampleFrequency / 1000))
```

We then add this to the timestamp of our previous most recent audio sample, g_latest_audio_timestamp, to obtain the timestamp of the most recent new audio sample.

After we have this number, we can use it to obtain the index of the most recent sample *in the history of all samples*. To do this, we multiply the timestamp of our previous most recent audio sample by the number of samples per millisecond:

```
const int32_t start_sample_offset =
    g_latest_audio_timestamp * (kAudioSampleFrequency / 1000);
```

Our buffer doesn't have room to store every sample ever captured, though. Instead, it has room for 16 times the DEFAULT_PDM_BUFFER_SIZE. As soon as we have more data than that, we start overwriting the buffer with new data.

We now have the index of our new samples *in the history of all samples*. Next, we need to convert this into theh samples' proper index within our actual buffer. To do this, we can divide our history index by the buffer length and get the remainder. This is done using the modulo operator (%):

```
// Determine the index of this sample in our ring buffer
const int capture_index = start_sample_offset % kAudioCaptureBufferSize;
```

Because the buffer's size, kAudioCaptureBufferSize, is a multiple of DEFAULT_PDM_BUFFER_SIZE, the new data will always fit neatly into the buffer. The modulo operator will return the index within the buffer where the new data should begin.

Next, we use the PDM.read() method to read the latest audio into the audio capture buffer:

```
// Read the data to the correct place in our buffer
PDM.read(g_audio_capture_buffer + capture_index, DEFAULT_PDM_BUFFER_SIZE);
```

The first argument accepts a pointer to a location in memory that the data should be written to. The variable g_audio_capture_buffer is a pointer to the address in memory where the audio capture buffer starts. By adding capture_index to this location, we can calculate the correct spot in memory to write our new data. The second argument defines how much data should be read, and we go for the maximum, DEFAULT_PDM_BUFFER_SIZE.

Finally, we update g_latest_audio_timestamp:

```
// This is how we let the outside world know that new audio data has arrived.
g_latest_audio_timestamp = time_in_ms;
```

This will be exposed to other parts of the program via the LatestAudioTimestamp() method, letting them know when new data becomes available. Because g_latest_audio_timestamp is declared as volatile, its value will be looked up from memory every time it is accessed. This is important, because otherwise the variable would be cached by the processor. Because its value is set in a callback, the processor would not know to refresh the cached value, and any code accessing it would not receive its current value.

You might be wondering what makes `CaptureSamples()` act as a callback function. How does it know when new audio is available? This, among other things, is handled in the next part of our code, which is a function that initiates audio capture:

```
TfLiteStatus InitAudioRecording(tflite::ErrorReporter* error_reporter) {
  // Hook up the callback that will be called with each sample
  PDM.onReceive(CaptureSamples);
  // Start listening for audio: MONO @ 16KHz with gain at 20
  PDM.begin(1, kAudioSampleFrequency);
  PDM.setGain(20);
  // Block until we have our first audio sample
  while (!g_latest_audio_timestamp) {
  }

  return kTfLiteOk;
}
```

This function will be called the first time someone calls `GetAudioSamples()`. It first uses the `PDM` library to hook up the `CaptureSamples()` callback, by calling `PDM.onReceive()`. Next, `PDM.begin()` is called with two arguments. The first argument indicates how many channels of audio to record; we only want mono audio, so we specify 1. The second argument specifies how many samples we want to receive per second.

Next, `PDM.setGain()` is used to configure the *gain*, which defines how much the microphone's audio should be amplified. We specify a gain of 20, which was chosen after some experimentation.

Finally, we loop until `g_latest_audio_timestamp` evaluates to true. Because it starts at 0, this has the effect of blocking execution until some audio has been captured by the callback, since at that point `g_latest_audio_timestamp` will have a nonzero value.

The two functions we've just explored allow us to initiate the process of capturing audio and to store the captured audio in a buffer. The next function, `GetAudioSamples()`, provides a mechanism for other parts of our code (namely, the feature provider) to obtain audio data:

```
TfLiteStatus GetAudioSamples(tflite::ErrorReporter* error_reporter,
                             int start_ms, int duration_ms,
                             int* audio_samples_size, int16_t** audio_samples) {
  // Set everything up to start receiving audio
  if (!g_is_audio_initialized) {
    TfLiteStatus init_status = InitAudioRecording(error_reporter);
    if (init_status != kTfLiteOk) {
      return init_status;
    }
    g_is_audio_initialized = true;
  }
```

The function is called with an `ErrorReporter` for writing logs, two variables that specify what audio we're requesting (`start_ms` and `duration_ms`), and two pointers used to pass back the audio data (`audio_samples_size` and `audio_samples`). The first part of the function calls `InitAudioRecording()`. As we saw earlier, this blocks execution until the first samples of audio have arrived. We use the variable `g_is_audio_initialized` to ensure this setup code runs only once.

After this point, we can assume that there's some audio stored in the capture buffer. Our task is to figure out where in the buffer the correct audio data is located. To do this, we first determine the index *in the history of all samples* of the first sample that we want:

```
const int start_offset = start_ms * (kAudioSampleFrequency / 1000);
```

Next, we determine the total number of samples that we want to grab:

```
const int duration_sample_count =
    duration_ms * (kAudioSampleFrequency / 1000);
```

Now that we have this information, we can figure out where in our audio capture buffer to read. We'll read the data in a loop:

```
for (int i = 0; i < duration_sample_count; ++i) {
  // For each sample, transform its index in the history of all samples into
  // its index in g_audio_capture_buffer
  const int capture_index = (start_offset + i) % kAudioCaptureBufferSize;
  // Write the sample to the output buffer
  g_audio_output_buffer[i] = g_audio_capture_buffer[capture_index];
}
```

Earlier, we saw how we can use the modulo operator to find the correct position within a buffer that only has enough space to hold the most recent samples. Here we use the same technique again—if we divide the current index *within the history of all samples* by the size of the audio capture buffer, `kAudioCaptureBufferSize`, the remainder will indicate that data's position within the buffer. We can then use a simple assignment to read the data from the capture buffer to the output buffer.

Next, to get data out of this function, we use two pointers that were supplied as arguments. These are `audio_samples_size`, which points to the number of audio samples, and `audio_samples`, which points to the output buffer:

```
// Set pointers to provide access to the audio
*audio_samples_size = kMaxAudioSampleSize;
*audio_samples = g_audio_output_buffer;

return kTfLiteOk;
}
```

We end the function by returning `kTfLiteOk`, letting the caller know that the operation was successful.

Then, in the final part, we define `LatestAudioTimestamp()`:

```
int32_t LatestAudioTimestamp() { return g_latest_audio_timestamp; }
```

Since this always returns the timestamp of the most recent audio, it can be checked in a loop by other parts of our code to determine if new audio data has arrived.

That's all for our audio provider! We've now ensured that our feature provider has a steady supply of fresh audio samples.

Index

TRAINING_STEPS, 186

U
underfitting, 23

V
validation, 24
validation_data, 48
val_loss, 49
val_mae, 49
vector, definition, 17

version(), 73
virtual machine (VM), running scripts on, 201

W
wake-word detection (see application building
    (wake-word detection example); training a
    model (wake-word example))
windowing, 18-20
Wizard of Oz approach, 398
writing tests, 369

About the Authors

Pete Warden is technical lead for mobile and embedded TensorFlow at Google. He was CTO and founder of Jetpac, which was acquired by Google in 2014, and previously worked at Apple. He was a founding member of the TensorFlow team, is on Twitter as @petewarden, and blogs about practical deep learning at *https://petewarden.com*.

Daniel Situnayake leads developer advocacy for TensorFlow Lite at Google. He cofounded Tiny Farms, the first US company using automation to produce insect protein at industrial scale. He began his career lecturing in automatic identification and data capture at Birmingham City University.

Colophon

The animal on the cover of *TinyML* is a crimson topaz (*Topaza pella*), a species of hummingbird found in northern South America. They live in tropical and subtropical forests, in the upper and middle canopy.

The male crimson topaz averages 8.7 inches tall, while the female is considerably smaller at 5.3 inches. Both males and females weigh about 10 grams. They are thought to be the second-largest species of hummingbird, after the giant hummingbird. Males are an iridescent red with a metallic-green throat and black head. The female's feathers are mostly green.

The crimson topaz, like other hummingbirds, feeds mainly on the nectar of flowering trees. By rotating their wings in a horizontal figure-eight pattern, the birds are able to perform active hovering flight, which is stationary flight at zero net forward speed. This allows them to drink the nectar of flowering plants while in midair. Many of these plants have tubular-shaped flowers and rely on the hummingbirds for pollination because bees and butterflies are unable to reach the pollen.

These hummingbirds are generally solitary, aside from breeding seasons twice a year. Females build tiny nests that stretch as their young grow, made with plant fibers bound by threads of spider silk. Females typically lay two eggs. Juveniles fledge about three weeks after hatching. The females care for their chicks for about six weeks.

The crimson topaz is common within its habitat, but they are not often seen because they are rarely near the ground. Many of the animals on O'Reilly covers are endangered; all of them are important to the world.

The cover illustration is by Karen Montgomery, based on a black and white engraving from *Lydekker's Royal Natural History*. The cover fonts are Gilroy Semibold and Guardian Sans. The text font is Adobe Minion Pro; the heading font is Adobe Myriad Condensed; and the code font is Dalton Maag's Ubuntu Mono.

CPSIA information can be obtained
at www.ICGtesting.com
Printed in the USA
JSHW030322271120
9856JS00006B/128